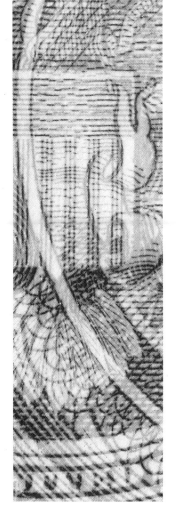

ESSENTIALS OF CASH MANAGEMENT

FIFTH EDITION

Co-Editors:

Dubos J. Masson, Ph.D., CCM
Principal Partner
The Resource Alliance

David A. Wikoff, Ph.D., CCM
Principal Partner
The Resource Alliance

Associate Editors:

Donald D. Aquila, CCM - Chair
Kent W. Crocombe, CCM - Vice Chair
Susan J. McComb, CCM
J. William Murray, CCM
Robert A. Westoby

A publication of the Treasury Management Association

Treasury Management Association

All inquiries should be addressed to:

Communications Department
Treasury Management Association
7315 Wisconsin Avenue, Suite 600W
Bethesda, Maryland 20814

ISBN 0-9614799-4-9

CONTENTS

EXHIBITS

FOREWORD

The best evidence that the scope of cash management continues to grow and change is *Essentials of Cash Management, Fifth Edition.* Developed as the current body of knowledge that constitutes the field of cash management, it has been expanded and upgraded to reflect the current cash and treasury management environment. A new chapter has been added on Electronic Commerce, with emphasis on EDI, FEDI, and EFT. An International Chapter includes new sections on banking in Canada, Europe, Pacific Rim, Latin America and the Middle East. A Financial Risk Management Chapter includes discussions on commodities, derivatives, and related accounting issues. Relationship Management encompasses financial institutions and service providers, as well as banks.

Beginning in 1986, four previous editions have been published. The primary use of the book remains as a study guide for the Certified Cash Manager (CCM) examination. *Essentials of Cash Management, Fifth Edition* is a valuable resource as well for anyone in treasury management. It is a helpful reference tool for veteran treasurers, vendors of cash and treasury management services, and college students and faculty interested in learning about careers in the treasury profession.

Essentials of Cash Management, Fifth Edition is the most comprehensive text of its kind. Its unique strength stems from the fact that it is developed by treasury practitioners drawing on their collective knowledge of current practices. As such, it is the treasury profession's own contribution to the literature in the field of treasury management.

Don Aquila, CCM, Chair
Body of Knowledge Task Force

EDITORS' ACKNOWLEDGEMENTS

The planning and writing of this text has been an arduous but rewarding process, and there have been many individuals who contributed their efforts to its completion. This project would not have been possible without the funding and support of the Treasury Management Association (TMA), headed by Don Manger (President, CEO). We would like to thank Jacqueline Callahan (TMA Senior Manager, Certification) for initiating the project and serving on the task force. We also want to thank Jean Marlowe (TMA Financial Editor), whose efforts as project manager were critical to the success of the many meetings and revisions required for this text; and Margaret Yao Pursell (TMA Director of Communications), who was in charge of the final publishing process. Their professionalism and friendship allowed us to complete a very difficult project with tight deadlines, and even have some fun while doing it.

The Body of Knowledge Task Force of volunteers for this project shared both their experience and insights to ensure that *Essentials of Cash Management, Fifth Edition* was both up-to-date and easy to understand. The BOK Task Force was chaired by Don Aquila (Thomas & Betts Company), with Kent Crocombe (Aladdin Industries) serving as Vice-Chair. Other task force members included Jacqueline Callahan (TMA), Sue McComb (Firstar Bank, Milwaukee), Bill Murray (First National Bank of Maryland), and Bob Westoby (Monsanto).

Others who contributed to this text include Paul Ruggeri of Sienna College, who worked on the initial outline; Kathleen Schrantz of KATTAIL Designs, who was responsible for graphics and design of the cover; Craig Nauman of TMA, who checked and validated all of the many calculations and formulas; and Arlene Chapman, CCM, (TMA Standards Manager), who reviewed chapters related to electronic commerce and relationship management.

Finally, we would like to thank our families for their understanding and support, especially when this project had us spending more time with each other than with them.

D. J. Masson
Dave Wikoff
Principal Partners, The Resource Alliance

ABOUT THE EDITORS

Dubos J. Masson and David A. Wikoff, Principal Partners of The Resource Alliance, have over 30 years combined experience in business consulting and management training. The Resource Alliance is a Colorado-based firm specializing in consulting and training in the areas of treasury management, sales management, electronic commerce, and business process redesign. The Resource Alliance's clients include financial institutions and corporations in a wide variety of industries.

ABOUT TMA

The Treasury Management Association (TMA) is the principal organization representing private sector treasury professionals.

TMA offers a wide range of continuing education, professional certification, industry standards programs, research, and publications for treasury professionals. Membership in TMA is open to corporate treasury practitioners as well as those who sell products and services to the treasury management profession, such as bankers, consultants, and academics. The mission of the Association is enhanced value of the treasury profession through professional knowledge, respect and recognition for the profession, a favorable business environment, and professional conduct.

CHAPTER **1**

The Role of Cash Management in Corporate Finance

OVERVIEW

This introductory chapter establishes the reason for the development of cash management as a separate discipline within a company's financial organization. It describes a number of forces and trends in financial institutions and corporate finance that continue to have an influence on the cash management environment in which the cash manager functions. The reader should focus primarily on overall trends in this chapter. This chapter introduces a number of terms and concepts that will be developed throughout the text.

LEARNING OBJECTIVES

Upon completion of this chapter and the related study questions, the reader should know:

1. The objectives of cash management.

2. What problems cash management solves.

3. How to identify major corporate financial objectives and the decisions that support them.

4. The major functions of cash management.

5. The place of cash management in the corporate financial organization.

6. The major historical developments in cash management.

OUTLINE

I.   **Overall Corporate Objective**

II. **Cash Management and the Operating Cycle of a Business**
     A.   Cash Management Objectives
     B.   The Operating Cycle and Cash Flow Timeline
     C.   Cash Flows
     D.   Tools of Cash Management

I. OVERALL CORPORATE OBJECTIVE

The primary objective of a corporation is to maximize shareholder value, which is the value of the owners' shares in the corporation. Shareholders entrust their assets to a corporation in order to earn an overall return that exceeds that available from similar investment alternatives. Shareholder value is directly enhanced through the efficient and profitable management of a company's operating cycle which is shown in Exhibit 1.1.

Financial goals and functions are vital to the achievement of the company's overall corporate objectives because they provide the financial resources required to sustain the operating cycle.

II. CASH MANAGEMENT AND THE OPERATING CYCLE OF A BUSINESS

The objectives of cash management are closely related to the management of the operating cycle and cash cycle of a business. The specific tools of cash management have evolved and are employed to attain stated cash management objectives.

A. Cash Management Objectives

An integral component of a company's financial activities is the cash management function. The general objective of cash management is the efficient utilization of cash in a manner which is consistent with the overall strategic objectives of the company.

The major objectives of cash management include:

- *Liquidity* - Maintaining the ability to pay obligations when they become due.
- *Cash Optimization* - Establishing systems and procedures that help minimize investment in non-earning cash resources while providing adequate liquidity.
- *Financing* - Assisting in obtaining both short- and long-term borrowed funds in a timely manner and at an acceptable cost.
- *Risk Management* - Monitoring and assisting in the control of a company's exposure to interest rate, foreign exchange, and other risks.
- *Coordination* - Ensuring that cash management goals are communicated and integrated with the strategic objectives and policy decisions of other areas of the company that have an impact on cash flows.

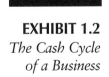

EXHIBIT 1.1

Operating Cycle of a Company

B. The Operating Cycle and Cash Cycle

The need for a cash management system arises out of the company's basic operating cycle. In cash management terms, this operating cycle translates into the cash flow timeline which is shown in Exhibit 1.2.

As generally illustrated, the business must first purchase the resources necessary to make its product or deliver its service. It then sells that product or service and finally collects the funds from the sale. The cash inflows and outflows occurring along the cash flow timeline are rarely for the same amount, nor do they occur at the same time. The challenge of cash management is to provide sufficient levels of cash at all phases of the cycle to insure its on-going operation.

EXHIBIT 1.2

The Cash Cycle of a Business

C. Cash Flows

There are three general types of cash flows that occur on or in relation to the cash flow time-line to achieve efficient liquidity management:

1. *Cash Inflows* - These are funds collected from customers or obtained from financial sources.

2.   *Concentration and Liquidity Management Flows* - Concentrated funds are those that are systematically transferred to create a centralized inventory of liquid reserves held as cash or invested in cash equivalents. Concentration funds include internal transfers among operating units of a company and between the company's various bank accounts.

3.   *Cash Outflows* - These funds are disbursed from liquid reserves to vendors, employees, lenders, shareholders, and other payees of the company.

D. Tools of Cash Management

The tools of cash management are designed to synchronize a company's cash flows, thereby promoting the efficient operation of the cash flow timeline. Products used in the collection, concentration, and disbursement of funds reduce the time periods between events occurring along the timeline. The shorter the overall cash flow cycle, the more liquidity a company is capable of generating. Increased liquidity not only reduces a company's risk of insolvency, but typically can increase its overall profitability.

The problems of the timing and unequal amounts of a company's cash inflows and outflows are addressed through the practices of cash management, which include the following day-to-day operations:

- *Collection* - Collecting funds from customers
- *Concentration* - Concentrating funds where they can be most efficiently deployed
- *Disbursement* - Disbursing funds to vendors, employees, and investors
- *Information* - Developing and maintaining appropriate information systems
- *Forecasting* - Forecasting to predict future funds flows
- *Investment* - Investing surplus funds
- *Borrowing* - Borrowing to meet short-term requirements
- *Financial Institution Relationships* - Managing financial institution relationships

III. THE FINANCE FUNCTION AND FINANCIAL DECISIONS

A company's financial functions and decisions significantly influence its cash management operations.

A. The Finance Function

The finance function plays a pivotal role in the achievement of a company's overall objective to maximize shareholder value. The principal roles of the finance function include the following:

1.   *Accounting* - The accounting function is the record-keeping function. Companies need to follow generally accepted principles of accounting to record their assets, liabilities, equity, revenues, expenses, and earnings.

2.   *Funding* - The funding function is responsible for raising capital to finance projects a company undertakes to produce earnings and enhance shareholder value.

3. *Capital Budgeting* - The capital budgeting function is responsible for the following:

- Quantitatively evaluating various alternative projects in which a company could invest its capital resources.
- Forecasting the rate of return of various projects in relation to one another and in relation to the company's cost of capital.
- Evaluating with senior management both the quantitative and qualitative costs and benefits of a project. Qualitative factors might include whether a project fits into a company's core strategy and whether it is in an area in which a company has a competitive advantage.

B. Corporate Financial Decisions

The most important financial decisions a corporation must make include the following:

1. *Investment Decisions* - Very few companies can raise unlimited capital for their projects, or have the management resources for an unlimited number of projects. They must decide how to allocate capital between the number and kinds of projects in which to invest. Investment projects may range from capital equipment to corporate subsidiaries and should be evaluated in terms of return and risk. In other words, the forecasted extra profits those projects will create must be weighed against the risk that the forecasted returns will not be achieved.

   Another type of investment decision is whether to sell a division or subsidiary or discontinue a product line because the company's capital resources can be more effectively deployed elsewhere.

2. *Financing Decisions* - A company must weigh several decisions when evaluating how to finance its projects. Decisions about a company's capacity to raise the total investment amount required and the appropriate mix of financing alternatives available are intertwined. A company's capacity to raise additional types of capital is influenced by its risk profile as perceived by outside investors or creditors. Its risk profile, in turn, is influenced by the existing mixture of the company's debt and equity.

3. *Dividend Decisions* - A company must decide how much of its earnings to distribute as cash dividends to stockholders and how much to retain and reinvest in operations. This decision is sometimes guided by shareholder expectations, which vary widely given a company's industry and stage of development. Dividend decisions and payouts may also be restricted by covenants contained in a company's debt agreements.

IV. FINANCIAL ORGANIZATION

Financial organization varies by company and is influenced by company size, industry group, and level of technology. The financial structure of a company should facilitate the achievement of its overall company objectives.

A. Finance Organizational Structure

In a large company, the treasurer and the controller typically report to the Chief Financial Officer (CFO). Some companies have a flatter organizational structure in which the following functions report to the CFO:

- Treasury
- Information systems
- Audit
- Strategic planning
- Financial analysis

Exhibit 1.3 illustrates how the cash manager typically fits into the treasury function of a large company.

EXHIBIT 1.3

Typical Organization of the Treasury Function

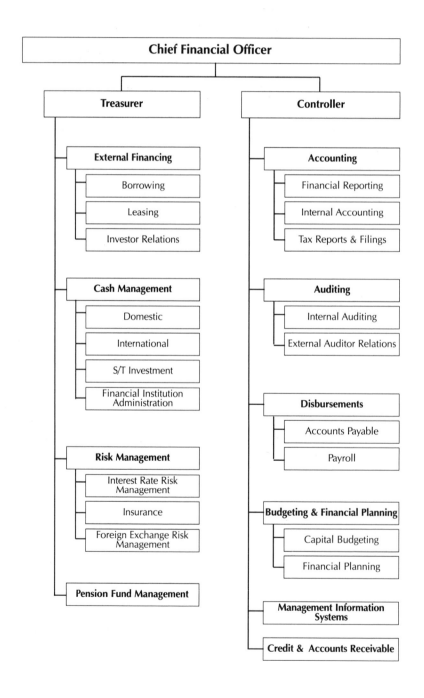

B. Responsibilities of the Key Players

The members of a company's financial staff have traditional roles in a typical company.

1. *Chief Financial Officer (CFO)* - The CFO is normally a member of the senior management team, reporting to the Chief Executive Officer (CEO). In a large company, the CFO usually oversees the treasury and accounting functions, and plays an important strategic planning role as the pivotal person in the capital budgeting and investment decision-making process. Selecting and rejecting investment projects is part of the way a company carries out its strategic plan. Final decisions on building a plant, buying or selling a subsidiary, or closing down a product line are typically the responsibility of the CEO or the Board of Directors. However, the CFO plays a central role in presenting and quantifying decision alternatives and measuring the financial results of those decisions once they are implemented.

2. *Treasurer* - The treasurer is usually responsible for arranging external financing, managing relationships with banks and other financial institutions, and overseeing day-to-day liquidity management. Other functions that may report to the treasurer include credit management, dividend disbursement, insurance and pension management. In a large company, some of these responsibilities may be delegated to an assistant treasurer.

3. *Controller* - The controller is normally responsible for accounts payable, internal accounting, preparation of financial statements, internal auditing, coordination with external auditors, preparation of budgets and tax filings, and monitoring budgeted capital expenditures.

4. *Internal Auditor* - The internal auditor is responsible for determining that controls and operating procedures are in place to protect a company from losses caused by inefficiency, inaccuracy, or fraud. The internal auditor may report to the controller, but may also report to the CFO or directly to the Board of Directors.

5. *Credit Manager* - The credit manager, who may report either to the controller or to the treasurer, is responsible for preserving and collecting accounts receivable, and implementing corporate credit policies, approving the extension of credit terms to customers, and establishing information systems to monitor accounts receivable.

6. *Cash Manager* - The cash manager is part of the treasury function and is concerned primarily with the management of day-to-day cash flows and banking relationships, as detailed in the following section.

V. THE ROLE OF THE CASH MANAGER

The responsibilities assigned to the cash manager vary from company to company, but several functions are typically included.

A. Cash Management Functions and Responsibilities

1. *Systems Design, Implementation, and Evaluation*
   • Analysis and design of cash management systems, their implementation, and ongoing evaluation

2. *Funds Management*
   - Monitoring the daily cash position
   - Controlling cash balances on deposit at financial institutions
   - Moving funds from concentration accounts and other cash pools to where they are needed

3. *Banking System Administration*
   - Managing bank relations and compensation for banking services
   - Conducting analytical reviews and feasibility studies of banking services

4. *Money Market Administration*
   - Short-term borrowing
   - Short-term investing

5. *Forecasting*
   - Projecting cash needs and excesses
   - Monitoring the accuracy of such projections

B. Reporting Relationships

In most companies, the cash manager reports directly or indirectly to the treasurer who, in turn, reports to the CFO. In a small company, the cash manager's job may be a part-time responsibility of the treasurer or assistant treasurer, but in a large company, a staff of several people may be devoted to cash management and banking relations.

C. Cooperation with Other Functions

Day-to-day monitoring of a company's cash position and maintenance of banking relationships are almost always within the scope of the treasury function. Other departments may have primary responsibility for some other functions, such as credit management and disbursements, that have a direct impact on cash management.

For example, the cash manager may share responsibility with the credit function for setting up and maintaining lockboxes to intercept and speed the collection of checks from customers. However, the credit function sometimes reports to the controller, not the treasurer. Successful cash management, therefore, requires teamwork and cooperation, and the cash manager must often play an informal, influencing role with managers of other departments.

VI. DEVELOPMENT OF CASH MANAGEMENT IN THE U. S.

Cash management in the U. S. has been an outgrowth of particular features of the domestic banking structure, mail system, and payment conventions. Though they may be changing as a result of recent developments and legislation, the features that have traditionally distinguished the U.S. from other countries include the following:

- a large number of banks
- a lack of comprehensive nationwide bank branching
- an extensive use of mail for payment
- a custom of paying most bills by check

Prior to 1950, interest rates were low and a corporate treasurer did not have a large variety of external investment opportunities. There was more money in the banking system than there was loan demand. Banks funded their loans with interest-free demand deposit accounts (DDAs) and invested the excess in safe, low-yielding government securities. Banks competed with each other far less than they do today. They were highly selective in their corporate lending, motivating treasurers to keep large excess balances to protect credit facilities.

A. The 1940s and 1950s

1. *The First Lockbox* - RCA was one of the first companies to arrange a collection system in 1947. It was designed to accelerate payments from dealers who were borrowing from RCA to finance their inventory of RCA products.

2. *The Accord and the Government Securities Market* - In 1951, the Federal Reserve Board of Governors reached an historic accord with the U.S. Treasury Department. It gave the Federal Reserve (Fed) the right to pursue an independent monetary policy. The Fed subsequently adopted a policy of purchasing only short-term Treasury bills, and no longer purchasing longer-term Treasury notes and bonds. The Treasury no longer had the Fed as a captive investor for notes and bonds and had to rely on a competitive market to raise funds. The Fed removing itself from the long-term side of the Treasury market also meant that the yield curve (the relationship between long- and short-term interest rates) was now determined as a result of competitive market forces rather than by government action. This marked the birth of a huge market of safe, liquid securities with short-, medium- and long-term maturities for companies with excess cash.

B. The 1960s

1. *Negotiable Bank Certificates of Deposit (CDs)* - By 1960, banks needed to buy funds and compete for deposits to support their growing loan portfolios. In 1961, the Fed authorized banks to issue negotiable certificates of deposit. The introduction of CDs provided a new source of funds for banks and an investment instrument for corporations.

2. *Diversifying Short-Term Investments* - Interest rates continued to rise in the 1960s. Treasurers diversified from low-yielding, liquid government securities into new instruments such as municipal obligations, banker's acceptances, commercial paper, and repurchase agreements.

3. *Managing Bank Balances* - Treasurers managed cash resources more efficiently, reduced idle bank balances and demanded more bank services for balances on deposit. In response, banks expanded their corporate services and developed more formal marketing programs.

4. *Lockbox Models* - Bank-operated lockboxes became increasingly popular as cash managers became more aware of collection float and its related cost. In the late 1960s, a model was developed for studying mail times between one city and another. The model optimized the location of lockbox sites in relation to the disbursement banks and mailing points used by bill payors.

C. The 1970s

1. *Remote Disbursement* - Remote disbursement was designed to take advantage of the inaccessibility of certain banks. These banks, generally located in geographically isolated locations, offered significant float gains to companies that used them for check disbursement. The remoteness of these banks created difficulty in physically presenting checks drawn on them in a timely manner. The Federal Reserve was granting credit to the depositing bank before the check could be collected from the remote bank on which it was drawn. The increasing use of remote disbursement throughout the 1970s, coupled with the Federal Reserve's concern over float costs and the financial health of banks used for this purpose, led to programs aimed at discouraging the practice.

2. *Controlled Disbursement* - Controlled disbursement was designed to take advantage of the Federal Reserve's presentment schedule. In a number of banks, the final presentment of checks from the Fed was sufficiently early in the day to enable a company to determine its total daily check clearings and fund this amount. The company could then make investment and/or borrowing decisions knowing there would be no additional clearings against the account that day.

3. *Funds Concentration* - Companies that processed credit card purchases established third-party services that aided in the creation of depository transfer checks (DTCs). The amounts deposited in local banks would be reported by the depositing units to the third-party services. The information would be consolidated and relayed to the concentration bank, which would create a DTC to transfer funds from the local banks. In later years, check depository transfers were replaced by electronic depository transfers.

4. *Bank Balance Reporting* - Banks began to offer services to gather and store bank balance and transaction information which companies could then directly access. Information from multiple banks could be consolidated into a single report.

5. *Transaction Details and Real-Time Reporting* - Customers began to get detailed transaction information on bank services. Banks offered information such as inbound money transfer amounts with accompanying reference information during the same working day in which they were received. Methods were developed for customers to initiate money transfers and other transactions using terminals in their offices.

6. *Electronic Payments* - Electronic payment alternatives began to be developed using the Automated Clearing House (ACH). The primary applications were direct deposit of payroll and collection of life insurance premiums.

7. *Commercial Paper* - Large corporations started to borrow by issuing short-term promissory notes (known as commercial paper) because it was less expensive than borrowing from commercial banks.

D. The 1980s

1. *Depository Institutions Deregulation and Monetary Control Act of 1980* - Also known as the Monetary Control Act, this was the most comprehensive banking legislation since the 1930s. A number of changes which it made were destined to have an impact on bank services and prices for years to come.

2. *Noon Presentment and Payor Bank Services* - In 1983 the Fed accelerated its presentment schedule by making second presentments later in the day, as part of the float-reduction program mandated by the Monetary Control Act.

3. *Electronic Corporate-to-Corporate Payments* - Banks began to promote corporate trade payments through the ACH. Companies saw the efficiency of electronic payments on the one hand, but were reluctant to give up disbursement float on the other.

4. *Electronic Commerce and Electronic Data Interchange* - Electronic Commerce (EC) is the exchange of business information from one organization to another in some type of electronic format and includes facsimile (fax), electronic mail (E-mail), and EDI communications. Electronic Data Interchange (EDI) is a formalized computer-to-computer communication for routine business transactions in a standard format. Financial EDI (FEDI) is EDI related to payments. The introduction of these new technologies has caused significant changes in treasury and cash management operations.

5. *Use of Personal Computers* - The introduction of the personal computer (PC) led banks and software firms to develop the treasury workstation. Software was developed to retrieve information from banks automatically and compile it into consolidated reports. The electronic spreadsheet replaced the paper spreadsheet.

6. *Integration of International Financial Markets* - Worldwide integration resulted from the global expansion of companies and banks and the development of international financial centers. Computer and communications technology played a crucial role in forging these links, in facilitating the enormous funds flows, and in increasing the importance of foreign exchange management. The Eurocurrency market developed initially in the 1960s, based on the accumulation of Eurodollars, which are U.S. dollars on deposit in financial institutions outside the U.S. The Eurodollar market broadened to become the Eurocurrency market, then expanded to become a worldwide non-U.S. currency market.

7. *Financial Product Innovation* - In the early 1980s, a number of capital market innovations were introduced. These new products included interest rate and currency swaps, futures, options, and asset-backed securities.

8. *Bank Creditworthiness* - Several instances occurred that raised concerns about a bank's creditworthiness. The Federal Reserve showed concern over the impact that a major bank failure would have on the payment system. Bankers, because of their exposure to other banks, were also concerned. Treasurers who had previously shown little interest started to scrutinize the financial condition of their banks.

   A key factor in judging a bank's creditworthiness is its level of capital. In recent years capital adequacy ratios have been developed on a global basis that could be used in evaluating a bank's relative financial condition.

9. *Cash Management Ethics* - In the early 1980s, the E. F. Hutton Company was involved in a widely discussed case concerning fair bank compensation. By channeling check deposits from Hutton branches through unsophisticated banks that treated ledger balances as though they were available balances, Hutton was effectively able to borrow interest free from the banks. The E. F. Hutton affair put the spotlight on some potentially questionable cash management practices.

E. The 1990s

1. *Payments System Risk* - Payments system risk is an issue closely related to bank creditworthiness because of an increase in money transfer volume on the Fedwire, the Clearing House Interbank Payments System (CHIPS), and the ACH. The Federal Reserve has taken numerous steps to reduce this risk.

2. *Electronic Payment of State and Federal Taxes* - The federal government, most state governments, and many local governments require the electronic payment of sales, withholding, income, and other taxes above a certain dollar limit. Electronic filing of tax returns and information is also offered by many government tax authorities.

3. *Interstate Banking* - Government regulations prohibiting interstate banking and branching are slowly being removed. The Interstate Banking and Branching Efficiency Act of 1994 allows banks to operate fully integrated banking systems nationwide beginning in June 1997, so long as a state has not taken legislative action to prohibit interstate mergers.

VII. CURRENT TREASURY ENVIRONMENT

The historical factors outlined above have played a significant role in shaping and reshaping the corporate financial function. Other general trends currently impacting the ongoing development of the treasury function include the following:

A. Quality Issues

The issue of quality has become an integral part of the overall corporate environment. Treasury departments have not been immune to this trend and are continuously challenged to provide a high level of quality results at an acceptable cost.

B. Reorganization of Treasury Operations

As the treasury function has evolved, treasury professionals have continually endeavored to use effectively the resources available to attain both financial and overall corporate objectives. A number of developments have led to a re-examination of how the treasury function is organized and the efficiency with which it operates. In many cases the restructuring of treasury operations has resulted in smaller staffing through automation and downsizing. The following are three common terms associated with these efforts:

1. *Re-engineering* - The concept of re-engineering involves a radical redesign of a particular business process with the goal of continuous process improvement. The redesign of treasury operations may include restructuring or eliminating traditional treasury processes.

2. *Benchmarking* - In the process of re-engineering the treasury function, it is valuable to seek out examples of other companies who have successfully redesigned their operation. The best practice in the field serves as a benchmark which can be used to compare and evaluate a company's existing process.

3. *Outsourcing* - One possible outcome of re-engineering the treasury operation may be the decision to have an outside provider perform part, or all, of a business function. This is known as outsourcing. For example, a company may decide to outsource its disbursement processing. It sends a data file containing payment information to an outside processor. The processor then initiates the specified payments on the company's behalf, using the designated method of payment (i.e., check, ACH, etc.).

Questions

These chapter questions are to test and review the information in the text and are not examples of CCM examination questions, nor are they in the examination format.

Answers can be found at the back of the book on p. 311.

1. What are the major objectives of cash management?

2. What is the relationship between the operating cycle and the cash flow timeline?

3. What are the three general types of cash flows which must be managed?

4. What is the purpose of using cash management tools?

5. What are the three principal roles of the finance function?

6. What are the three important corporate financial decisions?

7. Who are the key players (besides the cash manager) involved in the finance function?

8. What are the five cash management functions and responsibilities?

9. What are the key features which distinguish cash management practices in the U.S. compared to other countries?

10. What two disbursement products were introduced in the 1970s?

11. What banking legislation reshaped cash management in the 1980s?

12. What are the key issues in the current treasury environment?

CHAPTER 2

Accounting and Financial Concepts

OVERVIEW

This chapter reviews the basic principles of accounting and finance as they apply to cash management.

LEARNING OBJECTIVES

Upon completion of this chapter and the related study questions, the reader should know:

1. What the basic accounting concepts are, such as the income statement, the balance sheet, the statement of cash flows, and cash versus accrual accounting.

2. What the basic financial concepts are, such as the time value of money, capital structure, cost of capital, capital budgeting and liquidity.

3. What the cash flow timeline is, and how different types of float are associated with the timeline.

OUTLINE

I.   **Accounting Concepts**
    A. Accounting Principles
    B. Cash versus Accrual Accounting
    C. Accounting for Cash
    D. Financial Statements

II. **Financial Concepts**
    A. Time Value of Money
    B. Discount Rate/Opportunity Cost
    C. Capital Structure and Strategy
    D. Cost of Capital
    E. Capital Budgeting
    F. Liquidity Measures and Ratios
    G. Other Financial Ratios

III. **The Cash Flow Timeline and Float**
    A. Invoicing Float
    B. Payment Float

I. ACCOUNTING CONCEPTS

This section describes the basic accounting concepts that underlie the system of financial reporting and record-keeping used in the U.S. today.

A. Accounting Principles

Accounting provides the data necessary for measuring a company's performance and assessing its financial position. The accounting function records a company's assets, liabilities, shareholder equity, revenues, and expenses according to a detailed set of rules called **Generally Accepted Accounting Principles (GAAP)**. These principles are developed, agreed upon, and published in the form of Statements of Financial Accounting Standards (SFAS) by the **Financial Accounting Standards Board (FASB)**, an independent, self-regulating organization formed in 1973.

Adherence to those rules is important because investors, lenders, and trade creditors rely on consistent financial information for their decisions as to whether to invest or lend, or provide products or services on credit terms.

B. Cash versus Accrual Accounting

Some companies, particularly small ones, record their revenues, expenses, and earnings strictly on the basis of when cash is received or paid out. This is known as cash accounting. In cash accounting, all accounting entries are directly related to a cash inflow or outflow. Sales are recorded as the cash is received and expenses are recorded as they are paid. The other primary accounting method is accrual accounting, which recognizes revenues as they are earned and expenses as they are incurred, regardless of when the related cash flow occurs. The cash accounting approach tends to be used by small businesses.

The fundamental difference between cash and accrual accounting is the timing of the recognition of income or expenses, and the actual cash flows. With the accrual accounting system, revenues may be reported but not yet collected, and expenses may have been incurred but not yet paid. It is particularly important for the cash manager, who is mainly concerned with cash flows, to understand the distinction between accounting information and cash flows.

The following are some of the most important accrual accounting principles:

1. *Income Recognition* - Revenue is recognized on the income statement when sales are made. When sales are made on credit, accounts receivable are created on the balance sheet. This documents that revenue from sales has been recognized, but that funds have not yet been received. When funds are collected from the customer, the accounts receivable balance is decreased and the cash balance is increased, without any effect on income.

2. *Cost Recognition* - Costs incurred in a time period prior to the sale are added to the inventory value. They are not treated as expenses when there is a cash expenditure. The expense is recognized as part of the cost of goods sold in the accounting period of the sale, in order to match revenues and expenses.

3. *Capitalized Assets* - Capitalized assets are expected to have a life greater than one accounting cycle and are not fully expensed in the period in which they are acquired. The assets are carried on the balance sheet at their acquisition cost and depreciated.

4. *Depreciation and Amortization* - Accounting expense connected with a capitalized asset is recognized by depreciation in the case of fixed assets and amortization in the case of intangible, long-term assets. With both depreciation and amortization, the cost of the asset is allocated over its useful or legal life. Neither depreciation nor amortization measures a decline in the actual value of an asset. Both are non-cash expenses; therefore, the income statement for an accounting period understates the cash flow provided by operations by the amount of depreciation expense and/or amortization taken.

5. *Deferred Taxes* - Differences between recognition of revenue and expenses by the tax code versus by accrual accounting result in differences in the cash disbursement for income taxes and the taxes reported on the income statement. This difference is recognized as a deferred tax and appears on the balance sheet.

6. *Capital and Dividends* - A number of cash flows, such as capital asset additions or retirements and dividends, are neither income nor expenses. The addition of capital to the company, such as the issuance of debt or the sale of common stock, results in a cash inflow, but is not income. The cash flow for the repayment of principal in a debt obligation is not an expense. The payment of cash dividends to shareholders is a distribution of profits and not an expense.

7. *Management Discretion* - A company must exercise judgment on the allocation of expenses and revenues. There is potential for companies to adjust the value of revenues or expenses under the accrual system. Part of the external auditor's role is to render an opinion that revenue and expense recognition is according to GAAP.

C. Accounting for Cash

Cash as recorded on the company's accounting books is often different from the cash balance on the bank's books, primarily because of disbursement float (checks issued but not yet presented at the company's bank for payment).

Sometimes a company's books will reflect a negative cash balance, or a "red" book balance. There are two ways to avoid reporting these negative balances in the company's financial statements. Instead of reporting cash as a separate item, the combined total of cash and marketable securities can be reported on the balance sheet. This, of course, assumes that the amount of marketable securities is greater than the negative cash balance. Alternatively, the company can report the bank balance in the cash account, and report checks that have been issued but not yet presented for payment as a current liability under a title such as drafts payable or checks not cleared.

D. Financial Statements

The following types of accounting or financial statements are generally used to record revenues, expenses, assets and liabilities. They are prepared according to GAAP.

1. *Income Statement* - The income statement, or profit and loss statement, is a record of revenues and expenses, as illustrated in Exhibit 2.1. It describes the net change in the value of shareholder's equity resulting from operations over a specified period of time.

    • *Revenues* - Revenues represent the total amount derived from a company's sale of merchandise or services.

- *Cost of Goods Sold* - The cost of goods sold represents the expense of providing goods and services for sale. It includes labor and material directly used in manufacturing a product or providing a service, as well as other direct production and selling expenses.

- *Operating Expenses* - Operating expenses such as selling or administrative expenses are necessary for the conduct of the business, but not tied directly to the production of goods and services.

- *Depreciation* - Depreciation is generally considered an operating expense, but not a cash outlay. In order to determine cash flows from operations, depreciation must be added back to after-tax net income.

- *Operating Profit* - Operating profit, also known as operating income, is the profit after deducting the cost of goods sold and operating expenses from revenues.

- *Other Income/Expenses* - The income statement may include other income and expenses. These include extraordinary items, currency gains and losses, and amortization.

- *Net Income* - Net income is operating profit less the cost of debt financing and income taxes incurred during the accounting cycle, and adjusted for other income and expenses.

EXHIBIT 2.1
Sample Year-End Income Statement

Revenues	$ 15,000,000
Less: Cost of Goods Sold	9,200,000
Gross Profit	5,800,000
Less: Operating Expenses	4,000,000
Less: Depreciation	200,000
Operating Profit	1,600,000
Less: Interest Expense	300,000
Net Profit Before Taxes	1,300,000
Less: Provision for Income Taxes	450,000
Net Income	**$ 850,000**
Earnings Available for Common Shareholders	$ 850,000
Less: Common Stock Dividends Paid	250,000
Addition to Retained Earnings	$ 600,000
Earnings per Share (100,000 shares outstanding)	$ 8.50

2. *Balance Sheet* - A balance sheet is illustrated in Exhibit 2.2. The balance sheet or statement of financial condition reports the following as of a specific date:

- *Assets* - items of value owned by a company
- *Liabilities* - amounts owed by a company
- *Equity* - the value of the owners' position in a company

EXHIBIT 2.2

Sample Balance Sheets (Current and Prior Year)

ASSETS

	Current Year	Prior Year	Change
Cash	$ 1,500,000	$ 1,000,000	$ 500,000
Short-Term Investments	1,300,000	1,500,000	(200,000)
Accounts Receivable	1,700,000	1,300,000	400,000
Inventory	2,600,000	2,100,000	500,000
Pre-Paid Expenses	900,000	900,000	0
Total Current Assets	8,000,000	6,800,000	
Property, Plant, & Equipment	7,500,000	6,800,000	700,000
Total Assets	**$15,500,000**	**$13,600,000**	**$ 1,900,000**

LIABILITIES AND OWNERS' EQUITY

	Current Year	Prior Year	Change
Accounts Payable	$ 1,600,000	$ 1,200,000	$ 400,000
Short-Term Notes Payable	1,800,000	1,300,000	500,000
Total Current Liabilities	3,400,000	2,500,000	
Long-Term Debt	3,900,000	3,500,000	400,000
Total Liabilities	7,300,000	6,000,000	
Common Stock at Par Value	200,000	200,000	0
Paid-In Capital	3,600,000	3,600,000	0
Retained Earnings	4,400,000	3,800,000	600,000
Total Liabilities & Equity	**$15,500,000**	**$13,600,000**	**$ 1,900,000**

Assets - Assets are listed at historical cost on the balance sheet. Assets to be depreciated or amortized are shown net of accumulated depreciation or amortization. Assets are usually listed on the balance sheet in the order of decreasing liquidity, as follows:

- *Current Assets* - The basic current assets include cash, marketable securities, accounts receivable, and inventories. These current assets will normally be converted to cash within one year or within the accounting cycle. Current assets may also include prepaid expenses such as insurance premiums, which are prepaid a year in advance.

- *Intangible Assets* - Intangible assets are assets that lack physical substance. Examples are goodwill and patents. Intangible assets are amortized over their legal or useful life.

- *Fixed Assets* - Property, plant, and equipment are a company's investment in fixed assets such as buildings, machinery, and equipment. Fixed assets (also known as long-term assets or capital assets) cannot be turned into cash as readily as current assets.

Liabilities - Liabilities represent obligations of the firm. They are usually listed on the balance sheet in order of increasing maturity, as follows:

- *Current Liabilities* - Current liabilities include obligations such as accounts payable, short-term loans, wages payable, taxes payable, and the current portion of long-term debt (all due within one year or within the accounting cycle). Accounts payable (also referred to as trade payables) are amounts due to creditors for purchased items. Short-term notes payable are typically short-term bank loans or commercial paper.
- *Long-Term Liabilities* - Long-term liabilities are obligations such as term loans, mortgages, and bonds due beyond one year or accounting cycle.

Equity - Shareholder equity represents the book value committed by and belonging to the owners either in the form of shareholder capital or retained earnings. Retained earnings is the increase in shareholder equity that arises from retention of profits in the company.

The following equations always hold true:

$$\text{Total Assets} = \text{Total Liabilities} + \text{Shareholder Equity}$$

$$\text{Shareholder Equity} = \text{Total Assets} - \text{Total Liabilities}$$

3. *Statement of Cash Flows* - Under the accrual system, the accounting period when a revenue or expense item is recognized is often different from the accounting period when the cash transaction takes place. Although the income statement based on accrual accounting is a useful indication of the company's performance, lenders are concerned with the company's cash flow because cash, not earnings, repays debt.

    The Statement of Cash Flows provides an indication of the sources of a company's cash flow and how it is being used. It is divided into three sections—Operating, Investing, and Financing Activities.

    Exhibit 2.3 shows how a Statement of Cash Flows can be constructed from information in the income statement and balance sheet.

    Cash flow results from more than a change in net income. Among other items to consider are the following:

    - Changes in property, plant, and equipment resulting from additions or dispositions, and depreciation or amortization.
    - Changes in retained earnings from dividends paid.
    - Changes in assets and liabilities. Decreases in assets and increases in liabilities are sources of funds (cash). Increases in assets and decreases in liabilities are uses of funds (cash).

EXHIBIT 2.3

Sample Statement of Cash Flows

Cash Flows from Operating Activities		
Net Income		$ 850,000
Adjustments to Reconcile Net Income to Net Cash		
Depreciation	200,000	
Increase in Accounts Receivable	(400,000)	
Increase in Inventories	(500,000)	
Increase in Accounts Payables	400,000	
Net Cash Provided (Used) by Operating Activities		$ 550,000

Cash Flows from Investing Activities		
Capital Expenditures	(900,000)	
Decrease in Short-Term Investments	200,000	
Net Cash Provided (Used) in Investing Activities		($ 700,000)

Cash Flows from Financing Activities		
Net Borrowing - Bank Line of Credit Agreement	500,000	
Proceeds from Issuance of Long-Term Debt	400,000	
Dividends Paid	(250,000)	
Net Cash Provided (Used) by Financing Activities		$ 650,000

Net Increase (Decrease) in Cash		
Cash - Beginning of Year	$1,000,000	
Cash - End of Year	1,500,000	
Net Cash Increase (Decrease)		
		$ 500,000

The Statement of Cash Flows in Exhibit 2.3 shows that net income was the largest source of funds for the firm in question. Changes in current assets and current liabilities were also sources of funds. These funds were used to add to property, plant, and equipment and to pay dividends. Financing was a source of cash. Net cash was higher at the end of the year, compared to cash at the beginning of the year.

II. FINANCIAL CONCEPTS

There are several key financial concepts which are important for financial managers. These include time value of money, discount rate, cost of capital, capital budgeting, and liquidity measures and ratios.

A. Time Value of Money

Time value is one of the fundamental financial principles. A dollar today is worth more than a dollar tomorrow because a dollar today can be invested to earn a return. It follows logically that a dollar tomorrow is worth less than a dollar today because the opportunity to earn interest is foregone. The value of a cash flow at any point in time can be determined by using an appropriate interest rate and the number of time periods involved.

1. *Future Value* - The future value of $100 invested at 10 percent is $110 one year from now ($100 x 1.10), and $121 two years from now ($100 x 1.10 x 1.10).

Future Value = Value Today x (1+ Interest Rate)$^{\text{Number of Periods}}$

or

$FV = PV \times (1+ i)^n$

Where:
   FV = Future Value
   PV = Present Value or Value Today
   i = Interest Rate
   n = Number of Periods

Thus, the future value of $100 for two periods at 10 percent is calculated as follows:

Future Value $= \$100 \times (1 + .10)^2 = \$100 \times (1 + .10) \times (1 + .10)$
$= \$100 \times (1.210) = \$121$

2. *Present Value* - Present value is today's value of any sum to be received in the future. It is the inverse of the future value calculation and can be determined if the appropriate interest rate is known. This concept is useful for comparing different alternative cash flows to be received at a future date, or to determine how much an investor would be willing to pay for an investment that provides a particular future cash flow stream.

    For example, assume a company can purchase an investment that pays $100 at the end of three years. How much is this future payment worth if the appropriate rate of interest is 10 percent? This is determined to be $75.13, as follows:

$$\text{Present Value} = \frac{\text{Future Value}}{(1+ \text{Interest Rate})^{\text{Number of Periods}}}$$

$$= \frac{\$100}{(1 + .10)^3} = \$100 \times (1 +.10)^{-3}$$

$$= \frac{\$100}{(1.3310)} = \$100 \times (.7513) = \$75.13$$

This equation can also be expressed in the following algebraic format:

$$PV = \frac{FV}{(1 + i)^n}$$

Where:

PV = Present Value
FV = Future Value
i = Interest Rate
n = Number of Periods

3. *Net Present Value (NPV)* - The concept of net present value is useful to examine projects in which a company might invest. The net present value is the sum of the present values of all cash flows associated with the project over its useful life. Cash inflows are positive, while cash outflows are negative. If the sum of all cash flows (inflows and outflows) is positive, then the project is said to have a positive net present value. If the sum is negative, then the project has a negative net present value. If the firm were to invest in a project with a positive net present value, then the overall value of the firm would increase by the amount of the project's net present value.

Using the information from the previous example, if the company were to pay $70 to purchase the investment which paid $100 in three years, it would have a net present value of $5.13, calculated at follows:

NPV = Present Value of Cash Inflows – Present Value of Cash Outflows

NPV = $75.13 – $70.00 = $5.13

B. Discount Rate/Opportunity Cost

In determining present and future values, the interest rate used is generally referred to as the discount rate. The discount rate, also known as opportunity cost, represents the return the firm might earn on its next best alternative. Companies often use their cost of capital as a discount rate for evaluating their projects. Companies in riskier businesses tend to have higher costs of capital and to use higher discount rates in evaluating their projects. When a given project is evaluated with higher discount rates, the net present value is lower because each future cash flow is discounted at a higher rate.

Companies may use different discount rates for different types of projects. Low-risk, short-term projects may be evaluated using a short-term opportunity cost such as the company's short-term borrowing or investment rate. High-risk projects may be evaluated using a "risk-adjusted" discount rate which is greater than the company's normal opportunity cost. By using a higher discount rate for riskier projects, the company is, in effect, forcing riskier projects to earn a higher rate of return to compensate for the additional risk.

C. Capital Structure and Strategy

Each company must evaluate its own tolerance for leverage and risk and decide on a target mix between debt and equity. Investors demand higher returns for higher risks. Companies in different industries with different risk profiles attract investors with different risk and return expectations. Companies have the following incentives to finance with debt:

- The after-tax cost of debt is typically lower than the after-tax cost of equity because interest is tax deductible.
- From the point of view of existing shareholders, the less new stock is sold, the less equity interest in the company they give up. The sale of new stock dilutes the ownership of existing shareholders and reduces the earnings per share.

The use of debt to finance a company is called financial leverage. Investment projects with a return higher than the cost of debt can increase the company's earningsby leveraging the investment of the shareholders. However, if earnings decrease, the firm must still meet its legal obligation for debt service.

D. Cost of Capital

Companies tend to finance with a combination of equity and debt. Equity is typically more expensive than debt because the shareholders' position is generally considered riskier than that of the debt holders. Interest costs are a legal obligation, whereas the payment of dividends is discretionary and may be omitted in times of poor earnings, or delayed, in the case of preferred dividends. Also, interest on debt is tax-deductible, whereas dividends on common stock are paid out of after-tax earnings.

Many companies consider their weighted average cost of capital (WACC) to be an appropriate discount rate for evaluating projects whose risk profiles are consistent with the overall risk profile of the company as a whole. A weighted average cost of capital is calculated as follows:

WACC = (After Tax Cost of Debt x Percentage of Debt) + (Cost of Equity x Percentage of Equity)

Where:

After Tax Cost of Debt = Before Tax Cost of Debt x (1 - Marginal Tax Rate)

$$\text{Percentage of Debt} = \frac{\text{Market Value of Long-Term Debt}}{\text{(Market Value of Long-Term Debt + Market Value of Equity)}}$$

$$\text{Percentage of Equity} = \frac{\text{Market Value of Equity}}{\text{(Market Value of Long-Term Debt + Market Value of Equity)}}$$

Assume that a company's long-term capital structure is 40 percent debt and 60 percent equity. The company's average cost of debt is 12 percent. The company's marginal tax rate is 34 percent; therefore, the after-tax cost of debt is 12 percent x (1 − .34) = 7.92 percent. The company's cost of equity is 16 percent.

The WACC is calculated as follows:

$$
\begin{aligned}
\text{WACC} &= (.0792 \times .40) + (.16 \times .60) \\
&= .0317 + .0960 \\
&= .1277 = 12.77\%
\end{aligned}
$$

E. Capital Budgeting

Capital budgeting is the process of evaluating alternative investment projects by methods such as net present value, and weighing other non-quantitative factors such as the company's core strategy and where the company believes its competitive strengths lie. A company may compare the net present values of various projects using the WACC as the discount rate.

A company operating in several industries may use a higher assumed WACC and discount rate for its riskier businesses and a lower WACC for its less risky businesses. It may also evaluate projects by comparing their **internal rates of return (IRR)**. The IRR is the discount rate at which the net present value is equal to zero.

F. Liquidity Measures and Ratios

Liquidity is the ability to convert an asset into cash or cash equivalents without significant loss. A company may be said to be liquid if it is able to meet its near-term financial obligations on time. Managing corporate liquidity on a day-to-day basis is an important function of cash management.

1. *Sources of Liquidity* - The following are sources of liquidity:

    - cash flow from operations
    - available cash and easily liquidated short-term investments to take care of temporary cash shortages
    - unused short-term borrowing facilities

2. *Why Liquidity Is Needed* - According to traditional economics, there are three primary reasons a company needs liquidity. These are:

    - *Transactions Requirement* - A company's cash inflows and outflows are not perfectly synchronized. The transaction liquidity balance is a reserve containing cash and near-cash resources held to provide for future funds requirements.
    - *Precautionary Requirement* - A company's cash inflows and outflows are not known with perfect certainty. Furthermore, unanticipated cash needs may arise. The precautionary liquidity balance is a reserve in which cash and near-cash resources are held to provide for unexpected requirements for funds.
    - *Speculative Requirement* - Having extra liquid resources helps a company take advantage of investment opportunities which may arise, including changes in interest rates.

3.   *Determining the Appropriate Level of Liquidity*

Insufficient Liquidity - Among the costs associated with not having sufficient liquidity are the following:

- *Transaction Costs* - These are the brokerage and administrative costs incurred when securities are sold or a line of credit is exercised to replenish a company's cash balance.
- *Additional Interest Costs* - These are the costs that arise from having to make unanticipated borrowings. They may be significant if interest rates are generally rising, or if the company must pay higher rates due to increased risk or changed financial condition.
- *Costs of Delayed Payments* - These include damage to the company's credit standing, lost cash discounts, and interest penalties.
- *Cost of Lost Opportunities* - This is the opportunity cost of foregoing advantageous purchases or investment opportunities.

At the extreme, a company with inadequate liquidity may become insolvent, and be forced to seek court protection by filing for bankruptcy. The resulting liquidation or reorganization creates bankruptcy costs such as legal fees, low employee morale, a negative public image, and foregone investment opportunities.

Excess Liquidity - Too much liquidity also has disadvantages. The opportunity cost of holding too much cash arises from the inability to invest these resources more profitably.

Proper Levels of Liquidity - The dollar volume of cash inflows and outflows is a major determinant of the level of liquidity needed, but there are other important factors as well. Even slight timing differences between cash inflows and outflows can cause a large drain on cash resources. Individual remittances may be relatively large in proportion to the size of the company and, therefore, only a few days' delay in a customer payment can cause substantial problems. The company's sales may fluctuate from month-to-month while expenses are incurred at a steady rate. All of these factors require a company to maintain substantial cash reserves.

4.   *Measuring Liquidity* - Measuring liquidity is important to the company's internal management for determining the adequacy of the company's liquidity policies, setting policy guidelines, and reporting to outside creditors such as banks. Bankers, trade creditors, and rating agencies need to measure liquidity as part of their evaluation of a company's creditworthiness. Among the methods for measuring liquidity are the following:

Note: The following ratio examples use information from Exhibits 2.1 and 2.2. All dollar amounts are in thousands.

Current Ratio - The current ratio is defined as total current assets divided by total current liabilities. This ratio measures a company's ability to meet its current obligations, or the degree to which current obligations are covered by current assets.

$$\text{Current Ratio } = \frac{\text{Total Current Assets}}{\text{Total Current Liabilities}} = \frac{\$8,000}{\$3,400} = 2.35$$

Quick Ratio - The quick ratio is defined as cash plus short-term investments and accounts receivable divided by total current liabilities. It is also known as the "acid test" ratio and is considered a more conservative liquidity ratio than the current ratio. The ratio measures the degree to which a company's current liabilities are covered by the most liquid current assets. Note that inventory and prepaid expenses are not included in this ratio because they are the least liquid of the current assets.

$$\text{Quick Ratio } = \frac{\text{Cash } + \text{ Short-Term Investments } + \text{ Accounts Receivable}}{\text{Total Current Liabilities}}$$

$$= \frac{\$1,500 + \$1,300 + \$1,700}{\$3,400} = \frac{\$4,500}{\$3,400} = 1.32$$

Cash Flow to Total Debt Ratio - Cash flow to total debt is defined as net income plus depreciation divided by total long-term plus short-term debt. Short-term debt consists of short-term notes, debentures, commercial paper, or other short-term debt obligations. Studies of failed companies have found this ratio to be historically accurate in predicting financial failure. A relatively low ratio is indicative of an inability to repay debt.

$$\begin{array}{l}\text{Cash Flow to} \\ \text{Total Debt Ratio}\end{array} = \frac{\text{Net Income } + \text{ Depreciation}}{\text{Short-Term Debt } + \text{ Long-Term Debt}}$$

$$= \frac{\$850 + \$200}{\$1,800 + \$3,900} = \frac{\$1,050}{\$5,700} = .184$$

Cash Conversion Cycle - The cash conversion cycle approaches liquidity from a different angle. By adding the average age of the inventory (measured by days' inventory) and average days of accounts receivable (measured by days' receivables) and subtracting the average age of the accounts payable (measured by days' payables), this measure indicates how efficiently a company is using its current assets and liabilities. In essence, the cash conversion cycle is measuring the time it takes a company to convert a cash outflow (for payment of inventory purchases) into a cash inflow (collection of accounts receivable).

$$\text{Days' Inventory} \quad = \frac{\text{Inventory}}{\text{Cost of Goods Sold}} \times 365 = \frac{\$2,600}{\$9,200} \times 365 = 103.2 \text{ Days}$$

$$\text{Days' Receivables} = \frac{\text{Accounts Receivable}}{\text{Annual Sales}} \times 365 = \frac{\$1,700}{\$15,000} \times 365 = 41.4 \text{ Days}$$

$$\text{Days' Payables} \quad = \frac{\text{Account Payable}}{\text{Cost of Goods Sold}} \times 365 = \frac{\$1,600}{\$9,200} \times 365 = 63.5 \text{ Days}$$

$$\text{Cash Conversion Cycle} = \text{Days' Inventory} + \text{Days' Receivables} - \text{Days' Payables}$$

$$= 103.2 \text{ Days} + 41.4 \text{ Days} - 63.5 \text{ Days} = 81.1 \text{ Days}$$

In this example, the company cycles through its cash every 81.1 days.

Cash Turnover - Cash turnover is the number of cash conversion cycles per year.

$$\text{Cash Turnover} = \frac{365}{\text{Cash Conversion Cycle}} = \frac{365}{81.1} = 4.50 \text{ Times}$$

The cash conversion cycle and cash turnover are measures of efficiency that can be compared to those of similar companies in similar industries.

G. Other Financial Ratios

In addition to the liquidity ratios, other financial ratios are used to determine the company's creditworthiness and growth prospects. They can be used for comparison to other companies in the same industry. Such ratios include debt management and coverage ratios, and performance ratios. No single ratio tells the whole story, but groups of ratios considered together can be revealing. Analysis of key ratios is also an integral part of the evaluation of a company by rating agencies, such as Standard and Poor's or Moody's. Rating agencies may have their own unique ratios or may use different versions of standard ratios.

1. *Advantages* - Among the advantages of using traditional financial ratios for analysis are the following:

    • Ratios are easily computed from the information found in publicly available financial reports.
    • Ratios are familiar to most producers and users of financial information.
    • Historical trends and variability can be observed over time.
    • Financial ratio databases allow comparison between companies.

2. *Disadvantages* - Among the disadvantages of traditional ratio measures are the following:

    • Traditional ratio measures usually reflect accounting rather than economic values.
    • Ratios express static relationships that do not take the variability of cash flows into account, except to the extent that the ratios themselves may vary.
    • Financial ratios provide indications but not answers. The evaluation of the company's worth is a matter of judgment.
    • Ratios are affected by differing methods of depreciation and by window dressing, the practice of adjusting certain accounts just prior to the end of the accounting period to make financial statements look better.

3. *Debt Management and Coverage Ratios* - These ratios measure the use of debt and ability of a company to meet the interest payments associated with debt.

    • *Times Interest Earned (TIE Ratio)* - This is a coverage ratio which indicates how many times a company's operating profit could decline before a firm is unable to meet (or cover) its interest obligations. The higher this ratio, the greater the ability of a company to meet its interest obligations.

$$\text{TIE} = \frac{\text{Operating Profit}}{\text{Interest Expense}} = \frac{\$1,600,000}{\$300,000} = 5.33 \text{ Times}$$

    • *Long-Term Debt to Capital Ratio* - This ratio measures the percentage of long-term debt relative to all of the long-term capital used in the company's capital structure. Long-term debt would include long-term notes and bonds, term loans, and capitalized lease obligations. Equity capital would include all preferred and common equity accounts. The higher this ratio, the greater the proportion of debt a company is using in its long-term capital structure.

$$\text{LT Debt to Capital} = \frac{\text{Long-Term Debt}}{\text{LT Debt + Equity}} = \frac{\$3,900,000}{\$3,900,000 + \$8,200,000} = 32.2\%$$

    • *Total Liabilities to Total Assets* - This ratio measures the percentage of all liabilities relative to the total asset base of the firm. The higher this ratio, the more liabilities (as opposed to equity) the firm uses to finance its asset base.

$$\frac{\text{Total Liabilities}}{\text{to Total Assets}} = \frac{\text{Total Liabilities}}{\text{Total Assets}} = \frac{\$7,300,000}{\$15,500,000} = 47.1\%$$

4.   *Performance Ratios* - These ratios measure the ability of a company to generate profits on sales, or returns on assets or capital.

- *Return on Equity* - This ratio measures the earnings available to common shareholders (net income less any preferred stock dividends or amortization) as a percentage of the common equity. In this example, where the company has no preferred stock, sinking funds, or amortization, the earnings available to common shareholders is equal to net income. The higher this ratio, the greater the return to the common shareholders of the company.

$$\text{Return on Equity} \quad = \frac{\text{Earnings Available to Common Shareholders}}{\text{Common Equity}}$$

$$= \frac{\$850,000}{\$8,200,000} \quad = 10.4\%$$

- *Profit Margin on Sales* - This ratio measures the net income of a company as a percentage of its sales. The higher this ratio, the more after-tax profits the company generates on a given sales level.

$$\text{Profit Margin on Sales} \quad = \frac{\text{Net Income}}{\text{Revenues}} \quad = \frac{\$850,000}{\$15,000,000} \quad = 5.7\%$$

- *Return on Total Assets* - This ratio measures the net income of a company as a percentage of its total assets. The higher this ratio, the more after-tax profits a company is generating from its asset base.

$$\text{Return on Total Assets} \quad = \frac{\text{Net Income}}{\text{Total Assets}} \quad = \frac{\$850,000}{\$15,500,000} \quad = 5.5\%$$

III. THE CASH FLOW TIMELINE AND FLOAT

In Chapter 1, The Role of Cash Management in Corporate Finance, the cash cycle was defined as the time between the payment for materials used to make a firm's product and the time when its accounts receivable are collected. Float can be caused by any type of delay along the cash flow timeline. The cash flow timeline is illustrated in Exhibit 2.4.

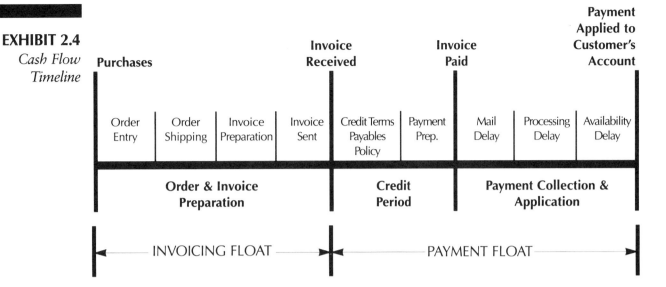

EXHIBIT 2.4
Cash Flow Timeline

A. Invoicing Float

Invoicing float is the delay between the purchase of goods and services and the receipt of the invoice by the payor.

B. Payment Float

Payment float is the delay between the receipt of the invoice by the payor, including the credit period, and the charging of the payor's account.

- *Collection Float* - The delay between the time a payor mails a check and the time the payee receives available funds.
- *Disbursement Float* - The delay between the time the check is mailed and the time it is charged to the payor's account.

A company benefits from shortening all types of float associated with cash inflows, and lengthening all types of float associated with cash outflows. In principle, this is true, except that companies generally do not extend disbursement float to the point of jeopardizing their vendor relationships. Other priorities such as cost containment and the quality of information provided to management have increased in relative value to float optimization in recent years.

QUESTIONS

These chapter questions are to test and review the information in the text and are not examples of CCM examination questions, nor are they in the examination format.

Answers can be found at the back of the book on p. 312-313.

1. What is GAAP?

2. What is a "red" book balance and how may its reporting be avoided?

3. What are the three basic financial statements?

4. What is the present value of $1,500 two years from now if the opportunity cost is 5 percent?

5. What are the primary incentives for a company to finance its capital structure with debt?

6. What are the three primary reasons a company needs liquidity?

7. What are the common ratios used to measure liquidity?

8. What is the cash conversion cycle?

9. What are the disadvantages of using financial ratios?

10. What is float and how can a company benefit from managing it?

CHAPTER 3

The U.S. Financial Environment

OVERVIEW

This chapter describes the role of the various types of financial institutions in the United States, the agencies that supervise them, and the legislation and regulations that impact the treasury function.

LEARNING OBJECTIVES

Upon completion of this chapter and the related study questions, the reader should know:

1. The principal functions of the following types of financial institutions: commercial banks, investment banking firms, savings banks, and finance companies.

2. The functions and structure of the following regulatory agencies: the Federal Reserve System, the Federal Deposit Insurance Corporation, and the Office of the Comptroller of the Currency.

3. How the banking system evolved through significant legislative developments.

4. How key Federal Reserve regulations impact a cash manager.

5. How relevant parts of the Uniform Commercial Code impact a cash manager.

OUTLINE

I. **Financial Institutions: Functions and Services**
    A. Commercial Banks
    B. Investment Banking and Brokerage Firms
    C. Thrift Institutions
    D. Credit Unions
    E. Mutual Funds
    F. Other Financial Institutions

II. **Regulatory Agencies**
    A. Federal Reserve System
    B. Office of the Comptroller of the Currency
    C. Federal Deposit Insurance Corporation
    D. Securities and Exchange Commission

E. Department of Justice
F. State Banking Boards and Commissions

III. **Federal Legislation**
A. Federal Reserve Act
B. Edge Act
C. McFadden Act
D. Glass-Steagall Act
E. Electronic Funds Transfer Act
F. Depository Institutions Deregulation and Monetary Control Act
G. Garn-St. Germain Depository Institutions Act
H. Expedited Funds Availability Act
I. Financial Institutions Reform, Recovery and Enforcement Act
J. Federal Deposit Insurance Corporation Improvement Act
K. Interstate Banking and Branching Efficiency Act

IV. **Federal Reserve Regulations**
A. Regulation D
B. Regulation E
C. Regulation J
D. Regulation Q
E. Regulation CC

V. **Uniform Commercial Code**
A. Article 3 - Negotiable Instruments
B. Article 4 - Bank Deposits and Collections
C. Article 4A - Funds Transfers
D. Article 5 - Letters of Credit

I. FINANCIAL INSTITUTIONS: FUNCTIONS AND SERVICES

This section discusses the functions of commercial banks and other types of financial institutions, as well as the services they offer.

A. Commercial Banks

Defined by law as a financial institution which accepts deposits and makes business loans, commercial banks offer a wide range of products and services. The term commercial bank is used to describe everything from small, single facility community banks with a few million dollars in assets to large, interstate institutions with hundreds of branches and billions in assets.

1. *Intermediation* - Central to an understanding of the difference between commercial banks and other types of financial institutions is the concept of intermediation. Banks are intermediaries between borrowers and investors (i.e., depositors). In this role, banks act as custodians for transaction and savings balances, as lenders of short-term credit, and as providers of a wide range of investment products.

   Among the services that commercial banks offer are the following:

   • *Deposit Accounts* - An important function of a commercial bank is to serve as a depository for cash. There are two basic types of depository accounts, demand and time. There are also interest-paying accounts that combine the features of demand and time deposits.

* *Demand Deposit Accounts* - Commonly referred to as checking accounts, Demand Deposit Accounts (DDAs) are a method by which an account holder uses a financial institution to transfer funds to a third party. The method of payment can be by check, wire transfer, or Automated Clearing House (ACH) transfer. By law (Regulation Q), interest cannot be paid on demand deposits held by businesses. The three exceptions to this regulation are sole proprietorships, government entities, and not-for-profit organizations. Balances held in demand deposit accounts may include:

  - *Transaction Balances* - Deposits held by companies as part of collection and disbursement activity.

  - *Compensating Balances* - Deposits held by companies in the form of collected balances which are used to pay for bank services.

  - *Correspondent Balances* - Balances from another bank held to facilitate check clearing, securities, letters of credit, and other transactions.

* *Time Deposits* - Deposits that must be held at a bank, thrift, or credit union for a specified period. Among examples of time deposits are the following:

  - *Savings Accounts or Passbook Savings Accounts* - Accounts that pay interest on balances. They are mainly held by individuals and not-for-profit institutions, but companies may also hold them.

  - *Certificates of Deposit* - Certificates of Deposit (CDs) are negotiable or non-negotiable obligations of a bank offered at either fixed or variable interest rates. Jumbo CDs are deposits of $100,000 or more; they are sold to individuals and companies. Maturities range from seven days to several years.

  - *Negotiable CDs* - Generally sold in $1,000,000 blocks to companies, money market funds, and other large investors. Being negotiable, they can be sold to another investor prior to maturity. Maturities range from 14 days to 5 years, but most have maturities of less than 12 months.

  - *Retail CDs* - Non-negotiable CDs sold to individual investors in amounts that vary from institution to institution. Maturities range from 3 months to 5 years.

* *Other Interest-Paying Accounts* - Accounts that have some of the features of both demand and time deposits. Among examples are the following:

  - *Negotiable Order of Withdrawal Accounts* - Accounts that offer unrestricted check writing and pay unregulated rates of interest. Negotiable Order of Withdrawal Accounts (NOWs) are limited to individuals, sole proprietorships, not-for-profit organizations, and governmental entities.

  - *Money Market Deposit Accounts* - Accounts that pay an unregulated rate of interest determined by the bank, and allow limited check-writing and electronic withdrawals. They are available to all types of businesses and individuals.

• *Credit Services* - Banks provide loans to companies of all sizes, not-for-profit organizations and individuals. The following are examples of credit services:

  * *Short-Term Loans* - Loans designed primarily for working capital purposes such as temporary or seasonal increases in inventory or accounts receivable. Short-term loans are expected to be repaid from the current assets they finance. Short-

term borrowing is often under a line of credit which allows a company to borrow up to a specified amount, repay, and borrow again at any time. (See Chapter 10, Borrowing, for additional information on short-term loans.)

* *Long-Term Loans* - Loans designed primarily for capital improvements such as plant and equipment. The source of repayment is generally expected to be earnings from the project being financed.

* *Leasing* - Banks provide leases as alternatives to the use of long-term loans for financing capital equipment. (See also Chapter 10, Borrowing.)

* *Mortgages* - Commercial banks provide mortgage financing for commercial and residential real estate.

- *Investment Banking Services* - Among the different types of investment banking services offered by commercial banks are the following:

  * *Commercial Paper* - Commercial paper (CP) consists of unsecured, short-term promissory notes issued by companies. Investment banks and commercial banks typically act as agents to place the commercial paper of their customers with investors. Commercial bank holding companies also issue commercial paper. (See also Chapter 9, Investments, and Chapter 10, Borrowing.)

  * *Loan Sales* - Banks structure lending facilities so that short-term loans can be sold to other banks and investors.

  * *Private Placements* - Banks work with their customers to place long-term loans with institutional investors such as insurance companies.

  * *Corporate Bonds and Equities* - Some banks underwrite corporate bonds and equities through investment and brokerage subsidiaries.

2. *Payments and Collections* - Banks assist companies by acting as clearing agents for checks, and by originating and receiving wire transfers and ACH transactions. (See also Chapter 4, The Payments System, and Chapter 6, Collections.)

3. *Guarantor* - Banks act as guarantors by agreeing to pay obligations in the event a customer is unable to do so. The role of guarantor is fulfilled by the following services:

- *Letters of Credit* - Letters of Credit (L/Cs) are documents issued by a bank on behalf of a corporate applicant guaranteeing the payment of a customer's draft up to a stated amount for a specified period provided certain conditions are met. In effect, the issuing bank substitutes its name and credit on behalf of its customer.

- *Standby Letters of Credit* - Standby L/Cs are issued on behalf of a bank's customer in favor of a beneficiary promising that the bank will pay the latter upon presentation of a letter stating that the bank's customer has not met the terms of the contract.

- *Credit Enhancement Standby Letters of Credit* - Credit enhancement standby L/Cs are issued by a bank assuring payment if the issuer (the borrower) defaults on commercial paper or some other underwritten facility.

- *Letters of Credit Confirmation* - L/C confirmations are issued by a bank at the request of a customer when that customer is unsure of the status of the original issuing bank. In such instances, another bank may confirm (i.e., guarantee) performance under the original letter of credit. In the event of default, the confirming bank is responsible for the payment.

4. *Agent or Fiduciary* - An agent is a bank or trust institution which manages assets whose title remains with the owner. A fiduciary is an individual or institution to whom certain property is given to hold in trust according to a trust agreement. Among examples of agent or fiduciary services are the following:

- *Trust Services* - Banks invest, manage, and distribute monies as instructed in wills, trusts, and estates.

- *Investment Management* - Banks manage portfolios of investments for their customers.

- *Corporate Pension Plans* - Banks act as agents for companies in establishing and managing employee pension programs.

- *Qualified Employee Benefit Plans* - Banks act as agents for qualified employee benefit plans.

- *Corporate Trustee* - As a trustee for a corporate bond or preferred stock issue, a bank monitors compliance with indenture agreements. These are formal agreements between an issuer of bonds and a bondholder.

- *Transfer Agent* - A transfer agent is an individual or company that keeps a record of the shareholders of a corporation by name, address, and number of shares. Banks serve as transfer agents by keeping records of the sale and purchase of stocks and bonds.

- *Registrar* - Banks serve as registrars by maintaining lists of current stockholders and bondholders for the purpose of remitting dividend and interest payments.

- *Paying Agent* - Banks receive funds from an issuer of stocks or bonds and, in turn, pay principal and interest to bondholders and dividends to stockholders.

- *Custody Services* - Banks provide safekeeping for securities. Under a custody agreement, a bank buys, sells, receives, and delivers securities at the customer's request.

5. *Consulting Services* - Banks provide consulting services for corporate customers in areas such as mergers and acquisitions, corporate financial structure, and cash management.

6. *Risk Management* - Fluctuations in exchange rates, interest rates, or prices of commodities can adversely impact a company's financial performance. For example, currency movements against the U.S. dollar can impact the profitability of a company that operates in international markets. To limit these risks, banks and other financial institutions offer a variety of products and strategies such as swaps, forwards, futures, and options. These instruments are known as derivatives because their value is derived from, or based on, an underlying asset's price movement. (See also Chapter 14, Financial Risk Management.)

7. *Broker and Dealer* - Banks act as brokers and dealers for certain permissible investment securities and foreign currencies, and trade for their own account as an extension of that role.

B. Investment Banking and Brokerage Firms

Investment banking and brokerage firms provide a wide range of services. Not every firm is a full service provider. Certain firms specialize more in investment banking, others more in brokerage; certain firms deal more with institutional customers, others more with retail customers.

1. *Stock and Bond Underwriting* - Underwriting is the principal function of investment banking. When an investment banking firm underwrites a stock or bond offering, it assures the issuer of a definite sum of money for the issue at a definite time. In purchasing the entire issue from the issuer, the underwriter assumes the risk of price and marketability. The investment banker's intermediation function is often described as having two components, origination and distribution. Underwriting is the origination function, and selling the securities to investors is the distribution function.

2. *Commercial Paper* - Investment bankers have traditionally acted as underwriters and dealers for commercial paper.

3. *Institutional and Retail Brokerage* - Stock brokerage, selling shares to institutional and retail customers, is the distribution side of the investment banker's intermediation function.

4. *Investment Research* - Investment banking firms have research analysts who generally specialize by industry and provide advice to large institutions and individuals.

5. *Investment Advisory and Portfolio Management* - Similar to commercial banks, investment banking firms provide investment advice and manage investment portfolios for large institutions and individuals.

6. *Risk Management* - Investment banking firms offer derivative products such as interest rate and currency swaps, forwards, options, and futures. They also offer foreign exchange services.

C. Thrift Institutions

Thrift institutions have traditionally been depositories that accept consumer deposits and lend money primarily in the form of home mortgage loans. The **Depository Institutions Deregulation and Monetary Control Act of 1980 (DIDMCA)** provided for a phase out of interest rate ceilings for thrift institutions and commercial banks, and allowed savings institutions to make commercial and consumer loans. There are two types of thrift institutions:

1. *Savings and Loan Associations* - Savings and Loans (S&Ls) are federally or state chartered and owned by either shareholders or depositors. Their deposits are federally insured by the **Savings Association Insurance Fund (SAIF)**, which is administered by the **Federal Deposit Insurance Corporation (FDIC)**, a regulatory agency described in detail in Sections II and III.

2. *Savings Banks or Mutual Savings Banks* - Historically, savings banks and mutual savings banks have been state chartered and owned by depositors, but the **Garn-St. Germain Depository Institutions Act** of 1982 allowed them to switch to a federal charter and to convert to stock ownership. Their deposits are insured by the **Bank Insurance Fund (BIF)**.

D. Credit Unions

Credit unions are not-for-profit financial corporations created by federal or state charter. Membership in a credit union is restricted to people with a common bond such as an employer, association, or community organization. Credit unions can provide retail financial services similar to those offered by other types of financial institutions. Members/owners often enjoy higher savings and lower lending rates. Deposits in most credit unions are insured by the National Credit Union Administration (NCUA) Share Insurance Fund.

E. Mutual Funds

Mutual fund providers sell shares to investors, offering those investors diversification and professional portfolio management. These providers include brokerage firms, banks, and investment companies. Shares may be redeemed through the provider which insures liquidity. Prices fluctuate with the performance of the fund. Money market mutual funds invest in short-term securities such as Treasury bills, certificates of deposit, and commercial paper.

F. Other Financial Institutions

A variety of other financial institutions specialize in certain types of lending:

1. *Industrial Credit and Capital Companies* - Subsidiaries of large industrial corporations raise funds in the commercial paper market and lend to companies and individuals. A captive finance company typically finances the purchase of its own company's products.

2. *Factors* - Factors provide short-term financing to companies by purchasing their accounts receivable at a discount and assuming the responsibility and the risk for collecting them.

3. *Insurance Companies* - Insurance companies are primarily long-term lenders to companies. Insurance companies have started to compete with banks for medium-term and short-term loans as well. They also provide leasing services, guaranteed income contracts, and universal life insurance policies with long-term savings features.

4. *Consumer Credit Companies* - Consumer loan and sales finance companies extend credit to individuals and businesses. The larger, well-known consumer finance companies raise funds in the commercial paper market.

II. REGULATORY AGENCIES

The United States has a dual banking system. It is regulated at the federal level and by state banking commissions. At the federal level, bank supervision is shared primarily by three agencies, the Board of Governors of the Federal Reserve System, the Federal Deposit Insurance Corporation (FDIC), and the Office of the Comptroller of the Currency (OCC). The Securities and Exchange Commission (SEC) and the Department of Justice have regulatory roles as well.

A. Federal Reserve System

The **Federal Reserve System (Fed)** is an independent agency of the U.S. government. The following is a description of the roles and structure of the Federal Reserve System:

1. *Roles* - The Fed has four principal roles. It acts as a supervisor of member banks and bank holding companies, as the manager of U.S. monetary policy, as a wholesaler of banking services, and as the fiscal agent of the U.S. Treasury.

- *Supervision* - The Board of Governors of the Federal Reserve System is charged with examination of state-chartered member banks and bank holding companies. It also regulates Edge Act banks, the U.S. banking activities of foreign owned banks, and the foreign activities of U.S. member banks.

- *Monetary Policy* - The Board controls the money supply through bank reserve requirements, the discount rate for bank borrowing at the Fed, and open market operations.

  * *Reserve Requirements* - All depository institutions must maintain a specified percentage of their deposits in cash or on deposit with the Fed. These deposits earn no interest. The required level of reserves is established by averaging reserve liabilities over a 14-day period. Reserve requirements are not changed often, but when they are, the effect is either an expansion or contraction of lendable funds and a resulting multiplier effect throughout the economy.

  * *Discount Rate* - The Fed sets the **discount rate** for its loans to depository institutions. The discount rate influences other interest rate movements such as the Fed funds rate and the prime rate.

  * *Open Market Activities* - One of the most influential roles of the Fed is exercised through the Federal Open Market Committee (FOMC). The FOMC is charged with promoting economic growth, full employment, stable prices, and a balance in international trade and payments. Its primary activities involve the sale and purchase of government securities. The sale of securities from the Fed's portfolio reduces the money supply by taking cash out of the economy. Conversely, buying securities increases the money supply.

- *Banking Services* - For a commercial bank, the Fed is both a regulator and a provider of services. It also oversees the payment system in the following ways:

  * *Check Clearing* - The Fed receives check deposits from depository institutions and then clears checks back to the drawee banks.

  * *Wire Transfers* - The Fed operates Fedwire, the domestic large-dollar wire transfer system.

  * *Automated Clearing House System* - The Fed is the main operator of the ACH, which processes and settles electronic payments.

- *Fiscal Agency* - The Reserve Banks and their branches function as the banker for the federal government. They maintain the Treasury Department's checking accounts, clear Treasury checks drawn against them, accept payments for federal taxes on behalf of the Internal Revenue Service (IRS), and act as fiscal agent for the Treasury Department to issue, redeem, and transfer ownership of government securities.

2. *Organization* - The Federal Reserve System has three components, the Board of Governors, the Federal Open Market Committee, and the 12 Federal Reserve banks and their branches.

- *Board of Governors* - Each of the seven members is appointed to a 14-year term by the President of the United States and confirmed by the Senate. Primary functions include formulation of credit and monetary policy, as well as supervision of the Federal Reserve banks, state-chartered member banks, and bank holding companies. The President appoints one governor as chairman and another as vice chairman; each serves a four-year term and may be reappointed.

The Board is advised by the following committees:

* *Federal Advisory Council* - Members represent the interests of commerce and industry.

* *Consumer Advisory Council* - Members represent the interests of the consumers.

* *Thrift Institutions Advisory Council* - Members represent the interests of savings and loan associations, mutual savings banks, and credit unions.

• *Federal Open Market Committee* - The FOMC implements monetary policy, principally by conducting open market operations. There are 12 committee members, including seven members of the Board of Governors, the president of the Federal Reserve Bank of New York, and presidents of four other Federal Reserve banks. They are appointed on a rotating basis.

• *Federal Reserve District Banks* - There are 12 Federal Reserve districts with one Federal Reserve bank serving each district. The 12 reserve banks have 25 branches, and there are additional regional check processing centers (RCPCs). Commercial banks in the region hold the stock of the Federal Reserve banks and are represented on their boards, but do not maintain control the way stockholders normally do. The Board of Governors appoints part of each reserve bank's board as well as its chairman. A map of the Federal Reserve System is shown in Exhibit 3.1.

EXHIBIT 3.1
*Federal
Reserve Check
Processing
Regions*

*Courtesy of
the Federal
Reserve*

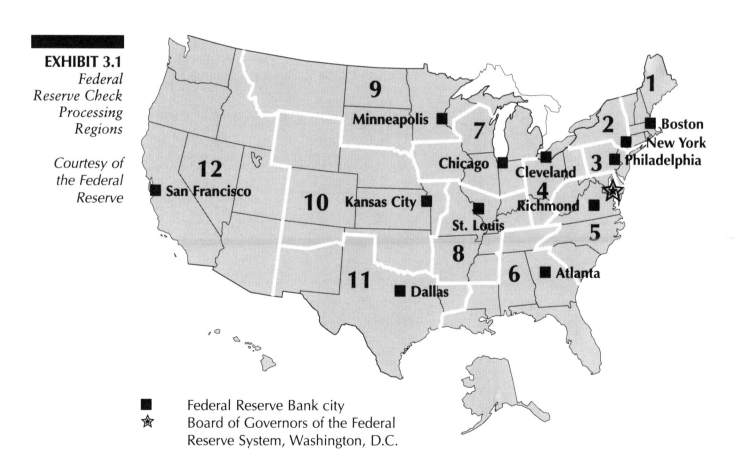

■   Federal Reserve Bank city
☆   Board of Governors of the Federal
     Reserve System, Washington, D.C.

B. Office of the Comptroller of the Currency

The Office of the Comptroller of the Currency (OCC) grants charters to, and regulates, supervises, and examines national banks. It monitors bank performance, issues supervisory agreements, and determines loan credit quality ratings.

C. Federal Deposit Insurance Corporation

The primary role of the Federal Deposit Insurance Corporation (FDIC) is to protect depositors from losses caused by bank insolvency.

1. *Deposit Insurance* - The following are among the rules and regulations governing deposit insurance:

   - The FDIC insures deposits up to $100,000 per personal or corporate depositor per institution in all federally chartered banks and most state banks. The deposit insurance premium rate charged is set by the FDIC on a risk assessment basis.

   - The FDIC manages two deposit insurance funds—the Bank Insurance Fund (BIF) for commercial banks and savings banks, and the Savings Association Insurance Fund (SAIF) for S&Ls.

   - The Federal Deposit Insurance Corporation Improvement Act (FDICIA) (1991) shifted the deposit insurance premium assessment system from a flat fee basis to a risk-based system. The Bank Insurance Fund (BIF) had been funded by a flat fee assessment which ignored the varying degrees of risk posed to the BIF by banks. FDICIA directed the FDIC to establish a premium assessment which took into account risk factors posed by banks.

2. *Supervision* - The FDIC supervises, examines, and regulates insured banks that are not Federal Reserve members.

3. *Role in Bank Failures* - One of the FDIC's most important roles is in determining the course of action in the event of bank failure. The FDIC usually makes the decision that a bank is insolvent, and the FDIC is usually appointed receiver. The agency is charged with finding a merger partner or liquidating the bank's remaining assets and paying insured depositors.

D. Securities and Exchange Commission

The Securities and Exchange Commission (SEC) is a federal agency which regulates and supervises the selling of securities to maintain a fair and orderly market for investors. Among its responsibilities are the following:

- Registering public offerings of debt or equity securities by banks or bank holding companies as well as all other corporations

- Setting financial disclosure standards for corporations that sell securities to the public

- Requiring filing of quarterly and annual financial statements by companies with publicly owned securities

E. Department of Justice

The Department of Justice reviews and approves proposed bank mergers and holding company acquisitions to determine their effect on competition as part of overall antitrust supervisory responsibility.

F. State Banking Boards and Commissions

Under the dual nature of the U.S. banking system, each state has its own banking boards and commissions. Among the responsibilities of these state agencies are the following:

- Issuing charters for new state banks

- Supervising and examining all state-chartered banks

- Reserving the right to approve all applications of banks operating within state borders to form holding companies, to acquire affiliates or subsidiaries, or to establish branch offices

- Reserving the right to impose liquidity requirements and minimum equity capital requirements on state-chartered banks

III. FEDERAL LEGISLATION

The following is a summary of selected bank legislation that demonstrates how the U.S. banking system evolved into its current form. The summary is arranged in chronological order.

A. Federal Reserve Act (1913)

Among the provisions of the Federal Reserve Act are the following:

- Provided the foundation for the current banking system.

- Granted the Fed supervisory power over member banks. Chartered national banks were required to become members and to comply with reserve requirements.

- Empowered the Fed to create a check collection and settlement system through member banks.

B. Edge Act (1918)

Among the provisions of the Edge Act are the following:

- Permitted U.S. banks to invest in corporations that engage in international banking and finance.

- Permitted the establishment of subsidiaries to conduct international banking business such as import and export financing, foreign exchange, letters of credit and documentary collections in other cities in the U.S. as well as overseas. This legislation has helped banks establish a presence and be closer to their customers in other cities, even though the units could not take in domestic deposits and were limited to providing services related to international trade.

C. McFadden Act (1927)

Among the provisions of the McFadden Act are the following:

- Established the state boundary as the primary limit for bank expansion by prohibiting banks from accepting deposits across state lines.

- Prohibited branching across state lines unless approved by state governments, thereby relegating to the states the power to decide the extent of bank branching within and outside state borders.

The following are two more recent legislative actions that have modified the McFadden Act:

- *The Douglas Amendment (1956)* - Allowed banks to merge across state lines if each state permitted it, but did not allow bank holding companies to acquire banks across state lines. Legislation enacted by individual states has allowed bank holding companies to acquire banks and bank holding companies in states both within and outside their regions.

- *The Interstate Banking and Branching Efficiency Act (1994)* - Phases out, over a three year period, the state barriers against branching established by the McFadden Act. Full interstate branching can be achieved in June 1997.

D. Glass-Steagall Act (1933)

Among the provisions of the Glass-Steagall Act are the following:

- Prohibited commercial banks from securities underwriting except for government issues.

- Prohibited securities firms from engaging in bank-like activities such as deposit gathering.

- Required the Fed to establish interest-rate ceilings on all types of accounts and prohibited the payment of interest on demand deposits. Provisions of this Act are incorporated in Federal Reserve Regulation Q.

- Created the Federal Deposit Insurance Corporation (FDIC) to guarantee the public's deposits up to a stipulated maximum amount.

E. Electronic Funds Transfer Act (1978)

Among the provisions of Electronic Funds Transfer Act (EFTA) are the following:

- Defined the rights and responsibilities of individuals using EFT services except for wire transfers.

- Limited customer liability for unauthorized banking transactions involving automated teller machines (ATMs) and point of sale (POS) terminals, provided the customer notifies the bank or other institution that issued the card.

Provisions of this act are incorporated in Federal Reserve Regulation E.

F. Depository Institutions Deregulation and Monetary Control Act (1980)

Among the provisions of the Depository Institutions Degregulation and Monetary Control Act (DIDMCA) are the following:

- Required all deposit-taking institutions to maintain reserves at the Fed.
- Made Fed services (such as the discount window short-term lending facility and check clearing) available to all deposit-taking institutions.
- Mandated the Fed to reduce and/or price payments system float.
- Priced previously free Fed services according to the standards of a tax-paying vendor.
- Provided for phasing out of Regulation Q interest rate ceilings over a five-year period ending in 1986.
- Permitted banks to offer Negotiable Order of Withdrawal (NOW) accounts, check writing accounts with an unregulated interest rate for individuals and not-for-profit organizations, and government entities.

G. Garn-St. Germain Depository Institutions Act (1982)

Among the provisions of Garn-St. Germain Act are the following:

- Extended the legal lending limit of banks to 15 percent of capital and surplus unsecured and 25 percent for secured loans.
- Allowed the FDIC to arrange mergers of banks across state lines when suitable intrastate partners could not be found.
- Allowed banks to offer accounts to compete with money market mutual funds. Allowed banks in need of capital to issue net worth certificates to the FDIC in return for promissory notes that could be held as assets.

H. Expedited Funds Availability Act (1988)

Among the provisions of Expedited Funds Availability Act (EFAA) are the following:

- Defined funds withdrawal time periods for deposited checks and payable-through drafts.
- Established payable-through draft and check return procedures.

Provisions of this act are incorporated in Federal Reserve Regulation CC.

I. Financial Institutions Reform, Recovery and Enforcement Act (1989)

Among the provisions of Financial Institutions Reform, Recovery, and Enforcement Act (FIRREA) are the following:

- Consolidated Federal Savings and Loan Insurance Corporation (FSLIC) resources under FDIC and established two insurance funds, the Savings Association Insurance Fund (SAIF) and the Bank Insurance Fund (BIF).

- Dismantled the Federal Home Loan Bank Board (FHLBB) and established the Office of Thrift Supervision (OTS) to assume the FHLBBs supervisory responsibilities.

- Established the Resolution Trust Corporation to make timely disposal of assets of failed S&Ls. The RTC was disbanded in 1995.

- Gave the FDIC increased flexibility to raise deposit insurance premiums charged to banks and savings and loan associations.

J. Federal Deposit Insurance Corporation Improvement Act (1991)

Among the provisions of the Federal Deposit Insurance Corporation Improvement Act (FDICIA) are the following:

- Established higher standards for financial institution safety and soundness in the wake of several bank failures during the late 1980s.

- Mandated the FDIC to declare insolvent any bank that failed to maintain equity capital equal to 2 percent of its assets.

- Required the FDIC to change its deposit insurance premiums from a flat fee basis to a risk-adjusted basis.

K. Interstate Banking and Branching Efficiency Act (1994)

Among the provisions of this act are the following:

- Permits bank holding companies to acquire a bank located in any state effective September 1995.

- Allows banks in one state to merge with banks in another state beginning June 1997, so long as neither state has taken legislative action to prohibit interstate mergers between the date of enactment and the end of May 1997.

- Allows banks to establish new branches in states where they do not maintain a branch if the host state passes a law expressly permitting such branches.

IV. FEDERAL RESERVE REGULATIONS

After legislation is passed by Congress, the implementation of a law is often directed to federal regulatory agencies. The following are examples of banking legislation affecting cash managers which are regulated by the Federal Reserve:

A. Regulation D

Imposes uniform reserve requirements on all depository institutions with different levels of reserves for different types of deposits. The Fed can use this regulation in controlling the supply of money.

B. Regulation E

Establishes the rights, liabilities, and responsibilities of parties to consumer-related electronic funds transfers (EFT) and protects consumers using EFT systems. Reg E also establishes the guidelines for documentation of electronic transfers.

C. Regulation J

Establishes procedures, duties, and responsibilities for check collection and settlement through the Federal Reserve System.

D. Regulation Q

Prohibits depository institutions from paying interest on corporate demand deposit accounts. Prior interest rate ceilings on all other deposit accounts were phased out in 1986 by the DIDMCA.

E. Regulation CC

Among the provisions of Reg CC are the following:

- Establishes policies on withdrawal of deposited funds, as provided in the Expedited Funds Availability Act (EFAA), and requires banks to disclose their withdrawal policies to their customers. Its intent is to prevent unnecessary delays in a depositor's access to funds.

- Establishes rules designed to speed the collection and return of checks and imposes a responsibility on banks to return unpaid checks expeditiously.

- Establishes endorsement standards for banks and companies to follow in depositing and clearing checks.

- Imposes the same return procedures that apply to checks to payable-through-drafts.

V. THE UNIFORM COMMERCIAL CODE

The Uniform Commercial Code (UCC) is a uniform set of laws governing commercial transactions enacted separately by each state. The UCC defines the rights and duties of the parties in a commercial transaction and provides a statutory definition of commonly used business practices. The four articles most relevant to the cash manager are as follows:

A. Article 3 - Negotiable Instruments

Among the provisions of Article 3 are the following:

1. *Negotiable Instruments* - Article 3 defines a negotiable instrument and the forms it may take, including a draft, a check, a certificate of deposit, and a note.

2. *Accord and Satisfaction* - Originally, this section was drafted to permit a check to constitute a payment made in full (i.e., accord and satisfaction) when a message to that effect was written on the face of the check and the check was deposited. However, this allowed for the possibility of inadvertent accord and satisfaction when the customer wrote "paid in full" on a check for a disputed claim—especially if the check was col-

lected through a lockbox. The revised section permits avoidance of inadvertent accord and satisfaction if the payee discovers the inadvertence and returns the check to the payor within 90 days.

3. *Unauthorized Signatures* - A bank's failure to examine a forged drawer's signature is not failure to exercise ordinary care to the extent that such failure does not violate the bank's procedures and that these procedures do not unreasonably vary from general banking practices. At the same time, a bank can only charge a customer's account for checks which are properly payable, and an unauthorized signature does not pass this test. However, a company may be held liable if it does not exercise ordinary care related to check issuance and does not notify the bank of multiple forgeries by the same wrongdoer in a timely manner.

B. Article 4 - Bank Deposits and Collections

Among the provisions of Article 4 are the following:

1. *Bank Parties* - Article 4 defines the various bank parties to the deposit and collection process and their respective rights and duties.

2. *Relationship Between Payor Bank and Customer* - Article 4 defines the following:

   • When a bank may charge a customer's account.

   • Bank's liability to a customer for failing to honor a good check.

   • Customer's right to stop payment.

   • Bank's option not to pay an item more than six months old (stale date).

   • Customer's duty to report unauthorized signature or alteration.

3. *Company Obligations* - A company has the duty to examine bank statements within a reasonable time, and to report to the bank any unauthorized signatures or alterations. This, coupled with the Ordinary Care provision of UCC3, makes it imperative that companies reconcile their accounts on a timely basis.

C. Article 4A - Funds Transfers

Article 4A provides a legal framework that outlines the risks, rights, and obligations of parties in connection with wire transfers through Fedwire, the Clearing House Interbank Payments System (CHIPS), and the Society for Worldwide Interbank Financial Telecommunications (SWIFT), as well as book transfers and wholesale credit transfers through the ACH and SWIFT. Among the provisions of Article 4A are the following:

1. *Security Procedures* - The bank must make security procedures for verifying payment orders available to the customer, and the bank and the customer must agree that those procedures are commercially reasonable. Some common security measures include the use of Personal Identification Numbers (PINs), callbacks, encryption, and message authentication.

2. *Consequential Damages* - Banks are not responsible for consequential damages, which are losses resulting from the action or error made by the bank beyond the simple loss

of funds. A bank incorrectly executing a payment order remains liable for interest losses or incidental expenses. The bank is liable for consequential damages only if it agrees to assume this liability in a written agreement with the customer.

D. Article 5 - Letters of Credit

Article 5 covers commercial letters of credit requiring documentary drafts or documentary demands for payment. It does not cover standby letters of credit. Among the provisions of Article 5 are the following:

- Defines a letter of credit, a documentary draft, or documentary demand for payment.

- Defines the roles of the issuer of the letter of credit, the applicant for whom the credit is issued, the beneficiary of the credit, the advising bank, and the confirming bank.

- Defines the issuer's obligation to the applicant, including the duty to examine documents to see that they comply with the terms of the credit. It also requires that the issuer must honor a demand for payment which complies with the terms of the credit.

QUESTIONS

These chapter questions are to test and review the information in the text and are not examples of CCM examination questions, nor are they in the examination format.

Answers can be found at the back of the book on p. 314-315.

1. What are the major roles of commercial banks?

2. What is the principal function of an investment banking firm?

3. Who charters savings and loan institutions?

4. In what ways are credit unions different from banks?

5. What are the four major roles of the Federal Reserve?

6. Who grants charters to national banks?

7. What are the two insurance funds are operated by the Federal Deposit Insurance Corporation (FDIC)?

8. What legislation permits U.S. banks to invest in corporations engaged in international banking and finance?

9. What legislation originally prohibited banks from accepting deposits across state lines, and what is the current status legislation in this area?

10. What legislation separates commercial from investment banking?

11. What legislation mandated the Federal Reserve to reduce and/or price float?

12. What legislation consolidated the two financial institution insurance funds under the FDIC?

13. What are the primary provisions of the Interstate Bank and Branching Efficiency Act of 1994?

14. What Federal Reserve regulation prohibits the payment of interest on corporate demand deposits?

15. What Federal Reserve regulation required the disclosure of check availability policies by banks?

16. What article of the Uniform Commercial Code (UCC) permits avoidance of inadvertent accord and satisfaction?

17. Under UCC Article 4, what is the maximum time a firm has to examine bank statements and report unauthorized signatures?

18. Under UCC Article 4A, is a bank responsible for consequential damages?

CHAPTER 4

Payments System

OVERVIEW

This chapter deals with the basic structure of the U.S. payments system which consists of paper-based and electronic payments. It is important to understand the mechanics of each of the major payment systems, the regulatory and institutional constraints, and the key corporate applications.

LEARNING OBJECTIVES

Upon completion of this chapter and the related study questions, the reader should know:

1. The mechanics and applications of the following principal paper instruments: checks, payable through drafts, preauthorized drafts, and depository transfer checks.

2. The mechanics and applications of the following principal electronic payment instruments: Fedwire, CHIPS, and ACH.

3. How the Federal Reserve and the banking industry define and measure payment system risk and what steps they are taking to reduce it.

OUTLINE

I. Overview of Payment Methods

II. Paper-Based Payment Instruments
   A. Domestic Check System
   B. Role of Drawee Bank
   C. Return Items
   D. Magnetic Ink Character Recognition Line
   E. How Checks are Cleared
   F. Ledger and Collected Balances
   G. Availability Schedules
   H. Federal Reserve Float
   I. Other Check-Like Payment Instruments

III.   Electronic Payment Methods
         A. The Automated Clearing House System
         B. Fedwire
         C. Clearing House Interbank Payments System
         D. Society for Worldwide Interbank Financial Telecommunications
         E. Payments System Risk

I. OVERVIEW OF PAYMENT METHODS

The primary method of payment in the United States is the paper check. However, while the majority of transactions are by check, the greatest dollar volume is transferred through one of three electronic payment networks: Fedwire, the Automated Clearing House (ACH), and the Clearing House for Interbank Payment System (CHIPS).

II. PAPER-BASED PAYMENT INSTRUMENTS

A. Domestic Check System

A check is a demand instrument used to transfer funds from the payor to the payee. It is important for a cash manager to know the terminology associated with checks as follows:

1.   *Payor* - The **payor** is the party who writes or draws the check to remit funds.

2.   *Payee* - The **payee** is the party to whom the check is made payable.

3.   *Drawee Bank* - The **drawee bank** is the bank on which the check is drawn, the payor's bank.

4.   *Signature* - A check requires the signature of the payor. Sometimes more than one signature is required. Also, some companies use mechanically-generated signature facsimiles, while others use computer-printed signatures.

5.   *Provisional Credit* - The payee receives ledger credit when the check is deposited. The credit is provisional, subject to final clearing of the check.

6.   *Check Clearing* - To effect final settlement, the check must be presented to and accepted by the drawee bank, the institution on which it is drawn. This process is called **check clearing**.

EXHIBIT 4.1
Steps in Check Clearing System

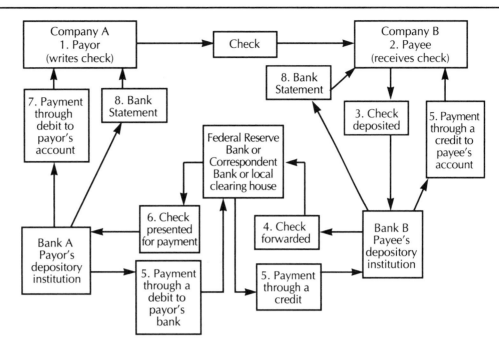

STEPS IN THE CHECK-CLEARING SYSTEM

Step 1:   Company A prepares and mails a check to Company B.

Step 2:   Company B receives and processes the check.

Step 3:   Company B deposits the check in its account at Bank B.

Step 4:   Bank B processes the check and transports it to a clearing system.

Step 5:   The clearing system gives value to Bank B in the amount of the check and subtracts value from Bank A for the same amount. The clearing agent (if any) can be the Federal Reserve System, a correspondent bank or a local clearing house.

Step 6:   The check is physically presented by the clearing agent to Bank A where the amount is deducted from Company A's account. This step may occur simultaneously with step 5.

Step 7:   This step does not come at a predetermined time in the cycle, but on the day of posting, Company A must have funds available in Bank A to cover the amount of the check.

Step 8:   Both banks provide reports to their respective companies in the form of periodic bank statements.

Exhibit 4.1 illustrates how a check is used to transfer funds from Company A (the payor) to Company B (the payee). The key event in the check clearing process is presentment, the delivery of a check to the payor's bank. At the time of presentment, value is subtracted from the bank's account with the Fed, correspondent bank, or other clearing institution. Normally, the amount is also subtracted from the payor's account the same business day.

B. Role of Drawee Bank

In the check clearing process, the drawee bank is responsible for inspecting the check for proper signature, alterations, appropriate dating, and stop payments.

The account is reviewed for active account status, adequate funds, whether or not there are holds in place (instructions not to debit the account or not to draw the account below a certain balance), or problems with the disbursement account.

C. Return Items

Return items are checks rejected by the drawee bank. The drawee bank has until midnight local time on the day following presentment to conduct a review of the check and authorize final payment. If the returned check exceeds $2,500, the drawee bank must notify the bank of first deposit of the return by 4:00 p.m. on the second business day following presentment. When the returned checks are received by the bank of first deposit, they may be redeposited or charged back to the depositor's account.

D. Magnetic Ink Character Recognition Line

The information necessary to process checks by machine is contained in the **Magnetic Ink Character Recognition (MICR)** line printed with special characters on the lower portion of the check. These characters can be read by scanning equipment. The MICR information is used by the depository institution to identify the drawee bank and to route the check back to the bank and the account on which it was drawn. The information contained in the MICR line of a business check is illustrated in Exhibit 4.2. The MICR line for a personal check has a different sequence.

The transit routing number is used by the depository bank to identify the drawee bank and to route the check back to this bank. The depository bank's reader-sorter equipment endorses and microfilms the checks, sorts them according to the clearing channels that will be used, and sends the clearing data to the bank's computers to allow deposit updating and float assignment.

When received by the drawee bank, the payor's account number is used by the drawee bank to debit the payor's account. The sequence number is used to provide account reconciliation services and to check for stop payments.

EXHIBIT 4.2
Sample Business Check

Name of Payor	Check No: 12345
	February 10, 19XX

Pay to the Order of:_____ NAME OF PAYEE _____

Dollars amount: _____ One thousand & thirty four _____ $1,034.00

Name of
Drawee Bank

Payor's Signature
_____

000012345	02	12	0001	2	0310987654	0000103400

Field 6 1 2 3 4 5 7

Transit Routing Number. The first four entries described below are collectively known as the transit routing number.

1. **Federal Reserve Bank Code** - Two digits (01 to 12) identify the drawee bank's Federal Reserve district. Numbers greater than 12 identify a non-bank depository institution such as a thrift.

2. **Federal Reserve Office** - The first digit identifies the Fed branch responsible for handling the drawee bank. The second digit is the availability classification.

3. **Bank Identification Number** - Four digits make up the bank's ABA identification number. That number designates the bank and location to which the item must be delivered. A number of banks have more than one identification number, which facilitates the handling of certain types of checks.

4. **Check Digit** - This digit, when combined with the other numbers, enables the computer to verify the accuracy of the routing number for the benefit of the automated routing process.

5. **Payor's Account Number** - This number is assigned to the payor by the drawee bank.

6. **Sequence Number** - Also called the auxiliary on-us field on a business check.
   - This number is frequently the check number.
   - It assists the drawee bank in providing a variety of account reconcilement services, for example sorting the cleared checks before returning them to the payor.
   - It may also be used for identification codes of divisions or subsidiaries.
   - It is a key to providing stop payment services.

7. **Encoded Amount of Check** - This number should agree with the amount placed on the check by the payor. The amount is typically encoded on the check by the bank in which the check is first deposited.

E. How Checks are Cleared

Check clearing is the process of presenting a check to the drawee bank to effect final payment. Checks are sent from one bank to another in cash letters. Often banks make direct sends to other banks or Federal Reserve banks in other districts. A variety of clearing channels are used.

1. *Cash Letter* - A **cash letter** is a bundle of checks accompanied by a list of individual items and dollar amounts, together with deposit tickets and other control documents. Checks are usually presented by a bank to the Fed or another bank via a cash letter.

2. *Direct Sends* - Banks often bypass the local Fed with **direct sends**, which are arrangements to send cash letters directly to correspondent banks or to a non-local Federal Reserve bank. These arrangements allow banks to meet various deposit deadlines, thereby achieving faster clearing times than they would by clearing them through the local Fed. The sending bank maintains a deposit account with the correspondent bank. The correspondent bank credits the account of the sending bank with the proceeds of the checks.

3. *Clearing Channels* - Selection of the appropriate check clearing channel to use is a function of deposit bank processing time, geographic location, and the availability schedules of clearing agents. **Availability** (i.e., when funds deposited will become available for use) is granted to the clearing bank if the check reaches the endpoint (or location established by the clearing agent) prior to a prearranged deposit deadline. **Availability schedules** define the number of days' delay for each endpoint. Channels that the bank of first deposit can use for clearing checks back to the payor bank include the following:

    *   *On-Us Check Clearing* - The payee deposits the check in the same bank on which it is drawn. Clearing the check is accomplished by charging the payor's account, crediting the payee's account, and returning the check to the payor.

    *   *Clearing Houses* - These are either formal or informal associations formed by banks in a geographic area to permit the exchange of items drawn on the other participants. Representatives from each bank meet daily to present checks to each other. The net value is transferred by debiting and crediting correspondent accounts or through reserve accounts each bank maintains with the local Fed. Nationwide clearing houses are being established to facilitate check clearing.

    *   *Federal Reserve Bank* - A key role of the Fed is to act as a check clearing agent. A bank deposits checks into its own account at the Fed. The Fed gives credit for the checks according to its availability schedule. It then sorts the checks and transports them to the drawee bank. When a check is presented to the drawee bank, the Fed subtracts the amount of the check from the drawee bank's Fed account. A bank may deposit checks at its local Fed or direct send them to other Federal Reserve banks.

    *   *Correspondent Bank* - The sending bank or bank of first deposit maintains a deposit account with the correspondent bank. The correspondent bank credits the account of the sending bank with proceeds of the checks.

4. *Drawee Endpoints* - The classification of drawee endpoints is as follows:

    *   *City Items* - Checks drawn on banks located in Federal Reserve cities.

    *   *RCPC Items* - Checks drawn on banks serviced by a Fed regional check processing center (RCPC).

- *Country Items* - Checks drawn on banks located outside the area served by a Fed city or RCPC.

- *High Dollar Group Sort Items* - Checks drawn on RCPC or country banks. High Dollar Group Sort (HDGS) is the Fed's program to expedite the processing of high-dollar checks through the system. The HDGS program automatically involves making a second presentment to banks with more than $10 million of checks presented from outside their Fed districts.

5. *Deposit Deadlines* - Each type of item has a specific deposit deadline that must be met if the clearing bank is to receive the designated availability.

6. *Same-Day Settlement* - Any bank can present a check at any other bank if the check is presented to the drawee bank by 8:00 a.m. local time. If this deadline is met, the Federal Reserve requires the drawee bank to settle in same-day funds by the close of Fedwire (6:30 p.m. ET). No presentment fee can be charged. This Fed rule is designed to improve competition in check collection services.

7. *Electronic Check Presentment* - With **Electronic Check Presentment (ECP)**, the MICR line on a check is captured by the depository bank and the data is transmitted to the drawee bank. The drawee bank uses this information to debit the funds from the payor's demand deposit account. The actual checks may be sent to the drawee bank for subsequent handling or be truncated. ECP accelerates the clearing of checks and thus the notification of checks being returned by the drawee bank.

F. Ledger and Collected Balances

Banks differentiate between ledger and collected balances in deposit accounts.

1. *Ledger Balances* - **Ledger balances** are bank balances that reflect all accounting entries that affect a bank account, regardless of any deposit float. Ledger balances are important for accounting purposes, but not usually for bank compensation. If the ledger balance is negative, there is a ledger overdraft. There is often a service charge and/or an interest penalty for such an overdraft.

2. *Collected Balances* - **Collected balances** are the difference between ledger balances and deposit float.

   - **Deposit float** is the sum of each check deposited, multiplied by its availability in days.

   - The collected balance reflects when availability is actually given for the deposit. For example, a $1,000 check deposited on Tuesday is granted one-day availability. This means that the bank gives the customer availability (the deposit becomes good funds) after a delay of one business day. While the ledger balance increases by $1,000 on Tuesday, the collected balance does not increase until Wednesday.

Checks are generally granted immediate (same day), one, or two business days' availability. Some remote locations may have three-day items. The assignment of availability is usually in whole numbers of business days. Checks presented for payment against the account are deducted from both the collected and ledger accounts on the same day. The ledger balance is usually larger than the collected balance. The collected balance may dip below zero without creating a ledger overdraft, but banks may consider a collected overdraft equivalent to a loan and charge interest and/or service fees.

3. *Deposit Float* - Among the ways that a bank can compute deposit float are the following:

- *Proof of Deposit or Item-by-Item* - **Proof of deposit (POD)** is a method by which banks assign availability to each check as it passes through the automated check processing system. Availability is assigned based on the time of deposit and endpoint. This is the most accurate method, and most major cash management banks have this capability.

- *Company Sample* - Some banks take a sample of check deposits for a specific company and track the average availability for a period of time. The float based on the sample is then applied to the company's deposits.

- *Bank Average* - Banks that lack POD capabilities often compute an average availability that applies to all checks. This average is applied to each customer. This method may or may not benefit a customer depending on whether its mix of check deposits has more or less float than average.

- *Negotiated Availability* - In some cases a bank and a company may negotiate an average availability that applies to all checks.

G. Availability Schedules

An availability schedule specifies when a bank or the Fed grants credit for deposited checks in the form of an increase in the depositor's available or collected balance. The assignment of availability is usually in whole business days, and checks are generally assigned zero, one, or two days' availability. The Fed has availability schedules for banks, and banks have availability schedules for their customers. Many banks have multiple availability schedules. The schedule a bank offers to a particular customer is a marketing decision.

An example of an availability schedule is shown in Exhibit 4.3. Other important concepts regarding availability schedules include:

1. *Ledger Cutoff Time* - A bank's **ledger cutoff time** is the time after which deposits are credited as of the following business day.

2. *Constructing the Schedule* - To construct the availability schedule, the clearing bank examines clearing times for important endpoints, determines clearing channels for each endpoint, calculates costs, and works back from deposit deadlines for those endpoints to establish its own deposit deadlines for customers.

	TR No.	Deposit Endpoint	Availability	Deposit Deadline	Days Covered
EXHIBIT 4.3 *Example of Availability Schedule*	0210-0000	NYC Banks	0	10:00 a.m.	Monday-Friday
	0531-0000	Charlotte RCPC	0	9:00 p.m.	Monday-Thursday
	1210-0000	L.A. City	0	1:00 a.m.	Monday-Friday
	0865-0000	St. Louis Country	1	6:00 a.m.	Monday-Thursday

Assuming a ledger cutoff of 5:00 p.m. and the above availability schedule, a company would receive ledger and collected balances as follows if its deposits were made on Monday at 8:00 a.m. or 8:00 p.m.:

Deposit Endpoint	8:00 a.m. Deposit Time		8:00 p.m. Deposit Time	
	Ledger Balance	Collected Balance	Ledger Balance	Collected Balance
NYC Banks	Monday	Monday	Tuesday	Tuesday
Charlotte RCPC	Monday	Tuesday*	Tuesday	Tuesday*
LA City	Monday	Tuesday	Tuesday	Tuesday
St. Louis Country	Monday	Wednesday	Tuesday	Wednesday

* The relationship between the bank's ledger cutoff, the time of deposit , and the endpoint deposit deadline determine the ledger and collected balances. In this example checks deposited between 9:01 p.m. Sunday and 5 p.m. Monday receive ledger credit on Monday and collected balance credit on Tuesday. Checks deposited between 5:01 p.m. Monday and 9 p.m. Monday receive ledger and collected balance credit on Tuesday. See also the discussion of availability and ledger cut-off on page 109.

3. *Factors Determining Availability* - The following factors influence the availability a bank assigns to a particular check:

    • *Drawee Location* - Checks drawn on banks in remote locations generally have longer availability times than those drawn on nearby banks.

    • *Time of Deposit* - Checks must reach the processing center by a certain time of day in order to receive the designated availability.

    • *Encoding* - If a company MICR-encodes the check dollar amount on the checks it deposits, the bank may grant faster availability, a later cutoff time, and/or reduced service charges.

    • *Reject Items* - Checks that are rejected by a bank's item processing equipment are likely to miss critical deposit deadlines and are likely to receive longer availability.

4. *Availability Adjustments* - Banks may make adjustments to a customer's availability in several ways:

- *As-of Adjustments* - An **as-of adjustment** is the adjustment of the value date of a transaction for the purpose of calculating collected balances to a date different from the date the transaction occurred. For example, if a bank originally granted one-day availability but actually cleared the check in two days, it would add one more day of float in calculating collected balances.

- *Fractional Availability* - A bank may experience an average availability of one day under normal circumstances, but its availability deadlines may be missed on five percent of the days of the year. Therefore, it assigns availability of 1.05 days to its customers.

- *Guaranteed Availability* - Some banks offer a guaranteed availability schedule, which is not subject to deposit adjustments. The customer is given the scheduled availability regardless of whether the bank experiences delays in clearing the checks.

H. Federal Reserve Float

In the process of clearing checks, banks will sometimes receive availability from the Fed before the Fed can generate the offsetting debit. The difference in timing between the availability granted a clearing bank and the actual presentment of the item to the drawee bank is called **Fed float**. As such, Fed float represents interest-free loans to banks and, indirectly, to companies. The 1980 Depository Institutions Deregulation and Monetary Control Act (DIDMCA) mandated both the reduction and pricing of this subsidy.

The amount of Fed float has been significantly reduced. Remaining Fed float is priced to banks through as-of adjustments, clearing balance requirements, or interest at the Fed funds rate. Some banks pass this charge on to their customers through as-of collected balance adjustments, explicit interest charges, or by granting fractional availability.

I. Other Check-Like Payment Instruments

A number of other payment instruments have check-like attributes and clear through the same channels. Among examples of these other check-like instruments are the following:

1. *Payable Through Draft* - A **payable through draft (PTD)** is a payment instrument resembling a check that is drawn against the payor and not the bank. The payor has a period of time in which to honor or refuse payment. Insurance companies often use PTDs for claim reimbursement because the PTD gives them an opportunity to verify the signature and endorsements before honoring it. The return process has very strict guidelines defined by both Fed Regulation CC and local clearing house rules. Regulation CC requires the same time for the return process as for checks. Some state or local governments use a form of PTD called a government warrant.

2. *Pre-Authorized Draft/Check* - The payor authorizes the payee to draw a draft/check against the payor's account. The payee, rather than the payor, initiates the transaction. Mortgage, insurance, and other recurring payments are often made in this way.

3. *Money Order* - The payor first purchases the money order from a third party (such as the Post Office or a bank). The draft then becomes the obligation of the third party.

4. *Travelers Checks* - Such instruments are prepaid drafts, similar to money orders. Two signatures are required by the purchaser: one at issuance and one at the time the check is used.

5. *Depository Transfer Checks* - Depository transfer checks (DTCs) are checks used in moving funds from one account to another account held by the same firm, usually in cash concentration systems. No signature is required, but for security there is often a payee restriction. Normally the payee can only be an account at the concentration bank.

6. *Sight Draft* - A **sight draft** is payable on demand and is usually presented in combination with other documents showing that the terms of the transaction have been met. Sight drafts are primarily used in foreign trade transactions.

7. *Time Draft* - This payment mechanism is like a sight draft but is not payable until a specified future date. **Time drafts** are used in foreign trade transactions that by contract call for delayed payments.

III. ELECTRONIC PAYMENT METHODS

A. The Automated Clearing House System

The **Automated Clearing House (ACH) system** was developed by the financial industry in the early 1970's as an electronic alternative to checks. In an ACH transaction, payment information is processed electronically instead of manually, thereby increasing reliability, efficiency, and cost-effectiveness. In addition, an ACH transaction is capable of transferring more information about a payment than is possible with a check.

1. *Structure* - The ACH is a network of regional associations, inter-bank associations, and private sector processors. Most regional ACHs are operated by the Fed. The majority of financial institutions are members of an ACH association.

   The National Automated Clearing House Association (NACHA) is the membership organization that provides marketing and education assistance and establishes the rules, standards, and procedures that enable financial institutions to exchange ACH payments on a national basis.

2. *Processing* - The ACH system is a batch process, store-and-forward system. Transactions received by most banks during the day are stored and processed later in a batch mode. This provides significant economies of scale. It also provides faster processing than paper checks, which must be physically handled. Banks are required to transmit and receive ACH transaction files electronically, including return items.

3. *Participants* - Exhibit 4.4 shows the parties in an ACH transaction.

EXHIBIT 4.4
ACH Transaction Participants

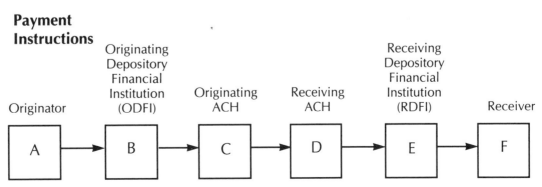

Payment Instructions

Originator	Originating Depository Financial Institution (ODFI)	Originating ACH	Receiving ACH	Receiving Depository Financial Institution (RDFI)	Receiver
A	B	C	D	E	F

4. *How an ACH Transaction Works* - Instead of using paper to carry the necessary transaction information (as a check does), an ACH transaction carries the information electronically. There are both ACH credit transactions and ACH debit transactions. ACH credit transactions move funds from the originator's account to the receiver's account. ACH debit transactions move funds to the originator's account from the receiver's account.

Exhibit 4.5 shows the steps in a typical ACH credit transaction in which Company A pays its payroll by direct deposit. An ACH debit transaction is identical to the credit transaction outlined in the exhibit, except that the file contains a code indicating that the account at the receiving depository financial institution (RDFI) is to be debited instead of credited.

EXHIBIT 4.5
An ACH Credit Transaction (Direct Deposit of Payroll)

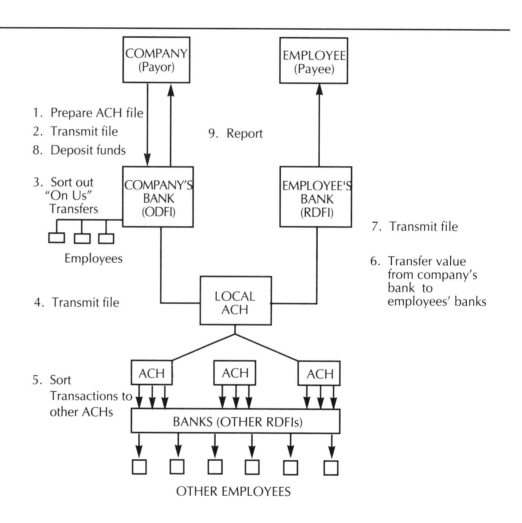

Step 1: A company prepares a file that may contain hundreds of payroll "checks." The file contains each employee's account number, the transit routing number of the employee's bank, the amount of the transfer, the transit routing number of the company's bank, the company's account number, and other pertinent information.

Step 2: The company transmits the file to its bank, the originating depository financial institution (ODFI).

Step 3: The company's bank sorts out on-us transactions for employees who have accounts with the bank and credits their accounts.

(Continued)

EXHIBIT 4.5

*An ACH Credit
Transaction
(Direct Deposit
of Payroll)*

(Continued)

Step 4: The company's bank merges the company's transactions involving other financial institutions with transactions from other firms. A combined file is transmitted to the ACH servicing the originating institution.

Step 5: The local ACH sorts out those transactions which involve banks in its area and sends the remaining transactions to other ACHs.

Step 6: The ACH gives value to the bank on a two-day settlement cycle.

Step 7: The ACH presents a file to the employee's bank containing all transactions pertaining to that bank. The amount the employee receives is credited to the employee's account.

Step 8: This step does not come at a predetermined time in the cycle. On or before the day the ODFI's account is debited, the company must have funds available in the bank to cover the transactions.

Step 9: Both banks provide reports in the form of periodic bank statements, and possible daily deposit and withdrawal reports.

5.   *ACH Payment Formats* - There are ACH formats for both consumer and corporate payments. All ACH payment formats move funds in essentially the same manner. The most appropriate format for a particular payment is determined by the relationship between the parties, the information exchanged, and the types of ACH payment services offered by the participating banks.

The format of an ACH payment message is identified by a three-letter standard entry class in the header of the message. The most commonly used formats are as follows:

- *Prearranged Payment or Deposit (PPD)* - The PPD format is the payment application by which consumers may authorize debits or credits to their accounts by a company or financial institution. These are normally recurring payments in fixed amounts.

   * *PPD Credits* - Examples of consumer credits are payroll, expense reimbursement, dividends, social security, retirement benefits, and tax refunds.

   * *PPD Debits* - Examples of consumer debits are rent and mortgage payments, subscriptions, dues and memberships, insurance premiums, installment debt payments, and utility payments.

- *Cash Concentration or Disbursement (CCD)* - CCD is an electronic payment format used for concentration and disbursement of funds within or between companies. A single 94-character record contains the standard entry class indicating the type of transaction, transit routing numbers for the originating and receiving financial institutions, and the payor's and payee's account numbers. CCD is the only corporate ACH format that does not have space for an additional addenda record, but it contains space for a reference number.

- *Cash Concentration or Disbursement Plus Addendum (CCD+)* - CCD+ is one of the formats used for the U.S. Treasury Vendor Express program and for corporate-to-corporate payments. It is useful when only a limited amount of information must be transmitted. This format is the identical to CCD but with an addenda record. The addenda record is a free-form data space for up to 80 characters of descriptive data. The CCD+ addenda record is also used to report federal and state tax payment information. The data appears in a standardized format, the Tax Payment (TXP) banking convention.

- *Corporate Trade Payment (CTP)* - This format is used for corporate-to-corporate payments. The CTP format consists of a standard ACH payment transaction and a message addendum for remittance information. The message addendum can carry remittance information in fixed-field format with up to 9,999 records, 80 characters each. CTP is scheduled to be discontinued in 1996.

- *Corporate Trade Exchange (CTX)* - The CTX format, like the CTP format, is designed for corporate-to-corporate trade payments. It consists of a standard ACH payment transaction and a variable-length message addendum designed to convey remittance information in the Accredited Standards Committee (ASC) X12 data standard. The addendum can accommodate 9,999 records, 80 characters each. CTX is useful for payments related to multiple invoices and substantial invoice detail.

The NACHA operating rules require all financial institutions participating in the ACH to accept all types of ACH entries and post the dollar amounts to the proper accounts, though many institutions do not have the capability to process addenda records. Addenda records contain remittance detail that follow the standard payment information in ACH payment messages.

6. *Corporate Applications* - The most frequently used corporate applications are in cash concentration and disbursement funding. Many companies use ACH debits to consolidate funds deposited in field banks. This is particularly well suited to corporate lock-box and retail branch deposits. By virtue of its next-day availability, an ACH debit may be used by creditworthy companies to fund disbursement accounts. This provides effective day-in-advance notification of the amount of funds required at the concentration bank, and it eliminates the timing problems associated with the late and/or large second presentments. In general, ACH payments can be used in place of more costly wire transfers when the amounts are known at least one day in advance.

7. *Settlement* - ACH transactions carry settlement dates that determine the availability of funds. Transactions are settled one or two business days after the payment information is entered into the payment system. Both the RDFI and the ODFI are settled simultaneously, thereby eliminating float. Among the conventions governing settlement are the following:

- Credit transactions are entered into the system one or two days prior to settlement.

- Corporate and consumer debits are entered one day prior to settlement. Large-dollar concentration debits usually are initiated as late as possible to allow the maximum dollar amount to be deposited.

- Cutoff times for input vary by originating bank.

- **Memo posting** is posting a credit or debit such as an ACH transaction on a memo basis early in the day when the actual credit or debit will not be posted until later in the day. This allows the beneficiary, such as an employee in a direct deposit of payroll program, use of the funds during the day.

- Some financial institutions and ACHs will accept files over the weekend for Monday settlement.

8. *Prenotification* - **Prenotifications** (prenotes) are zero-dollar entries that are to be sent through the ACH system at least ten calendar days prior to live entries. Prenotes provide a verification function at the receiving bank before entries for settlement are

processed. For example, when a company adds a new employee to its direct deposit payroll program, it uses prenotification to ensure that the bank's transit routing number and the employee's personal bank account number(s) are correct.

Until September 1996, prenotes are required for all PPD entries and are optional for CCD, CTP and CTX entries. After this date, they still may be used but will be optional for all entries. Companies originating ACH transactions should obtain prior consent that authorizes the ACH transaction process. For debits to consumer accounts, this consent must be in writing.

9. *Advantages of Using ACH* - The ACH system provides numerous advantages. These include:

   - *Reduced Banking Costs* - An ACH transfer is usually less expensive than a check and much less expensive than a wire transfer.

   - *Reduced Reconciliation and Cash Application Costs* - Because payments are automated, reconciliation time is reduced. Cash application costs are generally reduced compared to paper-based systems.

   - *Faster Inflows* - The use of ACH debits can accelerate cash inflow by reducing delays caused by invoicing, the mail, internal processing, and bank clearing channels.

   - *Control of Payment Timing* - The use of ACH debits and credits can increase control of payment initiation and funds availability.

   - *Easier Forecasting* - The control of payment timing can increase the accuracy of cash flow forecasts.

   - *Reliability* - ACH transactions reach their destination in a timely and predictable manner.

   - *Enhanced Service* - Customers and employees benefit from enhanced service such as automatic bill paying and direct deposit of payroll.

   - *Flexibility* - Input can be made using a wide variety of methods, such as data transmission or delivery of a magnetic tape.

10. *Disadvantages of Using ACH* - The following are considered disadvantages of the ACH system:

    - *Reduction in Disbursement Float* - The payor may lose float benefits accruing from invoicing, mail, processing, and check clearing delays.

    - *Loss of Control with Direct Debits* - Some payors have security and liability concerns regarding direct debits. However, some banks have systems designed to prevent unauthorized debit and credit activity or amounts in excess of preapproved limits.

    - *System Start-up Costs* - There can be significant development costs such as computer software and hardware, training of employees, education of customers, etc.

    - *Renegotiation* - Before switching to electronic payments, payors and payees often renegotiate payment terms.

B. Fedwire

The **Fedwire** is the Federal Reserve funds transfer system. It is a real-time method of transferring immediate funds and supporting information between two financial institutions using their respective Federal Reserve accounts. The system is reliable and secure but relatively expensive for companies compared to checks and ACH transactions.

1. *Communications and Settlement* - The Fedwire is both a communication and a settlement system operated by the Fed. Funds are moved almost instantaneously once the request has been received by the originating bank except for delays that might result from either a customer or bank temporarily reaching an overdraft limit. The transaction is final once it has been sent by the originating bank and receipt is confirmed by the Fed.

2. *Hours of Operation and Deadlines* - Fedwire is available from 8:30 a.m. to 6:30 p.m. ET. A bank's deadline for originating a transfer to a third party is 6:00 p.m. The deadline for a bank-to-bank transfer is 6:30 p.m. Banks establish earlier cutoff times for customers and other internal departments to allow for processing. In early 1997, Fedwire hours will be extended.

3. *Mechanics of a Wire Transfer* - Exhibit 4.6 shows the steps in a typical wire transfer. The entire process generally takes minutes.

EXHIBIT 4.6
Mechanics of a Wire Transfer

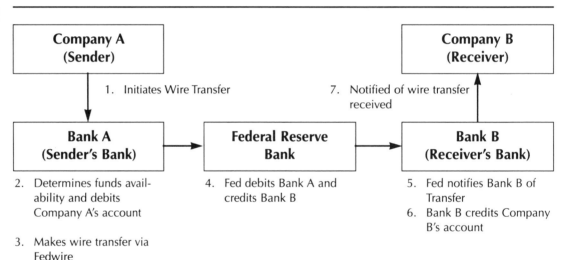

Step 1: Company A initiates a request to transfer funds to Company B. This is typically done through a PC or by a telephone call. Security procedures may include the use of Personal Identification Numbers (PINs), test key calculations or message authentication algorithms, dual authorization of the transfer, or callbacks to verify instructions. Most telephone calls are recorded for security purposes and to resolve disputes.

Step 2: Bank A checks to see if Company A has sufficient funds in its account. If it does, Bank A debits Company A's account. If not, appropriate credit approval must be obtained or the transfer must wait until sufficient funds are available.

Step 3: Bank A uses the Fedwire to transfer funds to Company B through Bank B.

Step 4: The Federal Reserve (Fed) debits Bank A's reserve account and credits Bank B's reserve account.

(Continued)

Step 5: The Fed notifies Bank B of the transfer, including account information for Company B. If Bank B is in a different Fed district from Bank A, the information is routed through the Fed's communication network to the appropriate receiving Federal Reserve Bank.

Step 6: Bank B credits Company B's Account.

Step 7: Company B is notified of the wire transfer received by Bank B via a telephone call, an information reporting system, or a mail or fax advice.

4. *Payment Finality* - In the event of the sending bank's failure to settle, the Federal Reserve guarantees the transferred funds to the receiving bank.

5. *Types of Fedwire Funds Transfers* - Among the different classifications of Fedwire transfers are the following:

- *Repetitive* - Repetitive transfers are used when a company makes a transfer frequently between the same debit and credit parties. The bank has a record of the debit and credit parties and receives electronic and telephonic instructions to make the transfer. A line number is used to identify each transfer. Only the date and dollar amount may be changed.

- *Semi-Repetitive* - With semi-repetitive transfers, the debit and credit parties remain the same but the description may be changed along with the date and dollar amount. Semi-repetitive transfers allow some of the control of repetitive transfers and some of the flexibility of non-repetitive transfers.

- *Non-Repetitive* - With non-repetitive transfers, the debit and credit parties are different each time. Additional security steps may be required.

- *Drawdown* - A company initiates instructions to debit its own or another party's account. The party being debited must authorize these transfers. Drawdowns are most frequently used as part of a company's concentration system.

6. *Expanded Wire Format* - By year-end 1997, the Fed is scheduled to complete the implementation of a new format for Fedwire which will align it with the Clearing House Interbank Payments System (CHIPS) and the Society for Worldwide Interbank Financial Telecommunications (SWIFT). More payment-related information can be communicated through Fedwire, and the expanded format will also carry information required by federal authorities to combat illegal money laundering activity.

7. *Wire Transfer Security* - Security in wire transfer is critical. Commercially reasonable security procedures are necessary in order to comply with Uniform Commercial Code Article 4A (UCC4A). Security procedures are generally outlined in a bank's wire trans-

fer agreement. Among examples of the types of security procedures that are commonly used are the following:

- Use of physical security and limited access at both the company and the bank

- Use of passwords and Personal Identification Numbers (PINs) to identify authorized users

- Use of repetitive wires to limit where funds can be transferred

- Use of dual release (one person enters the wire and another reviews and releases it)

- Use of electronic security methods such as encryption (the scrambling of a message by the sender and the unscrambling of the message by the receiver) and message authentication (a digital signature which prevents an unauthorized person from changing a wire)

8. *Pricing* - The total price to a user of a wire transfer varies significantly. Both the sending institution and the receiving institution may impose a charge.

C. Clearing House Interbank Payments System

The **Clearing House Interbank Payments System (CHIPS)** is an independent message-switching system operated by the New York Clearing House Association. It was established in 1970 to substitute electronic payments for paper checks arising from international dollar transactions such as Eurocurrency or foreign exchange between foreign and American banks. It is also used for payments under letters of credit and documentary collections and for third-party transfers. Other institutions outside New York City use their New York Edge Act subsidiaries as agents or have access to CHIPS through correspondents.

1. *Operation* - Transfers between member banks are received and authenticated during the day. Transfers are batched, and at the end of the day net amounts due to or from each of the settling participants are settled using the clearing banks or the Fed. Non-settling participants settle via correspondent banks. Transfers are executed on a same-day basis and may be unwound (i.e., reversed) only if a member bank cannot honor its net debit position.

2. *Finality* - The receiving bank that credits a customer and allows use of the funds bears the risk that the sending bank will not settle. A fund consisting of collateral posted by all members has been established to insure against the failure of a participant.

D. Society for Worldwide Interbank Financial Telecommunications

The **Society for Worldwide Interbank Financial Telecommunications (SWIFT)** is the major international interbank telecommunications network that transmits international payment instructions as well as other financial messages. It is not a funds transfer network. Messages are transferred requesting debits and credits to correspondent accounts (in addition to other types of messages). Settlement occurs through Fedwire, CHIPS, correspondent accounts, or other means. The formats and uses of SWIFT are being expanded to include things like balance reporting.

E. Payments System Risk

The Federal Reserve's concern with payments system risk started in the mid 1970s as payment volume grew and several large banks failed.

1. *Types of Risk* - Today's payment system creates four kinds of risk for banks:

    * *Systemic Risk* - The risk that the failure of one major bank could cause other banks to fail and cause a collapse of the payments system

    * *Credit Risk* - The risk that the party funding a transaction will default on its settlement obligation

    * *Operational Risk* - The risk of processing mistakes disrupting the system

    * *Fraud Risk* - The risk that someone might introduce a false item which might cause a loss for the disbursing party

2. *Daylight Overdrafts* - A **daylight overdraft** is an intra-day exposure occurring when an account is in an overdraft position during the business day. Banks may have daylight overdrafts in their Federal Reserve bank accounts, and companies may have daylight overdrafts in their accounts at commercial banks.

    Examples of transactions that inherently create daylight overdrafts include the following:

    * A bank may repay Fed funds borrowed for the previous night in the morning, but not receive the proceeds of new borrowings until the afternoon.

    * A bank customer that issues commercial paper may repay funds to investors in the morning, but not receive funds from investors until the afternoon.

    Controlling daylight overdrafts has been one of the primary elements in recent Federal Reserve measures to control risk among the large-dollar payment networks. The Fed has mandated that all banks using the large-dollar payment systems must have in place a sender net debit cap, which limits the intra-day overdraft that the bank can incur over all the large-dollar systems. The caps are based on a Fed schedule relating to a bank's self-evaluation of its overall creditworthiness as an institution, its credit policies, and operational controls. The self-evaluation must be approved by a bank's board of directors.

    The Fed has decided that pricing will be the primary approach for controlling the level of daylight overdrafts. In effect, this is a market, rather than a regulatory solution. The Fed is phasing in its pricing of daylight overdrafts to banks. It measures daylight overdrafts on a minute-by-minute basis and charges based on the magnitude and duration of the overdraft.

    Daylight overdraft limits have not had a major gridlock effect on corporate money transfers, though there are occasional delays when companies or banks reach their limits.

    In addition, the Fed has mandated that all banks must establish bilateral net credit limits which define the maximum amount of net payments that the bank receives from another bank over private networks such as CHIPS. The reason for the net credit limits is that payments on CHIPS are not settled until the end of the day. A higher amount of payments received and credited to beneficiaries means a higher exposure to the sending bank's failure to settle at the end of the day.

Questions

These chapter questions are to test and review the information in the text and are not examples of CCM examination questions, nor are they in the examination format.

Answers can be found at the back of the book on p. 315.

1. With a check, what is the difference between the payor and the payee?

2. What is the purpose of the Magnetic Ink Character Recognition (MICR) line?

3. What are the various methods used to clear checks?

4. What is a cash letter?

5. What is a direct send?

6. What is an on-us item?

7. What are High Dollar Group Sort (HDGS) items?

8. What is the difference between a ledger balance and a collected balance?

9. How is deposit float calculated?

10. What factors determine availability?

11. What is Federal Reserve float?

12. Why is a payable through draft (PTD) not a check?

13. What differentiates a time draft from a sight draft?

14. What are the most commonly used ACH formats?

15. When does settlement occur in an ACH transaction?

16. How does settlement through Fedwire differ from settlement through the ACH?

17. How does a repetitive wire transfer differ from a non-repetitive transfer?

18. What is the major difference between CHIPS and SWIFT?

19. Why is the Federal Reserve concerned about daylight overdrafts and what action has it taken to address this concern?

20. What are the various security procedures used to provide commercially reasonable security procedures for wire transfers?

CHAPTER 5

Credit and Accounts Receivable Management

OVERVIEW

This chapter describes the goals and processes of credit and accounts receivable management and their implications for cash management.

LEARNING OBJECTIVES

Upon completion of this chapter and the related study questions, the reader should know:

1. The objectives of the corporate credit and accounts receivable functions.

2. How the credit and accounts receivable functions fit into the corporate finance organization.

3. The forms of credit extension.

4. How companies make customer credit decisions.

5. The commonly used terms of sale, including credit terms.

6. How accounts receivable are measured and monitored.

7. How corporations develop credit policies.

8. How the costs and benefits of credit policies are calculated.

9. How accounts receivable may be financed.

10. How the cash application process works.

11. What legislation affects credit and collections.

OUTLINE

    I.   **Objectives of Credit and Accounts Receivable Management**

   II.   **The Credit and Accounts Receivable Management Functions**
        A.   Responsibility
        B.   Importance for a Cash Manager

I. OBJECTIVES OF CREDIT AND ACCOUNTS RECEIVABLE MANAGEMENT

The credit and accounts receivable areas of a company must work closely with other areas such as sales, customer service, billing, and accounting. The objectives of credit management include the following:

- Creating, preserving, and collecting accounts receivable

- Establishing and communicating a company's credit policies

- Evaluating customer creditworthiness and setting customer credit lines

- Establishing terms of sale consistent with overall company objectives

- Ensuring prompt and accurate customer billing in conjunction with the customer service or billing departments

- Maintaining up-to-date records of accounts receivable

- Following up on overdue accounts and initiating collection procedures when necessary

II. THE CREDIT AND ACCOUNTS RECEIVABLE MANAGEMENT FUNCTIONS

Accounts receivable are the result of a company's decision to sell goods and services on a non-cash basis. Accounts receivable are an asset of a company and represent an extension of credit (known as trade credit) to its customers.

A. Responsibility

The responsibilities of the credit and accounts receivable function include the following:

1. Credit policy is generally administered by the credit manager.

2. The sales or customer service areas may work with credit management in the development of credit policy because of its direct influence on sales volume and overall customer relationships.

3. Captive finance companies assume responsibility for credit management in some companies.

B. Importance for a Cash Manager

Working relationships with the credit function are important for a cash manager.

1. *Organizational Relationship* - While credit policy and collection of accounts receivable have a significant impact on the cash flow time line, these functions are not generally under the direct control of a cash manager.

2. *Need for Interaction* - A strong information link and a cooperative working relationship are needed between the credit and cash management functions for the following reasons:

   - *Customer Payments* - A cash manager is responsible for establishing and maintaining the banking network. The credit management function needs to have input to, and receive feedback from, this network regarding customer payments.

- *Forecasting* - The credit department is an important resource for a cash manager in forecasting, since credit policies affect the accuracy, nature and time frame of cash flow forecasts.

- *Cash Applications* - The cash manager or credit manager may also run the collections processing area that applies payments to customer accounts and generates the information required for posting to the accounts receivable ledger. This will be covered in greater detail later in this chapter.

III. CREDIT POLICIES

Company credit policies include credit standards, credit terms, and collection policy. If credit is to be offered, a number of decisions must be made by a company.

- *Credit Standards* - Granting credit has two stages, establishing credit standards and determining a customer's credit limit against those standards.

- *Credit Terms* - The terms of the sale must be clearly specified.

- *Collection Policy* - A company must establish policies and procedures to collect payment when a credit customer fails to pay according to the specified terms.

It is important that a company have written policies and procedures in place to ensure consistency and objectivity. After a company has established its basic credit policies, it must develop the procedures and information systems necessary to monitor the accounts receivable for compliance with credit terms and to detect changes in customer payment patterns.

A. Reasons to Offer Credit

The primary reason for a company to offer credit terms to its customers is to increase its sales. Companies may choose to offer credit for other reasons such as the following:

1. *Competition* - Matching competitor's terms may be a sales necessity.

2. *Promotion* - A company may offer special credit terms as part of a promotion program for a product.

3. *Credit Availability* - Some buyers may not have access to any other forms of credit. In tight credit times, seller trade terms or financing may be necessary.

4. *Convenience* - A buyer may prefer the convenience of an open account trade credit arrangement. Trade credit does not require the documentation or the explicit agreement on the repayment date that most forms of bank or finance company credit do.

5. *Profit* - A company extending credit may earn interest revenue above its cost of funds.

B. Credit Policy Constraints

A company's credit policy is influenced by the following:

1. *Industry Convention* - The credit terms customarily offered in many industries have not changed for a long time. It may be difficult for a seller to make a change from

convention unilaterally unless a buyer is offered some form of incentive such as a discount in return.

2.   *Contractual Obligations* - A covenant in a loan agreement may have a current ratio limitation. If accounts receivable are increased, working capital ratios could change, possibly causing a violation of a loan covenant.

3.   *Legal Issues* - The Robinson-Patman Act prohibits various forms of price discrimination. Also, state law may dictate terms for certain goods and services.

C. Financial Implications

For companies that offer credit, accounts receivable are unavoidable. A company's credit terms, together with the pattern of its sales and collections, determine the level of its accounts receivable.

1.   *Use of Capital and Liquidity* - Generation of accounts receivable represents a use of cash. Credit terms and any delays in customer payments must be financed and can cause a liquidity problem if the company does not have additional sources of financing available. Therefore, a company's ability to increase its investment in accounts receivable is directly related to its capacity to fund this increase.

2.   *Source of Liquidity* - Accounts receivable can also be a source of liquidity to the extent they can be used as the basis to obtain short-term borrowings or sold for cash to third parties.

D. Benefits and Costs

Credit policies create benefits and costs for the seller.

1.   *Benefits*
     • *Increased Sales* - The primary purpose of extending credit is to increase sales, resulting in increased profits for the company.

     • *Interest Income* - Funds received from interest on installment or other forms of credit sales are a benefit to the seller.

2.   *Costs*
     • *Credit Department Costs* - These may include personnel costs, data processing costs, and other costs required to sustain a department responsible for a company's overall credit function.

     • *Credit Evaluation* - This includes the costs of both obtaining and analyzing credit information.

     • *Accounts Receivable Carrying Cost* - Accounts receivable, like any other asset on the corporate balance sheet, have a cost. A company may consider that cost to be based on the weighted average cost of capital or the marginal cost of short-term borrowing.

     • *Discounted Payments* - When customers take advantage of an offered discount but the volume of sales does not increase, total net revenue is reduced. This loss of revenue may be partially offset by a reduction in accounts receivable carrying costs.

- *Selling and Production Costs* - A liberalized credit policy may contribute to an increase in sales, but sales and production expense may also increase at the same time.

- *Collection Expenses* - These include the cost of processing payments as well as the cost of pursuing accounts that are not being paid in a timely manner.

- *Bad Debts* - Accounts receivable that are determined to be uncollectable must be charged off. Most companies estimate their level of charge-offs by creation of a reserve account through periodic charges to bad debt expense. The timing and volume of bad debt expense and charge offs are important components of credit policy.

  The risk of accounts receivable write-offs can be reduced through the purchase of various insurance products designed to cover losses resulting from sales on credit. As with other costs, a company must evaluate the cost of this insurance versus the projected benefit.

- *Discrepancies in Payment*s - A reduction in revenue or additional costs can result when payments received are less than the amount invoiced. The reason for the reduced payment must first be determined through proper investigation and research. If a deduction is legitimate, a credit memo is issued to the customer which, in turn, reduces the company's revenues. If credit is not due, the amount deducted will be charged back to the customer. The company must then bear the additional administrative cost of monitoring and collecting any charged back amounts.

IV. CREDIT STANDARDS

It is important for a company to set and maintain its credit standards. This involves both the credit granting decision and the billing and collection policies.

A. Potential Errors in Credit Decision-Making

There are two types of potential errors associated with the granting of credit terms:

1. *Rejection of an Acceptable Credit Risk* - If a company rejects a customer who is a good risk, the company loses potential sales.

2. *Acceptance of a Substandard Risk* - If a company accepts a customer who does not pay according to the specified terms, the company incurs collection, monitoring and/or bad debt costs.

Making credit standards more stringent will in general reduce the frequency of the second type of error, but will also increase the frequency of the first type. In practice, the costs of these two types of errors are hard to quantify.

B. Information Sources

The type, quantity, and cost of information must be considered in establishing a company's method of analyzing credit requests. Credit information can be gathered in stages, and at each stage, the costs of additional information may be weighed against the expected benefits. Information sources can be internal or external.

1. *Internal Sources* - The most important sources of internally generated credit information include the following:

   • The company's credit application and agreement form completed by the applicant.

   • The company's own records regarding actual payment history of the applicant in question.

2. *External Sources* - A variety of external sources can be used to assist in determining the creditworthiness of a credit applicant.

   • *Financial Statements* - Audited financial statements provide important information on corporate credit applicants.

   • *Trade References* - Other companies are contacted to obtain their actual payment experiences regarding credit terms extended to the applicant.

   • *Banks or Financial Creditors* - The customer's bank or other financial creditors (commercial finance or leasing companies) can also be a valuable source of information about the customer's financial condition and available credit. Though banks or financial creditors are generally reluctant to discuss their detailed experience with trade creditors, they will generally provide standardized general credit information.

   • *Agencies* - There are local and nationwide agencies that collect, evaluate, and report information on the credit history of most companies. Their credit reports include past payment history, financial information, maximum outstanding credit amounts, length of time credit has been available, and any actions that have been necessary to achieve collection.

C. The Five C's of Credit

Qualitative and quantitative credit analysis naturally depends upon the type of information available and the tradeoff between cost and the benefit received. The traditional approaches are based on the following five C's of credit:

1. *Character* - The perceived honesty or integrity of an individual applicant, or of the officers of a corporate applicant, is used as an indication of the intent or willingness to pay. This can be evidenced by the company's payment history.

2. *Capacity* - A measure of a customer's current resources to pay the obligations when they become due, as measured by financial liquidity ratios.

3. *Capital* - A customer's short- and long-term financial resources that could be called upon if the immediate cash flow is insufficient to meet payment obligations.

4. *Collateral* - Assets or guarantees available to satisfy the obligation if payment is not made as required.

5. *Conditions* - The general economic environment and economic conditions existing for the customer and the seller affect the ability of the customer to pay and the willingness of the company to grant credit.

D. Quantitative Credit Analysis

Quantitative methods for both corporate and consumer credit analysis include:

1. *Business Credit Analysis* - Quantitative analysis of credit information begins with an examination of a credit applicant's financial statements, frequently through ratio analysis, to assess a customer's financial condition. The measures used most often include liquidity ratios (i.e., quick and current ratio), asset management ratios (i.e., total asset turnover and inventory turnover ratios), coverage ratios (times interest earned), and financial leverage ratios (i.e., debt to assets and debt to equity ratios). Ratios can provide valuable insight when evaluated in relation to industry standards published by credit rating agencies and other associations. Some commercial credit analysis can involve credit scoring, which is described below.

2. *Consumer Credit Analysis* - Major issuers of retail credit, such as department stores, use quantitative credit scoring models, often developing a different model for each billing region. These quantitative approaches are cost effective, and can aid in complying with consumer credit legislation which is discussed later in the chapter. Formal statistical analysis is often used to identify the factors that distinguish paying customers from non-paying customers.

3. *Credit Scoring* - One type of analysis, **credit scoring,** is a technique used to estimate the creditworthiness of applicants. Credit scoring follows three steps:

    *   Standard and high-risk accounts are defined based on historical data. Characteristics are compiled to differentiate between these two types of accounts. Variables such as monthly income, monthly obligations, and time on the job are used for a consumer credit applicant.

    *   Weighting of characteristics distinguishes between standard and high-risk accounts, thus creating an aggregate credit score that measures creditworthiness.

    *   Cutoff scores for credit granting are set. An applicant's actual credit score is then calculated in accordance with the established criteria. A score above the higher cutoff is granted credit, while one below the lower limit is denied credit. An applicant with a score between the two limits usually requires further analysis before a decision is made.

E. Billing and Collection Policies

The type of credit offered has an important influence on the characteristics of the collection system. The major objective of a collection policy is to speed the conversion of accounts receivable into cash, while minimizing collection expense and bad-debt losses.

1. *Invoicing* - The first step in collecting an account is to send prompt and correct invoices with the terms of payment clearly stated. Invoicing float is the delay between the purchase of goods and services and the receipt of the invoice. Delays in invoice generation or incorrect invoices can add days or even weeks to the cash flow timeline.

2. *Statements* - Most companies bill their wholesale customers by invoice with each shipment because that method helps both the buyer and the seller reconcile the invoice with the shipment and receipt of goods. A statement may be sent periodical-

ly as a reminder and a summary of outstanding invoices. Monthly statements listing goods or services purchased are common in retail consumer billing.

3. *Delayed Payments* - When payment is delayed beyond the due date, a company has the following options:

    -   Send a duplicate invoice

    -   Mail a form letter or series of form letters

    -   Make telephone calls, which will also determine if there is a perceived dispute or need for a duplicate invoice

    -   Visit the customer in person

    -   Suspend further sales until past due items are paid, i.e., put the customer on credit hold

    -   Negotiate with the customer for payment of past due amounts

    -   Claim or realize proceeds of any pledged collateral

    -   Attempt to negotiate additional corporate or personal guarantees or try to obtain a lien on specific assets

    -   Initiate direct legal action or turn delinquent accounts over to a collection agency

V. FORMS OF CREDIT EXTENSION

Trade credit can be extended to a customer in the following ways:

A. Open Account

This method, sometimes called open book credit, is the most common type of commercial trade credit in the U.S., and works as follows:

-   A seller issues an invoice, which is formal evidence of the obligation, and records the sale as an account receivable.

-   The customer is billed for each transaction by an invoice and/or by a monthly statement covering all invoices generated during the billing period.

-   Full payment of invoiced amounts are expected within the specified credit terms unless certain discounts or deductions are made available to the customer.

-   A buyer's creditworthiness is reviewed periodically, but the buyer does not need to apply for credit each time an order is placed.

B. Installment Credit

The amount of the sale, as well as any interest, is paid in periodic installments, usually in equal monthly amounts. Frequently, the seller requires the buyer to sign a contract specifying the terms of the obligation. This form of credit is most common for high-value consumer durables such as automobiles. A contract explaining credit terms and disclosing rates to retail customers is required.

C. Revolving Credit

Under **revolving credit terms**, credit is granted without requiring specific approval of each transaction as long as the account is current. The account is usually considered current if the credit outstanding is below an established credit limit and minimum payments have been made on time. The term revolving credit also refers to a type of bank loan which is described in Chapter 10, Borrowing.

D. Letter of Credit

The seller may require the buyer to open a commercial letter of credit (L/C) through a bank, wherein the bank promises and remits payment to the seller provided certain specified conditions are met by a certain date. This method is sometimes used domestically, but is more common in international trade.

A bank standby L/C may be required by a seller to secure credit sales made to a specific buyer. Unlike a commercial L/C, a standby L/C is not the intended mechanism for making payment. It is only drawn upon by the seller if the buyer fails to make payment as originally agreed.

VI. CREDIT TERMS AND CONSIDERATIONS

There are many different types of terms of sale, as well as important considerations for setting credit terms. A company offering or accepting credit terms must also consider the cost of that credit.

A. Common Terms of Sale

Terms of sale represent a contract between a buyer and seller. These terms stipulate the form and timing of payments, with many establishing a credit relationship between a buyer and seller. They are usually specified on an invoice or in legal documents. The following are the most commonly used terms of sale:

1. *Cash Before Delivery (CBD)* - CBD terms generally require full and final payment of an order prior to shipment. CBD is often used when the buyer is considered a greater credit risk than the seller is willing to accept or is unknown to the seller.

2. *Cash on Delivery (COD)* - Goods are shipped, and the buyer must pay upon delivery. The seller may have to pay the shipping costs to return the goods if the payment is not made.

3. *Cash Terms* - The buyer generally has a week to ten days to make the payment. This method is frequently used in sales of highly perishable items.

4. *Net Terms* - The seller specifies a net due date by which the full amount must be paid. For example, terms of Net 30 require that payment be made within 30 days. The actual due date is usually calculated from the invoice date, although other dates, such as the delivery date, are occasionally specified or used in determining the date payment is due.

5. *Discount Terms* - In addition to the specification of a net due date, the seller may also offer a discount if payment is made prior to the net due date. Terms of 2/10

Net 30 mean that the total amount is due within 30 days of the invoice date, but the buyer can take a two percent discount if payment is made within ten days.

6. *Monthly Billing* - A monthly statement is issued for all invoices dated prior to a cut-off date, such as the 25th of the month. Payment is due by a specified date the following month. Cash discounts may also be incorporated. For example, 1/10, Prox Net 30 means that a discount of one percent can be taken if payment is made by the 10th day of the following month. The total amount is due on the 30th day of the following month.

7. *Draft/Bill of Lading* - This collection method is also known as a documentary collection. The seller collects its payments through banking channels. Having shipped goods to the buyer, the seller sends shipping and title documents to its bank. The seller's bank sends the documents to the buyer's bank. The buyer gains possession of the documents upon paying its bank or upon signing a draft agreeing to pay at a future date. Finally, payment is remitted to the seller's bank for payment to the seller. This method is more common in international than domestic trade.

8. *Seasonal Dating* - Payment is due near the end of the buyer's selling season when the buyer has cash. This is a way for a manufacturer to provide short-term financing for a buyer's purchases. It is common in industries with distinct seasonality of sales such as toys, greeting cards, garden supplies, sporting goods, or textbooks. Sliding or scaled discounts may be available to the buyer to encourage early payment.

9. *Consignment* - Under a consignment agreement, the seller ships the goods to the buyer with no obligation to pay until the goods have been sold or used. The title to the goods remains with the seller until that date. In order to protect the seller's interests, the consigned inventory and the proceeds generated from its sale are generally accounted for on a separate basis.

B. Credit Term Considerations

The three considerations regarding credit terms are as follows:

1. *Penalty Fees* - In addition to offering credit terms, companies often assess a penalty fee for payments received past the due date. This fee is usually a percentage of the past due amount. The fee should be clearly stated at the time of the sale and shown on the invoice.

2. *Credit Limits* - The aggregate amount of credit to be granted to a customer must also be determined. A new customer that meets the standards is often granted credit at the lowest limit. After some time period of satisfactory payment performance the credit limit may be raised to the next level. Credit limits are usually reviewed periodically and as a result are subject to change.

3. *Eligibility for Discount* - Companies usually use the postmark date of the payment remittance or the date funds are received as the benchmark date for determining eligibility for discounts offered.

C. Cost of Trade Credit

In offering discounts, the seller must evaluate the cost of the discount versus the benefits gained from early payment. In the case of most net credit terms, there are no explicit costs to a buyer in taking full advantage of the terms offered by making payment on the appropriate due date. When discount terms are offered, there are also no explicit costs to trade credit, but there are implicit costs related to not taking an offered discount.

Standard accounting practices generally require purchases to be recorded net of any offered discounts. If the discount is not taken, the amount of the discount is accounted for as a cost of discounts foregone. The annualized cost to a buyer of not taking a discount can be calculated as a function of the amount of the discount and the number of additional days of credit gained by delaying payment until the net due date. The calculated percentage cost of not taking the discount can then be compared to other short-term borrowing alternatives.

If funds can be borrowed at a rate less than the cost of not taking the discount, then a buyer should borrow those funds and take the discount for early payment. If borrowed funds are more expensive (or not available), then the buyer should delay payment until the net due date. An example of this calculation for a company that is a net borrower is shown in Exhibit 5.1.

EXHIBIT 5.1

Annualized Cost of Trade Credit

$$\frac{\text{Annualized Cost}}{\text{of Trade Credit}} = \frac{\text{Early Pmt Discount}}{(1 - \text{Early Pmt Discount})} \times \frac{365}{(\text{Net Pmt Period} - \text{Discount Pmt Period})}$$

Example

Given terms of 2/10, Net 30, the cost of not taking the discount (i.e., paying the net amount on day 30, rather than the discounted amount on day 10) can be calculated as:

$$\text{Cost of Trade Credit} = \frac{.02}{(1-.02)} \times \frac{365}{(30 - 10)} = 37.24\%$$

If a buyer were able to borrow funds at a rate of less than 37.24%, then the buyer should do so, and take the discount for early payment. If borrowed funds cost more than 37.24% or if they are not available, then the buyer should delay payment until the net due date.

A company with excess cash reserves must compare this annualized cost to investment rates. If alternative investment rates available to the company exceed the annualized cost of trade credit, then the discount should not be taken and payment should be delayed until the net due date.

VII. ACCOUNTS RECEIVABLE MONITORING AND CONTROL

Monitoring and control of a company's accounts receivable are an important part of the overall credit policy and are the responsibility of the credit manager.

A. Purpose

Monitoring of accounts receivable should be performed on both an individual account and an aggregate level. A customer aging schedule is a useful method for tracking individual receivables, and a report of days' sales outstanding is a useful measure of total accounts receivable.

1. *Monitoring Individual Accounts* - Individual accounts should be monitored for the following reasons:

    • Some customers may intentionally delay payment until a follow-up is initiated.

    • A change in financial condition may alter the ability of a customer to make timely payments and may require a curtailment of future credit sales.

2. *Monitoring Aggregate Accounts Receivable* - Aggregate accounts receivable should be monitored because of the following reasons:

    • A significant change in the level of overall accounts receivable may be a symptom of a change in business that could affect a company's financing needs. These changes should be analyzed to determine underlying causes and any corrective actions that need to be taken. Potential variables that could create significant changes are:
      * variations in sales volume
      * modifications of credit standards policy
      * fluctuating economic conditions
      * response to actions of competitors

    • Aggregate accounts receivable also serve as the basis for forecasting the amount and timing of future cash receipts.

B. Days' Sales Outstanding

The most commonly used measurement of accounts receivable is **days' sales outstanding** (DSO), which is calculated by dividing accounts receivable outstanding at the end of a time period by the average daily credit sales for the period.

DSO is easy to calculate and gives a single number that, when compared to the stated credit terms or to a historic trend, provides an indication of a company's overall collection efficiency. It may, however, be distorted by changing trends in sales volume, payment pattern, or by a strong seasonality in sales.

Exhibit 5.2 describes a basic method for calculating DSO. The average sales of $3,444.44 is computed without considering the pattern of sales for the period.

EXHIBIT 5.2

Days' Sales Outstanding (DSO) Calculation

Assume

Outstanding Receivables of $285,000 at the end of Month 3
Credit Terms of Net 60
DSO Averaging Period of 3 months (90 days)
Credit Sales History:
  Month 1 = $ 90,000.00
  Month 2 = $ 105,000.00
  Month 3 = $ 115,000.00

DSO Calculation

$$\text{Average Daily Credit Sales} = \frac{(\$90,000.00 + \$105,000.00 + \$115,000.00)}{90} = \$3,444.44$$

$$\text{Days' Sales Outstanding (DSO)} = \frac{\text{Outstanding Accounts Receivable}}{\text{Average Daily Credit Sales}} = \frac{\$285,000.00}{\$3,444.44} = 82.74 \text{ Days}$$

Average Past Due Calculation

$$\text{Average Past Due} = \text{DSO} - \text{Average Days of Credit Terms}$$

$$= 82.74 \text{ Days} - 60 \text{ Days} = 22.74 \text{ Days}$$

C. Aging Schedule

An aging schedule is a list of the percentages and/or amounts of outstanding accounts receivable classified as current or past due, in 30-day increments. The schedule can be prepared at the aggregate level or on a customer-by-customer basis. The primary use of these schedules is to identify past-due accounts. This is important because the older an account receivable becomes, the less likely it is to be collected.

With credit terms of Net 30, the aggregate aging schedule in Exhibit 5.3 shows that 30 percent of the accounts receivable are past due. The aging schedule can be a more informative breakdown than DSO because it provides information on the distribution, not just a single average. However, the aging schedule suffers from the same potentially misleading signals as DSO when sales vary significantly from month to month. An example of an aging schedule is shown in Exhibit 5.3.

	Age of Accounts	Accounts Receivable	% of Accounts Receivable
EXHIBIT 5.3	0-30 days	$1,750,000	70%
Example of an	31-60 days	375,000	15%
Aging Schedule	61-90 days	250,000	10%
	91+ days	125,000	5%
	Total	$2,500,000	100%

D. Accounts Receivable Balance Pattern

An **accounts receivable balance pattern** is based on aging schedules. It specifies the percentage of credit sales in a time period, usually a month, that remains outstanding in the company's accounts receivable at the end of that and each subsequent time period. The normal balance pattern is identified by examining the company's collection history. The balance experience at any point in time is then evaluated for any shifts by comparing it to the normal balance experience.

Exhibit 5.4 gives an example of a firm whose sales are collected as follows:

5% of sales collected in the month of sale
40% of sales collected in the next month
35% of sales collected 2 months later
20% of sales collected 3 months later

At the end of March there are still $50,000 of accounts receivable outstanding (uncollected) from January's sales. This is determined as follows:

January Sales			= $ 250,000.00
Collected in:	January	= (.05 x $250,000)	= $ 12,500.00
	February	= (.40 x $250,000)	= $ 100,000.00
	March	= (.35 x $250,000)	= $ 87,500.00
	Total Collections		= $ 200,000.00

Total Outstanding Receivables from January Sales = $ 250,000 - $ 200,000 = $50,000

		Remaining Accounts Receivable from Month Sales at the End of March	Remaining Accounts Receivable as a % of Month Sales
Month Sales	Sales		
January	$250,000	$50,000	20%
February	$300,000	$165,000	55%
March	$400,000	$380,000	95%
April	$500,000		

EXHIBIT 5.4
Example of a Receivables Balance Pattern

The total outstanding accounts receivable balance at the end of March is:
$595,000 = ($50,000 + $165,000 + $380,000)

The estimate of cash inflows for April = 5% of April sales + 40% of March sales + 35% of February sales + 20% of January sales:

Estimated April Inflows =   (.05 x $500,000)
          + (.40 x $400,000)
          + (.35 x $300,000)
          + (.20 x $250,000)
         = $340,000

The balance pattern gives a more complete distribution of the collection experience. Furthermore, it is not directly affected by variation in sales; thus, it is not subject to misleading signals because of sales changes. The balance pattern can be used to project both accounts receivable levels and collections. Therefore, it can be a useful tool in the preparation of cash flow forecasts.

VIII. FINANCING ACCOUNTS RECEIVABLE

A major current asset for many companies is accounts receivable, which must be financed in some manner.

A. Unsecured Bank Borrowing

A company that offers trade credit may borrow unsecured funds from a financial institution to support additional accounts receivable if it has sufficient available credit capacity.

1. *Advantage* - The major advantage is that a company realizes the marketing benefits (i.e., increased sales) of extending credit and has the ability to control the approval of customers who purchase goods and services on credit.

2. *Disadvantage* - The major disadvantage is that a company absorbs the costs of running the credit operation, financing the accounts receivable, collection expenses, and bad-debt losses.

B. Secured Bank Borrowing

If a company cannot finance its accounts receivable with unsecured borrowings, it may be able to pledge its accounts receivable as collateral and borrow on a secured basis. The bank will select those accounts receivable it wishes to accept as collateral. A percentage of the accounts receivable pledged will be advanced to the company as a loan. The company will remit the funds owed to the bank upon collection of the receivables.

C. Captive Finance Company

A company may be able to create a wholly owned subsidiary to perform the credit operations and to obtain accounts receivable financing. Since the finance company is a subsidiary of the parent company, the advantages and disadvantages listed earlier apply. In addition, because of its greater liquidity, a **captive finance company** may be able to obtain financing at a lower cost than the parent company.

D. Third-Party Financing Institution

A company may collect the information necessary to complete a credit application and forward the completed application to a financial institution which makes the credit decision, and, at its option, grants or denies credit. Because of the administrative costs involved, this is most common for large-ticket items such as production machinery.

1.   *Advantage* - The advantage of this alternative is that a company avoids most of the costs of operating a credit department and frees up the funds that otherwise would be tied up in financing accounts receivable.

2.   *Disadvantage* - The disadvantage is that a company loses control over the type of customer accepted for credit and loses some of the marketing opportunities. A company may have to pay a fee in the form of a discount of the face value of the sale to compensate the third party.

E. Credit Card

A third party, usually a bank or another financial institution, may offer a credit card that a merchant accepts as payment. The agreement between the seller and the financial institution specifies that the seller is paid in cash at a discount of the face value of the purchase at a specified time after the credit card sale ticket is deposited.

1.   *Advantages* - The advantages of using credit cards are as follows:

   • The seller bears none of the direct costs of running a credit department.

   • Depending upon the agreement, the seller has little or no funds tied up in financing accounts receivable.

   • The third party and the seller have many options in sharing or absorbing bad-debt losses.

2. *Disadvantages* - The disadvantages in using credit cards for customer financing are as follows:

    - The seller loses control over the determination of acceptable credit customers.

    - The seller loses the promotional aspects of having its own list of credit customers.

    - A major direct cost is the discount of the face value of the transaction, which depends upon the average size of the sale, the total volume, and the type of business or organization.

F. Factoring

Another important third-party financing option is **factoring**, which is the sale or transfer of title of the accounts receivable to a factoring company. The factor provides credit evaluation and collection services. The degree to which factoring is considered acceptable and the degree to which it is actually used vary by industry and region.

1. *Recourse* - Most factoring is done without recourse to the seller. When factoring is done with recourse, the seller is still liable if the factoring company cannot collect an account receivable.

2. *Notification* - Most factoring is on a notification basis. The buyer is notified that the account has been sold and is informed to remit the funds directly to the factor.

3. *Advantages of Factoring* - Factoring has the following advantages:

    - It reduces or eliminates the cost of maintaining a credit department.

    - The factor absorbs the uncertainty in the timing of the payment and, if done without recourse, any extraordinary bad-debt losses.

    - Because of the ability to spread risks, the factor may be able to accept some credit customers that the seller would typically reject.

    - The factor may have better credit information and be able to make better credit decisions.

4. *Disadvantages of Factoring* - Disadvantages of factoring include the following:

    - The fees charged in a typical non-recourse agreement may be quite high.

    - The seller loses control over who is granted credit and may require its own credit operation to assess those customers rejected by the factor.

    - Some companies believe that having their receivables factored conveys a sign of financial weakness, though in some industries factoring is a standard practice.

G. Private Label Financing

With private label financing, a third party operates the credit function in the name of the seller rather than the seller administering its own credit card program. From the customer's perspective, the credit appears to be arranged through the seller.

1. *Advantages:*

   • The seller retains many of the promotional aspects of conducting its own credit function.

   • The seller has neither the costs of the credit operation nor the requirement to finance accounts receivable.

2. *Disadvantages:*

   • The seller does not receive the full face value of the sale.

   • The seller may lose the authority to decide on acceptable credit customers.

IX. CASH APPLICATION

Cash application is the process of matching and applying a customer's payment against outstanding accounts receivable. There are basically two kinds of accounts receivable systems: Open Item and Balance Forward.

A. Open Item

An open item system is most commonly used when the customer buying on credit is another company rather than a consumer. In an open item system, each invoice sent to a customer is recorded in the accounts receivable file. When a payment is received, it is necessary to match the payment with the specified invoices being paid and account for any payment discrepancies (discounts, allowances, adjustments, etc.). Remittance information, which typically accompanies payment, generally details which invoices are being paid, as well as any adjustments to the payment. This application process may be manual or automated or a combination of the two.

Many companies have automated cash application programs which take the payment and remittance information, and through a series of algorithms, apply the payments by matching them to specific invoices. A high rate of successful automated applications greatly reduces the amount of manual effort required to complete the application process.

Lockbox processors may provide payment and remittance data to a company to facilitate the cash application process. One common service is to capture the data in the MICR line of the check. Elements captured include the drawee bank's transit routing number, the payor's bank account number, and the check amount. The transit routing number and bank account number can be used to identify the customer (using an internal database), or additional information can be gathered from accompanying remittance data. The capture of this remittance data by the lockbox processor may be automated (using pre-encoded payment stubs) or manual. The additional remittance data may include such items as:

• invoice numbers
• amounts being paid
• customer account numbers
• remitter's name
• discounts and adjustments taken
• dates
• other pertinent information

Some lockbox processors access a company's accounts receivable system information during lockbox processing in order to look up such things as account numbers and other pertinent information. Others match payments and invoices to the extent possible prior to data being transmitted to the company using information provided by the company or on encoded payment stubs returned with the payments. These services are designed to increase a company's automated payment application rate, thereby increasing the overall efficiency of the application process.

B. Balance Forward

Balance forward systems are used most often by companies selling goods and services to individual consumers. In a balance forward system, a credit limit is established for each individual, and as purchases are made or services are provided, total accounts receivable outstanding increases. When payments are made, the accounts receivable balance is reduced by the amount of the payment. The use of a remittance document (bill or statement) which contains payment information in a machine-readable scan line facilitates the capture of information needed in the cash application process. Retailers and other companies which use credit cards for collections most often use these types of systems. Similar systems are also often used by utility companies. (See also Chapter 6, Collections.)

C. Electronic Data Interchange

Given the increased use of Electronic Data Interchange (EDI), a company's accounts receivable system must be able to process electronic payments and remittance information in order to use this information to properly apply payments. Because of the increased remittance information accompanying the payment in an EDI environment, the cash application rate may be increased through automation of the process.

X. LEGISLATION AFFECTING CREDIT AND COLLECTIONS

Many laws and regulations affect the area of credit and collections.

A. Pricing and Interest Charge Restrictions

Because the extension of credit is a benefit to the buyer, credit terms can be considered as a part of the price of the product or service being sold.

1. *Robinson-Patman Act (1936)* - The Robinson-Patman Act specifically prohibits price discrimination among customers where a cost basis cannot be demonstrated as the reason for price differences. Different credit terms are acceptable if they are industry practice or in cases in which cost differences can be substantiated.

2. *Usury Laws* - Usury laws, which vary significantly from state to state, restrict the interest rates that firms can charge on installment credit or penalty fees.

B. Consumer and Commercial Credit Legislation

A number of laws regulate the statement of terms, the credit analysis and approval process, and the collection practices that can be employed when selling on a credit basis to consumers.

Some of the more important federal legislation and regulations are as follows:

1. *Truth in Lending Act (1969)* - This act requires lenders to disclose the true annual interest rate and the total dollar cost on most types of loans.

2. *Fair Credit Reporting Act (1971)* - This act gives a borrower, an applicant for an insurance policy, or a job applicant the right to learn the contents of his or her own credit report at no charge, directly from the credit bureau, if credit is denied on the basis of that report. This act also allows any individuals to obtain a copy of their credit report, at any time, for a reasonable charge.

3. *Fair Credit Billing Act (1975)* - This act is an amendment to the Truth in Lending Act and protects charge account customers against billing errors by permitting credit card customers to use the same legal defenses against banks or other third-party credit card companies that they could previously use against merchants.

4. *Equal Credit Opportunity Act (1975)* - This act prohibits creditors from discriminating against credit applicants on the basis of sex, marital status, race, color, religion, national origin, age, or receipt of public assistance.

5. *Fair Debt Collection Practices Act (1978)* - This act is designed to eliminate abusive and unfair debt collection practices such as threats of financial ruin, loss of job or reputation, and harassing telephone calls.

C. Uniform Commercial Code

In general, revolving credit, installment credit, and sales finance transactions are covered by provisions of the Uniform Commercial Code (UCC), which is the model for many state laws.

D. Bankruptcy and Reorganization

Under the Federal Bankruptcy Reform Act of 1978, a company may file for liquidation under Chapter 7 or reorganization under Chapter 11. Individuals typically file for reorganization under Chapter 13. Reorganization allows a company to pay off debts gradually and operate under a court supervised plan for returning to financial soundness. Filing of a petition protects the debtor from a list of actions by creditors. The law established a federal bankruptcy court system with exclusive jurisdiction over bankruptcy cases.

Questions

These chapter questions are to test and review the information in the text and are not examples of CCM examination questions, nor are they in the examination format.

Answers can be found at the back of the book on p. 318.

1. What are the major objectives of credit management?

2. What are the three elements of a credit policy?

3. What is the effective cost of not taking a discount under terms of 3/20 Net 60?

4. What are the five C's of credit?

5. What is credit scoring?

6. What are revolving credit terms?

7. What is seasonal dating?

8. A firm has outstanding receivables of $125,000. Its credit terms are Net 30. If during the past three months sales are $75,000, $100,000 and $90,000, how many days' sales are outstanding?

9. What is factoring?

10. What federal legislation prohibits price discrimination?

11. What federal legislation requires disclosure of the true cost of a loan?

CHAPTER **6**

Collections

OVERVIEW

An organization must effectively develop systems to collect payments from customers. This chapter discusses the objectives of a collection system, the principal methods that companies and other organizations use to collect payments, and the role of the commercial banking system in the collection process.

LEARNING OBJECTIVES

Upon completion of this chapter and related study questions, the reader should know:

1. The objectives of a corporate collection system.

2. The components of collection float.

3. How a collection processing system is selected.

4. The differences among over-the-counter, mail, and electronic collection methods.

5. The service features of lockbox providers.

6. The differences between wholesale and retail lockboxes.

7. How a collection study works.

8. How to calculate the cost of float and the dollar savings from a lockbox.

9. The functions and applications of electronic and other collection systems.

OUTLINE

I. **Objectives of a Collection System**

II. **Collection Float**
    A. Components
    B. Measurement

III. **Collection System Considerations**
   A. Payment Practices
   B. Payments System
   C. Nature of the Business
   D. Payment Instrument Characteristics
   E. Float/Administrative Cost Tradeoff
   F. Wholesale and Retail Payments

IV. **Collection Methods and Products**
   A. Over-the-Counter/Field Deposit Systems
   B. Mail Processing Systems

V. **Types of Lockboxes**
   A. Wholesale Lockbox
   B. Retail Lockbox
   C. Whole-tail Lockbox

VI. **Issues Involved with Lockbox Selection**
   A. Lockbox Cost/Benefit Analysis
   B. Collection Studies
   C. How Lockbox Service Features Vary
   D. Lockbox Networks
   E. Electronic Lockbox

VII. **Image Technology**

VIII. **Electronic Collection Systems**
   A. Wire Transfers
   B. ACH Corporate-to-Corporate Payments
   C. Pre-authorized Payments

IX. **Other Collection Systems**
   A. Net Settlement Systems
   B. Retail Collection Systems

I. OBJECTIVES OF A COLLECTION SYSTEM

A collection system is a set of arrangements and management procedures used to gather and process customer payments. The broad objectives of a corporate collection system are the following:

- *Mobilize Funds* - Move funds collected from a customer (payor) into a company's (payee's) banking system as quickly and cost effectively as possible. To do this, a company's collection system must be well integrated with its cash concentration system.

- *Access Information* - Provide accurate and timely information on cash flows, the level of bank balances, and availability of funds in a manner that integrates easily with other parts of a company's treasury management information system.

- *Update Accounts Receivable* - Update accounts receivable records promptly and accurately. Credit management and treasury management systems must be linked closely together. Mistakes or failures to update customer files can jeopardize potential sales because of credit limitations and damage customer relationships.

- *Support Audit Trails* - Support audit trails for the company's internal and external auditors.

II. COLLECTION FLOAT

Collection float is the delay between the time the payor mails the check and the time the payee receives available funds at its financial institution. Converting accounts receivable expeditiously into collected funds requires minimizing collection float.

A. Components

Collection float has three components: mail, processing, and availability. Each represents a collection delay along the cash flow timeline.

- *Mail Float* - Mail float is the delay between the time a check is mailed and the date it is received by the payee or at the processing site. It usually ranges from one to five calendar days or more.

- *Processing Float* - **Processing float** is the delay between the time the payee or the processing site receives the check and the time the check is deposited at a financial institution. It can range from less than one day to three calendar days or more.

- *Availability Float* - **Availability float** is the delay between the time a check is deposited and the time a company's account is credited with collected funds. It typically ranges from zero to two business days, and is determined by the depository institution's availability schedule.

The components of collection float are illustrated in Exhibit 6.1.

EXHIBIT 6.1
Components of Collection Float

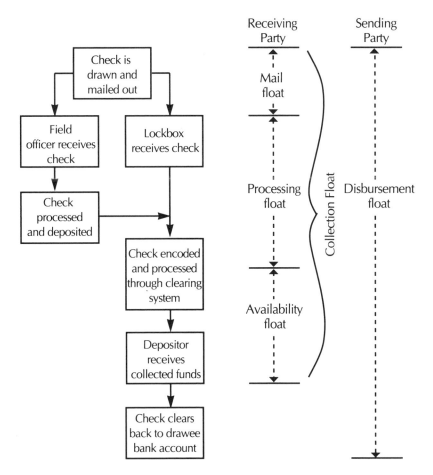

B. Measurement

Float is usually measured in **dollar-days** and is a function of the transaction's dollar amount and the number of days delay. The float on an individual check is calculated by multiplying the dollar amount by the number of days delay.

EXHIBIT 6.2

Example of Float Measurement

Batch	Dollar Amount	Calendar Days of Float	Dollar-Days of Float
1	$1,500,000	x 4 =	$ 6,000,000
2	4,500,000	x 2 =	9,000,000
3	3,000,000	x 6 =	18,000,000
	$9,000,000		$33,000,000

Note: In this example there are 30 calendar days in the month and the opportunity cost of funds is 9%.

$$\text{Average daily float} = \frac{\text{Total Dollar-Days of Float}}{\text{Total Calendar Days in Period}}$$

$$\text{Average daily receipts} = \frac{\text{Total Dollar Amount}}{\text{Total Calendar Days in Period}}$$

$$\text{Average delay} = \frac{\text{Total Dollar-Days of Float}}{\text{Total Dollar Amount}}$$

$$\text{Annual cost of float} = \text{Average Daily Float} \times \text{Opportunity Cost of Funds}$$

$$\text{Average daily float} = \frac{\$33,000,000}{30} = \$1,100,000$$

$$\text{Average daily receipts} = \frac{\$9,000,000}{30} = \$300,000$$

$$\text{Average delay} = \frac{33,000,000}{9,000,000} = 3.67 \text{ days}$$

$$\text{Annual cost of float} = \$1,100,000 \times .09 = \$99,000$$

Exhibit 6.2 provides a step-by-step analysis of float measurement as follows:

• Each of the three batches of checks has a different number of calendar days of float.

• The dollar-days of float are calculated for each batch and then for the total of the three batches.

• The average daily float is calculated by dividing the total dollar-days of float by the number of calendar days in the period.

- The average delay, or the average number of days of float, is calculated by dividing the total dollar-days of float by the total dollar amount.

- The annual cost of float is calculated by using a company's opportunity cost of funds. A company may consider its opportunity cost to be a marginal cost, such as interest on funds that have to be borrowed because receivables are still in collection. It may also use the opportunity cost of funds that could have been invested or its weighted average cost of capital.

III. COLLECTION SYSTEM CONSIDERATIONS

In designing a collection system, a company should take into consideration the following issues:

- commonly accepted payment practices

- the nature of the payments system

- the nature of its own business

- characteristics of the payment instrument used

- the cost of float and system administration

- the differences between wholesale and retail businesses

A discussion of each of these considerations follows.

A. Payment Practices

Checks are the most frequently used payment instrument for both corporate and consumer bill paying, though the use of electronic payments is increasing. Some believe that electronic payments will offer strong cost saving potential for corporate payors and receivers in the future. This is especially true if they become the predominant method of payment and are used as an integral part of an Electronic Data Interchange (EDI) business strategy. However, in today's environment, checks provide the payor with disbursement float and are an established way of doing business acceptable to most trading partners.

B. Payments System

The collection system must be designed in light of the particular strengths and limitations of a country's payments system. Four features that distinguish the U.S. payments system from that of most other countries are as follows:

- the widespread use of checks for the majority of payments

- unpredictable delays in the mail system

- a large number of small banks

- a lack of comprehensive nationwide branch banking

C. Nature of the Business

Often the collection method a company uses is determined by the nature of its business. A fast food store receives virtually all of its payments in cash. A time-critical transaction such as a securities settlement or a real estate closing, or simply a very large dollar amount, may require a wire transfer with same-day value. A supplier usually sends an invoice to its customer and receives a check as payment. The check is generally accompanied by information regarding invoices paid, partial payments, discounts, and deductions. Capturing this accompanying information determines, to a large degree, the method of collection.

D. Payment Instrument Characteristics

Each payment instrument has different characteristics and uses. Often the instrument used is a matter of negotiation between the payor and the payee. The most preferred method for the payee may not be best for the payor and vice versa.

1. *Cash* - Cash is the principal means of payment in many retail businesses. Cash provides the payee with immediate funds.

2. *Check* - A check is used for most corporate and consumer bill payments. Depending on when and how it is deposited and cleared, a check usually provides the payee with zero-to-two-day availability.

3. *Credit Cards* - The acceptance of credit cards by retailers is widespread. Increasingly, credit cards are also becoming a preferred method of payment among wholesalers. The payee is provided with zero-to-two-day availability.

4. *Debit Cards* - Consumer use of debit cards as a method of payment is growing in acceptance. Debit cards replace cash and check transactions. The payee is provided with zero-to-two-day availability.

5. *Automated Clearing House* - Consumer use of the Automated Clearing House (ACH) as a method of payment is growing in acceptance, as is the use of ACH by companies to pay trading partners. Settlement occurs one or two days after origination.

6. *Wire Transfer* - Wire transfer as a method of payment is primarily used by companies for large dollar transactions. The payee is provided with immediate funds.

E. Float/Administrative Cost Tradeoff

An optimal collection system minimizes the sum of float costs and processing and administrative costs. For example, if a company chooses to use a lockbox, it must determine the number and location of lockboxes. Additionally, each customer must be assigned to a specific lockbox if more than one is used. Adding more collection points generally reduces float, but increases administrative and processing costs.

F. Wholesale and Retail Payments

The following is a discussion of the different issues involved with wholesale versus retail payment collection:

1. *Wholesale* - Wholesale, or corporate-to-corporate, payments are generally for large amounts and in response to specific invoices. Often several invoices are paid with

one check. Usually detailed information is required of the invoices paid, discounts taken, returns and allowances. Wholesale collection systems emphasize float reduction and timely handling of information related to the invoices being paid.

2. *Retail* - In retail systems, payors are generally consumers. Payments are often small-dollar amounts, and frequently involve installments or recurring payments. Because of the large number of items to be handled, processing cost is a more critical consideration than float reduction.

IV. COLLECTION METHODS AND PRODUCTS

Companies collect payments from their customers over-the-counter, through the mail, and through electronic networks. For an overview of these three systems, see Exhibit 6.3.

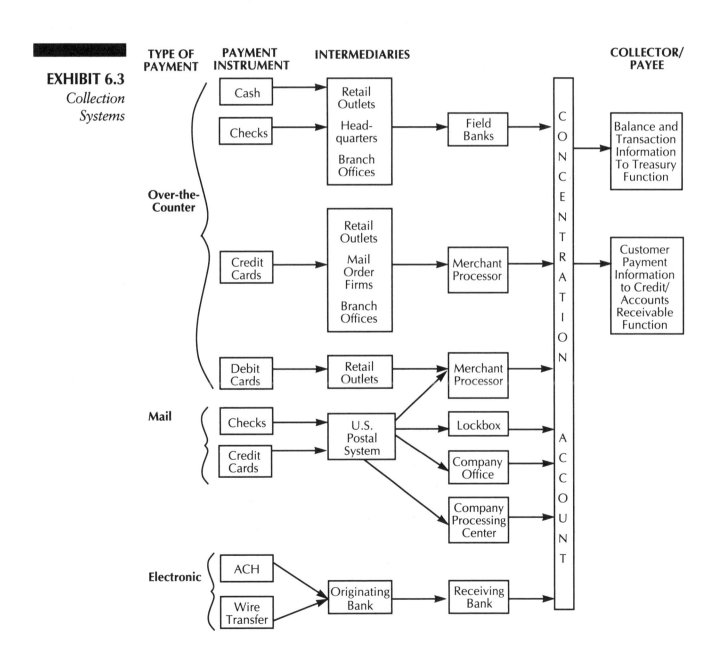

EXHIBIT 6.3
Collection Systems

A. Over-the-Counter/Field Deposit Systems

Various businesses may collect receipts over-the-counter at field locations. Methods used by retail establishments to collect at the point-of-sale include cash, checks, debit cards, and credit cards. A wholesale customer or its agent may deliver checks or cash to a vendor's office. Alternatively, a vendor, or its agent, may pick up checks or cash from the customer when making a delivery. Field units include local offices, stores and restaurants. An important design issue is the selection of banks for deposits made by field units. These banks are called deposit or collection banks. The following factors should be considered in the selection of deposit banks:

1. *Location* - A deposit bank close to the field unit offers convenience and increased cash handling security for the local manager.

2. *Branch Banking* - Where statewide, regional, or interstate branching is available, collections may be simplified by using branches of the same bank. This reduces the company's administrative and cash concentration costs. The company may, however, lose some flexibility in selecting convenient deposit bank locations and incur a risk in relying on only one bank.

3. *Compensation* - The compensation of field banks can be by fees, balances, or a combination of both. Levels of account analysis statement detail vary from bank to bank.

4. *Deposit Reconciliation Services* - A bank with multiple branches may offer deposit reconciliation services, also called branch consolidation services. These services enable deposits from multiple locations to be credited to a single corporate account with a bank. Magnetic Ink Character Recognition (MICR) encoded deposit tickets identify each location and enable the bank to produce a report of deposits by location on a daily, weekly, or monthly basis.

5. *Preprocessing Check Deposits* - A bank may charge a company less and offer better availability for checks when the dollar amounts are MICR-encoded before they are deposited.

6. *Cash Processing* - A company that accepts cash has two options for making cash deposits:

    • *Branch Deposits* - An employee of the company can take cash to a nearby bank or bank branch for deposit. When the amounts are large, there is a security risk in this method.

    • *Centralized Cash Processing* - With centralized cash processing, an armored courier is used to pick up cash from a company's locations and deliver it to a money processing site. This method is most common for large amounts because it reduces security risks. Use of armored services may result in cash being held overnight at the courier facility before deposit.

    Companies can save fees by putting bills of the same denomination in currency straps, by putting each denomination of coin in standard rolls, or by filling Fed standard bags with loose coins of a particular denomination in similar standard, defined amounts. If the cash is delivered in mixed denominations, the bank may charge extra for verification.

    Banks may charge for these services in different ways such as the amount of time required to verify the deposit, the dollar amount of the deposit, or the number of straps or bills and deposits processed.

B. Mail Processing Systems

Companies receive checks from individual consumers and from other businesses in the mail directly or through lockboxes. For payments received in the mail, a company may use either its own processing center or a lockbox. Deciding which method to use depends primarily on the volume of checks processed and the dollar amounts of the checks.

1. *Company Processing Center* - With a **company processing center**, a company does its own processing and deposit preparation. It is typically used by a company with a large volume of relatively small-dollar payments.

    Advantages - The following are among the advantages of a company processing center relative to a lockbox:

    - A company maintains total control over the operation.

    - It is easier to make changes in an internal system than it is in a lockbox processor.

    - Processing is customized to meet a company's needs rather than standardized to meet the needs of a lockbox processor.

    - Updating of payor information may be faster.

    - With large volume and small dollars, a company may find internal processing less expensive than paying a third party for the same amount of work because a company can realize the same economies of scale as a lockbox processor.

    - A company is assured of future processing capability, as opposed to relying on a lockbox processor that may eliminate the service.

    Disadvantages - The following are among the disadvantages of a company processing center relative to a lockbox:

    - A company has to staff and equip the processing center. Check volume must be sufficient for a company to have a cost-efficient operation and peak volume must be accommodated.

    - A company may lack a contingency site to prevent an interruption in payment processing.

    - Compared to a lockbox, there may be a greater time lag between processing the items and depositing the checks.

    - A company processing center may not receive mail through a unique ZIP code, resulting in longer mail times.

    - A company processing center is likely to be located where the company has operations, which is not necessarily at a point that minimizes mail float.

2. *Lockbox* - A processor receives mail at a specified lockbox address, processes the remittances, and deposits them in the payee's account. Lockboxes are one of the more important cash management tools.

Advantages - The following are among the advantages of a lockbox relative to a company processing center:

- *Float Reduction* - A lockbox is designed to reduce the three components of collection float as follows:

  * *Mail Float* - Mail float is usually reduced because a lockbox processor uses its own unique ZIP code to further speed mail delivery. Also, a lockbox processor may make more frequent mail pickups.

  * *Processing Float* - Processing float is usually reduced because remittances are mailed directly to the lockbox processor, eliminating a company's intermediary role in receiving and processing checks and delivering them to the bank. Further, many lockbox processors operate 24 hours a day, seven days per week, with emphasis on peak periods. In effect, lockbox operations specialize in the efficient processing of remittances and deposits.

  * *Availability Float* - Availability float is usually reduced because lockbox processors schedule work to meet critical availability deadlines. These are deadlines by which checks must reach the bank's proof and transit area. For example, 8 a.m. could be the deadline for receiving same-day availability for checks drawn on banks in the same city, or next-day availability for checks drawn on banks in outlying cities.

- *Efficient Processing* - A lockbox provides efficient processing through economies of scale. Trained staff process the work for a particular account, and others are trained to back up these specialists.

- *Audit and Control* - A lockbox establishes an external audit trail for payments received, and segregates check processing from other accounts receivable functions. A lockbox may be required by company auditors even when it is not economically justified based on float reduction.

Disadvantages - The following are among the disadvantages of a lockbox relative to a company processing center:

- *Operational Control* - A company has less control over the operation than with a company processing center.

- *Cost* - A company with very high volume may be able to run its own processing center at a cost that is lower than the cost of a lockbox.

V. TYPES OF LOCKBOXES

There are three different types of lockboxes as follows:

A. Wholesale Lockbox

Among the characteristics of a wholesale lockbox are the following:

- A **wholesale lockbox** is used for corporate-to-corporate payments.

- The typical wholesale lockbox customer usually receives a small-to-moderate number of large-dollar remittances.

- The most important concerns are to minimize collection float and to provide accurate and timely information on payments received.

- Processing is usually manual and labor intensive.

- Payments are usually made for specific invoices.

- Invoices are sometimes partially paid, and often one payment is for several invoices.

- Adjustments are often made by the payor for discounts, returns, and allowances.

- There is not a standard format for the remittance information accompanying the payment.

- Therefore, each company's remittance information requirements may be different.

While processing varies by processor, the typical steps in a wholesale lockbox operation are illustrated and described in Exhibit 6.4.

EXHIBIT 6.4
Example of Wholesale Lockbox Processing

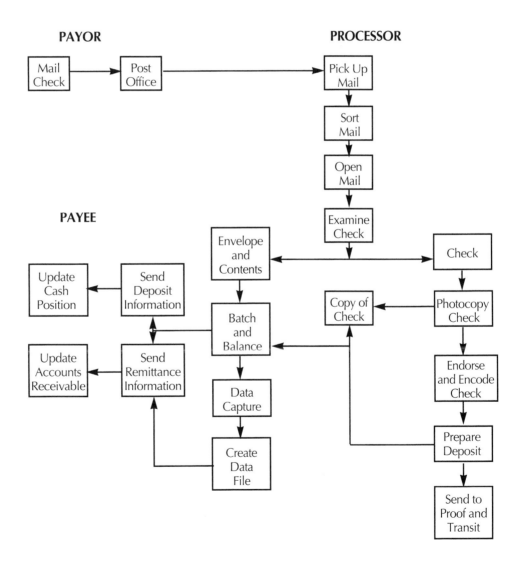

Step 1: *Mail Check* - The payor is instructed by a company to mail checks to a lockbox address.

Step 2: *Pick Up Mail* - Mail is picked up from a postal facility throughout the day and night.

Step 3: *Sort Mail* - The processor sorts mail by lockbox number.

Step 4: *Open Mail* - The mail is opened.

Step 5: *Examine Checks* - Checks are examined for acceptable payees, postdated checks, and missing signatures.

Step 6: *Separate Checks and Advices* - Checks are separated from remittance advices and other contents.

Step 7: *Photocopy Checks* - If required, the checks are photocopied.

Step 8: *Prepare Deposit* - Check amounts are added, balanced, and deposit tickets are prepared.

Step 9: *Endorse and Encode Checks* - Checks are encoded with a dollar amount and endorsed.

Step 10: *Clear Checks* - Checks are sent to the proof and transit department for clearing.

Step 11: *Send Deposit and Remittance Data* - The processor provides both deposit information, such as the amount of deposit and availability, and remittance information, such as invoices paid, deductions, and discounts taken.

  * Detailed deposit information, often including a breakdown of the total amount by days of availability, is usually transmitted daily to the company or to its concentration bank either by telephone or electronic means.

  * The lockbox processor may also capture remittance data either electronically or manually from the check or remittance advice and transmit it to the company. Detailed remittance data may be sent by courier, by mail, or electronically.

B. Retail Lockbox

Among the characteristics of a retail lockbox are the following:

• A **retail lockbox** is used by companies that receive large volumes of relatively small-dollar remittances, usually from consumers.

• Minimizing costs is generally more important than reducing collection float because of the large volume of small-dollar payments.

• A standard remittance advice, sometimes called a return document, usually accompanies the check.

• A retail lockbox operation is generally highly automated, including specialized equipment that opens the envelopes and removes the contents.

- A retail lockbox often uses Optical Character Recognition (OCR) and Magnetic Ink Character Recognition (MICR) equipment to scan checks and remittance advices.

- The return document has a scan line which contains information such as the payor's account number, the total amount due, the minimum amount due, and the due date.

- The data on the scan line is captured and usually transmitted electronically to the company to update accounts receivable.

- The dollar amount of the check may be automatically encoded during the scanning process.

C. Wholetail Lockbox

A **wholetail lockbox** combines aspects of both wholesale and retail lockbox operations. It is able to process both payment types. An example is a utility company which has as its customers both consumers, who return a standardized remittance document which can be processed automatically, and businesses, which remit documents that require manual handling. Automated cash application data can be combined and sent to the company in a single transmission. Wholetail lockboxes are often characterized by customized processing and data capture requirements.

VI. ISSUES INVOLVED WITH LOCKBOX SELECTION

A. Lockbox Cost/Benefit Analysis

The economic benefit of using a lockbox is usually a tradeoff between reducing collection float and paying fees to a lockbox processor over and above internal processing costs.

- *Float Savings* - A lockbox can create float savings by reducing some combination of mail, processing, and availability time.

- *Fixed and Variable Costs* - Lockboxes have both fixed and variable cost components. The company should compare both the fixed and the variable costs per item between a lockbox and a company processing center. Lockbox providers have many ways of charging, but the following are some basic concepts:

  * *Fixed* - Fixed monthly charges may include fees for preparing deposit tickets, renting the post office box, sending remittance data to the company, balance reporting, and account maintenance. Often several of those charges are wrapped into a lockbox maintenance charge. There may also be a charge for transferring funds to a concentration bank.

  * *Variable* - Variable costs may include per-item deposit and processing charges and the charges for transmitting remittance data, photocopying, and microfilming. These and other custom processing charges are often on a per-item basis. Some costs, for example, deposit ticket preparation, may be considered either fixed or variable, depending on the lockbox processor.

- *Calculation of Net Benefit* - The net benefit from a lockbox is equal to the reduction in float opportunity costs plus the reduction in internal processing cost minus lockbox processing costs. Float opportunity cost is a function of the dollar amount of the collected items, the total collection time of items, and the current investment/ borrowing rate.

Exhibit 6.5 is an example of a lockbox cost/benefit analysis, including the tradeoff between the savings from float reduction and the cost of a lockbox.

EXHIBIT 6.5

*Example of
Lockbox
Cost/Benefit
Analysis*

This exhibit shows the lockbox savings and associated costs for a company with $108,000,000 annual sales ($9,000,000 per month). Each of the items is assumed to be a batch of checks with average size of $9,000; the annual volume of checks is 12,000. The company's annual opportunity cost is 9%. The company's internal check processing cost assuming no lockbox is $.25 per item. The lockbox processor charges $10,000 per year plus a processing cost of $.50 per item.

WITHOUT LOCKBOX

Batch	Dollar Amount	Calendar Days of Collection Float Without Lockbox	Total Dollar-Days
1	$1,500,000	x 4 =	$ 6,000,000
2	4,500,000	x 2 =	9,000,000
3	3,000,000	x 6 =	18,000,000
Total Deposits	$9,000,000	Total Float without Lockbox	$33,000,000

Divided by 30 calendar days = Average Daily Float	$ 1,100,000
Times Opportunity Cost/Investment Rate = Annual Cost of Float (9%)	$ 99,000

WITH LOCKBOX

Batch	Dollar Amount	Calendar Days of Collection Float With Lockbox	Total Dollar-Days
1	$1,500,000	X 3 =	$ 4,500,000
2	4,500,000	X 1 =	4,500,000
3	3,000,000	X 5 =	15,000,000
Total Deposits	$9,000,000	Total Float with Lockbox	$ 24,000,000

Divided by 30 calendar days = Average Daily Float	$ 800,000
Times Opportunity Cost/Investment Rate = Annual Cost of Float (9%)	$ 72,000

Annual Cost of Float Without Lockbox	$ 99,000
Annual Cost of Float With Lockbox	($ 72,000)
Lockbox Float Savings	$ 27,000
Fixed Lockbox Cost	($ 10,000)
Variable Lockbox Cost: 12,000 checks x $0.50	($ 6,000)
Saving of Internal Lockbox Processing Cost: 12,000 x .25	$ 3,000
Net Dollar Benefit of Lockbox	$ 14,000

B. Collection Studies

The objective of a collection study is to minimize combined mail, processing, and availability float. These studies use remittance data (customer remittance envelopes, photocopies of checks, and bank statements) to compile the following information for analysis:

- location of remitting customers
- geographic concentration of remitting customers
- location of customers with largest payments
- intercity mail times
- bank availability schedules
- difference between company and bank processing costs
- administrative costs associated with using lockboxes

1. *Mail Time Studies* - Treasury consulting firms do periodic studies to compare mail times for various combinations of cities. These services generally report mail times between central city post offices for a uniform distribution of mailings throughout the week. If necessary, adjustments can be made for non-surveyed mail points and day-of-the-week mail experience.

   The results of mail time studies are combined with information from banks' availability schedules to compare both city-average and banks' availability statistics. Banks or consultants use this data in conjunction with analysis of a company's actual remittances to determine which cities or combinations of cities are the most effective collection sites.

   Computer analysis is performed to produce close to an optimal solution and can be attractive for a company with many banking relationships that is willing to consider many different combinations of cities.

2. *Processing Cost* - A collection study should take into account not only float but the difference in processing costs between a company processing center and a lockbox, and the price differences among lockbox processors.

3. *Site Selection* - In doing a study, a firm will usually select a number of potential sites based on the following criteria:

   - *Availability* - A lockbox in a Federal Reserve city or Regional Check Processing Center (RCPC) point generally gets faster availability than one in a Federal Reserve country point.
   - *Mail Center* - A lockbox is usually best located in a city with a major airport and a major postal processing center.
   - *Customer Base* - A lockbox is usually best located near high concentrations of customers.
   - *Service Quality* - Processors may be pre-screened for service quality before they are included in a study. The overall quality of service and responsiveness to a company's inquiries is as important as mail time and availability performance. A number of processors have dedicated customer service representatives and guaran-

teed response times for answering inquiries. A company must evaluate the ability of a processor to serve its particular needs.

4. *Lockbox Processor Selection* - In selecting a lockbox processor, there are a number of considerations.

- *Processor Characteristics* - Among the characteristics to consider are the following:
  * payment processing capabilities
  * check processing procedures
  * availability schedules
  * data transmission capabilities
  * deposit and balance reporting capabilities
  * its postal facility's mail processing capabilities

- *City and Processor Selection* - A company may first select lockbox cities based on a lockbox study, and then select processors within those cities, but there are other factors to consider that could modify the decision. Some processors may try to demonstrate features such as processing time and availability schedules that are better than the average for their cities and win customers from cities with marginally better mail times.

- *Relationship Banks* - Having a lockbox at a bank where there is an existing relationship may allow the company to strengthen that relationship. Protecting access to credit facilities and making better use of operating balances for bank compensation are two examples. An existing relationship may give an advantage where there are small differences in the study.

C. How Lockbox Service Features Vary

In selecting a lockbox processor, a cash manager should determine how the lockbox operation meets the company's particular needs. Meeting a company's requirements is a more important characteristic than the technology used. The company should consider the following service features in evaluating each processor:

1. *Mail Time Performance* - As mentioned earlier, mail time performance varies considerably among cities. Among the reasons for this are total mail volume, post office proximity to the airport and the lockbox processor, post office processing capabilities, and airline routes serving the city. A more desirable site has a post office that processes mail 24 hours per day, sorts bar-coded envelopes automatically, reads non-bar-coded envelopes with OCR equipment, and makes a unique ZIP code available to a lockbox processor.

2. *Unique ZIP Codes* - Most processors offering lockbox services have a unique ZIP code for lockbox remittances. Depending on their capabilities for fine sorting, this feature may speed processing of incoming mail and save several hours of mail and processing float daily.

3. *Deposit Deadlines* - Incoming lockbox work should be processed expeditiously so that deposit deadlines are met and the best possible availability achieved. Related

service features include frequent mail pick-ups and ample peak-time staffing when the bulk of the mail is received. These features are helpful to the extent that they are designed to meet critical check clearing deadlines. As deadlines approach, an effective lockbox operation should search for and immediately process large-dollar items. Sometimes, the number of deposits per day is a matter of negotiation. It is a trade-off. Each company must decide whether the cost of more frequent deposits is justified by the item volume and dollar amount in relation to the potential improvement in availability.

4. *Availability* - Banks may offer several availability schedules. A company should be aware of which availability schedule is applicable. A better availability schedule may be offered for a premium price or when it is merited by overall relationship profitability. The availability a company will receive from a bank does not necessarily agree with the independent studies done on the city and the bank.

   Some banks assign availability in the lockbox area, but regardless of where it is assigned, the company may bear the risk of as-of adjustments or fractional availability if the bank incurs a float loss in clearing a check. Some banks guarantee availability to the company even if there is a delay. A bank that guarantees availability may perform better than another bank that offers a better availability schedule but charges back any float losses.

5. *End-Point Analysis* - An end-point analysis, in which all checks drawn on banks in selected cities are broken down by days of float, is an effective way to measure and compare different banks' availability.

6. *Direct Sends* - Direct sends improve the availability of funds. Detailed knowledge of the bank's direct send program helps a company understand the availability schedule.

7. *Ledger Cutoff Time* - The cutoff time for giving ledger credit on the same day a check is deposited can vary. In evaluating a lockbox bank, it is important to look at the total collection time rather than just availability. The ledger cutoff can influence the availability received, but total collection time may not change. The ledger cutoff must be considered in conjunction with the availability schedule.

   For example, a check with one-day availability before the ledger cutoff may have zero-day availability if processed right after the ledger cutoff. In this case, there is no difference in total collection time. A check might also be available in one day before and after the ledger cutoff. In this case, there will be an increase of one day in the total collection time if the check is not processed before the cutoff time. It is important to understand the relationship between a bank's ledger cutoff, its availability schedule, and the time of day the lockbox is processed.

D. Lockbox Networks

Lockbox networks may involve several processors in different cities or a single processor with multiple locations. A network permits a company to have a number of collection points and get consolidated remittance data. Funds concentration is simplified and a company may deal with fewer processors.

E. Electronic Lockbox

Banks provide electronic lockboxes for companies to receive payments from their customers by wire transfer or through the ACH. As a company starts to receive an increased volume of electronic payments, it may want a consolidated report of ACH, wire transfer, and lockbox receipts in the same format. This information may be available in paper reports, through a bank's information reporting system, or through data transmission. A number of banks are equipped to transmit information in the Bank Administration Institute (BAI) format and the Accredited Standards Committee (ASC) X12 821 Financial Information Reporting transaction set, as well as their own proprietary formats.

VII. IMAGE TECHNOLOGY

Image technology is used to facilitate processing of both wholesale and retail payments. This technology allows paper documents to be scanned, converted to a digital image, and stored for subsequent handling and processing. The data capture process is enhanced through the use of Intelligent Character Recognition (ICR), which reads handwritten or typed information, and OCR, which reads pre-printed information. The documents scanned can be both checks and remittance advices. Potential benefits of applying image technology to the remittance processing function include reduced overall processing costs, increased productivity, improved accuracy, and the ability to capture data for automated posting to accounts receivable.

Regarding the latter benefit, the degree of data capture automation achievable with image technology is generally higher with retail than with wholesale payments because of the presence of a standard return document. Wholesale payments often do not contain the seller's original invoice or OCR advice. Instead, a buyer may enclose its own payment document, a check stub with limited information, or nothing at all. As a result, any machine-readable data is often supplemented with manual-entry data for wholesale remittances.

In addition to the actual processing of items, image technology can be applied to the delivery and storage of remittance data output. A lockbox provider can transmit to a company images of its deposit and detailed payment information or supply this data on a CD-ROM. Among companies that can benefit from this feature are those that must research payment information to respond to a high volume of customer service inquiries.

VIII. ELECTRONIC COLLECTION SYSTEMS

A company can receive a payment via wire transfer or ACH. Wire transfers are typically used for large payments that must be received with good value on the same day. Electronic payments through the ACH are less expensive than wire transfers, but payment instructions must be submitted to the bank one or two days prior to settlement.

A. Wire Transfers

Wire transfers are used for large-dollar payments when speed and finality are important.

B. ACH Corporate-to-Corporate Payments

A company can pay a bill through the ACH network provided that the originating and receiving banks have ACH capabilities. Debits as well as credits can be originated.

Companies generally consult with their trading partners in advance to determine which payment formats are appropriate, as well as to negotiate the timing of ACH payments.

1. *Applications* - Though most bills are paid by check, companies may collect a portion of their payments by ACH. A number of companies have initiated comprehensive programs to originate payments through the ACH. The following are examples of applications:

    *   *Federal Government* - The U.S. Treasury Department's Vendor Express program is used to pay government vendors electronically. The Department of Defense also pays its vendors electronically.

    *   *Manufacturer's Suppliers* - Many suppliers to manufacturing companies are receiving payments through the ACH as part of a more comprehensive EDI program including purchase orders and invoices.

    *   *Dealers with Floor Plans* - Automobile, truck, farm equipment suppliers, and floor plan lenders have utilized the ACH network extensively to debit dealers. A floor plan is a loan to a dealer to finance inventory which is paid back when the financed item is sold.

    *   *Debit Programs* - Companies can also collect funds by debiting their customers' bank accounts. This is typically done in one of two ways. Either a supplier notifies a customer in advance of the date and the exact amount of the debit. Or, as an alternative, a buyer can notify the supplier of the desire to make a payment. The supplier then originates an ACH debit.   The latter option offers the customer greater control.

2. *Advantages* - Potential benefits of ACH corporate-to-corporate payments for the payee include:

    *   *Float* - Reduction of collection float.

    *   *Cost* - Reduction of receivables processing cost; lower overall cost compared to either a check payment or wire transfers.

    *   *Forecasting* - Improved cash flow forecasting.

3. *Disadvantages* - Despite possible cost savings opportunities in the long run, there are many potential deterrents to the use of ACH corporate trade payments. Among the disadvantages are the following:

    *   *Trading Partner Negotiation* - The buyer (payor) and the seller (payee) must agree to make the switch.

    *   *Float* - When a company starts to receive payments electronically, there must be agreement on when the effective use of funds is being transferred under the existing system, and what the settlement date of the ACH transaction should be.

        For example, the payor may currently pay bills by check 25 calendar days after the invoice date and may on average be debited four days after mailing the check. The payee may or may not receive availability at the same time the payor is debited. The payor and the payee negotiate a settlement time for an ACH transaction that puts each party in approximately the same economic position as when checks were used to settle invoices.

- *ACH Formats* - Several different formats are currently used for corporate-to-corporate payments. (See also Chapter 4, The Payments System.)

- *Set-Up Costs* - Preparation to receive ACH corporate-to-corporate payments can be time consuming; it also may require an investment in software and communications equipment.

- *Control* - A company may be reluctant to give someone outside the company the authority to debit its bank account.

4. *Preparation* - A company preparing to receive ACH corporate-to-corporate payments for the first time should take the following steps:

- *ACH Formats* - Review ACH payment formats with the payor. Take advantage of descriptive literature and other educational tools provided by the payor.

- *Bank Capabilities* - Discuss ACH receiving and translating capabilities with the bank where payments will be received.

- *Payment-Related Information* - Consider alternative ways that are available to receive payment-related information. Compare the capabilities and costs of banks and value-added networks (VANs) to transmit full details related to the payment. A company may want to consider buying translation software to enable automated receipt of ACH remittance information to update its accounts receivable system.

  There is still debate about the preferable alternative. Some favor sending the payment and payment information together through a bank while others favor sending the payment through a bank and the payment information through a VAN. (See also Chapter 13, Electronic Commerce.)

C. Pre-authorized Payments

Pre-authorized debits are a payment method in which the payor approves in advance the transfer of funds from the payor's bank account to the payee's bank account. These payments are often for the same dollar amount and at the same time each month, but variable dollar amounts and schedules are possible. Where there is payment variability, notice of the withdrawal is generally sent to the customer ten days prior to the transfer of funds.

Pre-authorized payments can be made through the ACH, or if the payee's bank is not a member of the ACH, by pre-authorized drafts/checks. Consumer payments are governed by Federal Reserve Regulation E and National Automated Clearing House Association (NACHA) rules; corporate-to-corporate payments are governed by UCC4A and NACHA rules.

1. *Applications* - Pre-authorized payments are used by both consumers and corporations. Corporate payments are made to pay suppliers and trading partners. Consumer payments are commonly made for the following applications:

- insurance payments

- utility payments

- mortgage payments

- installment loan payments

- cable payments

- association dues

- health club dues

- distributor/dealer payments

- equipment lease payments

2. *Advantages* - Among the advantages of pre-authorized payments are the following:

- Eliminates mail float.

- Eliminates invoicing.

- Reduces processing float because deposits do not need to be prepared.

- Eliminates availability float because of immediate availability on settlement day.

- Results in fewer delinquent payments.

- Reduces tendency of customers to change vendors or terminate services once pre-authorized debits have been implemented.

- Reduces cash application costs.

3. *Disadvantages* - Among the disadvantages of pre-authorized payments are the following:

- Requires additional costs and time to educate customers.

- Involves overcoming reluctance on the part of customers to have their bank accounts debited by another party.

- Even though no invoices are required, there may be cost and time involved in preparing and sending billing statements because of regulatory requirements or customer service considerations.

- Requires up-front time and effort to set up each customer's standard monthly payment instructions, including the correct bank transit routing number and customer account number.

IX. OTHER COLLECTION SYSTEMS

A. Net Settlement Systems

In some industries, companies make exchanges and buy and sell from each other. For example, Airline A accepts a ticket from Airline B in exchange for a passenger making a change in reservations. Through a clearing system, it returns the ticket and is reimbursed by the airline that originally wrote the ticket. These clearing systems process transaction information and allow participants to make periodic net settlements with each other.

B. Retail Collection Systems

There are a number of alternative retail collections systems that may have benefits for companies such as improving cash flow, reducing paperwork, reducing per item transaction costs, and increasing the accuracy and timeliness of accounts receivable updating. Among these systems are the following:

1. *Credit Cards* - Credit cards are a frequently used payment method. They are accepted both electronically and manually as follows:

    *   *Electronic Acceptance* - Using a stand-alone credit card authorization/draft capture terminal or a magnetic stripe reader integrated into the merchant's cash register system, the merchant swipes the presented card through the reader so that the magnetic stripe on the back of the card is read. (The use of the term merchant here refers to a seller of goods and services.) This stripe contains, among other things, the cardholder's account number and name. Once the dollar value of the sale is entered into the terminal, the transaction is routed via telephone lines to the **merchant processor** for authorization. If approved, a receipt is printed for the customer to sign. The terminal accumulates transaction information throughout the day, and, at settlement time, transmits the accumulated transaction information to the merchant's processor. Within two business days, the merchant processor credits the merchant's checking account for the total dollar amount of the accumulated transactions. Electronic acceptance has become the predominate method of processing credit card transactions.

    *   *Manual Acceptance* - Using a paper sales draft and a telephone, the merchant records the sales transaction information on the draft and obtains an authorization from a voice operator or an audio response unit. If approved, the merchant obtains the cardholder's signature on the draft. The merchant can mail or deliver the drafts to its processor. These funds will be available to the merchant usually within one, two, or three business days.

    *   *Charges* - Regardless of the method of acceptance, at the end of the month, the merchant processor deducts a fee (discount) and other charges from the merchant's checking account. Availability and discount amounts are pricing decisions determined by the processor and the merchant. Other charges may include such items as terminal rental, authorizations, and supplies.

    *   *Authorizations and Chargebacks* - A credit card payment is not guaranteed, even when authorized. An authorization indicates that the cardholder has available credit but it does not indicate that the right person is using the card. A merchant may receive a chargeback (i.e., a returned transaction) for as long as six months after funds have been received. When fraud occurs, the time may be even longer. Signature verification is necessary to determine if the authorized person is using the card.

2. *Debit Cards* - **Debit card** products work like credit cards except that the transactions post to bank deposit accounts as withdrawals rather than to credit card accounts as future amounts owed. Debit cards settle in one of the following ways:

    *   *On-Line* - A Personal Identification Number (PIN) is required to initiate the transaction. Positive authorization is received from the cardholder's bank. The merchant receives zero to two day's availability.

- *Off-Line* - There are two types of off-line programs:

    * *National Association Debit Cards* - The purchaser's bank deposit account is automatically debited. Availability is usually two days.

    * *Proprietary Cards* - Settlement for proprietary cards is through the ACH. Availability is usually one day.

3. *Automated Teller Machine Networks* - Vendors that deal with a large number of retail customers may be able to make arrangements with banks for bills to be paid at Automated Teller Machines (ATMs). The payment is transferred manually or electronically from the customer's account to the vendor's account at the time of sale, or when the customer decides to pay the monthly bill.

4. *Telephone Banking* - Vendors can make arrangements with financial institutions that offer telephone banking services to have consumers call in to authorize the debiting of their accounts. The call may be to an operator or through a push-button phone audio response system. Smart or screen telephones with added capabilities are increasingly used to facilitate this process.

5. *Bill Paying Services* - Individuals usually use these services to make payments to companies, primarily utilities and retailers. Generally, a company wishing to receive payments through this mechanism works with a financial institution or a third party vendor offering the service. An individual, however, may decide independently to pay a company this way. In either case, the consumer initiates a payment with a bill paying service, rather than the company initiating the transaction, as is the case with ACH pre-authorized payments. Methods for initiating bill paying services include ATMs, phones, and personal computers (PCs).

6. *Home Banking* - Home banking services are offered by financial institutions or can be part of a personal financial software system which connects the user to a third party provider. Generally, these services are PC-based products with a broad array of capabilities which may include bank account inquiry, account transfers, and bill paying services. As more of these services are used by consumers, companies must adapt their collection systems to receive and process these types of payments.

7. *Agents* - Retailers and financial institutions may act as agents for collecting monthly payments related to service providers such as cable and utility companies.

8. *Smart Cards* - Smart cards are plastic cards which have integrated computer or micro-computer chips embedded within them. Smart cards are an emerging technology capable of storing important data, including monetary value that is capable of being electronically replenished. The cards can be used as stored value devices which enable cardholders to make fewer cash transactions. From a collections standpoint, smart cards operate in a manner similar to credit or debit card electronic transactions.

Questions

These chapter questions are to test and review the information in the text and are not examples of CCM examination questions, nor are they in the examination format.

Answers can be found at the back of the book on p. 319.

1. What are the major objectives in establishing a collection system?

2. What are the three major collection methods?

3. What are some key considerations in designing a collection system?

4. What elements compose collection float?

5. What determines availability float?

6. A company has provided the following information:

Batch	Dollar Amount	Calendar Days of Float	Dollar-Day of Float
1	$100,000	3	$ 300,000
2	$350,000	4	$ 1,400,000
3	$210,000	2	$ 420,000
			$ 2,120,000

If the company's opportunity cost is 7% and there are 30 calendar days in the month, what is the annual cost of float?

7. What determines the selection of a mail payment processing system?

8. What are the major advantages of a lockbox?

9. What is the difference between a wholesale and a retail lockbox?

10. The company in Question 6 is considering using a lockbox, which would reduce float as follows:

Batch	Dollar Amt.	Calendar Days of Float	Dollar Days of Float
1	$100,000	1	$ 100,000
2	$350,000	2	$ 700,000
3	$210,000	1	$ 210,000
			$ 1,010,000

The lockbox processor will charge $1,000 per year and a processing cost of $.30 per item. The current internal processing cost is $.20 per item. The annual volume of checks is 6,000. If the annual float cost without the use of a lockbox is $4,947 (see Question 6), is a lockbox appropriate for this company?

11. What is the purpose of lockbox studies?

12. What is an electronic lockbox?

13. What is an over-the-counter/field deposit collection system?

14. What is a pre-authorized debit?

15. What system would benefit companies in the same industry that buy and sell from each other on a regular basis?

16. What impact will image technology have on collection systems?

17. What are the major types of retail collection systems?

18. What is a whole-tail lockbox?

19. What are the key applications in ACH corporate-to-corporate payments?

CHAPTER 7

Cash Concentration

OVERVIEW

This chapter discusses why companies concentrate cash, the objectives of a cash concentration system, the principal funds concentration mechanisms, and how to minimize costs in a cash concentration system.

LEARNING OBJECTIVES

Upon completion of this chapter and related study questions, the reader should know:

1. The objectives of a cash concentration system.

2. The important considerations in designing a concentration system.

3. The advantages and disadvantages of the principal funds transfer mechanisms used in cash concentration.

4. The cost components of a cash concentration system.

5. How a company can minimize costs in a cash concentration system.

6. How to reduce risk and increase control in a cash concentration system.

OUTLINE

I. **Objectives of a Cash Concentration System**

II. **Concentration System Considerations**
    A. Collection System
    B. Disbursement System
    C. Funds Transfer Alternatives
    D. Banking Network

III. **Cash Concentration Cost Components**
    A. Excess Bank Balances
    B. Transfer Charges
    C. Administrative Costs

IV.   **Techniques to Reduce Concentration System Costs**
    A.   Improve Transfer Timing
    B.   Reduce Transfer Costs
    C.   Compare Transfer Costs

V.   **Risks and Controls**
    A.   Punctuality
    B.   Fraud
    C.   Bank Overdraft
    D.   Bank Failure

I.   OBJECTIVES OF A CASH CONCENTRATION SYSTEM

Cash concentration is the movement of funds from outlying depository locations to a central bank account, commonly referred to as a concentration account, where the funds can be managed more efficiently.   Among the objectives in designing a cash concentration system are the following:

- *Simplify Cash Management* - A cash concentration system enables a cash manager to focus on fewer accounts in the day-to-day management of corporate liquidity.

- *Improve Control* - By separating deposit gathering from disbursement control, tracking, and forecasting, a cash concentration system is able to place the control of funds in the hands of key financial managers.   In addition, it provides an audit trail for incoming deposits.

- *Pool Funds* - By concentrating cash from multiple accounts, a company can buy larger blocks of short-term securities which tend to earn higher yields.   Concentrated funds may also be used to reduce debt or take advantage of supplier discount opportunities.

- *Minimize Excess Balances* - Cash concentration enables a company to reduce excess bank balances.

- *Reduce Transfer Expenses* - If a cash concentration system is properly designed, it should reduce the expense of transferring funds from field banks to a concentration bank.

II.   CONCENTRATION SYSTEM CONSIDERATIONS

Among a company's concentration system considerations are its collection system, disbursement system, funds transfer alternatives, and banking network.

A.   Collection System

The design of the concentration system is in part a function of the collection system used by a company.   The two major types of collection systems are:

1.   *Over-the-Counter/Field Banking Systems* - Some companies receive payments from customers in a number of locations.   Examples include companies with regional sales offices and retailers.   These types of companies deposit over-the-counter cash and checks in field banks.   Field banks are outlying depository banks which are usu-

ally located near retail outlets, regional offices, or subsidiary operations. Although field banking systems vary, most have the following features:

- *Multiple Banks* - A company with many locations needs a convenient local depository for each location.

- *Local Banks* - A field banking system may use community banks if these are closest to the field offices.

- *Limited Need for Daily Deposit and Balance Information* - Because sales and deposit information is often sent directly to company headquarters or a concentration bank by the company's field units, headquarters may require fewer deposit and balance reporting services from field banks. Generally, field offices do not use field banks extensively for cash management services.

- *Local Deposits* - Deposits consist mainly of coin, currency, and local checks. Coin and currency are usually given immediate availability. Local checks may take one day to clear; on-us items may clear faster.

2. *Lockbox Systems* - In a lockbox system, a company collects payments through one or more locations and transfers available funds to a concentration bank. A company may have several lockbox sites to optimize collection float, and may also use separate lockboxes for different subsidiaries. Though lockbox systems vary, most have the following characteristics:

    - *Relatively Few Collection Points* - The trend for most companies has been toward the use of fewer lockboxes.

    - *Regional and Money Center Banks and Third-Party Processors* - A lockbox system often uses regional or money center banks and third-party processors.

    - *Corporate Services* - Standard capabilities of lockboxes include daily reporting of transaction details and ledger and collected balances, and moving funds by wire transfer or the Automated Clearing House (ACH). Bank lockbox providers may offer a company credit facilities and a variety of cash management services.

    - *Deposit Availability* - Because a lockbox often processes a large portion of checks drawn on non-local endpoints, a portion of a company's daily deposit may not be available for one or two business days from the day of deposit.

A typical concentration system, incorporating both a field banking system and a lockbox system, is illustrated in Exhibit 7.1.

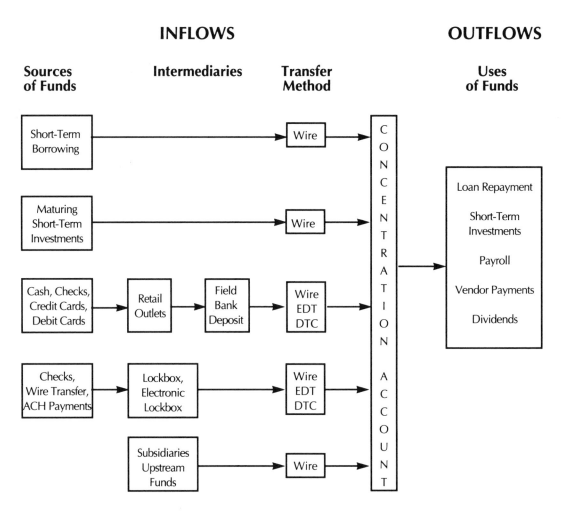

EXHIBIT 7.1

Example of a Concentration System

3. *Electronic Payments* - Corporate-to-corporate payments through the ACH are growing as the use of Electronic Data Interchange (EDI) continues to expand. While electronic payments are not likely to eliminate the need for field banking or lockbox systems, many companies can expect to receive a portion of their corporate-to-corporate payments through the ACH.

    With electronic payments, a company's bank can be located anywhere, because mail float is no longer an issue. This reduces the number of banks needed and the cost of cash concentration transfers.

B. Disbursement System

The design of a concentration system is also a function of the disbursement system used by a company. The two major disbursement systems are as follows:

1. *Centralized Check Issuance* - In this type of system, headquarters controls disbursement accounts and is responsible for check writing and account reconciliation. Efficient concentration is crucial in order to fund these disbursement accounts.

2. *Decentralized Check Issuance* - In this type of system, checks are written on local disbursement banks and account reconciliation is performed at the local level. Since

funds remain at the local deposit banks for disbursement, concentration concerns are reduced.

C. Funds Transfer Alternatives

The most frequently used mechanisms for concentration are electronic depository transfers (EDTs), wire transfers, and depository transfer checks (DTCs).

1. *Electronic Depository Transfers* - An **Electronic Depository Transfer** (EDT) is an ACH transaction used for cash concentration. It is the most common method used today.

    - *Concentration Payment Origination* - EDTs can be originated by field offices and field banks or they can be originated by a headquarters office or concentration bank. A field office can either provide a debit authorization to a field bank and regularly notify headquarters of the amount to be transferred from the field bank, or notify the concentration bank of the amount to be transferred.

      Some large retail networks transmit information on cash receipts from point-of-sale (POS) terminals to headquarters. Headquarters then transmits ACH debit instructions to a concentration bank.

    - *Notifying the Concentration Bank* - Among the ways a field unit or lockbox provider can send deposit information to the concentration bank are by voice, push-button phone, and personal computer. This information can be transferred as follows:

      * *Through a Third-Party Vendor* - Several third-party providers specialize in gathering deposit information from field units. Deposit data may be transmitted to both a concentration bank for EDT preparation and company headquarters for follow-up of non-reporting units. In some cases, deposit data are sent to headquarters, which then notifies the concentration bank as to the amounts to be transferred.

      * *Through Headquarters* - In some companies, managers call headquarters directly or convey the deposit data to headquarters via a terminal. Deposit data are then relayed to a concentration bank by headquarters.

      * *Through the Concentration Bank Directly* - Some banks are able to receive deposit reports directly from field units or lockbox providers. With this capability, EDTs are prepared by a concentration bank.

    - *ACH Format* - EDTs are transmitted in CCD format.

    - *Advantages* - Among the advantages of EDTs are the following:

      * *Cost* - EDTs normally cost less than DTCs, particularly when there are a large number of transfers. Pricing generally includes a charge per transfer, and may include a charge for each transmission.

      * *Settlement* - One-day settlement is the industry norm.

    - *Disadvantages* - Not all banks are members of the ACH system. As a result, some transfers may have to be made by DTC.

2. *Wire Transfers* - Wire transfers are an alternative for concentrating large dollar amounts where same-day value and finality are critical concerns. Among the methods for transferring funds by wire are the following:

   - Either the local manager or the headquarters staff may request a deposit bank to wire funds to a concentration bank.

   - A field or lockbox bank may have standing instructions to transfer funds in excess of a specified balance on a periodic basis. Standing instructions set the amount, frequency, and destination of the transfer.

   - Headquarters may send transfer instructions to a concentration bank to wire funds from a field or lockbox bank. This is known as a **drawdown wire.** A company gives standing instructions to a lockbox or field bank authorizing a concentration bank to initiate the wire transfers.

   Deposit information that is related to the wire transfer can flow to headquarters through deposit reports, telephone, or data transmission.

   Among the advantages and disadvantages of wire transfer are the following:

   - *Advantages* - Wires provide immediate funds and help reduce excess balances at deposit banks. They are typically used when large amounts of immediately available funds are deposited in a lockbox or a field bank.

   - *Disadvantages* - Wires are the most expensive funds transfer mechanism.

3. *Depository Transfer Checks* - A **Depository Transfer Check (DTC)** is a paper instrument used by a company to transfer funds from one of its outlying depository locations to its concentration account. It is an unsigned, restricted-payee instrument payable only to the bank of deposit for credit to a specific company account. Instead of writing and depositing checks to concentrate funds, a corporate headquarters or field office instructs a concentration bank to prepare DTCs drawn on field banks for deposit into the concentration account. After DTCs are deposited, they clear in the same manner as regular checks. Availability is one or two days. The use of DTCs continues to decline.

   An example of EDT and DTC clearing is found in Exhibit 7.2.

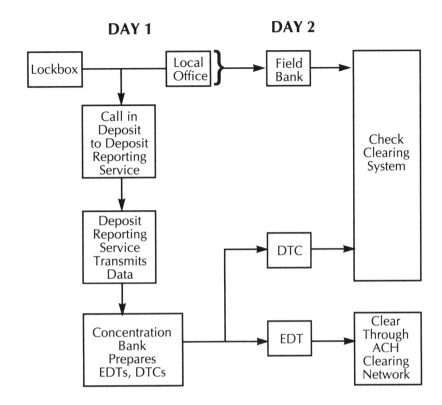

EXHIBIT 7.2
*Example of
EDT and DTC
Clearing*

D. Banking Network

The number of banking relations will impact the transfer and administrative costs of a company's concentration system. If branches of a single bank can be used, the number and costs of concentration transfers can be reduced. In addition, administrative tasks like account reconciliation are simplified. The growth in statewide and interstate branch banking will benefit companies by reducing concentration costs.

III. CASH CONCENTRATION COST COMPONENTS

Among the examples of cash concentration cost components are **excess bank balances**, transfer charges, and administrative costs.

A. Excess Bank Balances

Balances are said to be in excess when the average collected balance in an account is above the level that a bank requires for compensation or the level that a company has chosen to maintain at a bank. There is an opportunity cost associated with excess balances. (See also Chapter 16, Relationship Management.)

1. *Determining Required Balances* - Among the methods for determining required balances are the following:

   • *Account Analysis* - Most large banks provide an **account analysis** statement showing the price of each service used, the volume of activity, and the compensation required. Banks may be compensated with balances, fees, or a combination of both.

- *Estimates for Field Banks* - Some small field banks may not have the capability to provide account analyses. Therefore, a company may have to determine a fair compensating balance. Using estimated per item service costs, average volume, and a reasonable earnings credit rate, a company can compute a target compensating balance for a field bank.

2. *How Excess Balances Arise* - Among the reasons excess balances arise are the following:

    - *Deposit Reporting Delays* - Deposit reports by field units may be delayed by local management or the deposit information gathering system. Excess balances may result from delayed concentration transfers.

    - *Clearing Delays* - If concentration is done with EDTs or DTCs, there can be one or more days of float between transfer initiation and clearing or settlement. Excess balances may be created when immediately available funds are deposited, or when checks deposited in field or lockbox banks clear before the concentration transfers clear back to the deposit account.

    - *Transfer Initiation Delays* - A company or a company's concentration bank may be delayed in preparing transfers. For example, if an EDT is not originated in time to meet the bank's deposit deadline, settlement will be delayed an extra day.

B. Transfer Charges

In concentration systems, there are various transfer costs associated with the banking system and reporting services. Among typical service charges are the following:

1. *Deposit Bank Charges* - A deposit bank may charge for depositing funds, outgoing wires, EDT and DTC clearings, deposit reports, account maintenance fees, and overdrafts.

2. *Concentration Bank Charges* - A concentration bank may charge for receiving wires, originating and depositing EDTs and DTCs, for receiving and reporting deposit information, and for account maintenance.

3. *Third-Party Vendor Charges* - A company may use vendors to assist in concentration. Vendors charge for collecting deposit information from field units or lockbox providers, and for transmitting data to a concentration bank and/or company.

C. Administrative Costs

Among the administrative costs involved with operating a concentration system are the following:

1. *Managing Deposit Reporting* - A major administrative responsibility is receiving and monitoring daily deposit reports from local managers, lockbox providers, and concentration banks.

2. *Cash Transfer Scheduling* - **Cash transfer scheduling** is deciding when and how much to transfer. Cash transfer scheduling is a routine decision if a company's poli-

cy is to transfer the entire amount of the daily deposit. Otherwise, there is a cost associated with deposit monitoring and decision making.

3.   *Overdrafts* - Cash concentration systems have occasional overdrafts caused by misdirected transfers, returned items, or missed deposit deadlines. Also, sometimes a check deposited at a field or lockbox bank is returned after the amount was included in the concentration transfer. In these cases, a field office may reimburse a field bank for a returned item, or reduce the next concentration transfer by the amount of the returned item.

4.   *Timely Local Deposits* - Ensuring that deposits are made in field banks in time to receive same-day ledger credit accelerates the availability of funds and reduces expenses related to overdrafts.

IV. TECHNIQUES TO REDUCE CONCENTRATION SYSTEM COSTS

Among the techniques to reduce concentration system costs are improving transfer timing, reducing transfer costs, and comparing transfer costs.

A. Improve Transfer Timing

Excess balances can be reduced by removing information delays, anticipating deposits, and by using a faster transfer mechanism. An explanation of each of these techniques follows.

1.   *Remove Information Delays* - There are sometimes delays in informing a concentration bank of required transfers, thereby adding extra float to the process. To overcome these delays, a company may do the following:

  •   *Establish Cutoff Times* - Cutoff times encourage transfer reports to be made to meet a concentration bank's schedule.

  •   *Require Timely Reports* - Banks offer services which help monitor non-reporting locations, as well as the timeliness of reporting locations.

2.   *Anticipate Deposits* - **Anticipation** is the initiation of a transfer before cash becomes available at the deposit bank. Given the possibility of abuses of this technique or of occasional accidental overdrafts, it should not be practiced without written agreement with the banks involved. The following are the two most common forms of anticipation:

  •   *Availability Anticipation* - The transfer is initiated on the basis of deposit information. There is little risk of ledger overdraft with this method because the ledger balance is known with virtual certainty when the transfer is initiated. However, there is a risk of drawing on uncollected funds since the collected balance is not always predictable due to potential delays in the clearing system or returned items.

    An example of availability anticipation is a local manager who reports a Monday deposit of $100,000 in checks, then originates a $100,000 EDT on Monday with one-day settlement.

  •   *Deposit Anticipation* - In this form, the transfer is initiated on the basis of expected deposits that have not yet been reported. This technique is often used by retailers. This form of anticipation requires a good forecasting system, timely deposit processing at the local level, and administrative time to forecast daily receipts and reconcile transfers to deposits.

An example of deposit anticipation is a field bank which expects to receive $15,000 in cash on Monday morning from weekend sales. A $15,000 EDT from the field bank to the concentration bank is originated on Friday with Monday settlement. The EDT clears on Monday when the field deposit is made.

3. *Use Faster Mechanisms* - The use of wire transfers results in immediately available funds while EDTs or DTCs are available only after a one- or two-day time delay. In many cases, EDTs may become available more quickly than DTCs.

B. Reduce Transfer Costs

Two ways to reduce costs are to transfer less often and use less expensive transfer mechanisms.

1. *Transfer Timing* - Examples of reducing transfer costs by changing transfer timing are as follows:

   • *Less than Daily* - While daily transfers are the norm, many companies transfer less often than daily if the deposit amounts do not justify the expense.

   • *Average Daily Deposit Less than Target* - If the target balance is $50,000 and the daily deposit is $10,000, then transferring once a week or even less often may be sufficient.

   • *Deposits Grouped Toward Certain Days of the Week* - For companies whose receipts are deposited on certain days of the week, it is more cost effective to transfer on these days.

   • *Balance Averaging* - Banks compute monthly average collected balances for compensation purposes. However, since a number of banks are now charging for uncollected funds on a daily basis, as opposed to a monthly average basis, balance averaging is not always an option.

   Balance averaging can reduce costs in a concentration system because it allows for the following:

   * Reduction in the number of transfers and related transfer costs
   * Initiation of larger transfers on critical days
   * Reduction in excess balances through anticipation

2. *Transfer Mechanisms* - Examples of reducing transfer costs by changing transfer mechanisms are as follows:

   • *EDT versus Wire Transfer* - For some companies, deposits may be mostly checks with delayed availability such as lockbox deposits. In these cases, it would be more cost-effective to use a less expensive mechanism such as an EDT or DTC on the day of deposit instead of initiating a wire transfer on the day funds become available.

- *Repetitive Wire Transfers* - Repetitive wire transfers are usually less expensive than non-repetitive transfers, thereby reducing concentration costs.

3. *Target and Threshold Concentration* - A company can manage its balance level in field banks with a system of either target or threshold balances. Many bank concentration systems offer headquarters the flexibility to change the amounts reported by field units, thereby adjusting the amount transferred.

    - *Target Concentration* - With **target concentration**, a target balance is set and all funds above that balance level are transferred to the concentration bank. This system maintains balances at the desired level. It could involve transfers as frequently as daily.

    - *Threshold Concentration* - With **threshold concentration**, balances are allowed to build up to a predetermined level, then most or all of the funds are transferred to the concentration bank. This method helps to minimize the number of transfers required. A cash manager can monitor the average balances that result from this system and, over time, make the necessary adjustments.

4. *Deposit Reconciliation Services* - A bank may offer deposit reconciliation services. With this service, deposits from multiple locations are credited to a company's account with the bank, which may be a regional or main concentration account. MICR-encoded deposit tickets identify each location, and enable a bank to produce a daily, weekly, or monthly deposit report. This service reduces the number of transfers and bank accounts that must be maintained, thereby decreasing concentration system costs. Deposit reconciliation will become more useful to a cash manager as statewide branching and interstate banking become more widespread.

C. Compare Transfer Costs

In determining whether to use an EDT, a DTC, or a wire transfer to concentrate funds, it is important to establish the value of the accelerated funds. By comparing this value to the costs of the alternative transfer methods, the appropriate transfer mechanism can be selected.

For example, assume the following:

1. Total costs for an EDT are $1.00.
2. Total costs for a wire transfer are $20.00.
3. Available funds for transfer are $100,000.
4. The opportunity costs of funds is 10%.
5. A wire transfer accelerates funds one day faster than an EDT.

Funds Value = Available Funds x Days Accelerated x Opportunity Cost
= $100,000 x 1 x .10/365
= $27.40

Because the funds value, $27.40, exceeds the incremental costs of a wire transfer ($20.00 - $1.00 = $19.00), it is advantageous for the company to use a wire transfer rather than an EDT.

Another approach for determining the minimum wire transfer required to break even is as follows:

$$\text{Minimum Transfer} = \frac{\text{Wire Cost} - \text{EDT Cost}}{\text{Days Accelerated} \times \dfrac{\text{Opportunity Cost}}{365 \text{ Days}}}$$

$$= \frac{\$20.00 - \$1.00}{1 \text{ Day} \times \dfrac{.10}{365 \text{ Days}}}$$

$$= \$69,350$$

As long as the wire transfer amount is larger than $69,350, the additional cost of the wire transfer is justified.

V. RISKS AND CONTROLS

Among the risk and control issues in designing a concentration system are the following:

A. Punctuality

The primary operational risk of a concentration system is the failure to make deposit calls and/or report deposits accurately by a concentration bank's clearing deadline. Many banks offer services that allow companies to monitor deposit reporting.

B. Fraud

A potential for fraud exists when a local employee does not deposit the amount reported. This type of fraud may go undetected for a period of time. Preventive measures include the following:

- Require more than one type of report from field offices such as a sales report that allows a comparison to deposits. Require that these different reports be prepared and reviewed by different staff daily.

- Conduct unscheduled audits of field offices.

- Instruct field banks not to allow overdrafts, to return any items that can result in overdrafts, and to notify headquarters of these actions.

C. Bank Overdraft

The failure to make a single transfer from a deposit bank to a concentration bank could be sufficient to cause overdrafts at the concentration bank.

D. Bank Failure

Field deposit systems typically have many banks, and a company may be at risk if one fails. Timely concentration limits this risk. To reduce this risk further, a cash manager needs to monitor the creditworthiness of each bank in a company's concentration system.

Questions

These chapter questions are to test and review the information in the text and are not examples of CCM examination questions, nor are they in the examination format.

Answers can be found at the back of the book on p. 321.

1. What are the objectives of a cash concentration system?

2. What is EDT?

3. What other electronic alternative is available for concentration other than an EDT, and when is it generally used?

4. What is a depository transfer check (DTC)?

5. What are the major cost components of a cash concentration system?

6. What can cause excess balances?

7. What is anticipation?

8. What is threshold concentration?

9. A company provides the following information:
    - EDT costs total $1.00
    - Wire transfer costs are $22.00
    - A wire accelerates availability one day
    - Opportunity cost of funds is 8%

    What is the minimum wire transfer required to break even?

10. What are some ways fraud may be prevented in a concentration system?

11. Why is the pooling of funds a valuable objective of cash concentration?

12. What are some of the key considerations in designing a cash concentration system?

CHAPTER 8

Disbursement and Accounts Payable

OVERVIEW

This chapter discusses the objectives of a disbursement system, the principal methods and products used for disbursements.

LEARNING OBJECTIVES

Upon completion of this chapter and the related study questions, the reader should know:

1. The objectives of disbursement and accounts payable management systems.

2. The components and calculation of disbursement float.

3. How corporate disbursement activities are organized.

4. The various disbursement products and their applications.

5. The accounts payable functions.

6. Check reconciliation and complementary services.

OUTLINE

I. **Disbursement and Accounts Payable System Objectives**
   A. Reduce Costs
   B. Access Information
   C. Maintain Relationships
   D. Control and Fraud Prevention
   E. Manage Disbursement Float

II. **Disbursement Float**
   A. Mail Float
   B. Processing Float
   C. Clearing Float

III. **Disbursement System Considerations**
   A. Centralization versus Decentralization
   B. Control and Fraud Prevention

I. DISBURSEMENT AND ACCOUNTS PAYABLE SYSTEM OBJECTIVES

The basic goal of managing a disbursement and accounts payable system is to properly disburse funds to vendors, suppliers, employees, and other payees in a timely and cost-effective manner. More specifically, the objectives of a disbursement and accounts payable system are the following:

A. Reduce Costs

An important objective of a disbursement system is to reduce a company's net cost of making payments. These costs include:

1. *Opportunity Costs* - Opportunity costs include the following:

   • The cost of excess borrowing or lost investment income when idle balances exist in disbursement accounts.

   • The costs of missed or early payments, which include:

     * The costs of paying bills late, such as lost discounts and ill will.

     * The opportunity costs of paying bills early, such as interest income lost or extra interest expense incurred.

2. *Transfer Costs* - Transfer costs are the costs of transferring funds to the bank accounts from which disbursements are made.

3. *Overdraft Costs* - Overdraft costs include the monetary costs of overdrawing disbursement accounts as well as possible damage to the banking relationship.

B. Access Information

Obtaining timely and accurate information about the status of disbursement accounts and disbursement clearings enables the company to effectively manage its cash position.

C. Maintain Relationships

It is important that good relationships are maintained with vendors and other payees.

D. Control and Fraud Prevention

Funds should be protected from unauthorized use through controls such as a written policy establishing authority, responsibilities, and separation of duties.

E. Manage Disbursement Float

Disbursement float should be managed in light of company objectives and policies.

II. DISBURSEMENT FLOAT

Disbursement float results from the delay between the time when a payor mails the check and the time when the funds are debited from the payor's account. This form of float is essentially the same as collection float, plus any clearing system slippage. Disbursement float has the following components:

A. Mail Float

Mail float is the delay between the time a check is mailed and the date the check is received by the payee or at the processing site. Mail float is the same for both collections and disbursements.

B. Processing Float

Processing float is the delay between the time the payee or processing site receives the check and the time the check is deposited. Processing float is the same for both collections and disbursements.

C. Clearing Float

Clearing float is the delay between the time the check is deposited and the time it is presented to the payor's bank for payment. It has two components:

1. *Availability Float* - The delay between the time a check is deposited and the time the company's account is credited with collected funds. Availability float is the same for both collections and disbursements.

2. *Clearing Slippage Float* - The difference between the time the payee receives collected funds and the time the payor's account is debited. This is not a component of collection float and may be highly variable depending on inefficiencies in the check clearing system.

The components of disbursement float are illustrated in Exhibit 8.1.

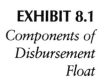

EXHIBIT 8.1

Components of Disbursement Float

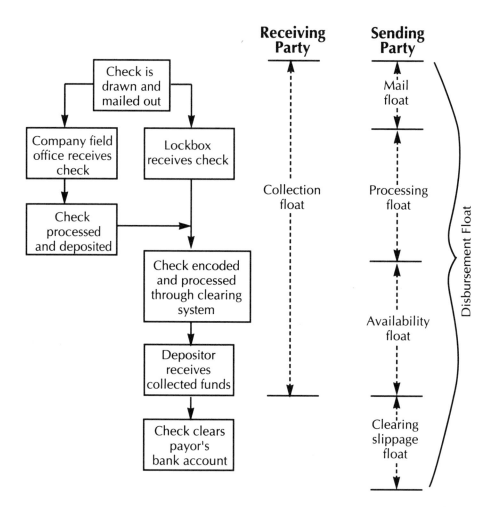

III. DISBURSEMENT SYSTEM CONSIDERATIONS

There are several considerations in planning and managing a disbursement system.

A. Centralization versus Decentralization

Disbursement systems may be centralized or decentralized. The advantages and disadvantages of each are as follows:

1. *Centralized Check Issuance* - In this type of system, headquarters controls disbursement accounts and is responsible for check writing and account reconciliation.

Advantages:
- Bank and internal costs may be reduced.

- Idle cash at local banks is minimized; excess cash is concentrated and available for investment or loan repayment.

- Payment of bills can be scheduled to coordinate with the cash inflows of the firm.

- Information about a company's cash position can be obtained easily and quickly.

- As fewer individuals have access to the system, there is less likelihood of unauthorized disbursements.

Disadvantages:
- Payments to suppliers may be delayed and the organization may miss a discount because invoices must be sent to a central location for processing.

- Disbursement float may increase and payees may perceive that it is being increased at their expense.

- Problem resolution requires coordination between headquarters and field offices.

2. *Decentralized Check Issuance* - In this type of system, check issuance and account reconciliation are performed at the local level. The checks are generally drawn on a local disbursement bank.

   Advantages:
   - In decentralized corporations, it may be more efficient for the local manager to have total control over disbursement activities.

   - Relationships with payees may be better because checks are drawn on local banks and the local manager can resolve payment disputes more easily.

   Disadvantages:
   - Idle balances in disbursement accounts may result in significant excess balances for the company as a whole.

   - Disbursement float may be lower when disbursements are made to local vendors.

   - Information about a company's day-to-day aggregate cash position may be more difficult to obtain. More company accounts may need to be monitored.

   - There may be a greater likelihood of unauthorized disbursements because more people have access to the system.

   - There may be additional transfer, reconciliation and administrative costs for maintaining local disbursement accounts.

3. *Local Checks Written on a Centralized Disbursement Bank* - In this system, check issuance and account reconciliation are performed at the local level, but headquarters is responsible for choosing disbursement banks and funding disbursement accounts.

   Advantages:
   - The number of bank relationships is minimized compared to a decentralized system.

   - Excess balances in field locations are reduced compared to a decentralized system.

- There are more opportunities for volume discounts on disbursement bank charges compared to a decentralized system.

- The local manager has greater autonomy compared to a centralized system.

- There is local control of payment timing compared to a centralized system.

- Vendor relationships are improved compared to a centralized system.

Disadvantages:
- There is less control over when checks are written compared to a centralized system.

- Higher administrative costs may result from a dual system, including local check writing, headquarters monitoring, and management of centralized accounts.

- Use of a non-local bank is required for checks sent to local vendors, compared to a decentralized system.

B. Control and Fraud Prevention

Disbursement fraud has become an increasingly significant problem. Technological advances have increased the sophistication of check fraud. These advances include color copiers, high-resolution laser printers and hand-held document scanners for use with a personal computer. Control and fraud prevention measures include the following:

1. Formal, written policy and procedures for each type of disbursement.

2. Separation of functional authority for collection and disbursement.

3. Separation of expense approval, check-signing authority and account reconciliation.

4. Use of check stock printed on safety paper and/or use of difficult to reproduce watermarks.

5. Use of reputable printing companies.

6. Storing checks and signature plates in a secure area with limited access.

7. Using a printing process that does not require preprinted check stock (i.e. laser printing of checks and MICR lines).

8. Use of positive pay, a service that matches check serial numbers and dollar amounts to a database to determine the checks to be paid.

9. Setting a specific dollar amount limit for each type of account. Checks issued above this limit are returned to the depositor as unauthorized.

10. Increasing the use of electronic payment methods.

C. Disbursement Networks

Disbursement networks are systems of check mailing locations and drawee banks based on disbursement studies and are designed to maximize disbursement float. Disbursement networks are not widely used. The cost and control benefits of making disbursements from just one or two banks often outweigh the float benefits of using a greater number of banks.

D. Compliance with Trade Terms

Lengthening mail float does not benefit a company unless it is given credit for having paid the bill on the postmark date. The postmark date may settle a technical dispute, but a vendor might view a substantial delay in receiving good funds as a late payment.

E. Funding Disbursement Accounts

The cash manager needs to be sure that disbursement accounts are funded to pay checks presented but at the same time, do not have excess balances.

F. Special Payment Types

1. *Freight Payments* - A few banks and third parties offer a specialized payment service in which freight payment specialists pay all of a shipper's freight bills, audit bills for possible overcharges and duplicate payments, and provide reports that help the company compare costs for different routes and carriers.

2. *Tax Payments*

    *   *Federal Tax Deposits* - The method for collecting and accounting for taxes withheld by employers from individuals' salaries and wages, as well as corporate business and excise taxes, is being changed to an electronic system called **Electronic Federal Tax Payment System (EFTPS)**. Effective January 1995, the largest taxpayers were mandated to make all tax deposits electronically. In succeeding years, additional organizations are to be mandated. By 1998, most organizations are scheduled to make these deposits electronically.

        The primary mechanism for electronic deposits is the Automated Clearing House (ACH). Either debits or credits may be used. Wire transfers are allowed for all mandated taxpayers. Until a company is required to make these deposits electronically, it can continue to use the current Federal Tax Deposit paper coupon system (Form 8109) through its banks or participate on a voluntary basis in the electronic deposit system. Once a company is mandated to use the electronic system, it can no longer use the paper coupon system as an alternative.

    *   *State Tax Payments* - Many states require companies with tax payments above certain amounts to remit taxes electronically. This may be done with an ACH credit or debit, with some states permitting the use of a wire transfer as well. The standard payment format for state tax payments via the ACH is known as TXP, but usage and specific conventions vary from state to state.

IV. DISBURSEMENT PRODUCTS AND METHODS

There are several disbursement products or methods which cash managers can utilize to manage the disbursements process.

A. Zero Balance Accounts

Zero Balance Accounts (ZBAs) are used by many companies to help manage their disbursement processes.

1. *Description of a ZBA* - A **zero balance account** (ZBA) is a disbursement account on which checks are written, even though the balances in the accounts are maintained at zero. Checks debited to a ZBA for payment are covered by a transfer of funds from a master account located in the same bank. Funding of the ZBA account is automatic and involves only an accounting entry by the bank. Depending on each bank's capabilities, multi-tiered ZBAs may be available. Debits and transfers are posted to each account, and entries to bring the balance to zero are made through the respective tiers at the end of each day.

2. *How ZBAs Work* - Credits and debits are posted just before the close of business, when a credit from the master account is posted to bring the balance back to zero. If there is a credit balance in the ZBA account, the ZBA will be debited and a credit made to the master account.

3. *ZBAs in Multi-Division Companies* - ZBAs may be used to allow companies with multiple divisions and subsidiaries to write checks on separate accounts and to segregate different types of payments such as payrolls, dividends and accounts payable. The cash manager can control the balances and funding of a master account and its associated ZBAs as if they were all one large account. This reduces idle balances and the need for multiple manual transfers.

B. Controlled Disbursement

Another method used to minimize balances in disbursement accounts is controlled disbursement.

1. *Description*

    *   **Controlled disbursement** is a bank service that provides same-day notification, usually by early or mid-morning, of the dollar amount of checks that will clear against the controlled disbursement account that day. The disbursement bank must receive its final cash letter of the day from the local Fed early in the morning so that the checks can be sorted and the company notified of its funding requirement. Payor bank services are often used to aid in this process.

    *   Companies generally find better rates for short-term investments early in the morning; consequently, they require check clearing information as early as possible.

    *   Under the Federal Reserve's High Dollar Group Sort (HDGS) program, the local Reserve Bank automatically makes a second daily presentment to drawee banks with more than $10 million in presentments from banks outside their Fed district. The second, later presentment involved in this program makes the management of controlled disbursement more difficult.

    *   Controlled disbursement accounts must also deal with same-day presentment items. These are checks drawn on the disbursement bank which are directly presented from another bank by 8:00 a.m. According to Fed regulations, these checks must be paid the same day they are presented. These same-day presentment items may need to be handled by a different processing method than the rest

of the controlled disbursement checks. Banks also have the option of designating the local Federal Reserve Bank as the clearing point for same-day presentment items. This approach may eliminate some of the processing problems.

2. *Payor Bank Services*

- **Payor Bank Services** is an information service of the Federal Reserve which electronically notifies controlled disbursement banks early in the morning of all checks that will be presented that day. There are typically two notifications: the first early in the morning, and the second no earlier than 9:30 a.m., E.T. Banks are then prepared to notify customers after an appropriate processing time.

- Fed banks and branches are not uniform in their ability to provide Payor Bank Services.

3. *Discrepancies After Notification*

- There is risk of presentment after the morning notification. A check missed by the Fed in the Payor Bank Services notification but discovered the same morning will be presented that day. There is also the possibility that a check will be presented over-the-counter, through a bank's branch network, or in a direct send from another bank.

- Some banks offer a controlled disbursement option to prevent problems caused by late presentments. The bank guarantees that the final presentment amount will be equal to the morning notification, and makes whatever adjustments are required to the account the next day.

4. *Funding Controlled Disbursement Accounts*

- A controlled disbursement account is normally funded from a corporate concentration account. The account can be funded either by the corporate customer or the bank. The transfer is usually on a same-day basis.

- If concentration and controlled disbursement accounts are in unrelated banks, a wire transfer or the ACH can be used for funding. For applications that are not wire transfers, credit approval may be required, and the company may have to keep a balance equal to one day's average clearing.

5. *Credit Risk*

- Controlled disbursement poses credit risk for a bank, with important implications for a company.

- When the bank on which checks are actually drawn is funded on a same-day basis with a wire transfer or from another account at the same bank, there is very little credit exposure. This is because the bank can return any checks if funds are not sufficient.

- Two situations in which a bank has credit exposure are:
  * With delayed funding, there is risk that an electronic depository transfer (EDT) or depository transfer check (DTC) may be returned by the bank on which

these items are drawn. By the time the returned EDT or DTC reaches the disbursement bank, it may be too late to return any disbursement checks being funded by the EDT or DTC. The disbursement bank is owed funds and becomes a creditor of the company.

* With the use of an affiliated bank for disbursing with funding through the parent bank, there is no problem if the affiliate bank is funded directly on a same-day basis by a wire transfer. However, if the company funds the parent bank and the parent bank automatically funds the affiliate with immediate funds, there is a potential overdraft problem at the parent bank. Since the affiliate bank does not have an overdrawn account, it cannot legally refuse to pay the checks even though there may be an overdraft at the parent bank.

• Such risks make it very likely that a bank will undertake a credit review of a company that wants to use its controlled disbursement service and in some cases, a formal credit facility may be required. When an affiliate bank is used, an agreement may be required that allows checks to be returned if sufficient funds are not available at the parent bank.

6. *How to Select a Controlled Disbursement Bank* - In addition to overall relationship considerations, several service considerations should be evaluated in the selection of a controlled disbursement bank. Disbursement float remains important for the company, but in recent years other considerations have become more important. They include:

• *Timeliness of Reporting* - This is important because a company wants to make investing or borrowing decisions as early as possible.

• *Processing Accuracy* - Processing errors can result in over- or underfunding of the disbursement account.

• *Volume Capacity* - Check processing capacity should be sufficient, so that reporting deadlines can be met.

• *Reporting Detail and Reconciliation Services* - Reports should contain adequate detail and be timely enough to meet a company's information needs.

• *Price* - Service pricing should reflect fair and reasonable compensation.

• *Customer Service Support* - Bank customer service staff should provide prompt and knowledgeable responses to a company's requests.

C. Payable Through Drafts (PTDs)

A payable through draft (PTD) is a payment instrument resembling a check that is drawn against the payor, not the bank, and on which the payor has a period of time to honor or refuse payment. Some important aspects of PTDs and their use are as follows:

• The deadline under Federal Reserve Regulation CC for approval or rejection of a PTD is the same as for a check.

• PTDs are frequently used for insurance claims and other field office disbursements that require final headquarters approval. They give a company time to ensure that all terms have been met or expenditures authorized.

• Electronic payable through drafts are ACH debits to a company's account in which the company is notified in time to pay or reject each item. They are used for similar purposes as paper payable through drafts.

D. Multiple Drawee Checks

Multiple drawee checks, also known as payable-if-desired (PID) checks, are checks that can be presented for payment at a bank other than the drawee bank. Both bank names appear on the check.

1. *Applications* - Examples include payroll in states that require employees to be paid by checks payable in the state, payroll for employees on assignments away from the company office, and dividend checks.

2. *Banking Arrangements* - Balances are usually maintained at the alternate payment bank to compensate it for cashing multiple drawee checks. The alternate bank will require indemnity from the paying company for any loss relating to those checks. Some banks are unwilling to provide this service.

E. Imprest Accounts

An **imprest account** is an account maintained at a prescribed level for a particular purpose or activity, and periodically replenished to the prescribed level. For example, a field office may have an imprest account for local disbursements with a balance sufficient for one or two months' expenses. Based on an established time frame or level of imprest account balances, the office submits expenses to headquarters for approval, and headquarters reimburses the imprest account.

F. Electronic Disbursement Methods

Electronic disbursements via the Fedwire and ACH (see also, Chapter 4, Payments System) are used for payments from corporations to individuals, from individuals to corporations, and from corporations to corporations. The item volume of such payments is low compared to checks, but is expected to increase as the value of float declines, and the emphasis on expense control increases. The increasing use of electronic commerce (see also Chapter 13, Electronic Commerce) will also stimulate the growth of these forms of electronic disbursements.

V. ACCOUNT RECONCILIATION AND COMPLEMENTARY SERVICES

Banks provide account reconciliation services to meet companies' information and control requirements. The following services are available:

A. Sort Only

In a sort only service, a bank sorts the checks by check serial number for a company.

B. Partial Reconciliation

In a **partial reconciliation** service, a bank lists all checks paid in numerical order by check serial number, or date paid. For each item, the paid report shows the check serial number, dollar amount, and date paid. The listing is available as a paper report and/or electronic form.

C. Full Reconciliation

In a **full reconciliation** service, a company supplies an electronic file of checks issued to its bank and the bank matches checks paid against the file. The bank supplies a listing, either as a paper report and/or electronic form, of checks paid and outstanding in check serial number order.

D. Positive Pay

The **positive pay service** is used to combat check fraud. With this system, the company transmits a file of checks to the bank soon after issuance. The bank matches check serial numbers and dollar amounts and pays only those checks that match.

A similar system known as **reverse positive pay**, occurs when the bank transmits to a company on a daily basis, a file of the checks presented for payment. The company matches this file to its list of checks issued and notifies the bank of any items it wishes to have returned.

E. Inquiries and Stop Payments

Stop payments can be initiated by a company either by voice, electronically, or in writing. Written confirmation may be required by the bank for telephone instructions. Many banks offer information reporting systems which allow customers to electronically inquire about the status of checks written. (See also, Chapter 11, Information and Technology Management.)

F. Check Retention (Check Safekeeping)

In a **check retention service**, a bank retains paid checks for periods that typically range from one to six months. Microfilm records are usually maintained for seven years. Copies of checks can be obtained when needed.

G. High-Order Prefix (Divisional Sort)

The high-order prefix sorting service allows a single account to be used by a company with multiple units. Codes identifying the various units are included in the check serial numbers. Reports are available showing unit subtotals.

VI. ACCOUNTS PAYABLE DEVELOPMENTS

There are several developments which have an important impact on the operation and management of the accounts payable area.

A. Integrated or Comprehensive Payables

An **integrated or comprehensive payables service** is the outsourcing of all or part of a company's accounts payable and/or disbursements functions. There are several approaches to managing an integrated or comprehensive payables service:

- One approach is to have a company send a single data file to a third party containing a listing of all its payments to be made. The file contains information on when to issue a disbursement and to whom, as well as instructions on the payment method to be used (i.e., check, wire, or ACH).

- Alternatively, the third party maintains a database of a company's payees that includes detailed information such as preferred payment methods, specific remittance information, and receiving financial institutions. The database is periodically updated as new payees are added or an existing payee's remittance profile changes (i.e., payee switches to ACH instead of check for its standard payment type). In such cases, as a company makes a disbursement, it sends to the third party only limited payment information.

- With either approach, the third party either issues the payments immediately or warehouses them until a future date as instructed by the data file. A company using these types of services is outsourcing much of its disbursements function and potentially reducing the overall costs of its accounts payables operations.

B. Procurement Cards

Many companies are implementing the use of **procurement or purchasing cards for** the purchase of supplies, inventory, equipment, and service contracts. Though companies have long used credit cards for travel and entertainment expenses, the use of credit cards for routine procurement is a relatively new development. Companies that have implemented such systems have been able to reduce the costs involved in purchasing, while still maintaining adequate levels of control.

C. Imaging Services

Image processing is being used in a variety of disbursement services. The checks are optically scanned and converted into digital information. Both the front and the back of a check may be captured. Check images (all of them or selected ones) may be transmitted to a company's computer and stored there. They may also be sent to a fax machine. The check images may also be stored in a bank computer which a company can access to view or retrieve the images. Any of these methods allows a company faster access to check information.

Imaging services are particularly useful in conjunction with positive pay services. They help a company identify potential unauthorized check activity and make critical pay/no-pay decisions on checks in a timely manner. Photocopies of checks can be obtained in a more timely fashion, allowing companies to respond quickly to inquiries from customers, employees, and vendors.

Some financial institutions are capturing check images on CD-ROM as a substitute for microfilm or microfiche.

Questions

These chapter questions are to test and review the information in the text and are not examples of CCM examination questions, nor are they in the examination format.

Answers can be found at the back of the book on p. 322.

1.   What are the major objectives of a cash disbursement system?

2.   How may disbursement systems be organized?

3.   What are the components of disbursement float?

4.   What are the various ways of controlling and preventing check fraud?

5.   What is controlled disbursement?

6.   What is a zero balance account (ZBA)?

7.   What is the Electronic Federal Tax Payment system?

8.   How does same day settlement impact controlled disbursement?

9.   Who provides payor bank services?

10.   What factors should be examined in the selection of a controlled disbursement bank?

11.   What is Positive Pay?

12.   What is the difference between a partial and full reconciliation?

13.   How does controlled disbursement cause credit risk for a bank?

14.   What are the two basic approaches to managing an integrated or comprehensive payables service?

15.   What are procurement cards and what is their benefit to a company?

16.   How are imaging services used in disbursements?

CHAPTER **9**

Short-Term Investments

OVERVIEW

This chapter describes why a short-term investment program is important and how investment policies and procedures are determined. It includes a description of investment risks, frequently used short-term investment instruments, and examples of short-term investment strategies and guidelines. This chapter discusses investment instruments from the investor's point of view, while Chapter 10, Short-Term Borrowing, discusses investment instruments from the borrower's or issuer's point of view.

LEARNING OBJECTIVES

Upon completion of this chapter and the related study questions, the reader should know:

1. Why companies hold short-term investments.

2. How authority and responsibility for short-term investments are usually assigned in a company.

3. What typical company investment guidelines are and how they are determined.

4. What factors influence short-term investment yields.

5. How prices are quoted for short-term investment instruments and how yields are calculated according to money-market, bond-equivalent, and effective annual yield quoting conventions.

6. The term-structure of interest rates, and how yield curves change under various market environments.

7. The most frequently issued short-term government, agency, municipal, bank, and corporate short-term investment instruments.

8. The differences between active and passive short-term investment strategies, and other more specific strategies such as matching, riding the yield curve, and dividend capture.

OUTLINE

I. WHY COMPANIES HOLD SHORT-TERM INVESTMENTS

Companies hold short-term investments for a variety of reasons.

A. Temporary Excess Funds

One of the primary reasons for a company having a short-term investment portfolio is the existence of temporary excess funds. The following can generate temporary excess funds for a company:

1.   *Positive Cash Flow* - A company may gradually accumulate excess cash through positive operating cash flow.

2.   *Seasonality* - A company may generate a large portion of its cash in one period, and invest some of that cash for use in other periods.

3. *Sale of Assets* - An asset may be sold to produce liquid funds that will be reinvested in a future period.

4. *Timing of Long-Term Financing* - Equity or bond offerings must be large enough to be economical, and their timing is determined primarily by market conditions. A company may raise funds that will not be needed until a future period.

B. Liquidity Reserve

A company that needs reserve liquidity to manage temporary cash shortages resulting from seasonality or working capital imbalances may accomplish this by holding a portfolio of short-term investments. The reserve can be provided by investments, unused short-term borrowing capacity, or some combination of the two. Reserve liquidity is one of the primary reasons companies have short-term investment portfolios.

C. Income Generation

A further reason for a company having a short-term investment portfolio is the generation of investment income within the constraints imposed by the need for acceptable risk management consistent with the company's overall risk policy.

II. INVESTMENT ISSUES

There are several key issues which companies must consider related to the management of short-term investments.

A. Requirements for Investment Policies and Guidelines

A company can incur opportunity costs or lose principal through poor investment judgment, assumption of imprudent risks, assignment of investment responsibilities to unqualified personnel, and poor internal controls. Because of these risks, a company should have clearly defined and published investment guidelines. These include not only the criteria for acceptable investments, but also specific personnel responsibilities for defining policy, carrying out day-to-day investing, reviewing performance, and auditing. These guidelines should be reviewed on a regular basis.

B. Investment Objectives

A company's basic investment objectives typically include:

1. *Liquidity* - A short-term investment portfolio is one of several ways to enhance corporate liquidity.

2. *Risk Minimization* - All investments have some degree of risk. Investment alternatives with higher returns usually have higher risks. Controlling risk involves identifying the risks and determining the relationship between risk and return.

3. *Return* - Investments should generate acceptable returns. The level of return considered acceptable may vary by company depending on factors such as risk tolerance and resources available for selecting and monitoring investments.

C. Factors that Influence Investment Policies

A company's investment policies and decisions are influenced by factors such as the following:

1. *Purpose* - Companies have different objectives for short-term investments, ranging from providing a source of liquidity to generating income for the company.

2. *Timing* - A portion of a company's funds may be required at all times as a liquidity reserve, while other funds may be designated for future uses. Therefore, investments with different maturities may be appropriate for various segments of the portfolio.

3. *Tax Status* - A company's effective tax rate determines the after-tax return from taxable investments and the desirability of tax-exempt investments. The tax impact must be considered in decisions on the timing of investment gains and losses.

4. *Staffing* - Carrying out an active, internally managed short-term investment program requires internal resources, including staff and systems. Alternatively, a company may find it more advantageous to utilize the expertise of an outside investment management firm.

5. *Investment Restrictions* - There may be legal restrictions, industry guidelines, or internal policies that restrict the types of instruments in a company's short-term investment portfolio.

6. *Reporting Requirements* - A company may have to report additional information on certain types of short-term investments on its balance sheet to satisfy the requirements of shareholders, creditors, or industry regulators.

D. Responsibility

It is important to determine the responsibility for both short-term investment policy and the implementation of that policy.

1. *Policy* - In most companies, investment policy is determined and monitored by the board of directors, the finance committee of the board of directors, or the executive committee.

2. *Implementation* - Implementing and influencing the investment policy may be the responsibility of the treasurer, the cash manager, a specialized investment manager, or an investment staff.

E. Investment Guidelines

The development, implementation, and periodic review of investment guidelines are critical factors in the management of short-term investments.

1. *Acceptable Instruments* - A company generally has a list of acceptable short-term investment instruments based on the following factors:

    *   *Maturity* - This is considered an important investment guideline since the prices of longer-maturity, fixed-income securities are volatile. Prices of fixed-income securities typically move inversely with interest rates. In addition, the longer the maturity, the greater the effect of rate movements on price.

- *Quality* - The credit quality of many instruments can be determined by ratings assigned by credit rating agencies. There are rating systems for corporate bonds, bank issues, banks, municipal obligations, commercial paper, preferred stock, and money market funds.

  * In some cases, such as buying unrated commercial paper or loan participation, the investor must analyze and evaluate the credit quality of the borrower.

  * In other cases, a financial intermediary may provide credit support or credit enhancement by issuing an instrument such as a standby letter of credit to guarantee the obligation of the borrower. The obligation then assumes the credit rating of the institution providing the credit enhancement.

- *Marketability* - Holding marketable securities provides a source of liquidity for a company. A security is marketable if it can be sold in large volumes quickly and without making a substantial price concession. A large, active secondary market for a security ensures its marketability. Securities for which there is a limited secondary market are therefore less liquid and may carry higher yields.

2. *Diversification* - An important risk-reduction technique is diversification in terms of issuer, instrument type, maturity, or other investment characteristics. Investment policies may include a limitation in the percentage of the portfolio, dollar amount, or both for securities of a single issuer or instrument or category of instrument.

3. *Acceptable Dealers and/or Issuers* - Companies may have guidelines specifying acceptable dealers, banks, or other financial institutions. There may also be restrictions relating to specific issuers or criteria related to their size and/or reputation.

4. *Investment Authority* - Instruments that may be bought or sold must be specifically defined in terms of type, dollar amount, and maturity.

See Exhibit 9.1 for an example of investment guidelines.

EXHIBIT 9.1
Example of Investment Guidelines

Investment Objectives

To invest in high-quality, short-term debt obligations in order to achieve the maximum yield consistent with safety of principal and maintenance of liquidity. Liquidity and preservation of capital are the primary considerations. Yield is important but secondary to these objectives.

Responsibilities

The treasurer shall have the responsibility to manage the short-term investments within the terms of the policy set by the board of directors, maintain a reasonable relationship between short-term borrowings and short-term investments, and maintain a level of liquidity adequate to meet the company's financial obligations.

Approved Instruments

The following are approved investment vehicles with attached limitations:

1. U.S. Government and Agency Securities - no limits
2. Money Market Funds - up to $1 million may be invested in any one fund
3. Banker's Acceptances - may be up to 40% of the portfolio
4. Repurchase Agreements - may be up to 20% of the portfolio
5. Commercial Paper - may be up to $2 million per issuer. Commercial paper holdings may not exceed 50% of the portfolio.
6. Certificates of Deposit - may be up to 50% of the portfolio and further limited to an approved schedule of banks.

Constraints

Diversification	Foreign-denominated securities may not exceed 10% of the portfolio. Options and futures contracts may only be used to hedge underlying exposures.
Credit Quality	All domestic commercial paper purchased must be rated A-1/P-1. All domestic CDs must be rated the equivalent of AA or higher.
Maturity	The portfolio should have an appropriate mix, with 65% of the portfolio having no longer than a two-month maturity. The remaining maturities may not exceed two years.
Safekeeping	Securities purchased by the company are to be delivered against payment and held in a custodian account by one of the company's principal banks.

III. MARKETS FOR INVESTMENTS

Investment markets are generally divided into short-term and long-term markets. For a company, investments of temporary excess funds are generally the responsibility of the treasury function, with the individual responsible dealing primarily in the short-term rather than the long-term markets.

A. Short-Term (Money) Market

This market consists of debt instruments that usually mature in one year or less. The short-term or money market is a group of markets for common instruments such as Treasury bills,

Federal agency securities, municipal notes, commercial paper, banker's acceptances (BA), negotiable certificates of deposit, loans to security dealers, repurchase agreements (repos), and Fed funds. At the center of the market are a group of U.S. and foreign government securities dealers, some of which are large financial institutions, a number of commercial paper dealers, bankers acceptance dealers, and money brokers specializing in short-term instruments.

B. Long-Term (Capital) Market

This market consists of debt instruments (bonds) that typically mature in more than one year, as well as equity instruments (stocks). While investment in long-term securities is not normally part of a short-term portfolio, bonds maturing within a year, or preferred stock may be included. In addition, a short-term investor may evaluate the long-term securities of a company to better understand the overall risk profile for that company.

IV. INVESTMENT INSTRUMENTS

A company has a wide variety of short-term investment options with differing credit quality, yields, maturities, and marketability.

Securities are typically issued in either registered or bearer form. A security issued in registered form is issued in the name of the investor and only that party (or the legal agent) can collect interest and principal or sell the security. With a security issued in bearer form, the name of the investor is not recorded and the holder of the security is entitled to interest and/or principal payments or to sell the instrument.

A. U.S. Treasury Securities

U.S. Treasury securities are generally a significant portion of a company's portfolio of short-term securities.

1. *Characteristics* - The U.S. Treasury securities market is a large, actively traded, and liquid market that appeals to a broad spectrum of investor groups. U.S. Treasury securities are sold to finance the federal government. Characteristics of U.S. Treasuries include:

   - *Treasury Auctions* - Virtually all Treasury offerings are sold at auction. When a Treasury instrument is to be offered, the Treasury issues a notice of the new offering, inviting bids. Banks and broker/dealers, and other private and governmental entities tender bids for specific amounts of securities at specific yields. The securities go to those bidders offering the highest price (i.e., lowest yield/interest cost to the Treasury). This is known as a Dutch auction process.

   - *Form of Issue* - All Treasury securities are registered and issued in **book entry** form. The physical securities do not move when they are traded. They remain in a vault at the Federal Reserve Bank of New York. Book entries are made when ownership changes.

   - *Liquidity* - Treasury securities are actively traded in the secondary market in large volume with low transaction costs.

   - *Credit Risk* - Treasuries are considered to be free from credit risk.

   - *Taxation* - Interest income on Treasuries is exempt from state taxation.

- *Yields* - Yields on Treasury securities are generally the benchmark against which rates and prices in the other fixed income securities markets are compared. Other investment alternatives generally trade at yields above those of government securities.

2. *Securities* - In its financing operations, the Treasury issues the following:

- *Treasury Bills (T-bills)* - T-bills are the most liquid securities in the money market because of the volume issued, their credit quality, and short maturities. They are issued each week on a discount basis in maturities of 13, 26, and 52 weeks. T-bills are available in a minimum denomination of $10,000 and in multiples of $1,000 thereafter. They are usually traded in round lots of $1,000,000. The discount rate on T-bills is quoted in terms of the actual number of elapsed days divided by 360.

- *Treasury Notes (T-notes)* - T-notes are issued with original maturities of 2, 3, 5, 7, and 10 years. The minimum denomination for new issues of two and three year notes is $5,000, while longer maturities have a $1,000 minimum. All notes are available in $1,000 increments above their minimum amounts. As in the case of T-bills, T-notes are usually traded in round lots of $1,000,000. T-notes are interest bearing securities on which interest is paid semiannually. Interest is calculated on the actual number of elapsed days using a 365-day year.

- *Treasury Bonds (T-bonds)* - T-bonds are similar to T-notes, but with maturities ranging from 10 to 30 years.

B. Federal Agency Securities

Many agencies of the U.S. government issue securities either to fund their operations, or as intermediaries between different types of financial markets. With the exception of those instruments issued by the Government National Mortgage Association, federal agency securities do not carry the same "full faith and credit" guarantee that U.S. Treasury issues carry.

1. *Characteristics* - Federal agencies act as financial intermediaries. They borrow funds and use them to make various types of loans to specific classes of borrowers. Characteristics of federal agency securities include:

- *Liquidity* - Although agency issues are smaller than Treasury issues, the liquidity of most agencies compares favorably with other money market instruments. Agencies trade at higher yields than Treasuries of the same maturity.

- *Credit Risk* - While credit risk exists, agency securities represent reasonable risk. Most agency securities are not direct or indirect obligations of the government and thus do not carry the "full faith and credit" guarantee of U.S. Treasury obligations. They are, however, obligations of entities dealing largely with federally regulated institutions and often involve federal sponsorship and, in some cases, guarantees.

- *Taxation* - Interest income earned on many agency issues is exempt from state and local taxation.

2. *Securities* - The major federal agency securities are the following:

- *Federal Farm Credit Bank (FFCB)* - The Federal Farm Credit System is a cooperatively owned nationwide system of banks and associations that provides mortgage loans, short- and intermediate-term credit, and related services to farmers and ranchers. The Federal Farm Credit Bank issues securities on a consolidated basis under the name of the Federal Farm Credit System. FFCB securities are not guaranteed either directly or indirectly by the U.S. government, but the risk of default is considered to be low. Interest derived from these securities is subject to federal taxation but exempt from state and local taxation.

- *Federal National Mortgage Association (FNMA or Fannie Mae)* - FNMA is a privately owned corporation whose function is to buy government-insured or guaranteed and conventional mortgages. To finance its mortgage purchases, FNMA relies primarily on the sale of debentures and short-term discount notes. FNMA securities are not backed by the full faith and credit of the federal government, but the risk of default is considered to be low.

- *Government National Mortgage Association (GNMA or Ginnie Mae)* - GNMA is a wholly government-owned corporation within the Department of Housing and Urban Development that makes real estate investment more attractive to institutional investors by administering mortgage-backed securities programs. Those programs provide a vehicle for channeling funds from the securities and bond markets into the mortgage market, thus increasing the overall supply of mortgage credit available for housing. GNMA guarantees timely payment of principal and interest on private issues backed by pools of mortgages which carry the full faith and credit of the U.S. Government.

- *Student Loan Marketing Association (SLMA or Sallie Mae)* - SLMA is a stockholder-owned corporation which was established to help finance the education needs of students. This is accomplished by providing liquidity to banks, S&Ls, educational institutions, state agencies and other lenders to increase the amount of funds available for educational purposes. These issues are not backed by the full faith and credit of the U.S. government.

- *Federal Home Loan Mortgage Corporation (FHLMC or Freddie Mac)* - The FHLMC was created to promote the development of a nationwide secondary market in conventional residential mortgages. FHLMC may purchase mortgages only from financial institutions that have their deposits or accounts insured by agencies of the Federal government. FHLMC sells its interest in the mortgages it purchases through mortgage-backed securities. These are not backed by the full faith and credit of the U.S. Government.

C. Municipal Securities

Municipal securities are debt securities issued by state and local governments or their agencies. Agencies of state and local governments include school districts, housing authorities, sewer districts, municipally owned utilities, and authorities running toll roads, bridges and other transportation facilities.

1.   *Bonds and Notes* - Municipalities generally issue bonds or notes.

- *Bonds* - Most municipal securities are long-term bonds. State and local governments generally sell long-term bonds to finance the construction of schools, housing, pollution-control facilities, roads, bridges, and other capital projects. An ongoing secondary market for municipal bonds exists but is not as active as the market for newly issued bonds.

- *Notes* - Municipal notes are municipal debt obligations with an original maturity of two years or less. These notes are generally issued to help overcome a temporary cash shortage and are usually related to the anticipation of receiving future revenues or taxes.

2. *Revenue and General Obligation Securities* - Municipal securities fall into two broad categories. These are:

- *General Obligation Securities* - General obligation securities have the full faith, credit, and taxing power of the issuing entity securing the payment of principal and interest. This usually means that the securities are backed by all of the issuer's resources and its pledge to levy taxes.

- *Revenue Securities* - Payments of interest and principal on revenue securities are made from specific sources such as tolls, user charges, or rents paid by those who use the facilities financed by the proceeds of the security issue. Sometimes they are credit enhanced by the use of letters of credit or other guarantees.

D. Bank Instruments

Domestic and foreign banks issue short-term certificates of deposit (CDs), time deposits, and banker's acceptances that typically offer higher yields than Treasuries.

1. *Certificates of Deposit*

- *Institutional CDs* - Institutional CDs are interest-bearing debt issues of financial institutions in the U.S., with original maturities ranging from seven days to several years. These are also referred to as domestic CDs and generally have maturities of less than one year. The minimum investment is $100,000, but institutional CDs are usually traded in $1,000,000 units. Since most institutional CDs held by companies are negotiable, there is an active secondary market for these instruments. Though there are a wide variety of different types of CDs, the basic types are as follows:

  * *Fixed-Rate CDs* - The interest rate is established at the time of issue. Interest is paid at maturity for CDs that mature in less than one year and semiannually for those maturing in more than one year.

  * *Floating (Variable) Rate CDs* - Interest is adjusted periodically to reflect prevailing interest rates. For example, on six-month CDs, interest is paid and the rate is reset every 30 days. For CDs with maturities of one year or longer, interest is paid and the rate is reset every three months. The rate is a spread over a widely-used index rate such as the 90-day T-bill or a composite of the London Interbank Offered Rate (LIBOR) from several banks.

- *Yankee CDs* - Yankee CDs are U.S. dollar-denominated CDs issued by foreign banks through their branches in the U.S. market.

- *Eurodollar CDs* - Eurodollar CDs are U.S. dollar-denominated CDs issued by banks outside the U.S. Though the primary issuers are European banks, Eurodollar CDs may be issued by any bank located outside of the U.S., including foreign branches of U.S. banks. Original maturities are usually less than two years, though most have maturities of six months or less. There is a large secondary market for Eurodollar CDs. Eurodollar CDs offer marginally higher yields than domestic CDs because they are slightly less liquid and expose the investor to sovereign risk. Sovereign risk is the risk that a foreign country will not allow an obligation to be paid. (See also Chapter 15, International Cash Management.)

2. *Eurodollar Time Deposits* - Eurodollar time deposits are non-negotiable, fixed-rate time deposits with maturities ranging from overnight to several years that are issued by banks outside the U.S. Most have maturities in six months or less. Eurodollar time deposits offer higher yields than similar domestic time deposits because of sovereign risk.

3. *Banker's Acceptance* - A banker's acceptance (BA) is a negotiated short-term instrument used primarily to finance the import, export or domestic shipment of goods or the storage of readily marketable staples. The debt obligation on the part of the bank is evidenced by a time draft drawn by the borrower that is then accepted by the bank on which it is drawn. By accepting the draft, the bank becomes directly obligated for payment of the draft on the maturity date. By substituting its own credit for that of the borrower, the bank creates a readily marketable instrument that can be discounted in the money market. (See also Chapter 10, Short-Term Borrowing, and Chapter 15, International Cash Management.)

E. Repurchase Agreements

The availability of repurchase agreements (repos) adds considerable liquidity to the government securities market.

1. *Repos* - A **repurchase agreement (repo)** is a transaction between a securities dealer and an investor in which a dealer sells the security to an investor with an agreement to buy the security back from the investor at a specific time and at a price that will result in a predetermined yield to the investor. The investor is providing the dealer short-term funds, while the dealer is providing the investor short-term securities. Repo transactions are done overnight, for a specified number of days, or as a continuing open contract.

2. *Reverse Repos* - In a **reverse repurchase agreement (reverse repo),** a company holding securities in its short-term portfolio sells securities to a dealer with an agreement to buy them back at a specific price at a specific time. The company lends the dealer securities and the dealer lends money to the company. This is essentially a short-term borrowing arrangement where a company uses the securities as collateral for the loan.

3. *Purpose* - The repo mechanism helps the liquidity of the government securities market overall. A repo helps dealers finance their inventory of government securities, and a reverse repo helps dealers borrow the inventory to make deliveries. The repo market itself is highly liquid, and repos offer returns slightly above Treasuries for investors.

4. *Risk* - In a repo transaction the investor takes collateral, but is still exposed to the creditworthiness and business practice of the dealer. If a dealer fails, the investor in a repo could lose the amount invested. Also, the investor must continually monitor the value of the collateral to make sure it does not drop below the value of the repo.

Investors may take collateral in the following ways, in decreasing order of safety:

- Physical delivery of securities to an acceptable custodian.

- Formal acknowledgment by an acceptable custodian that it is holding securities for the investor's account.

- Delivery of a letter from a dealer to an investor stating that collateral is being held for an investor's account.

F. Corporate Obligations

Several types of corporate debt and equity obligations are suitable for short-term investment portfolios.

1. *Commercial Paper* - Commercial paper (CP) is an unsecured promissory note issued for a specific amount to mature in 270 days or less. It is issued by corporations, financial institutions, and other borrowers.

    - Commercial paper may be interest-bearing or discounted; it is usually discounted.

    - Issuers sell CP directly to investors or through dealers. Dealers include securities firms and commercial banks.

    - The issuer's obligation may be backed by a standby letter of credit, which is similar to a guarantee, from a bank or insurance company with a high credit rating.

    - Commercial paper is rated by credit rating agencies based on factors such as liquidity, cash flow potential, earning trends, position in the industry, quality of management, and backup credit facilities.

    - Commercial paper which is unrated is also sold by some dealers. Unrated commercial paper is issued by companies that lack the credit quality required for a rating. Substantially higher yields are available on unrated CP, but the investor incurs greater credit risk and must analyze and follow the issuer's creditworthiness.

2. *Preferred Stock* - Preferred stock is a type of equity instrument that has preference over common stock in its share of a company's earnings and assets. Preferred dividends are paid before common stock dividends can be paid, and like common stock offer a tax advantage to corporate investors. Currently, a corporate investor can exclude 70 percent of stock dividends received from current income as long as the stock is held for at least 46 days.

    Generally, preferred stock is considered a long-term investment, but there are several types of preferred stock which are designed to be suitable for short-term investors. They usually feature some type of adjustment to the stated dividend amount which is expressed as a percentage and is tied to an interest rate index in order to provide a stable price. The most common types of preferred stocks suitable for short-term investments are as follows:

    - *Adjustable-Rate Preferred* - Adjustable-rate preferred stock has a dividend rate that is adjusted quarterly, based on current treasury yields.

    - *Money Market Preferred* - Money market preferred stock, also known as auction-rate preferred, adjusts the dividend rate every 49 days, which is beyond the minimum holding period for the corporate dividend exclusion. The dividend rate adjustment is based on current Treasury yields. Securities dealers are invited by the issuer to bid in a Dutch auction every seven weeks. Existing holders may retain their shares and receive dividends at the new rate.

G. Collateralized Mortgage Obligations

Collateralized Mortgage Obligations (CMOs) are a type of mortgage-backed derivative security. In many cases these securities are backed by federal agency securities issued by the GNMA, FNMA, and the FHLMC. The securities are combined with options and/or futures to provide different types of cash flow streams to an investor. Though many types of CMOs are safe and generally stable investments, some may be highly volatile in a changing interest rate environment.

H. Money Market Mutual Funds

These funds are professionally-managed portfolios of short-term or money market securities with daily withdrawal privileges. Money market mutual funds can provide a company with a professionally-managed marketable securities portfolio at a low management cost. These funds can also be useful in providing a minimum benchmark for judging investment performance. There may be different management fees or service charges depending on the investor's balance, level of activity, or services provided.

V. YIELD

Yield is a measure of what an investment earns, expressed as an annual percentage rate of return. Given the purpose of a short-term investment portfolio, yield can be of secondary importance to liquidity and safety of principal.

A. Factors that Influence Yields

The five factors that explain the major influences on yield among potential investments are maturity and yield curves, marketability, default risk, price risk, and tax status.

1. *Maturity and Yield Curves* - The relationship between market yield and maturity is illustrated by a yield curve, as shown in Exhibit 9.2. A yield curve depicts the differences in yield on securities that are identical except for their dates of maturity.

    - *Normal Yield Curve* - The typical relationship between interest rates and the prices of debt instruments is inverse. As rates rise on current issues, the prices of existing issues fall. The longer the maturity, the greater the risk of a price decline. The most common shape of the yield curve is upward-sloping, reflecting increased risk and return over time.

    - *Inverted Yield Curve* - Long-term yields may be lower than short-term yields when short-term interest rates are expected to fall. Investors buy long-term securities to lock in good long-term yields. This demand drives long-term rates down. At the same time, borrowers, awaiting lower long-term rates in the future, continue to push short-term rates up through short-term borrowing. The resulting downward-sloping yield curve is less common than an upward-sloping yield curve.

EXHIBIT 9.2
*Sample Yield
Curves*

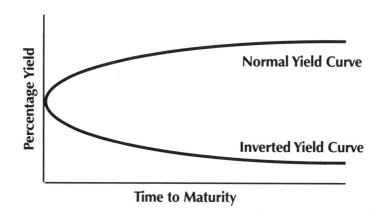

2. *Marketability* - The marketability of securities affects the yield, because investors require a higher yield as compensation for holding securities that are more difficult to sell.

3. *Default Risk* - Investors require higher yield to compensate for the risk that the principal will not be repaid under the original terms. The greater the likelihood of default, the higher the risk premium, and the higher the expected yield. A risk premium is the extra yield above the yield of a risk-free security that investors require as compensation for assuming the additional risk. U.S. government securities are considered to have no default risk, and other short-term securities are evaluated in comparison to them. Credit rating services attempt to quantify relative default risk through evaluation and assignment of credit ratings.

4. *Price Risk* - Price risk is the uncertainty over the price at which a security can be sold prior to maturity and is a function of interest rates. An increase in rates will cause the price to fall. A decrease in the rates will cause the price to rise. Generally, securities with longer maturities are subject to more price risk than similar securities with shorter maturities.

5. *Tax Status* - The tax status of an investment has an impact on its yield.

   • The interest income from obligations of the U.S. government is exempt from state income taxes, while the income from obligations of state and local governments is generally exempt from Federal income taxes. Securities issued by a given state are often exempt from taxes in that state, but may not be exempt from taxes in other states.

   • Tax-exempt securities provide a lower pretax yield than taxable securities of similar maturity and default risk. When comparing taxable and tax-exempt instruments, the tax-exempt yield is usually converted to a taxable equivalent yield as follows:

$$\text{Taxable Equivalent Yield} = \frac{100 \times \text{Tax-Exempt Yield}}{1 - \text{Marginal Tax Rate of Investor}}$$

This taxable equivalent yield can then be used to compare the tax-exempt instrument with other taxable investments. An example of a calculation of taxable equivalent yield is shown in Exhibit 9.3.

EXHIBIT 9.3
Example of Taxable Equivalent Yield Calculation

Assuming a corporate investor's marginal tax rate of 34 percent, the taxable equivalent yield for an investment with a tax-exempt yield of 6 percent is determined as follows.

$$\text{Taxable Equivalent Yield} = \frac{100 \times \text{Tax-Exempt Yield}}{1 - \text{Marginal Tax Rate of Investor}}$$

$$\text{Taxable Equivalent Yield} = \frac{100 \times .06}{1 - .34} = 9.09\%$$

B. Yield Characteristics

Not all rates quoted in the markets are comparable. Investors and borrowers have a problem in comparing all of their financing and investment alternatives because rates for various financial instruments are quoted and priced differently, and interest payments are timed differently.

1. *Interest-Bearing Instruments* - Some instruments, for example, certificates of deposit (CDs), and Eurodollar deposits, pay interest in arrears, or at the end of the financing period and are thus called interest-bearing instruments.

2. *Discount Instruments* - Other instruments, such as Treasury bills and banker's acceptances, are discounted; the investor pays the face value of the instrument minus the interest (the discount) and receives the face value at maturity. The discount is the face value multiplied by the discount rate, times the number of days divided by the year basis (360 or 365).

    • A discount rate understates the yield of an instrument because it is calculated on the face value, whereas yields are computed as a percentage of purchase price.

    • The investor's yield for the investment period is the discount divided by the price paid (the face value minus the discount).

3. *Year Basis* - Most short-term instruments, commercial paper and Treasury bills, for example, pay interest calculated on a 360-day basis. Treasury bonds and Treasury notes pay interest on a 365-day basis.

4. *Nominal Yield* - The quoted yield on an annual basis for most instruments is a simple annual rate, called a nominal yield, and does not reflect compounding.

5. *Money Market Yield* - Money market yield (MMY) is the nominal yield quoted on a 360-day basis.

6. *Bond Equivalent Yield* - Bond equivalent yield (BEY) is the nominal yield quoted on a 365-day basis.

7. *Effective Annual Yield* - The most reliable way to compare all of these instruments is to calculate their **effective annual yields.** Effective annual yields assume compounding and are calculated on a 365-day basis. Because of compounding, effective annual yields are higher than simple annualized yields. By assuming compounding, an effective annual yield assumes that the investor always has the opportunity to reinvest funds at the same rate.

C. Yield-Quoting Conventions

To compare the yields on two different investment instruments, it is often necessary to convert from one yield quoting convention to the other. A simpler way is to convert both to an effective annual yield.

An easy way to remember the different conventions and how they relate to each other is to remember the logic of the sequence above, starting with the discount basis, converting to the simple annualized (but not compounded) money market yield on a 360-day basis, moving to the still non-compounded, bond-equivalent yield calculated on a 365-day basis, and finally moving to the effective annual yield, both compounded and calculated on a 365-day basis. A summary of the yield-quoting conventions is provided in Exhibit 9.4.

EXHIBIT 9.4
Summary of Yield-Quoting Conventions

Yield-Quoting Convention	Characteristics
Nominal Yield	Annualized Not Compounded 360- or 365-Day Basis
Money Market Yield	Annualized Not Compounded 360-Day Basis
Bond Equivalent Yield	Annualized Not Compounded 365-Day Basis
Effective Annual Yield	Annualized Compounded 365-Day Basis

D. Yield Calculations

The following formulas and sample calculations show the relationships among the dollar discount, the discount rate, the purchase price, and the discount rate for a T-bill. The calculation for determining the yield on a commercial paper issue is similar to that of a T-bill.

1. *Purchase Price for a Discounted Instrument* - The dollar discount is equal to the discount rate multiplied by the face or redemption value. This value is then multiplied by the number of days to maturity divided by the appropriate year basis. For T-bills, 360 is used as the year basis.

$$\text{Dollar Discount} = (\text{Discount Rate} \times \text{Face Value}) \times \left(\frac{\text{Days to Maturity}}{360} \right)$$

The Discount Rate on a period basis is equal to the discount divided by the face value. To annualize that rate, divide by the number of days to maturity and multiply by 360.

$$\text{Discount Rate} = \left(\frac{\text{Dollar Discount}}{\text{Face Value}} \right) \times \left(\frac{360}{\text{Days to Maturity}} \right)$$

The Purchase Price is equal to the Face Value minus the Dollar Discount

$$\text{Purchase Price} = \text{Face Value} - \text{Dollar Discount}$$

Examples of the calculation of the purchase price and the discount rate for T-bills are provided in Exhibits 9.5 and 9.6 respectively.

EXHIBIT 9.5
Example of T-Bill Purchase Price Calculation

The purchase price of a 91-day $100,000 T-bill sold at a 7.91% discount rate is calculated as follows:

$$\text{Dollar Discount} = (\text{Discount Rate} \times \text{Face Value}) \times \frac{\text{Days to Maturity}}{360}$$

$$\text{DD} = (\text{DR} \times \text{FV}) \times \frac{\text{DM}}{360}$$

$$= (.0791 \times \$100{,}000) \times \frac{91}{360} = \$1{,}999.47$$

$$\text{Purchase Price} = \text{Face Value} - \text{Dollar Discount}$$

$$\text{PP} = \text{FV} - \text{DD}$$

$$= \$100{,}000 - \$1{,}999.47 = \$98{,}000.53$$

EXHIBIT 9.6
Example of T-Bill Discount Rate Calculation

The discount rate on a 182-day $100,000 T-bill which is currently selling at a price of $95,875.00 is calculated as follows:

Dollar Discount   = Face Value - Purchase Price

$$DD = FV - PP$$

$$= \$100,000 - \$95,875 = \$4,125$$

$$\text{Discount Rate} = \frac{\text{Dollar Discount}}{\text{Face Value}} \times \frac{360}{\text{Days to Maturity}}$$

$$DR = \frac{DD}{FV} \times \frac{360}{DM}$$

$$\text{Discount Rate} = \frac{\$4,125}{\$100,000} \times \frac{360}{182} = 8.16\%$$

2. *Money Market Yield for a Discounted Instrument* - The money market yield (MMY) states the annual yield of a discounted security on a short-term interest-bearing basis with a 360-day year.

$$\text{Money Market Yield} = \left(\frac{\text{Dollar Discount}}{\text{Purchase Price}}\right) \times \left(\frac{360}{\text{Days to Maturity}}\right)$$

This calculation represents a two-step process. The dollar discount divided by the purchase price is the formula for period yield, which is then annualized. A period yield is the effective yield for a particular period such as a week, a month, or a year. A 30-day instrument with a simple annual yield of 12% has a period yield of 1%. An example of this calculation is provided in Exhibit 9.7.

EXHIBIT 9.7
Example of Money Market Yield Calculation

The money market yield of a 91-day $100,000 T-bill sold at a discount rate of 7.91 % as presented in Exhibit 9.5 is calculated as follows:

$$MMY = \frac{\text{Dollar Discount}}{\text{Purchase Price}} \times \frac{360}{\text{Days to Maturity}}$$

$$= \frac{DD}{PP} \times \frac{360}{DM}$$

$$= \frac{\$1,999.47}{\$98,000.53} \times \frac{360}{91} = 8.07\%$$

3. *Converting to Bond Equivalent Yield from a Discount Rate or Money Market Yield -* The following formula and calculation shows how the yield on a discounted security can be converted to the bond equivalent yield (365 days). Note also that there are several ways to calculate the bond equivalent yield.

$$\text{Bond Equivalent Yield} = \left(\frac{\text{Dollar Discount}}{\text{Purchase Price}}\right) \times \left(\frac{365}{\text{Days to Maturity}}\right)$$

or

$$= \text{Money Market Yield} \times \left(\frac{365}{360}\right)$$

or

$$= \frac{365 \times \text{Discount Rate}}{360 - (\text{Discount Rate} \times \text{Days to Maturity})}$$

An example of this calculation is provided in Exhibit 9.8.

EXHIBIT 9.8
Example of Bond Equivalent Yield Calculations

The bond equivalent yield of the previous 91-day $100,000 T-bill example with a 7.91% discount rate is calculated as follows:

$$\text{BEY} = \frac{\text{Dollar Discount}}{\text{Purchase Price}} \times \frac{365}{\text{Days to Maturity}}$$

$$= \frac{D}{PP} \times \frac{365}{DM}$$

$$= \frac{\$1,999.47}{\$98,000.53} \times \frac{365}{91} = 8.18\%$$

or

$$= \text{MMY} \times \frac{365}{360} = 8.07\% \times 1.0139 = 8.18\%$$

or

$$= \frac{365 \times \text{Discount Rate}}{360 - (\text{Discount Rate} \times \text{Days to Maturity})}$$

$$= \frac{365 \times .0791}{360 - (.0791 \times 91)} = 8.18\%$$

4. *Calculation of Commercial Paper Nominal Yield* - The calculation of the yield on commercial paper is similar to that of the BEY for a T-bill. Like T-bills, commercial paper is normally sold on a discount basis, but the nominal yield is calculated using a 365-day basis.

$$\text{Commercial Paper Nominal Yield} = \left(\frac{\text{Dollar Discount}}{\text{Purchase Price}} \right) \times \left(\frac{365}{\text{Days to Maturity}} \right)$$

An example of this calculation is provided in Exhibit 9.9.

EXHIBIT 9.9

Example of Commercial Paper Nominal Yield Calculation

The nominal yield of a 45-day, $100,000 commercial paper issue selling at a price of $98,750 is calculated as follows:

$$\text{Dollar Discount} = \text{Face Value} - \text{Purchase Price}$$

$$D = FV - PP$$

$$= \$100,000 - \$98,750 = \$1,250$$

$$\text{Commercial Paper Nominal Yield} = \frac{\text{Dollar Discount}}{\text{Purchase Price}} \times \frac{365}{\text{Days to Maturity}}$$

$$CPY = \frac{D}{PP} \times \frac{365}{DM}$$

$$= \frac{\$1,250}{\$98,750} \times \frac{365}{45} = 10.27\%$$

---

5. *Algebraic Notation for Yield Equations* - All of the yield formulas presented in this chapter can also be presented in a general algebraic notation format. These formulas are shown in Exhibit 9.10.

EXHIBIT 9.10
Yield Equations in Algebraic Format

The yield equations in this chapter expressed in a general algebraic format are as follows:

$$D = (DR \times FV) \times \left(\frac{DM}{360}\right)$$

$$DR = \left(\frac{D}{FV}\right) \times \left(\frac{360}{DM}\right)$$

$$PP = FV - D$$

$$MMY = \left(\frac{D}{PP}\right) \times \left(\frac{360}{DM}\right)$$

$$BEY = \left(\frac{D}{PP}\right) \times \left(\frac{365}{DM}\right)$$

or

$$BEY = MMY \times \left(\frac{365}{360}\right)$$

or

$$BEY = \frac{365 \times DR}{360 - (DR \times DM)}$$

$$CPY = \left(\frac{D}{PP}\right) \times \left(\frac{365}{DM}\right)$$

Where:
D = Dollar discount
DR = Discount rate
PP = Purchase price
FV = Face value (redemption value)
DM = Days to maturity
MMY = Money Market Yield
BEY = Bond Equivalent Yield
CPY = Commercial Paper Nominal Yield

VI. INVESTMENT STRATEGIES

A short-term investment strategy may be either passive or active, depending on the company's objectives.

A. Passive Strategies

With a passive strategy the investor does minimum decision making and keeps funds liquid at all times. Passive investment strategies are appropriate for companies that want to be assured that their principal is safe, and do not have the resources and risk tolerance to warrant a more active strategy.

- Overnight investment is the most basic passive investment strategy. Funds available (the amount that exceeds the target bank balance) are invested daily in an instrument or a fund that a financial institution manages for overnight investments. Many banks provide this service in the form of a sweep account that automatically transfers excess balances into an interest-earning account. For many companies, sweep accounts represent the primary investment method.

- Companies can carry out their own overnight investment programs by investing in instruments such as repos, Eurodollar time deposits, or commercial paper. Overnight investment programs typically produce the lowest available rates, but they also entail minimal risk and time commitment.

B. Active Strategies

Active investment strategies require the investor to decide regularly how and where short-term funds are to be invested. The more popular active short-term investment strategies include:

1. *Matching* - **Matching** is the purchase of a security with a maturity on the date that funds are required to meet an obligation.

   - The investor can have an incentive to invest for longer periods because in a normal, upward-sloping yield curve environment investing for longer maturities produces higher yields.

   - An accurate forecast of future cash flows is required to ensure that the security can be held to maturity. If cash is required sooner than expected, the security may have to be sold at a loss because of marketability problems or interest rate changes.

   - Because of these risks, companies normally match fund a portion, but not all, of their short-term investment reserves.

2. *Riding the Yield Curve* - In contrast to matching, the investor may choose to ride the yield curve, buying highly liquid and marketable securities such as T-bills that mature on a day different from the day a payment must be made. With such a strategy, the investor aims to take advantage of the current yield curve. There are two ways that this can be done.

   - *Normal Yield Curve/Long Maturity* - With a normal yield curve, longer-term securities offer higher yields. To take advantage of this, the company purchases a security that matures at a time beyond a known cash need. At the time of sale to cover the cash outflow, the security has a shorter maturity than it did when it was purchased. Unless interest rates have risen considerably, the price of the security will be higher when it is sold than when it was purchased. The investor's yield is higher than it would have been with a security maturing on the date cash was needed.

   - *Inverted Yield Curve/Short Maturity* - With an inverted yield curve, shorter-term securities offer higher yields. The investor buys a security that matures before the known cash need, and reinvests the proceeds when it matures. As long as the yield curve does not shift, the investor earns higher rates by rolling over shorter-term investments than on an investment whose maturity matched the time cash was required.

   An example of a riding-the-yield-curve strategy is illustrated in Exhibit 9.11.

EXHIBIT 9.11

Riding the Yield Curve

Assume a company has a cash need in 30 days. The discount rate is 8.0% on T-bills with 30 days to maturity and 8.5% on T-bills with 60 days to maturity:

The bond equivalent yield (BEY) on a matching strategy is:

$$= \left[\frac{365 \times DR}{360 - (\text{Discount Rate} \times \text{Days to Maturity})} \right]$$

$$BEY = \left[\frac{365 \times DR}{360 - (DR \times DM)} \right]$$

$$= \left[\frac{365 \times .08}{360 - (.08 \times 30)} \right] = 8.17\%$$

The bond equivalent yield from riding the yield curve (buying the 60-day T-bill and selling it after 30 days) is:

$$\text{Price Paid} = 100 \times \left[1 - \frac{(\text{Discount Rate} \times \text{Days to Maturity})}{360} \right]$$

$$= 100 \times \left[1 - \frac{(.085 \times 60)}{360} \right] = 98.58$$

$$\text{Sale Price} = 100 \times \left[1 - \frac{(.08 \times 30)}{360} \right] = 99.33$$

$$\text{Bond Equivalent Yield} = \left[\frac{(\text{Sale Price} - \text{Price Paid}) \times 365}{\text{Price Paid} \times \text{Holding Period}} \right]$$

$$= \left[\frac{(99.33 - 98.58) \times 365}{98.58 \times 30} \right] = 9.26\%$$

Note that here the yield has improved by 1.09% or 109 basis points. While no additional default risk has been incurred, reinvestment or interest rate risk has. If the yield curve does not shift over the investment horizon, the company realizes a higher yield than that afforded by other strategies.

On the other hand, riding the yield curve can provide lower yields than matching if market interest rates change during the investment horizon. For example, if interest rates rose during the 30-day investment period so that when the 60-day bill was sold, the 30-day T-bill discount was 9.5%, the yield would be below the yield on the matching strategy. The new sale price and bond equivalent yield are:

$$\text{Sale Price} = 100 \times \left[1 - \frac{(.095 \times 30)}{360} \right] = 99.21$$

$$\text{Bond Equivalent Yield} = \left[\frac{(99.21 - 98.58) \times 365}{98.58 \times 30} \right] = 7.78\%$$

This results in a loss of 0.39% or 39 basis points when compared to a matching strategy.

3.   *Dividend Capture* - Companies may increase the yield on their short-term investment portfolios through a dividend capture or dividend rollover program. Under this type of tax-motivated trading program, a company buys a stock just before the ex-dividend date (the first date on which a new holder of the stock does not receive the last declared dividend). The stock is held for a period long enough to receive the dividend, and at least 46 days to qualify for the 70 percent exclusion from taxable income.

4.   *Swaps* - Swaps are exchanges of securities for other securities of similar credit quality to improve yields. In considering swaps, it is usual for an investment portfolio to have specific guidelines on the amount of securities in each credit quality category and a carefully managed maturity structure.

   For example, the investor analyzes the yield curve to determine the increase in yield that would result from extending a maturity; i.e., selling a security and buying one with similar credit quality but longer maturity. The investor must then determine whether the increased yield justifies assuming the additional market exposure.

   The type of swap explained here is different from interest rate and currency swaps, which are described in Chapter 14, Financial Risk Management.

5.   *Derivatives* - Yields may be enhanced or protected by the use of derivative instruments such as options. Some types of derivatives, however, are speculative in nature and increase the riskiness of an investment. Derivative strategies should be used with caution, and only when all of the risk parameters are fully understood and well communicated within a company. Company investment policies may require that derivatives only be used to hedge an underlying exposure. (See also Chapter 14, Financial Risk Management.)

Questions

These chapter questions are to test and review the information in the text and are not examples of CCM examination questions, nor are they in the examination format.

Answers can be found at the back of the book on p. 325.

1. What are the major purposes of having a short-term investment portfolio?

2. What are some of the factors that influence a company's investment policy?

3. What are the three major areas that influence the acceptability of a financial instrument for inclusion in the short-term investment portfolio?

4. What are the two major categories of financial markets?

5. What is meant by "book entry"?

6. What are the three major U.S. Treasury securities?

7. What are Federal agency securities?

8. What are the two broad categories of municipal securities?

9. What makes municipal securities an attractive investment?

10. What are Eurodollar CDs?

11. When are banker's acceptances used?

12. What is a repo?

13. What is the maximum time-to-maturity for commercial paper?

14. What is money market preferred stock?

15. What are the four factors that influence yield?

16. What is an inverted yield curve?

17. What is the purchase price of a 182-day, $100,000 T-bill sold at a 4.53% discount rate?

18. What is the bond equivalent yield of the T-bill in Question 17?

19. What bank product is frequently used in an overnight investment strategy?

20. What are the major active investment strategies?

21. Why do companies use investment guidelines and how are they determined?

CHAPTER 10

Borrowing

OVERVIEW

This chapter covers borrowing objectives, strategies, and alternatives. It discusses the principal types of borrowing alternatives used by companies and how lines of credit and commercial paper offerings are priced. It also covers the legal considerations and mechanics of borrowing.

LEARNING OBJECTIVES

Upon completion of this chapter and the related study questions, the reader should know:

1. A company's borrowing objectives and strategies.

2. The principal features of borrowing alternatives.

3. How to calculate the all-in cost for lines of credit and commercial paper.

4. The most common provisions of loan agreements.

OUTLINE

I.   **Corporate Borrowing Strategy and Objectives**
     A. Overall Borrowing Strategy
     B. Short-Term Borrowing Objectives

II. **Variables Affecting the Cost of Borrowing**
     A. Loan Pricing
     B. Credit Ratings
     C. Credit Enhancement

III. **Short-Term Borrowing Alternatives**
     A. Line of Credit
     B. Revolving Credit Agreement
     C. Commercial Paper
     D. Banker's Acceptance
     E. Asset-Based Borrowing
     F. Securitization
     G. Loan Sales and Participations
     H. Master Note

I. CORPORATE BORROWING STRATEGY AND OBJECTIVES

A. Overall Borrowing Strategy

For a company to realize its long-term financial objective, it must have access to capital. Capital is made up of debt and equity. Both debt and equity involve a trade-off between risk and return. Debt represents a legal liability of the company to repay a creditor an amount of borrowed funds, while shareholder equity represents an ownership claim in the company made by an investor. The cost of debt is represented by an interest rate; the value of equity is represented by either a stock price or the value of assets. Interest cost is a tax-deductible expense, while the dividends paid on equity shares are not tax-deductible. The acquisition of debt may influence the operation of the company through loan agreement covenants, while shareholders exert control through the exercise of specified voting rights.

Leverage is the relationship between debt and equity in a company's capital structure. The more debt there is, the greater the financial leverage, or the more a company is using borrowed funds. The use of debt represents a means of maximizing shareholder value whenever the return on the project for which the borrowed funds are used exceeds the cost of debt. For this reason, a company's borrowing program is often coordinated with capital budgeting, the process by which a company's management decides on its investment projects.

In formulating a borrowing strategy, management must decide when to assume the liability of debt, for what purpose, from what sources, and at what cost. In addition, it must take into consideration the mix between:

- debt and equity
- short and long-term debt
- fixed and floating-rate debt
- secured and unsecured borrowing
- on- and off-balance sheet financing

One of the challenges for a cash manager is balancing a company's need for short-term financing to cover cash flow shortages and working capital requirements, with a company's need for long-term financing to raise funds for capital projects.

B. Short-Term Borrowing Objectives

On a day-to-day basis, a cash manager is concerned primarily with the short-term borrowing needs of a company. Short-term borrowing objectives include the following:

- *Maintaining Availability of Credit* - This objective involves establishing adequate credit facilities to insure the availability of borrowed funds to meet short-term cash requirements.

- *Optimizing the Cost of Funds* - This objective involves optimizing the overall cost of funds, the major component of which is interest cost.

- *Minimizing Risk* - This objective involves minimizing and balancing the risks of unfavorable interest rate movements and unavailability of debt financing.

- *Maintaining Flexibility* - This objective involves maintaining as much flexibility as possible among alternative sources of borrowed funds available to the company.

II. VARIABLES AFFECTING THE COST OF BORROWING

Money, like any other commodity, has a cost associated with its use. The cost of borrowing is dependent upon the following variables:

A. Loan Pricing

When a company obtains borrowed funds from a financial institution in the form of a loan, the key variable is pricing. The price of borrowed funds is usually expressed in terms of an interest rate. An interest rate is a function of a base rate plus a spread. A spread is an adjustment for risk that is related to the overall creditworthiness of the borrower. The sum of these two components is referred to as the **all-in rate**. Rates can be either fixed or variable. A fixed rate remains unchanged during the term of the debt, while a variable rate is subject to periodic adjustments.

Another factor affecting pricing is the lender's use of either a 360-day or 365-day year basis in the calculation of interest cost. Certain methods of borrowing have traditionally used one year basis over the other.

Lenders may use a variety of **base rates** in determining pricing. Examples of typical base rates are as follows:

1. *Prime Rate* - Traditionally, prime has been the rate at which commercial banks loaned money to their most creditworthy corporate customers. When a company borrows above prime, it is expressed as prime plus a number of **basis points** above prime (e.g., prime + 150 basis points or prime + 1.5 percent).

2. *London Interbank Offered Rate* - The **London Interbank Offered Rate (LIBOR)** is the rate offered by banks in the Eurodollar market for short-term placement of U.S. dollar-denominated funds by other banks. LIBOR is quoted for a full range of short-term maturities including 30, 60, 90, and 180 days. It is the most commonly used base rate for international lending and is used as a base rate for U.S. lending as well.

3. *Other Base Rates* - Other base rates include the U.S. Treasury Bill rate, the Fed funds rate, banker's acceptance rate, the certificate of deposit rate, and even a financial institution's weighted average cost of funds. Companies with top credit ratings can usually negotiate rates at spreads over LIBOR, U.S. Treasuries, or Fed funds, which amount to an effective cost below prime.

B. Credit Ratings

When a company obtains financing from the capital markets in the form of corporate bonds or commercial paper, one of the key variables affecting the cost of borrowing is a company's overall creditworthiness. An indication of this creditworthiness is the credit rating assigned by various rating agencies. Although a credit rating applies to a specific debt issue, it can be a useful tool in assessing a company's overall creditworthiness. Credit agencies rate corporate bonds and commercial paper based on factors such as current earnings, leverage, future prospects of the company, and the amount of collateral assigned to the debt issue in question. Some of the major credit agencies providing these types of ratings are Fitch; Duff & Phelps; Moody's; and Standard & Poor's.

C. Credit Enhancement

Another key variable affecting the cost of borrowing for a company issuing corporate bonds or commercial paper is credit enhancement. **Credit enhancement** is a process in which a third party with a higher credit rating, guarantees the debt obligations of a borrower using such contractual agreements as an indemnity bond or letter of credit. As a result, the borrower's debt assumes the credit rating of the guarantor, which may reduce the borrowing cost or enhance the marketability of the debt to investors.

III. SHORT-TERM BORROWING ALTERNATIVES

Short-term debt instruments mature in less than one year. They are generally used to finance current assets such as accounts receivable and inventory.

A. Line of Credit

A **line of credit** is an agreement between a lender and a borrower in which the borrower has access to funds up to a specified amount during a specific period of time. A line of credit may be used to provide short-term financing, to back up commercial paper, or to provide a liquidity cushion. Some firms with seasonal borrowing requirements have lines of credit in which the maximum amount available varies over the year.

1. *Key Characteristics* - Among the key characteristics of a line of credit are the following:

   • Lines of credit are either uncommitted or committed. Uncommitted lines are usually made available for a one year period and can be canceled at any time by the lender. This line of credit may also be referred to as a money market or demand line of credit. When a committed line is used, there is usually a formal loan agreement with the lender that specifies the terms and conditions under which the credit facility will be available. A committed line of credit typically requires compensation in the form of balances or fees. Under a committed facility, the lender is obligated to provide funding up to the credit limit stipulated in the agreement as long as the borrower is not in default.

- Borrowing against the line is commonly in the form of notes or advances drawn for varying short-term maturities (i.e., overnight, seven days, 60 days, etc.).

- Lines of credit may be unsecured or secured. Secured lines require the borrower to pledge some form of collateral.

- To assure the lender that the line is not being used as a permanent source of financing, a cleanup period of 30 to 60 days is sometimes required. No outstanding borrowings are allowed during the agreed upon cleanup period. This requirement has become less common in recent years.

2. *Effective Rate for a Line of Credit* - Line of credit pricing is negotiated between the parties. The lender may take into account other aspects of the overall lender/borrower relationship in pricing the line. There are three basic pricing components to lines of credit:

   - *All-in Rate* - This rate consists of a risk spread that is added to a **base rate** such as prime, the Fed funds rate, or LIBOR. This rate is normally variable and will adjust in relation to changes in the base rate.

   - *Commitment Fee* - For committed lines, the lender charges a percentage fee, either on the total amount of the commitment or on the unused portion of the commitment. Payment is usually made quarterly. Fees vary, depending on the creditworthiness of the firm, the stated purpose of the line, and the term of the line.

   - *Compensating Balances* - Some lenders also require compensating balances, though this practice has become less common in recent years. In a compensating balance arrangement, the balance requirement can be specified as a percentage of the total commitment, the unused amount of the commitment, or outstanding loan amount. If **compensating balances** are required, their effect is to reduce the amount of the funds that can be used by the borrower, thereby increasing the effective annual interest rate.

To compute the effective borrowing rate for a line of credit, the following formula is used:

$$\text{Effective Annual Borrowing Rate} = \left(\frac{\text{Total Interest Paid} + \text{Total Fees Paid}}{\text{Average Usable Loan}} \right) \times \left(\frac{365}{\text{\# of Days Loan is Outstanding}} \right)$$

Where:
- Total Interest Paid is calculated as the all-in rate times the average loan amount outstanding.
- Total Fees Paid include all commitment fees, placement fees, and any issuance costs.
- Average Usable Loan is the net amount of borrowed funds available after any prepaid interest and/or compensating balances are deducted.
- Number of Days Loan is Outstanding is the effective term of the loan or the time over which the funds are borrowed.

This formula can also be represented in an algebraic format as follows:

$$i = \left(\frac{I+F}{L}\right) \times \left(\frac{365}{t}\right)$$

Where:

i = The effective annual borrowing rate

I = Total interest paid (in dollars)

F = Total fees paid

L = Average usable loan

t = Number of days loan is outstanding

An example of this calculation is provided in Exhibit 10.1.

EXHIBIT 10.1

Effective Annual Borrowing Rate Calculation

1. A company has an average loan outstanding of $1,000,000.
2. The total line of credit is a commitment for $3,000,000.
3. The lender requires no compensating balances.
4. The commitment fee is 0.25% based on the unused portion of the line.
5. The interest rate charged is set annually with a spread of 2% over prime. Prime is assumed to be 8%.
6. Year basis used is 365.

The effective annual borrowing rate is:

$$\text{Effective Annual Borrowing Rate} = \left(\frac{(.10 \times \$1,000,000) + (.0025 \times \$2,000,000)}{\$1,000,000}\right) \times \left(\frac{365}{365}\right)$$

$$= \left(\frac{\$100,000 + \$5000}{\$1,000,000}\right) \times (1) = 10.5\%$$

The effect of the commitment fee in this example adds 50 basis points to the interest rate of 10%. Had there been compensating balance requirements, the average amount of compensating balances would have been subtracted from the amount of funds in the denominator to determine the amount of the usable funds.

B. Revolving Credit Agreement

A **revolving credit agreement** is a facility which allows the borrower to borrow, repay, and reborrow up to a defined amount. Revolving credits are contractual commitments with loan agreements, including covenants. Usually there is a commitment fee on the unused portion, as well as a facility fee.

C. Commercial Paper

Commercial paper (CP) is an unsecured promissory note issued by companies for a specific amount, with maturities ranging from overnight to 270 days. Limiting the maturity of commercial paper avoids the Securities and Exchange Commission (SEC) registration requirement for securities whose maturities exceed 270 days.

The following are key characteristics of commercial paper:

1. *Rate* - Commercial paper is generally issued on a discount basis, similar to T-bills. The actual rate paid by a company is market-based and is a function of the issuing company's credit rating, size of the issue, and general short-term interest rates. Companies with the highest credit rating can usually raise funds by issuing commercial paper at a lower effective rate than borrowing against a commercial bank line of credit. When commercial paper is issued, there are underwriting or agency fees and charges related to a back-up line of credit, but these are usually small relative to the size of the CP issue. In contrast, a financial institution that makes a loan and keeps that loan on its balance sheet must also factor in administrative costs and capital requirements as part of the interest rate charged to the borrower.

2. *Distribution* - Commercial paper is usually sold through dealers, either investment banking firms or commercial banks. Some companies sell commercial paper directly to investors.

3. *Back-up Lines of Credit* - Some commercial paper borrowers arrange backup lines of credit that may be used if market conditions are not conducive to issuing or refinancing commercial paper. Another alternative to a backup line is to obtain a bank standby letter of credit.

4. *Credit Rating* - Commercial paper of a specific issuer can be rated by the major credit rating agencies.

5. *Effective Cost for Commercial Paper* - The effective cost for commercial paper needs to take into account the discount rate, the dealer fee, and, in some cases, the cost of a backup line or letter of credit. An example of this calculation is provided in Exhibit 10.2.

EXHIBIT 10.2
Effective Cost for Commercial Paper Calculation

1. A company is issuing $20,000,000 of commercial paper with a 30-day maturity at a discount rate of 8%.
2. The paper is sold through a dealer at an annual charge of 1/8 of 1%.
3. The company has a backup line of credit in the amount of $20,000,000, and pays an annual commitment fee of 0.25% on the line.
4. Since this commercial paper is sold at a discount, the company will receive only $20,000,000 less 30 days worth of interest at 8%. The amount of usable funds is:

$$\text{Usable Funds} = \text{Face Value} \times \left[1 - \left(\text{Discount Rate} \times \frac{\text{Maturity}}{360} \right) \right]$$

$$= \$20,000,000 \times \left[1 - \left(.08 \times \frac{30}{360} \right) \right] = \$19,866,667$$

(Continued)

EXHIBIT 10.2

*Effective Cost
for Commercial
Paper
Calculation
(Continued)*

(Note that the maturity is divided by 360, following the U.S. convention for this instrument.)

The interest cost is the difference between the face value of $20,000,000 and the funds received, $19,866,667, which equals $133,333.

The dealer cost and annual cost of the backup line of credit are calculated as:

$$\text{Pro-Rated Dealer Cost} = (\text{Annual Dealer Charge x Face Value}) \times \left(\frac{\text{Maturity}}{360}\right)$$

$$= (.00125 \times \$20,000,000) \times \left(\frac{30}{360}\right) = \$2,083$$

$$\text{Annual Backup Credit Line Cost} = (\text{Commitment Fee Rate} \times \text{Face Value})$$

$$= (.0025 \times \$20,000,000) = \$50,000$$

$$\text{Pro-Rate Backup Credit Line Cost} = (\text{Annual Credit Line Cost}) \times \left(\frac{\text{Maturity}}{360}\right)$$

$$= (\$50,000) \times \left(\frac{30}{360}\right) = \$4,167$$

Most commercial paper users issue new commercial paper on a fairly continuous basis, so the pro-rated figures for both the dealer cost and the cost of the back-up line of credit are the most appropriate in determining total issue costs.

Total Issue Costs = Interest Cost + Pro-Rated Dealer Cost + Pro-Rated Backup Credit Line Costs

or $133,333 + $2,083 + $4,167 = $139,583

The effective annual interest cost is determined by dividing the total costs by the amount of usable funds and annualizing this rate. The effective annual cost of the issue to the company is:

$$\text{Effective Annual Cost of Issue} = \left(\frac{\text{Total Issue Costs}}{\text{Usable Funds}}\right) \times \left(\frac{365}{\text{Maturity}}\right)$$

$$= \left(\frac{\$139,583}{\$19,866,667}\right) \times \left(\frac{365}{30}\right) = 8.55\%$$

D. Banker's Acceptance

A **banker's acceptance** (BA) is a negotiated short-term instrument used primarily to finance the import, export or domestic shipment of goods or the storage of readily marketable staples. BA financing has the following characteristics:

- A debt obligation is evidenced by a time draft drawn by the borrower that is then accepted by the bank on which it is drawn. By accepting the draft, the bank becomes directly obligated for payment of the draft on the maturity date.

- By substituting its own credit for that of the borrower, the bank creates a readily marketable instrument that can be discounted in the money market. The discounted proceeds are advanced to the borrower who is obligated to pay the full draft amount to the accepting bank at maturity. The accepting bank is, in turn, obligated to pay the investor who purchased the BA.

- The all-in rate for acceptance financing includes the discount rate plus the BA commission. This often compares favorably with other short-term borrowing rates. (See also Chapter 15, International Cash Management.)

- Acceptance financing is often provided to a buyer or seller in connection with a letter of credit, but acceptances can be created to finance open account transactions as well.

E. Asset-Based Borrowing

Some financial institutions specialize in a form of secured lending based on the pledging of accounts receivable and inventory as collateral for a loan. The following are examples of asset-based borrowing:

1. *Accounts Receivable* - Accounts receivable represent the most common form of asset-based borrowing.

    - In the case of accounts receivable financing, the lender evaluates the type of customers who buy from the borrower by analyzing the volume of customer purchases, delinquency rates, and the level of bad debt write-offs. The lender also monitors the borrower's accounts receivable aging schedule to determine the timeliness of customer payments.

    - As a result of this evaluation, an advance rate is determined. The advance rate is stated as a percentage of accounts receivable outstanding. This percentage, when applied to the amount of pledged accounts receivable, determines the maximum amount that can be borrowed. For example, a lender may restrict a borrower's loan amount to 80 percent of their accounts receivable.

    - Sometimes the lender requires the borrower's customers to remit payments directly to the lender. These payments are then applied to the outstanding loan balance.

2. *Inventory* - Inventory represents the other most common form of asset-based borrowing.

    - As with accounts receivable financing, borrowing is limited by the advance rate and is calculated as a percentage of inventory. In determining the advance rate, the lender has to take into consideration the risk that the borrower will not be able to sell the inventory for reasons such as fluctuating market conditions, changes in commodity prices, spoilage, or obsolescence.

    - Generally, inventory lenders are more willing to advance against finished goods rather than work in process. They may also be willing to lend against raw materials. Sometimes different advance rates are determined for these different types of inventories.

3. *Factoring* - Factoring is the sale of or transfer of title to accounts receivable to a third party (factor). A factor is a financing institution that discounts acceptable

accounts receivable with or without recourse to the borrower.

- In some cases, the borrower's customers are notified to remit their payments directly to the factor. For this service, the factor charges a percentage commission on the amount of receivables discounted.

- The borrower may collect funds from the factor on the average due date, or pay additional financing charges for earlier funding.

4. *Floor Planning* - This type of financing is used frequently to support the inventory of dealers who specialize in high cost durable goods such as automobiles, trucks, farm equipment, and major appliances. The lender advances funds to the manufacturer to pay for the dealer's inventory purchases. To secure the amount owed to it by the dealer, the lender will retain legal title to the goods until they are sold. The proceeds from the sale are then used to repay the loan.

F. Securitization

Securitization is a financing technique in which a company issues debt securities backed by a pool of selected financial assets such as mortgages, auto loans, credit card receivables, or equipment leases. Assets suitable for debt securitization have the following characteristics:

- Provide a predictable cash flow stream required to pay off the securities.

- Have a low level of historical loss experience.

Securitization is a type of off-balance sheet financing. Neither the debt nor the assets securing the financing appear on a company's balance sheet. By removing debt financing from the balance sheet, securitization improves a company's financial structure.

Sometimes securitized issues are credit enhanced. These issues usually receive a higher credit rating. Among typical methods of credit enhancement are the following types:

- Over-collateralization by selling assets that have a higher present value than that of the securities.

- A letter of credit from a financial institution with a higher credit rating than the company issuing the securities.

- A spread account, which is a reserve built from an excess of cash flow from underlying assets over cash flow required for debt service.

- Recourse to the issuer should the securitized assets not provide the projected cash flow to pay off the debt.

G. Loan Sales and Participations

Among the key characteristics of loan sales and participations are the following:

- In a loan sale program, a lender makes a loan and sells all or a part of that loan to investors. The lender may sell the loan at a spread below the rate paid by the borrower. For example, the borrower may pay the lender eight percent and the lender may sell the loan to the investors at a 7-7/8 percent yield. A loan sale program can be a useful funding source for a company with financing needs that cannot justify or qualify for a commercial paper program.

- In a participation, a loan commitment is made by more than one lender. Loan advances and payments are then divided between the participants on a pro-rata basis. Loan servicing is usually provided by one of the participants, called the lead bank or agent.

H. Master Note

This type of borrowing is between highly rated companies and the trust departments of financial institutions. The borrowing company creates a note with a maturity of two or three years. It specifies a maximum and a minimum amount that the trust department will lend to the company. The pricing is often set at a small spread above the company's commercial paper rate. The amount loaned and the rate are set and confirmed on a daily basis.

I. Trade Credit

Trade credit is a financing tool that is created when a company is granted credit terms on its purchases from its vendors. The most common form is an open account in which the buyer (i.e., borrower) is generally given a specified period of time to pay for goods or services purchased from a supplier (i.e., the creditor). Trade credit can be an important part of a company's overall financing strategy. (See also Chapter 5, Credit and Accounts Receivable Management.)

J. Export Financing Programs

Export and import financing is available from both commercial lenders and through various programs offered by the Export Import Bank of the United States (Eximbank). (See also Chapter 15, International Cash Management.)

IV. MEDIUM- AND LONG-TERM BORROWING ALTERNATIVES

From an accounting perspective, anything maturing beyond one year is considered long-term. For the purposes of borrowing, however, a distinction is made between medium- and long-term debt. Medium-term debt is generally considered to mature between two and 10 years from the date of issuance. Long-term debt typically has a maturity of more than ten years.

A. Medium-Term Notes

Medium-term notes are a form of debt and are usually sold in two- to ten-year maturities. Many companies are increasingly using medium-term notes to finance their debt.

B. Bonds

A bond is an interest-bearing or discount certificate of debt that obligates the issuer to repay the face amount of the bond plus interest.

Bonds have the following components or characteristics:

- A bond indenture is an agreement among all the parties to a bond issue. It defines details of the issue such as terms and conditions, covenants, events of default, subordination, sinking fund, property to be pledged, if any, and the duties of the trustee.

- Bonds are administered through a trustee. The trustee is responsible for ensuring that the bonds are authentic, ensuring that sinking fund and interest payments are properly paid and applied, and administering redemption. In the event of default, the trustee represents the bondholders in legal proceedings.

- Bonds are rated by a number of services according to factors such as the financial strength and future prospects of the company and the amount of security assigned to the bond. The ratings apply to the bonds themselves, not the company.

- Bonds are usually traded publicly through securities dealers and securities exchanges, but may also be sold directly to institutional investors.

- Bonds may be either secured or unsecured. Secured bonds are collateralized by a specific asset or revenues from a specific project. Secured debt gives the investor a lien against a corporate asset. Bonds may be secured by various assets including inventories, real estate, or fixed (capital) assets. Unsecured bonds, called debentures, offer no collateral. Debenture holders have a general claim against a company but not against a specific asset.

- Bonds are either senior or subordinated in relation to other debt obligations. Holders of senior bonds have first claim on the assets of a company in the event of liquidation. Relative to senior debt, all other debt is subordinated or junior. The more junior the debt, the greater the risks and subsequent borrowing costs to a company.

- A subordinated debenture is an unsecured bond on which payment to the holder will take place only after the senior debt has been fully paid, in the event of corporate liquidation. In the event of liquidation, holders of secured debt, whether senior or junior, will be paid off before holders of unsecured debt. Then senior unsecured debt holders will be paid out before the subordinated debenture holders.

- A call feature on a bond allows the issuer to retire the security before maturity. Bondholders must sell the security back to the company at par (face value) or a predetermined premium over face value. A call provision is often useful for the issuer if there is a good possibility that interest rates will fall during the life of the bond. The firm can call the bond and refinance with less expensive debt.

C. Special Types of Bonds

Examples of special types of bonds are as follows:

1. *Municipal Bonds* - Municipal bonds are bonds issued by a state or local government entity. Interest earned on municipal bonds is generally not taxable by the U.S. government or the jurisdiction that issued it, which can make them very attractive to certain investors.

2. *Industrial Revenue Bonds* - **Industrial Revenue Bonds** (IRB) are a special classification of municipal bonds issued by a government entity often for the purpose of financing specific projects that it or a private company manages.

3. *Junk Bonds* - Junk bonds are high-yield, below investment grade securities. Junk bonds are high risk because they are typically issued by companies which are already highly leveraged.

4. *Zero-Coupon Bonds* - These are bonds which make no periodic interest payments, but only a single payment of face value at maturity. Due to this single payment feature, they are generally sold at deep discount from their face value.

5. *Eurobonds* - **Eurobonds** are bonds issued outside the country where the currency of those bonds is domiciled. For example, dollar-denominated Eurobonds are bonds issued in U.S. dollars outside the U. S.

6. *Foreign Bonds* - Foreign bonds are issued in the country of their currency by nonresidents of that country. Foreign bonds, which are issued in currencies other than an issuer's principal operating or functional one, are used to finance the issuer's international operations.

D. Debt-Equity Hybrids

Debt-equity hybrids have both debt and equity characteristics. The following are types of debt-equity hybrids:

-   *Convertible Bonds* - **Convertible bonds** are bonds that are convertible into shares of a company's common stock at a defined price. They provide the borrower with a lower interest rate than non-convertible bonds because of the equity potential.

-   *Equity Warrant* - An **equity warrant** is a long-term option to buy a stated number of shares of stock at a specified price (exercise price). At the time of their issuance, warrants usually have an exercise price greater than the then current market price of the stock. They may be purchased separately in the open market, but are generally part of a debt or preferred stock issue and are included to make the security issue more attractive. The value of a warrant moves in relation to the value of the underlying stock.

E. Term Loan

Term loans are made for a fixed period of time, typically two to ten years, usually to support equipment purchases and more permanent capital financing. Repayment schedules vary depending on the type of loan and the nature of the project being financed. Some repayment schedules require periodic interest payments with repayment of principal upon maturity. Others allow the borrower to repay and reborrow as is the case in a revolving credit line.

F. Leasing

Leasing is an alternative to term lending and is used extensively as a means of financing equipment. Among the characteristics of leasing are the following:

-   In a typical leasing arrangement, the lessor actually owns the equipment and is leasing it to a lessee.

-   In leasing, typically 100 percent of the equipment's cost is financed, and payment amounts can be fixed or variable.

- A leasing arrangement can be structured as either on- or off-balance-sheet. On-balance-sheet is referred to as a capital lease; off-balance-sheet is referred to as an operating lease. Accounting and tax issues must be evaluated to determine a lease's proper classification.

- Leasing offers tax advantages to both parties. The lessor realizes the benefit of depreciation, and the lessee has tax deductible operating expenses.

- There are different end-of-term options, some of which might allow the lessee to return, purchase, or re-lease the equipment.

G. Private Placement

A private placement is a direct sale of securities by a company to institutional investors such as insurance companies or pension funds. Private placements have the following characteristics:

- Private placement securities are not registered with the Securities and Exchange Commission (SEC).

- Terms and conditions are spelled out in an agreement called a note-purchase agreement.

- A private placement can be arranged by an investment lending firm, a commercial bank, or the borrower.

- Private placements are usually less costly for the issuer to arrange than publicly issued debt, and may offer longer and more flexible terms than commercial bank term loans.

V. REPAYMENT OF PRINCIPAL

Corporate debt can be structured to allow for any schedule of principal and interest payments. In general, the repayment of debt should reflect the cash flows related to the underlying asset or project being financed.

The two most common methods of debt repayment are as follows:

A. Amortization

Amortization is the repayment of the loan principal in installments over the life of the loan. Among the characteristics and options of amortization schedules are the following:

- Many loans are amortized over their life to require the borrower to pay off the principal gradually, rather than at one point in time. This reduces the lender's risk by shortening the amount of time the principal is outstanding.

- An amortization schedule may be matched to the cash flows expected from the project or equipment being financed. Amortization schedules may also vary depending on the type and maturity of the loan.

- Some schedules provide for equal installments over the life of the loan, and others (e.g., mortgages) have equal payments incorporating both principal and interest over the life of the loan.

- Some schedules allow a **grace period** where the repayment of principal does not begin until some specified future date. For example, an eight-year loan with a two-year grace period would mean that principal payments would not commence until the third year of the loan.

- Some schedules have **balloon payments** where the majority of the principal balance is due in the final years of the loan term. For example, a 10-year loan may require that only 10 percent of the principal amount be amortized over the first five years of the loan. The remaining 90 percent balloon payments would then have to be amortized over the final five years or be refinanced.

- Some schedules have **bullet payment maturities** in which the entire principal is due on the final maturity date.

B. Sinking Fund

A **sinking fund** is used to insure that adequate funds are available to pay a bond issue at its maturity. Periodic payments are accumulated in a separate custodial account that is used to redeem the securities. A sinking fund assures investors that adequate funds are available to meet payments at maturity.

VI. LEGAL ASPECTS OF BORROWING

A. Loan Agreements

Among the primary components of a loan agreement as follows:

1. *Covenants* - **Covenants** are provisions in loan agreements that restrict the borrower's activities in ways that protect the lender during the term of the agreement. Examples of covenants in loan agreements include the following:

   - *Financial Ratios*
     * Maximum debt to equity ratio
     * Minimum interest coverage ratio
     * Minimum net worth
     * Minimum current ratio or working capital

   - *Borrower Limitations*
     * Limitations on capital expenditures
     * Limitations on incurring other debt or lease obligations
     * Limitations on payment of dividends
     * Limitations on mergers and acquisitions
     * Limitations on sale or pledge of assets
     * Limitations on stock or debt repurchase

- *Borrower Obligations*
    * Requirement to properly and environmentally maintain properties
    * Requirement to maintain adequate insurance coverage

2. *Events of Default* - Among the characteristics of events of default are the following:

    - Default includes such events as non-payment of interest or principal when due, material adverse changes in the condition of the borrower, and violation of specified covenants.

    - An event of default allows the lender to demand payment of the outstanding debt prior to its maturity, to terminate the agreement, or both.

    - The agreement may specify a time period in which a covenant violation may be corrected before it results in an event of default.

    - Waivers of covenant violations or events of default may be negotiated and granted at the lender's discretion.

3. *Representations and Warranties* - Among characteristics of representations and warranties are the following:

    - Representations and warranties typically refer to the conditions that must exist before and at the time the loan agreement is executed.

    - They include the valid legal existence of the borrowing corporation, a resolution by the borrower's board of directors authorizing the borrowing, and the authority of the corporate officers signing the loan agreement.

    - They may include a requirement that the company is in compliance with Employee Retirement Income and Security Act (ERISA), and an indemnity protecting the lender from environmental liabilities. In such instances, the requirement of indemnity may appear either as a covenant or a representation and warranty.

B. Promissory Notes

Promissory notes are often used for borrowings under lines of credit. A promissory note is an unconditional promise to pay a specified amount plus interest at a specified rate either on demand or on a certain date. A promissory note can be issued for each individual borrowing or for a total line against which multiple borrowings are made.

A **grid note** is a type of promissory note used to simplify the paperwork connected with the loans. A company signs one comprehensive promissory note for the total amount of the line of credit. Any loans or repayments under the terms of the note are simply recorded on the note as a way of monitoring the current amount of debt outstanding.

Questions

These chapter questions are to test and review the information in the text and are not examples of CCM examination questions, nor are they in the examination format.

Answers can be found at the back of the book on p. 327.

1. What are the major objectives of a company's borrowing program?

2. What is LIBOR?

3. What is credit enhancement?

4. What is a committed line of credit?

5. A firm has an average loan outstanding of $200,000 on a $500,000 line of credit. There is a commitment fee of 0.25% on the unused portion of the line, and the interest rate on the borrowed funds is 7.0%. If there is no compensating balances requirement, what is the effective annual interest cost of the loan?

6. How are lines of credit used in conjunction with commercial paper?

7. A company issues $1,000,000 of commercial paper with a 60-day maturity at a discount rate of 6%. The paper is sold through a dealer for a charge of 1/4 of 1%. There is no backup line of credit. What is the effective annual percentage cost of issuing the commercial paper?

8. What is a loan participation?

9. What are the two characteristics which show that an asset is suitable for securitization?

10. What is a bond indenture?

11. What is the difference between an operating lease and a capital lease?

12. What is a sinking fund?

13. Why will a company issue convertible bonds?

14. What may the lender do if a default occurs?

CHAPTER 11

Information and Technology Management

OVERVIEW

This chapter introduces the reader to the basics of information technology as it is used by cash managers to perform a variety of daily tasks. It covers the objectives of information management, the different types of internal and external data sources and their applications, the different kinds of technology that are available, and the security, database management, and disaster recovery issues involved with the use of **Treasury Management Information Systems** (TMIS) technology.

LEARNING OBJECTIVES

Upon completion of this chapter and the related study questions, the reader should know:

1.   The objectives of daily cash management.

2.   The TMIS processing tasks and timeframes.

3.   The different sources and uses of both internal and external TMIS data.

4.   The basic levels of TMIS technology.

5.   Examples of advanced TMIS technology and their capabilities.

6.   The benefits and costs of TMIS technology.

7.   Database management, security, and disaster recovery issues involved with information management.

OUTLINE

I.   **Objectives of Information Management**

II.   **TMIS Processing: Tasks and Timeframes**
   A. Processing Tasks
   B. Processing Timeframes

III. **TMIS Internal Data: Sources and Uses**
   A. Internal Sources of TMIS Data

      B. Types of Internal Data

      C. Uses of Internal Data

  IV. **TMIS External Data: Sources and Uses**

      A. External Sources of TMIS Data

      B. Types of External Data

      C. Multi-Bank Reporting

      D. Uses of External Data

      E. External Information Formats

  V. **Reporting Mechanisms**

  VI. **Treasury Workstations**

      A. Concepts

      B. Capabilities

      C. Modules

  VII. **Information Reporting Systems**

      A. Concepts

      B. Capabilities

      C. Modules

  VIII. **Transaction Initiation**

      A. Types of Transactions

      B. Mechanisms

  IX. **TMIS Benefits and Costs**

  X. **TMIS Security**

      A. Database Management Issues

      B. Security Risks

      C. Security Safeguards

      D. Disaster Recovery Issues

I. OBJECTIVES OF INFORMATION MANAGEMENT

Cash management is information management. One of the key responsibilities of a cash manager is to prepare a daily cash position. This task requires access to timely and accurate information on the following:

- bank balances (ledger, collected, available)

- cash inflows (collections and concentration)

- cash outflows (disbursements)

- maturity status of short-term investments

- maturity status of short-term debt

A cash manager obtains this information from a variety of internal and external sources. Internal sources may include other areas of the company such as sales, purchasing, credit, accounts receivable, accounts payable, and accounting. External sources include financial institutions and third-party information providers.

The objectives of daily cash management are as follows:

- *Determine Cash Requirements* - A **daily cash position** assists a cash manager in determining a company's cash needs. If additional cash is required to meet short-term obligations, it may be necessary to access lines of credit or sell marketable securities. If excess cash is available, it may be invested.

- *Track Activity* - As part of preparing a daily cash position, a cash manager obtains information about a wide variety of individual transactions such as incoming and outgoing wire transfers, the collection of large accounts receivable, the clearing of large disbursement items, and Automated Clearing House (ACH) credits and debits. This information is often used to identify exception items, resolve problems, and monitor internal or external fraud.

- *Identify Opportunities* - A daily cash position enables a cash manager to take advantage of trade payment, investment, and debt repayment opportunities.

- *Update Forecasts* - A daily cash position enables a cash manager to compare forecasted cash flows to actual cash flows. These variances are used to update forecasts. As part of this process, a cash manager may also adjust target or compensating balances at financial institutions.

- *Update Management Information* - Because the daily cash position represents financial data that is compiled from a wide range of sources, it also is often used to update management information such as performance measurements, long-term forecasting, and budget analysis. However, while management information is gathered daily, it is usually reported weekly, monthly, or quarterly, depending on the size and needs of the company.

While the uses of information and technology in the treasury function involve more than just the preparation of a cash position, it is this daily activity which has been the driving force behind the development of **Treasury Management Information System** (TMIS) technologies.

II. TMIS PROCESSING: TASKS AND TIMEFRAMES

A. Processing Tasks

Typical of the TMIS tasks which a cash manager performs on a daily basis are the following:

- Obtain account balances and transaction detail from external sources
- Obtain from appropriate sources internal information that impacts the cash flow timeline
- Consolidate the external and internal information into the cash position worksheet
- Integrate data on current day transfers and large transactions
- Determine cash position
- Initiate transfers
- Execute investment and/or borrowing decisions
- Update the cash position worksheet and the short-term cash forecast

B. Processing Timeframes

The timeframes for treasury reporting vary depending on the type of industry, the size of the company, and the degree to which management relies on financial information for decision-making. The following are examples of different timeframes and reports:

- Daily - Cash position
- Weekly - Short-term cash forecast
- Monthly - Account analysis summary
- Quarterly - Investment and debt maturity schedule
- Annually - Bank relationship review

III. TMIS INTERNAL DATA: SOURCES AND USES

A. Internal Sources of TMIS Data

One of the ways to view the treasury function is as a clearing house for financial information. In this role, a cash manager is responsible for:

- compiling information from a wide range of internal and external sources
- sorting, storing, and analyzing this information
- reporting information to management

In performing the task of compiling internal information, a cash manager must communicate with other areas of the company such as sales, purchasing, credit, accounts receivable, accounts payable, payroll, and accounting. The method of communication with these other areas is increasingly electronic in that information is stored, edited, shared, and retrieved using compatible computer systems connected through either a local area network (LAN) or a wide area network (WAN).

B. Types of Internal Data

Examples of the kind of internal information that is exchanged between treasury and other areas of the company are the following:

- *Sales Summary Reports* - Information on weekly or monthly sales, both actual and projected
- *Purchase Summary Reports* - Information on weekly or monthly purchases, both actual and projected
- *Cash Receipt and Disbursement Forecast* - Information on actual and anticipated collections and disbursements
- *Aging Schedules* - Information on the aggregate status of accounts receivable, as well as information on large individual collection items which are outstanding
- *Investment Schedules* - Information on the sale and purchase of short-term investments
- *Debt Repayment Schedules* - Information on the issuance and repayment of short-term borrowings

C. Uses of Internal Data

Among the accounting and planning uses of internal data are the following:

- *Preparation of a Cash Journal* - The recording of individual debits and credits
- *Updating General Ledger* - The posting of transactions to their proper accounts
- *Cash Forecasting* - The preparation of forecasts
- *Funds Flow Between Operating Units* - The tracking of cash flows between different operating units of a company or between different subsidiaries of a parent company
- *Monthly Budget Analysis* - The comparison of planned to actual, including variances

IV. TMIS EXTERNAL DATA: SOURCES AND USES

A. External Sources of TMIS Data

On a day-to-day basis, a cash manager needs information from external as well as internal information sources. The primary external information sources are a company's financial institutions.

B. Types of External Data

Information gathered from external sources falls into one of two categories as follows:

1. *Prior Day and Historical Information* - Examples of prior day and historical information are as follows:

   - *Balance and Transaction Activity* - Information on current ledger and collected balances, one and two-day float, debit and credit detail, and adjustment items (average balances and a balance history may also be reported)
   - *Target Balance Activity* - Information on the status of **target balances**
   - *Investment and Borrowing Activity* - Information on investment purchases and sales, as well as loan drawdowns and repayments
   - *International Transaction Activity* - Information on international wire transfers, drafts, letters of credit, and foreign exchange transactions
   - *Custody Activity* - Information on securities safekeeping and approaching maturities
   - *Check Inquiry* - Information on the clearing status of individual items that have been issued
   - *Stop Payment Activity* - Information on the status of stop payment requests

2. *Current Day Information* - Examples of current day information are as follows:

   - *Lockbox Deposits* - Information on lockbox deposits as well a float breakdown of the deposits
   - *Controlled Disbursement* - Information on the amount of check clearings that need to be funded

- *Cash Concentration Reports* - Electronic Depository Transfer (EDT) activity and exception reports, such as identifying sending locations that have not reported daily deposits (may also be available on prior day reports)

- *Wire Transfers* - Information on both incoming and outgoing wire transfers

- *ACH Transactions* - Information on ACH debits and credits

- *Money Market and Foreign Exchange Rates* - Information on same day market activity for purposes of investment, borrowing, and foreign currency exchange

C. Multi-Bank Reporting

Multi-bank reporting is a service used by companies with two or more banking relationships. An arrangement is established by which one of the company's financial institutions or a third party reporting service gathers and consolidates the account balances and transaction activity from each of the company's financial institutions. The method by which multi-bank reporting is gathered is commonly referred to as **data exchange**.

D. Uses of External Data

The uses of external data vary depending whether or not it is for an immediate purpose or for other reasons. Examples of different uses for the same data are shown in Exhibit 11.1.

EXHIBIT 11.1
Uses of External Data

Type of Information Accessed	Immediate Uses	Other Uses
Lockbox Detail	Update Accounts Receivable	Verify Transactions
Concentration Bank Deposits	Initiate Transfers	Update Cash Scheduling
Controlled Disbursement	Fund Accounts	Manage Disbursement Float
Transaction Detail	Track Individual Debits and Credits	Detect Internal or External Fraud
Short-Term Investments	Access Daily Market Information	Review Investment Strategy
Short-Term Borrowing	Initiate Line of Credit Drawdown	Update Cash Forecasting
Account Analysis	Monitor Target Balances	Monitor Bank Pricing

E. External Information Formats

The two standardized formats for transmission of external data are the Bank Administration Institute (BAI) format and the Accredited Standards Committee (ASC) X12 821 Financial Information Reporting transaction set. The BAI format is the older and more commonly used. However, there is a migration toward ASC X12 821, which is an Electronic Data Interchange (EDI) transaction set. (See also Chapter 13, Electronic Commerce.)

V. REPORTING MECHANISMS

The four most common types of reporting mechanisms are as follows:

1. *Telephone Reporting* - At its least automated level, reporting involves the use of a telephone to gather information from external sources. This may involve a telephone call initiated either by a financial institution or a company. Likewise, it may involve either gathering information manually via person-to-person contact or accessing an automated information system via a Touch-Tone telephone. Telephone reporting is often used to gather prior day information such as ledger and collected balances, and transaction totals, as well as current day information such as lockbox deposits, controlled disbursement clearings, and cash concentration detail.

2. *Facsimile Transmission* - Reporting may involve the use of a manual or automated facsimile (fax) transmission initiated by a financial institution. As with telephone reporting, a fax transmission can be used to report prior and current day information.

3. *PC/Terminal Access* - PC/terminal access involves the use of either a personal computer (PC) or terminal to gather information from both external and internal sources. PCs and terminals can be used to gather a variety of prior and current day information. Some systems have interactive capabilities, thereby enabling the user to initiate transactions. The software used to operate PC/terminal access systems can reside either on a financial institution's computer or a company's PC, depending on the application.

4. *CPU-to-CPU Transmission* - Reporting may involve the use of a central processing unit (CPU) for the purpose of transmitting a data file from one type of CPU to another. The CPU may be a mainframe, a PC, or a minicomputer. This is the most automated type of reporting mechanism.

Use of any one of these mechanisms does not exclude use of the others. In many cases, a cash manager compiles information on a daily basis using a combination of these methods.

VI. TREASURY WORKSTATIONS

A. Concepts

A **treasury workstation** is typically a PC which has software that gathers information from both internal and external sources, then compiles the data for purposes of analysis and decision-making. A treasury workstation can either be stand-alone or part of a LAN or WAN. In addition to automating a number of manual tasks, a treasury workstation enables a cash manager to prepare and distribute financial information in a variety of customized spreadsheets and management reports. Treasury workstation software can either be purchased from a vendor or developed in-house.

B. Capabilities

Treasury workstation technology has three basic components as follows:

1. *Modularity* - Treasury workstation software is modular in design. Among the basic modules included in many programs are balance reporting, cash forecasting, investment portfolio management, and debt scheduling. Additional modules offer the user

choices such as general ledger interface, word processing, electronic mail (E-mail), foreign exchange management, and letters of credit application. See Exhibit 11.2 for examples of modularity.

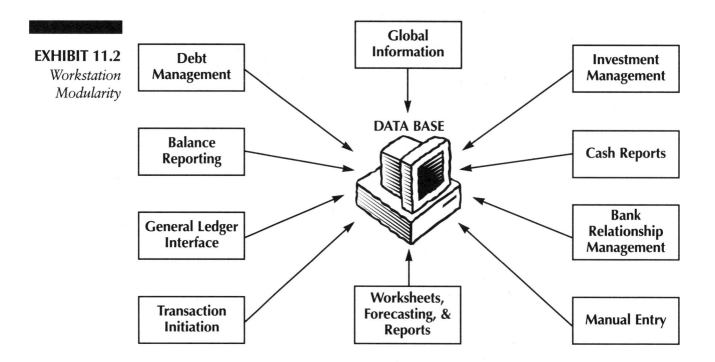

EXHIBIT 11.2
Workstation Modularity

2. *Data Integration* - A treasury workstation is capable of integrating a wide range of information from both internal and external sources. The data is downloaded into the computer and organized in a spreadsheet. Prior to the development of treasury workstations, these tasks had to be performed manually.

3. *Database Management* - Treasury workstations also provide the user with database management. This feature allows the user to determine how information is stored and organized. It also allows the user to customize spreadsheets and financial reporting.

C. Modules

A treasury workstation enables a cash manager to monitor, measure, and manage information both faster and in ways that were not possible before the invention of the microprocessor. Exhibit 11.3 shows examples of treasury workstation applications.

EXHIBIT 11.3
Treasury Workstation Modules

Treasury Workstation Module	Treasury Application
Account Balance Report	Monitor Ledger and Collected Balances
Target Balance Report	Manage Compensating Balances
Cash Position Worksheet	Manage Cash Position
Transaction Detail Report	Monitor Individual Debits and Credits
Investment	Manage Short-Term Investments
Borrowing	Monitor Debt Repayment
Letters of Credit	Issue Letters of Credit

VII. INFORMATION REPORTING SYSTEMS

A. Concepts

Information reporting systems are products offered by financial institutions or third-party providers which enable an authorized individual to access a wide range of daily balance and account activity information, as well as to initiate transactions.

B. Capabilities

Information reporting systems, like treasury workstations, offer the user modularity. However, unlike treasury workstations, information reporting systems do not offer such capabilities as data integration or database management. Information reporting systems are sometimes referred to as "window" products. Data is often obtained through multiple points of access. However, the technology is migrating toward a single point of access commonly referred to as an **electronic window**. (Use of the term window in this context should not be confused with Microsoft© Windows™, a computer operating system.)

C. Modules

As with treasury workstations, information reporting systems provide the user with a variety of modules. The modules commonly available are shown in Exhibit 11.4.

EXHIBIT 11.4
Information System Reporting Modules

Prior Day Information Modules	Current Day Information Modules
Account Balances	Lockbox Deposits
Float Information	Controlled Disbursement Totals
Debits/Credits	ACH Debits and Credits
Loans/Investments	Wire Transfers
Cash Concentration Totals and Detail	Money Market Data
International Transactions	Foreign Exchange Data

VIII. TRANSACTION INITIATION

Increasingly, cash managers are using more automated methods for initiating transactions once they have compiled and analyzed data and completed the daily decision-making process. Using these methods for transaction initiation increases security issues for a company. Steps need to be taken to prevent either authorized or unauthorized users from executing fraudulent transactions.

A. Types of Transactions

Among examples of the types of transactions that can be initiated are the following:

- Wire transfers
- Cash concentration transfers
- ACH debits and credits
- Stop payments
- Letters of credit
- Investment purchases and sales
- Loan drawdowns
- Foreign exchange transactions

B. Mechanisms

As with data gathering, several mechanisms can be used to initiate transactions. Among the most common are the following:

- Touch-Tone telephone
- Fax
- Terminal access
- PC
- Mainframe computer

IX. TMIS BENEFITS AND COSTS

Exhibit 11.5 compares some of the benefits and costs of TMIS technology.

EXHIBIT 11.5
TMIS Benefits and Costs

Benefits	Costs
Improves productivity	Start-up and training expense
Expedites data gathering, compiling, and analysis	Hardware and software costs
Increases forecasting accuracy	Administrative, maintenance, and overhead expenses
Reduces borrowing expense	Telecommunications charges
Improves investment earnings	Transaction service charges
Improves management reporting	Security expense

X. TMIS SECURITY

A. Database Management Issues

One of the major issues for all companies is who is allowed access to treasury information systems. Determining who has access involves not only the issue of confidentiality, but of technical competency. A user must have a working knowledge of how to:

- set up a database correctly

- enter, edit, and update data accurately

- protect the database's security and integrity at all times

B. Security Risks

The three most common types of risk are as follows:

1. *Loss of Data* - One of the most common risks for all computer users is loss of data. This can occur in a variety of ways:

    - a power surge or failure

    - a computer crash

    - a bug within a software program

    - an intentional tampering with data by an authorized user

    - an error on the part of the user

    - a misplaced or lost disk

    The degree of risk depends on the nature of the information that is lost and the amount of time involved in restoring it—if it can be restored at all.

2. *Unauthorized User Access* - There are two different types of unauthorized user access as follows:

    - The first type is someone within the company who is able to access information by logging on to a computer in the treasury area or by means of a company's LAN.

    - The second type of unauthorized user is someone outside the company who is able to access information either accidentally or intentionally.

    The risks in both cases are the same: access to confidential information, intentionally altering or destroying data, and initiating unauthorized or fraudulent transactions.

3. *Computer Viruses* - A computer virus is a software program that is designed to corrupt or destroy data. Some viruses are relatively harmless and may affect only a small portion of a software program—sometimes just the current screen. Other viruses are far more malicious in intent as they are designed to sabotage an entire information system. While anti-virus protection programs are readily available, these programs are not always fail-safe.

C. Security Safeguards

The following are examples of security safeguards:

1. *Create a Security Officer/Administrator Position* - Assigning specific responsibility for TMIS security to a designated individual is one of the basic safeguards. This individual should be responsible for developing, monitoring, and enforcing information security policies and procedures.

2. *Develop Written Policies and Procedures* - Another standard safeguard is a formal set of policies that spells out all procedures for approval and access levels, system maintenance, and protection of passwords. As with all such written policies, they are only effective if they are used, enforced, and periodically updated.

3. *Establish Physical Security* - Physical security includes both protection of hardware and software. Actions range from simply storing computer systems and software in a secure place to restricting physical access to certain areas. The degree of physical security, as with all safeguards, depends upon many factors, including the risks involved, the costs, personnel constraints, and the practicality of imposing such controls.

4. *Institute Basic Access Requirements* - Among access requirements are the following:

    *   Requiring user identification and authorization such as a password and personal identification number (PIN)

    *   Monitoring event logging (generate a log of who accesses the system and at what time)

    *   Limiting sign-on attempts

    *   Activating automatic log-off procedures when the system is not in use

5. *Establish Different Levels of Access* - An additional safeguard is to establish different levels of access. The following is an example of a levels-of-access policy:

    *   At the first level, some employees are only allowed access to inquiry functions. Inquiry functions permit authorized users to view information, but prevents them from inputting or editing data.

    *   At the second level, authorized users can view, input, and edit information, but are not allowed to initiate transactions.

    *   At the third level, authorized users have the authority to view, input, edit, and initiate.

6. *Require Backup Storage* - Backup storage can be accomplished in many different ways depending on the system. Among examples of the different methods of backing up data are the following:

    *   floppy diskettes

    *   tapes

    *   removable hard drives

    *   transmission by a LAN to another microprocessor

    *   transmission to a mainframe

7. *Institute Computer Virus Protection Methods* - Virus protection methods include all of the following:

   • Using virus protection programs

   • Prohibiting installation of electronic mail on the operating system

   • Prohibiting downloading from public bulletin boards

   • Establishing an approved software program policy

   • Buying software from reputable dealers

   • Prohibiting installation of copied or pirated software

8. *Use Electronic Security* - Two of the most common methods of electronic security are the following:

   • *Encryption* - **Encryption** is a process which electronically scrambles a message so that it cannot be read by someone who might intercept it. These coded messages must be translated when received. Both hardware and software are available for this purpose.

   • *Message Authentication* - **Message authentication** is a digital signature. It is used to protect the integrity of a message and ensure that it has not been tampered with. The sender calculates a message authentication code in a unique manner and transmits it with the message. The receiver duplicates the calculation. A match indicates the transaction is valid.

D. Disaster Recovery Issues

Treasury departments should have a documented disaster recovery plan in place, ranging from what to do in the event of a minor system failure to a major natural disaster. Companies may enter into agreements with financial institutions, third party service bureaus, or strategic partners to provide backup in the event of a disaster. As with written policies, a disaster plan is only effective if it is periodically reviewed and tested.

Questions

These chapter questions are to test and review the information in the text and are not examples of CCM examination questions, nor are they in the examination format.

Answers can be found at the back of the book on p. 329.

1. What are the objectives of daily cash management?

2. What are the typical tasks a cash manager performs on a daily basis?

3. What are the types of internal data exchanged between the treasury area and other areas of the company?

4. What are the sources of current day information for the cash manager?

5. What is multi-bank reporting?

6. What are the four most common types of reporting mechanisms?

7. What is a treasury workstation?

8. What types of modules are often found in treasury workstation systems?

9. What types of transactions can be initiated through a treasury workstation?

10. What are the primary benefits and costs associated with TMIS technology?

11. What are the most common security risks with TMIS systems?

12. What are the basic types of security safeguards for TMIS systems?

13. What is disaster recovery?

CHAPTER 12

Forecasting Cash Flows

OVERVIEW

This chapter describes the objectives of forecasting, the forecast horizons, and the principal techniques used for forecasting.

LEARNING OBJECTIVES

Upon completion of this chapter and the related study questions, the reader should know:

1. The objectives of cash forecasting.

2. The distinction between short- and long-term forecasting.

3. How to explain steps in the forecasting process such as data selection, source selection, forecast method selection, and forecast validation and implementation.

4. The various forecasting methods, and how to apply them to the forecasting of cash flows.

OUTLINE

I. Objectives of Cash Forecasting

II. The Forecasting Process
   A. Forecasting Horizons
   B. Cash Flow Components
   C. Degree of Certainty
   D. Data Identification and Organization
   E. Forecast Method Selection
   F. Forecast Validation

III. Forecasting Methods
   A. Receipts and Disbursements Forecast
   B. Distribution Method
   C. Pro Forma Statements
   D. Adjusted Net Income
   E. Statistical Forecasting

I. OBJECTIVES OF CASH FORECASTING

One of the more important tasks of the cash manager, forecasting cash flows involves predicting cash flows for the purposes of liquidity management and financial control. The objectives of cash forecasting include the following:

- *Liquidity Management* - Forecasting the net cash position over different time horizons is essential in scheduling maturities of borrowings and investments, as well as in anticipating borrowing requirements.

- *Financial Control* - Predicted cash flows provide a standard of measurement and comparison for actual cash flows. Variance analysis can help identify unpredicted cash flows, such as: unacceptable inventory changes, delays in accounts receivable collection, mis-timing of payments, and other problems. Identification of these problems allows corrective measures to be taken quickly and the negative consequences of these problems to be minimized.

- *Strategic Objectives* - Cash flow forecasts are used to identify a company's future funding requirements and support its strategic objectives and policies.

- *Capital Budgeting* - Forecasts of revenues, expenditures, and funding are required in evaluating potential projects and determine a company's capital budget.

- *Cost Management* - Cash forecasts can help management to best utilize available cash in the face of conflicting goals and trade-offs. By minimizing borrowing costs and excess bank balances and optimizing short-term investment income, overall financial results can be improved.

- *Currency Exposure* - Companies conducting business internationally use various forecasting techniques to determine foreign cash flows and assess their degree of foreign currency exposure.

II. THE FORECASTING PROCESS

Development of a particular forecast depends on the forecast horizon. The forecaster's understanding of the company regarding its size, business, and structure, as well as sources of information and forecasting tools, is also important. Computer spreadsheets are used extensively in the forecasting process. The factors involved in the forecasting process are as follows:

A. Forecasting Horizons

The time horizon over which information is to be forecast is an important consideration. Cash flow forecasting is done for periods ranging from one day to several years. The forecast horizon can be thought of as a continuum, with valid distinctions between short-, medium-, and long-term forecasts.

1. *Short-Term Forecasting* - Short-term forecasts predict cash receipts and disbursements and the resulting funds balances on a daily or weekly basis (usually for periods up to a month). Short-term forecasts aid in scheduling cash concentration transfers for field and lockbox accounts, funding disbursement accounts, and making short-term investing and borrowing decisions. Without such forecasts, borrowing could be excessive, thereby creating a need for a higher line of credit and related fees. Short-term forecasting is also important in setting and managing target balances which must be maintained in certain bank accounts to compensate for bank services.

2. *Medium-Term Forecasting* - Cash flow forecasts from one to 12 months are often referred to as the cash budget and are usually based on an adjusted net income approach. This forecast tracks the projected inflows (collections from sales and other sources of funds) and outflows (expenses and other uses of funds) on a monthly basis and is used to determine the company's need for short-term credit or the availability of funds for short-term investments. It can also be used as a benchmark for performance over the period by comparing actual cash flows to projected cash flows from the cash budget.

3. *Long-Term Forecasting* - Long-term forecasts cover any period beyond one year. They take into consideration projections of long-term sales and expenditures as well as the market environment. Such forecasts are strategic in that they relate to long-term financial planning for the company. They are also used by financial institutions and rating agencies for credit analysis and evaluation.

B. Cash Flow Components

The factors determining the magnitude and timing of cash flow components will influence the selection of appropriate forecasting techniques. Therefore, to properly develop a cash flow forecast, the cash flows need first to be divided into their major components.

One approach is to split cash flows into those related to receipts (inflows) versus those related to disbursements (outflows). Cash flows can be further segregated by product line, type of customer, or region. Disbursements can be further split into categories such as interest payments, dividend payments, payroll, large-dollar vendor payments, or small-dollar vendor payments.

C. Degree of Certainty

The next step in the process is to categorize cash flows by the degree of certainty attached to each component to be forecast:

1. *Certain Flows* - For many companies, a significant number of cash flows are known in advance. Examples of certain cash flows include interest, royalty, and tax payments.

2. *Predictable Flows* - Cash collections from credit sales are an example of a cash flow component that can be predicted with reasonable accuracy. The cash flow on a given day depends on factors such as the recent history of credit sales. A prediction of future cash flows can then be made on the basis of past observations. Disbursements such as payroll are also easy to forecast based on records of hours worked and projected float on payroll checks. Similarly, patterns of clearings of vendor checks can also be determined on the basis of past clearing times.

3. *Less Predictable Cash Flows* - Some cash flows are more difficult to forecast accurately. Examples may include sales of a new product, temporary damage repairs pending settlement of insurance claims, or the cost of settling a strike. The experience and judgment of the forecaster are important in these instances.

D. Data Identification and Organization

The identification of data to be used in the forecast is an important part of the forecasting process. Some of the considerations are as follows:

1. *Sources* - Information is available from external and internal sources, including the company's banks, field managers, sales managers, and the accounts payable or accounts receivable departments.

2. *Identification* - The identification of sources is affected by the degree of centralization or decentralization in the company's structure. In a decentralized company, local managers usually have the most current financial data related to their operation. A centralized company is less dependent on local sources.

3. *Account Structure* - The bank account structure used by the company is also important. For example, zero-balance accounts (ZBAs) can help to facilitate cash flow forecasting as compared to a standard single account system.

4. *Reporting Requirements* - In order to ensure the usefulness of the data selected, it is essential that the data be precisely defined and accurately reported in a timely manner.

5. *Data Selection* - Data selection is an important step in forecasting cash flows. The choice involves the organization of available data to be included in the forecast.

6. *Prior Period Data* - In predicting cash flows from credit sales, data from prior periods can be used. Individual customer payment histories may be used, or information may be broken down by other categories such as credit rating, internal credit score, size, industry, or location.

E. Forecast Method Selection

The process of selecting a method of forecasting involves several steps, as follows:

1. *Establishing Data Relationships* - Any statistical relationship between the available data and the cash flow components to be forecast should be determined before selecting the appropriate forecasting method. This determination can come from forecaster intuition, past experience, viewing the data graphically, or more formal quantitative statistical techniques. Cash disbursements can be modeled as a function of invoices received for payment. Cash collections can be based on a prior period's credit sales.

2. *Selecting a Method* - A forecasting method is selected after the relationship is established between the input data and the cash flow to be forecast. For example, a daily cash disbursement forecast suggests the specific identification and grouping by type of payable.

3. *Testing Relationships* - Sample input data is used to test the accuracy of the selected method. The result is a model used to forecast cash flows.

4. *Managing the Costs of Forecast Systems and Data* - Forecasting models should be cost effective. Any forecasting system or model must be maintained along with the data required to produce the forecast. Sophisticated computer-based models may require systems support and personnel to provide data input. The cost of a more

detailed analysis must be weighed against the expected improvement in the accuracy of the forecast.

F. Forecast Validation

Validation of a forecast model is required and should be done on three levels.

1. *In-Sample Validation* - In-sample validation tests how well the model works using the historical data from which the model was developed. From this forecast, variances are calculated between actual and predicted values.

2. *Out-of-Sample Validation* - Out-of-sample validation tests the accuracy of the model using data not involved in the model's estimation. For example, if three years (36 months) of monthly data are available, the model is estimated using the first 30 months of data. The model can then be validated by comparing the model's predictions to actual values over the remaining six months of data.

3. *Ongoing Validation* - Continuing feedback from projected versus actual comparisons allows continuous evaluation and refinement of the model.

III. FORECASTING METHODS

The forecasting method to be used for a given forecast is generally dependent on the forecasting horizon. Short-term forecasts based on information relating to receipts and disbursements that will occur in the near future are used by many companies. There are a number of methods which incorporate individual cash flow details to develop accurate short-term cash projections. Two of the more important methods for short-term forecasting include receipts and disbursements forecasts and distribution forecasts. Medium- and long-term forecasting methods include **pro forma statements** and adjusted net income. Long-term forecasts generally use methods which project cash flows and funding requirements on an annual basis. Finally, statistical techniques may be applied across all time horizons.

A. Receipts and Disbursements Forecast

The **receipts and disbursements forecast** is a basic method used for short-term cash forecasting. It begins with the creation of separate schedules of cash receipts and cash disbursements. Both schedules are prepared on a cash basis rather than an accrual basis. This method can be accurate in the short-term and near medium-term, especially when based on accounts receivable and accounts payable data.

*   *Receipts Schedule* - A receipts schedule consists of a projection of collections from customers (cash sales or payments on accounts receivable) and unearned income such as interest or dividends received from investments. Included in a receipts schedule are proceeds from the sale of assets and other non-recurring cash inflows.

*   *Disbursements Schedule* - A disbursements schedule involves a forecast of purchases and other cash outflows, such as payroll, taxes, interest, dividends, rent, and payments of principal.

*   *Completed Forecast* - To complete the forecast, the receipts and disbursements schedules are combined, and a minimum cash balance is determined for the company.

In Exhibit 12.1, a company has determined its minimum cash requirements to be $50,000 to cushion it against unexpected expenses or to allow it to take advantage of unanticipated opportunities. The beginning cash is the ending cash from the prior month. The final two lines of the forecast represent the forecasted surplus or deficit cash position each month. With this information, a company can better manage its borrowing and investing activity.

EXHIBIT 12.1
Receipts and Disbursements Forecast

$ Amounts in $1,000	January	February	March
Cash Receipts	$1,000	$1,100	$ 950
Cash Disbursements	(870)	(1,450)	(1,000)
Net Cash Flow	130	(350)	(50)
Beginning Cash Balance	100	230	(120)
Ending Cash Balance	230	(120)	(170)
Minimum Cash Req. (Target Balance)	(50)	(50)	(50)
Financing Needed (Deficit)		$170	$220
Investable Funds (Surplus)	$180		

B. Distribution Method

The **distribution method** is used in many short-term cash forecasting situations.

- The distribution forecast is the total estimated cash flow allocated over the forecast horizon. The total is spread over the days in the forecast horizon by multiplying the total by estimates of the proportions that will occur on each day.

- These proportions can be estimated by taking a simple average of the amount of the cash flow that occurs on a given day. Actual historical patterns are used to determine these proportions.

- Regression analysis can be used if the amount of the cash flow that occurs on a particular day is influenced by more than one factor. For example, the amount of cash flow may depend on the day of the month and the day of the week in question.

- The distribution method is accurate, allows seasonality and trends to be incorporated, and is easily and inexpensively prepared. However, a large amount of data is usually required to estimate the proportions used to spread the total, and proportions may need to be revised if conditions change.

Exhibit 12.2 is an example of forecasting using the distribution method.

EXHIBIT 12.2

Forecasting Using the Distribution Method

A company has used regression analysis to estimate the proportion of dollars that will clear on a given business day. It has determined that this proportion depends on the number of business days since the checks were distributed. The estimated proportions are given below.

Business Days Since Distribution	Percentage of Dollars Expected to Clear
1	13%
2	38%
3	28%
4	13%
5	8%
Total	**100%**

Therefore, if $100,000 in checks is distributed on Wednesday, May 1, the checks are estimated to clear according to the schedule below.

Date	Business Days After Distribution	Day of the Week	Percentage of Dollars Clearing	Forecasted Dollars Clearing
May 2	1	Thursday	13%	$13,000
May 3	2	Friday	38%	$38,000
May 6	3	Monday	28%	$28,000
May 7	4	Tuesday	13%	$13,000
May 8	5	Wednesday	8%	$ 8,000
		TOTAL	**100%**	**$100,000**

C. Pro Forma Statements

Projected income statements and balance sheets can form the basis of predicted cash flows over a longer forecast horizon. They are based on the percentage-of-sales method, as illustrated in Exhibit 12.3.

Percentage-of-Sales - With the **percentage-of-sales** method, financial statements are projected based upon future sales and the historical relationship between sales and balance sheet items such as cash, accounts receivable, inventory, and accounts payable.

The percentage-of-sales method can be developed in the following way:

1. Generate the sales forecast, working closely with sales managers, product managers and the top management of the company.

2. Determine the items on the balance sheet and income statement that can be assumed to be a constant percentage of sales. The percentage can be estimated from the most recent year's financial statements.

3. Assume that the other balance sheet and income statement items are either constant or updated, based on available information. For example, the level of long-term debt is projected on the basis of the current amount outstanding plus scheduled changes.

After these projections are generated, total projected assets usually do not equal total liabilities and equity. If the assets are less, a company has a cash surplus. If the assets are greater, a company has a cash shortage that will have to be financed through debt or equity.

EXHIBIT 12.3

Forecasting with Pro Forma Financial Statements

Assume the following income statement and balance sheet (in thousands) represent a company's actual position as of December 31, 199X.

Income Statement

Sales	$ 2,000	
Cost of Goods Sold	(1,500)	[75% of Sales]
Selling & Admin. Exp.	(200)	[10% of Sales]
Depreciation	(100)	
Interest Expense	(38)	
Income Before Taxes	162	
Taxes	(55)	[34% Tax Rate]
Net Income	$ 107	

Balance Sheet

Cash	$ 100	Payables	$ 50
Receivables	300	Notes (at 12%)	150
Inventory	200	Bonds (at 10%)	200
Net Fixed Assets	400	Common Equity	600
Total Assets	$1,000	Total Liab. & Equity	$1,000

To generate the percentage of sales forecast, the following assumptions are made (all numbers are in thousands):
- Sales will increase by 10% to $2,200 in 199Y
- Cost of goods sold, selling and administrative expenses, payables, and all current assets are a constant percentage of sales
- Additional fixed assets in the amount of $100 will be purchased
- Depreciation will be $50
- Notes will be reduced to $100 at the beginning of the year
- Dividends will be $24

(Continued)

EXHIBIT 12.3

Forecasting with Pro Forma Financial Statements

Projected Income Statement (in thousands) - Year Ending December 31, 199Y		
Sales	$ 2,200	
Cost of Goods Sold	(1,650)	[75% of Sales]
Selling & Admin. Exp.	(220)	[10% of Sales]
Depreciation	(50)	
Interest Expense	(32)	[.12 x 100 + .10 x 200]
Income Before Taxes	248	
Taxes	(84)	[34% Tax Rate]
Net Income	$ 164	
Dividends	(24)	
Retained Earnings	$ 140	

Projected Balance Sheet (in thousands) December 31, 199Y				
Cash (5% of Sales)	$ 110	Payables (2.5% of Sales)	$	55
Receivables (15% of Sales)	330	Notes		100
Inventory (10% of Sales)	220	Bonds		200
Net Fixed Assets (NFA) (Prior NFA + New NFA – Depreciation) ($400 + $100 – $50)	450	Common Equity (Prior Common Equity + Retained Earnings) ($600 + $140)		740
Total Assets	$ 1,110	Total Liab. & Equity	$	1,095

Note that the $15 difference between Total Assets and Total Liabilities and Equity is the amount by which projected uses of funds exceeds the projected sources of funds. This difference is usually plugged back into cash (subtracted in this case) to balance the balance sheet. If the amount of cash cannot be reduced, then the company must find additional sources of funds, usually short-term borrowing.

The same answer can be generated using the adjusted net income approach, illustrated in Exhibit 12.4. Here, net cash flow is projected liabilities and net worth minus projected assets.

Adjusted Net Income					
Sources of Cash (in thousands) Cash Flow from Operations (Projected Net Income + Depreciation) ($164 + $50)		$ 214	**Uses of Cash (in thousands)** Increases in Assets (Cash + A/R + Inventory + New Fixed Assets) ($10 + $20 + $30 + $100)		$ 160
Decreases in Assets (no decreases)		0	Decreases in Liabilities (Decrease in Notes) ($150 – $100)		50
Increases in Liabilities (Increase in A/P) ($55 – $50)		5	Dividends (Projected Dividends) ($24)		24
Total Sources		$ 219	Total Uses		$ 234
Net Cash Flow = –$15					

EXHIBIT 12.4

Forecasting with the Adjusted Net Income Method

D. Adjusted Net Income

The **adjusted net income method** identifies sources and uses of funds. Examples of sources and uses of funds are:

Sources
- Cash flows from operations (net profit plus non-cash charges)
- Decreases in assets
- Increases in liabilities

Uses
- Increases in assets
- Decreases in liabilities
- Capital expenditures
- Dividend payments

The projected sources and uses of funds are calculated from the company's financial statements in order to derive projected cash flows. Non-cash charges (such as depreciation) and changes in balance sheet accounts are added back to the forecast of net income to forecast the net cash flow. Net cash flow is equal to the sources minus the uses.

E. Statistical Forecasting

Statistical forecasts describe the relationship between the cash flow component to be predicted and one or more input variables. Statistical forecasting is useful when there is a large population to be sampled. It also can be applied to the analysis of trends. Two of the more important statistical techniques are:

1. *Time Series Forecasting* - A time series model seeks to forecast a variable based only on past observations of that variable. The primary types of **time series forecasting** applicable to cash forecasting are discussed below.

   Simple Moving Average - **Simple moving average**s base a forecast on a rolling or moving average of past historical values. In a five-day moving average (shown in Exhibit 12.4), the amount of cash flow for day 6 is predicted by taking the simple average of the cash flows from the five previous days (days 1-5). To forecast day 7, the five previous days' actual values (days 2-6) are averaged together. A forecast prepared using a simple moving average will always lag any trend in the actual cash flow. Also, the longer the moving average, the greater the smoothing of individual data point variances, and the shorter the moving average, the less the smoothing of individual data point variances. While this approach may be useful in helping to identify cyclical or other patterns in past data, it does not take these patterns into account in the determination of the forecast value.

   Exponential Smoothing - **Exponential smoothing** is a variation on a simple moving average that is somewhat easier to use in actual application. Rather than calculating a moving average, the exponential smoothing technique uses the previous forecast value, the most recent actual value, and a user-determined value known as the smoothing constant. This smoothing constant is typically designated as " α " (referred to as alpha) and may range between 0 and 1. Using the formula below, setting α closer to 0 will result in more weight being placed on the historical values of the series rather than the most recent actual cash flow, resulting in greater smoothing of the series. Setting α closer to 1 will result in more weight being placed on the most recent actual value, resulting in less smoothing of the series. The forecaster must determine how much smoothing is required and choose the smoothing constant, α, accordingly. The most common form of the exponential smoothing formulation is:

Next Period Forecast = Current Period Forecast + [α x (Forecast Error)]

Where:
Forecast Error = Current Period Actual − Current Period Forecast

This formula can be expressed more formally as:

$$F_{t+1} = F_t + [\alpha \times (X_t − F_t)]$$

Where:
F_{t+1} = Cash flow forecast for the next period (t+1)
F_t = Cash flow forecast for the current period (t)
α = Smoothing constant ($0 \le \alpha \le 1$)
X_t = Actual cash flow for the current period (t)

As in the simple moving average forecasts, a simple exponential smoothing forecast will lag trends in the data. To correct for this, and to allow for seasonality in the forecast, more complex extensions of exponential smoothing allow the user to incorporate these factors.

Exhibit 12.5 shows a forecast using both the moving average and exponential smoothing techniques.

	Moving Average Forecast			Exponential Smoothing Forecast	
Day	Actual Cash Flow	Forecast (N=5)	Error	Forecast (α = .4)	Error
1	$110,000				
2	120,000				
3	115,000				
4	122,000				
5	126,000				
6	124,000	$118,600	$5,400	$118,600*	$5,400
7	129,000	121,400	7,600	120,760	8,240
8	133,000	123,200	9,800	124,060	8,940
9	132,000	126,800	5,200	127,640	4,360

For example, the moving average forecast for day 6 is:
($110,000 + 120,000 + 115,000 + 122,000 + 126,000)/5 = $118,600
Which results in a forecast error of $124,000 – $118,600 = $5,400

The exponential smoothing forecast for day 7 is:
$118,600 + (.4 × $5,400) = $120,760
Which results in a residual of $129,000 – $120,760 = $8,240

* The exponential smoothing forecast for day 6 is assumed to be the average of the previous five observations.

2. *Regression Analysis* - **Regression analysis** is a statistical technique that systematically identifies the relationship between a variable to be predicted (the dependent variable) and other data which may be available (explanatory or independent variables). Though there are many forms of regression analysis, the most basic is that of a simple linear regression model. This approach essentially determines a line that best represents the relationship between a single dependent variable and a single explanatory variable. Regression analysis (especially the more complex type) is most often done using a computer program which determines the relationship between the variables in question though a series of mathematical algorithms and which can also display the relationship in a graphic format.

Questions

These chapter questions are to test and review the information in the text and are not examples of CCM examination questions, nor are they in the examination format.

Answers can be found at the back of the book on p. 331.

1.   What are the objectives of cash forecasting?

2.   What are the major steps involved in the forecasting process?

3.   What are the two major short-term forecasting methods?

4.   One long-term forecasting method is the use of pro-forma statements. What is the technique that is used to prepare a pro-forma statement?

5.   In the adjusted net income method, what are the major sources and uses of cash?

6.   What are the primary types of time series forecasting?

7.   The following cash flow information is provided:

Day	Cash Flow
1	100
2	150
3	250
4	210

What is the moving average forecast for day 5?

8.   How does exponential smoothing differ from the simple moving average forecast?

9.   What are the steps in selecting a forecasting method?

10.   What are the three types of forecast validation?

11.   What is regression analysis?

CHAPTER 13

Electronic Commerce

OVERVIEW

This chapter describes the basics of electronic commerce (EC) and its relationship to electronic data interchange (EDI) and electronic payments. The costs, benefits, and barriers to electronic commerce are discussed, as well as the standards for sending and receiving electronic messages. The roles of the various software and service providers are described, in addition to the impact of EC on a company.

LEARNING OBJECTIVES

Upon completion of this chapter and the related study questions, the reader should know:

1. What electronic commerce is and how it relates to EDI and electronic payments.

2. How companies implement EDI.

3. The benefits and costs of electronic commerce, as well as barriers to its implementation.

4. How electronic commerce standards and software are used.

5. The role of value added networks (VANs) and value added banks (VABs) in electronic commerce.

6. How electronic commerce impacts a company.

OUTLINE

I.   **Basics of Electronic Commerce**
    A. Definitions
    B. Types of EFT Systems
    C. Relationship Between EDI, FEDI and EFT
    D. Factors Influencing the Use of EDI

II. **Benefits and Costs of EC and EDI**
    A. Benefits
    B. Costs
    C. Additional Barriers

I. BASICS OF ELECTRONIC COMMERCE

The majority of business documents and payments transacted between companies in North America are paper-based and move through the postal system. Electronic commerce is an alternative to this paper system and is being implemented in various forms by many companies. Electronic commerce, tied with re-engineering efforts, is enabling some companies to form closer ties and become strategic partners with their vendors and customers.

Among the benefits of EC are the following:

- information moves faster, and with greater accuracy
- costs related to paper processing are reduced
- inventories may be lowered
- customer and supplier relationships are redefined
- treasury functions and duties are changed

A. Definitions

There are several important definitions related to the area of electronic commerce, as follows:

1. *Electronic Commerce* - **Electronic commerce** (EC) is the exchange of business information from one organization to another in an electronic format. It usually entails the electronic connection of any person, application or computer to another in some mutually agreed standard. EC includes unstructured electronic messaging such as facsimile (fax) or electronic mail (E-mail) as well as electronic data interchange (EDI) formats. The range of electronic commerce is shown in Exhibit 13.1. At one end of the continuum are totally unstructured messages such as fax transmissions and E-mail. At the other end, are highly structured messages, including EDI. Enabled E-mail represents a middle ground between unstructured E-mail and more structured EDI messages. This format is created by agreements among E-mail users to maintain specific standards for transmission of business data via E-mail messages.

EXHIBIT 13.1

Electronic Commerce

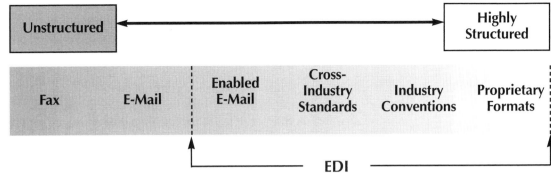

2. *Electronic Data Interchange* - **Electronic Data Interchange** (EDI) provides a vehicle for the electronic movement of business data in a standard format from one company's application system (such as an order entry system, purchasing system, or billing system) to another company's application system. EDI allows senders to generate the EDI messages directly from their applications. EDI allows receivers to bring data into their applications without the need to re-enter any of the information.

    Though this definition of EDI generally excludes fax and E-mail, which are more unstructured in nature, certain forms of these transmissions meet the definition of EDI. They utilize a standard format to provide for the communication of data between business applications.

    There are three basic types of EDI:

    *   *Cross-Industry EDI* - Cross-industry EDI is a format standard that addresses the needs of many different users in many industries. For example, when a company sends a cross-industry EDI purchase order to another company that conforms to the same standard, the receiving company can capture the purchase order data directly in a business application without re-entering data.

    *   *Industry Convention EDI* - Industry convention EDI is a specific format standard or a subset of the more generic cross-industry EDI standards used within a particular industry. Examples of industries which utilize these types of EDI standards include grocery, retail, automotive, electrical manufacturing, and chemical production and distribution.

    *   *Proprietary EDI* - Proprietary EDI is developed by one company for exclusive use by its trading partners. Many companies using proprietary formats are moving toward the use of cross-industry or industry convention standards.

3. *Electronic Funds Transfer and Financial EDI* - These are subsets of EDI. The distinguishing feature that characterizes electronic funds transfer (EFT) is the exchange of value which requires the involvement of financial intermediaries such as banks to send and receive electronic payments. Examples of EFT include wire transfers and automated clearing house (ACH) payments.

    Financial EDI (FEDI) is the electronic transmission of payments and payment-related information in standard formats between company trading partners and/or their banks. FEDI includes electronic format for invoices, initiation of payments, lockbox deposit reports, and remittance information sent either directly to a trading partner or processed through a financial or communications intermediary.

B. Types of EFT Systems

Several types of EFT systems are available in the U.S. These are covered in full detail in Chapter 4, Payment Systems.

1. *Fedwire* - Fedwire is a real-time method of transferring cash value from one bank to another using Federal Reserve account balances. In an electronic commerce application, wire transfers are initiated by the payor either through a standard EDI transaction set to its bank or by using its bank's treasury information system. The receiver of a wire transfer can receive electronic notification of the incoming funds from its bank, either through a standard EDI transaction set or through its bank's treasury information system.

2. *Automated Clearing House Transfers* - The Automated Clearing House (ACH) system is a computer-based clearing and settlement facility for interchange of electronic debits and credits among financial institutions. The ACH system offers several types of standardized EDI formats for the transmission of payment and remittance information.

C. Relationship Between EDI, FEDI and EFT

Exhibit 13.2 shows the relationship between companies and financial and communications intermediaries engaging in non-financial EDI, Financial EDI and EFT. For example, a company may send an EDI invoice to a customer. The customer (payor) sends a Financial EDI payment instruction to its bank. The customer's bank sends electronic payment information to the seller's bank through the ACH system. The seller's bank notifies the seller of the received payment through an electronic deposit report. The payment-related information transmission is an example of Financial EDI.

Exhibit 13.2 also shows two third-parties which assist companies in the transmission of EDI messages.

• *Value-Added Network (VAN)* - One of these parties is a **Value-Added Network** or VAN. A VAN is a communications intermediary which provides various services to the users of EDI or EC. VANs make it easier for companies to implement EDI and to add new EDI trading partners. They also provide ongoing support services.

• *Value-Added Bank (VAB)* - The other party is known as a **Value-Added Bank** or VAB. A VAB is a bank which provides non-financial EDI services in addition to payment-related FEDI service for its customers. In essence, this type of bank offers services similar to those of a VAN.

There is also an issue of whether payment and remittance information should be transmitted together or separately. Generally, use of a VAB or some of the more complex ACH formats allows payment and remittance information to flow together. Using a VAN or direct transmission generally requires that the remittance information be split from the payment by the sender and sent separately. The payment must move through a financial intermediary and recombined later with the remittance information by the receiver. For most applications, this matching of payment and remittance information can be accomplished. Many companies are successfully using either of these methods for managing their electronic payments process.

EXHIBIT 13.2
Relationship Between EDI, FEDI, and EFT

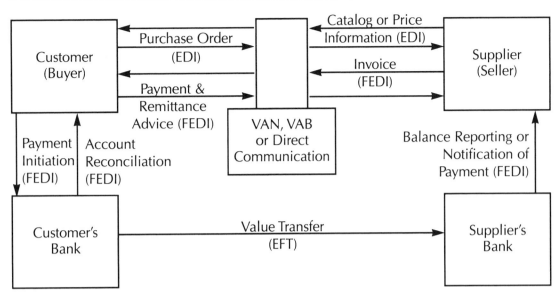

EDI, FEDI, and EFT - Parties and Applications

Mode	EDI Electronic Data Interchange	FEDI Financial EDI	EFT Electronic Funds Transfer
Parties Involved	Company-to-Company Company-to-VAN/VAB VAN/VAB-to-VAN/VAB VAN/VAB-to-Company	Company-to-Company Company-to-Bank Bank-to-Bank Bank-to-Company	Bank-to-Bank (Value Transfer)
Applications	Catalog Price Information Request for Quote Purchase Order PO Acknowledgement Production Schedule Shipping Information	Invoice Payment & Remittance Advice Payment Initiation Lockbox Information Balance Information Account Information Reconcilement Info. Account Analysis	ACH Debits ACH Credits Wire Transfers CHIPS SWIFT

D. Factors Influencing the Use of EDI

Companies implement EDI for a number of reasons and the actual design of their EDI systems vary widely, depending on the number of trading partners, the volume and type of EDI transactions used by the company, and whether they are an originator or receiver of EDI transactions. Three primary reasons for EDI use by companies are as follows:

1. *Reaction to a Request from Customer or Supplier* - Some companies implement EDI at the request (sometimes at the mandate) of key customers. These companies are generally suppliers to a company which is already a heavy user of EDI. This type of EDI implementation is often done on a small scale initially, using a PC and off-the-shelf software. Over time, the use of EDI at these companies may grow, but in the

early stages, they are doing EDI only with one or more major customers and are usually referred to as EDI spokes.

2. *Pro-Active EDI Implementation* - Other companies implement EDI as a result of observing the use of EDI by other companies in their industry, or perhaps from observing EDI use by customers or suppliers. These companies choose to implement EDI before they are forced to by customers or other factors. The EDI implementation is usually done after an analysis of the benefits and costs, as well as surveys of potential trading partners. The desire to reduce costs and remain competitive is usually a strong motivator for EDI use in these companies.

3. *Large Scale EDI Implementation* - Some companies implement EDI on a large-scale in order to maintain, or possibly increase, their competitive edge. Historically, these companies have been large manufacturers and retailers who benefited from the cost reductions, improved productivity, or decreased order lead times from EDI. Companies that encourage many of their suppliers to implement EDI are referred to as EDI hubs. Though these hubs often start as EDI originators, sending EDI purchase orders to their suppliers, they generally also become EDI receivers as their trading partners begin to send EDI invoices in response to purchase orders. One of the major challenges for a large EDI hub is to provide the necessary support and training for the many EDI spokes with which it deals.

II. BENEFITS AND COSTS OF EC AND EDI

Among the benefits which may accrue to companies which implement EC or EDI are the following:

A. Benefits

1. *Improved Productivity* - Once data is entered at the beginning of a transaction, the same data can be moved from one application to another without manual intervention. Filing, matching, sorting and retrieving are no longer manual processes with EDI, and stuffing, stamping, and mailing are eliminated.

2. *Reduced Cycle Time* - With the absence of mail time delays and minimal processing delays, EDI transactions can move rapidly. EDI facilitates just-in-time (JIT) inventory management in many companies, generally resulting in lower levels of inventory. In turn, JIT inventory makes it possible to achieve significant reductions in cycle times (elapsed time to convert purchased raw materials into finished goods) for many processes.

3. *Lower Error Rates* - Since data is not re-entered, error rates can be reduced by the implementation of EDI. For example, using EDI for receiving remittance information may allow for greater accuracy in the posting of payments to the accounts receivable ledger.

4. *Improved Cash Forecasting* - In an EDI environment mail time is usually eliminated and processing of data is faster. These factors, combined with faster and more reliable payment via either ACH or Fedwire, make it possible to eliminate, or greatly reduce, uncertainty in cash flow timing. This ultimately results in better cash forecasts and improved working capital management.

5. *Acknowledgment* - With EDI it is possible to receive notification that a message has been received by the other party. This acknowledgment that a customer has received an invoice (which is not available in a mail-based system), can help to resolve issues of payment timing between buyer and seller.

6. *Redesign and Re-engineering* - EDI implementations are often closely tied to redesign and/or re-engineering efforts in a company. EDI can be a valuable tool in these processes.

B. Costs

Among the costs which need to be considered in the implementation of EDI are the following:

1. *Software* - EDI or other electronic data must be integrated with data from existing applications. This usually requires modification of current business software applications. In addition, the data must be translated from the company's current format into a recognized EDI format. When standard EDI formats are used, there are commercially available software packages that perform the translation process.

2. *Hardware* - EDI requires computer equipment to operate. A company may choose to use existing hardware, or to install new systems for the EDI implementation. Extra computer security hardware such as key locks, equipment utilized for encryption and authentication, or removable data storage may be necessary to protect data.

3. *Communications* - EDI data must be sent from one party to another. This communication may be done either directly (usually over telephone lines) or through a VAB or VAN. Regardless of how the data is transmitted, the relevant costs must be determined. The company needs to consider the cost of communications software and hardware (modems, communications interfaces) in this process.

4. *Encryption and Message Authentication* - Additional software and/or hardware may also be required for security measures such as encryption and authentication. Encryption is a process whereby sensitive information (account numbers, dollar amounts, access codes, etc.) is scrambled to prevent unauthorized use. The data encryption standard (DES), the encryption format adopted by government and industry, requires that information scrambling take place before transmission. A message authentication code is a unique security code, often used in transactions (especially those related to payments) to ensure that the information has not been tampered with, and that the sender of the message is in fact an authorized originator.

5. *Education and Training* - EDI often requires that a company train both its internal personnel and any of its trading partners which are not knowledgeable about EDI. This can be a significant expense for a company adding EDI to a major application or using EDI with a large number of trading partners.

6. *Trading Partner Selling and Support* - Benefits of EDI accrue only when a significant number of transactions are converted from paper. This requires the company to solicit trading partners willing to send and receive EDI messages and to support those trading partners in their EDI implementations.

7. *Negotiating with Trading Partners* - Implementing EDI may affect the timing of payments, and credit terms may need to be renegotiated with trading partners. Beyond

the impact of a change in payment timing, the negotiation itself may be a costly and protracted process, especially if legal or audit concerns need to be addressed.

C. Additional Barriers

Besides the readily identifiable costs of doing EDI, there are additional barriers to EDI implementation, usually a result of moving from paper-based systems to electronic-based systems.

1. *Convenience of Paper-Based Systems* - The U.S. Postal Service delivers to all addresses in the U.S. for a uniform postage fee and provides low-cost delivery of paper-based messages and payments. Virtually all companies and individuals have access to the postal delivery system, as well as a bank or other financial intermediary to handle the payment part of the cycle.

2. *Versatility of Check Processing System* - The check-paper system is versatile in the way ancillary information can accompany the payment instrument. A check, for example, can be accompanied by any required documentation such as a copy of the invoice.

3. *Tradition of Paper-Based System* - Legal, audit and processing structures surrounding paper-based systems have been developed over many years. Almost all of the Uniform Commercial Code, as well as most accounting and legal standards, are based on paper and signatures for reporting and control purposes. Although there has been some consideration of EDI in legal and audit systems, it is still in the early stages.

4. *Dual Systems May be Required Initially* - For a variety of reasons, many companies implementing EDI and/or electronic payments find they must continue to use dual systems (both paper and EDI) after EDI implementation.

5. *Number of EDI Capable Banks* - The number of banks or other financial intermediaries which are capable of handling complex EFT formats is limited, but growing. This means that companies trying to make electronic payments to suppliers may find that many of their suppliers' banks cannot process the payment and related information in electronic formats. Initial programs have been undertaken by several banking and clearing house organizations to increase the number of EDI-capable banks.

III. EDI INFRASTRUCTURE

In order to move towards an electronic environment in transaction processing, a cost-effective infrastructure is required. This infrastructure includes four primary elements:

1. Standard formats for common business documents
2. EDI software
3. Communication networks and standards
4. Computer hardware

A. EDI Standards

To send documents electronically, companies must agree on a specific data format and structure for electronic messages. In the early days of EDI, some companies announced a proprietary format and communication interface and either encouraged or mandated trading partner participation. Proprietary data formats and technical requirements are adequate when a company deals with a small number of partners. When a company has many EDI partners, a common standard becomes a necessity.

1. *Development of EDI Standards* - EDI standards have developed from proprietary standards to the current cross-industry and international standards.

    • *ASC X12 Standards* - The development of the current U.S. standards for EDI began in 1968 with efforts of the transportation industry to establish standards for communications between and within railroads, ocean carriers, air carriers, and motor carriers. Based on this early work, EDI standards were also developed in the grocery and retail industries. In 1979, ASC X12 (Accredited Standards Committee X12 of the American National Standards Institute) was formed to develop general EDI standards which could be used in a variety of industries. Now all of the various industry standards are under the jurisdiction of ASC X12, which acts as a coordinating body for the further development and support of EDI cross-industry standards in North America.

    • *Industry Conventions of ASC X12 Standards* - Several industry groups (i.e., automotive, chemical, communications, health care) have decided to adopt ASC X12 standards for their industries. Rather than develop independent standards, industry groups may define subsets of generic X12 standards that fit the needs of their industries. This practice is expected to continue in other industries with common requirements.

    • *UN/EDIFACT Standards* - Parallel efforts in EDI standards development have been proceeding in many countries, leading to the development of the UN/EDI-FACT standards (United Nations Rules for EDI for Administration, Commerce and Transport). UN/EDIFACT comprises a set of internationally agreed-upon standards, directories, and guidelines for the electronic interchange of structure data that relates, in particular, to trade in goods and services between independent computerized information systems. UN/EDIFACT standards are widely used in Europe and are also used in some Asian countries.

2. *ASC X12 Structure* - An ASC X12 format standard consists of rules for translating one or more business documents into electronic messages.

    • A transaction set is the electronic equivalent of a paper business document or form. Transaction sets are formed using specific rules for formatting the information in the business document.

    • Within a transaction set, a group of related information, such as a line item in the purchase order, is called a data segment. A transaction set consists of at least three data segments and usually many more.

    • Data segments consist of pieces of data called data elements, such as price, unit of measure, and quantity. Data elements are defined in a data dictionary.

3. *ASC X12 Financial Transaction Sets* - By convention, ASC X12 transaction sets are identified by a number and a name. The following are some of the common EDI transaction sets used in the finance area:

    • *810 Invoice* - This allows the user to convey invoice data such as unit price, quantities purchased, and terms of sale from a seller to a buyer.

- *820 Payment Order/Remittance Advice* - This transaction set has a dual purpose. It initiates a money transfer to a payee and/or provides the payee with information describing the purpose of the associated payment. The 820 allows multiple invoices to be paid in a single payment. It also includes the amount of discounts and other payment adjustments.

- *821 Financial Information Reporting* - This transaction set is designed as a bank-to-corporate account reporting mechanism. It provides account level totals for such things as ledger and collected balances, float dollars, and total debits and credits. It can be tailored to meet a user's need for account reconciliation and transaction information reporting.

- *822 Customer Account Analysis* - This transaction set provides the customer with account analysis information (services, volumes, balances, service charges, etc.). It is designed primarily for transmission from a bank to its corporate customers. The Treasury Management Association (TMA) service codes can be used in the 822 to identify bank services and associated charges.

- *823 Lockbox Information* - This transaction set conveys check data from lockboxes, including remittance detail (i.e., payers, invoices, and amounts being paid), deposit totals, and funds available.

- *824 Application Advice* - This transaction set is designed to accommodate the business need of reporting the acceptance, rejection, or acceptance with change, of information received from another transaction set. In the finance area, this transaction set can be used to notify a payor of changes in information received in an 820 Payment Order/Remittance Advice.

- *828 Debit Authorization* - This transaction set can be used by a company to authorize its financial institution to honor an ACH debit on its account by another company. This allows greater control for the buyer, as it can specify certain payees sellers, certain time periods, dollar limits, and even specific debit transactions.

- *835 Health Care Claim Payment/Advice* - This transaction set is used in the health care industry to transmit medical claim payment and remittance information.

- *997 Functional Acknowledgment* - This transaction set is used to notify a transaction originator that the transmitted transaction sets were received and that they were in compliance with ASC X12 standards.

4. *NACHA Standard Formats for ACH Payments* - ACH transactions use standardized formats. There are several different formats for various ACH applications. The most commonly used ACH formats are as follows:

- *Prearranged Payments or Deposits (PPD)* - This format is used primarily for consumer payments such as deposit of payroll and social security payments. In an EDI environment, companies would generate payment instructions for direct deposit of payroll from their payroll systems, and provide their financial institutions with the payroll data in an electronic format.

- *Cash Concentration or Disbursement (CCD)* - This format is used for cash concentration purposes and for some corporate-to-corporate payments. In an EDI environment, a company may use its treasury information system to generate a listing of required concentration transfers and send this to its financial institution in an electronic format. Since it contains only limited space for ancillary payment information, this format is not often used for corporate-to-corporate trade payments.

- *CCD Plus Addenda (CCD+)* - The CCD+ format combines the widely used CCD record with an addenda record providing limited space to add a segment of an ASC X12 820 remittance advice. The segment can identify, in standard format, the invoice being paid or give other reference information needed to apply the payment. The Federal government's Vendor Express uses the CCD+ format and has been recently expanded to also use the (Corporate Trade Exchange) CTX format.

- *Tax Payment Format (TXP)* - This format is a special version of the CCD+ designed for the electronic payment of taxes to state and federal governments.

- *Corporate Trade Payments (CTP)* - This format was an initial attempt to provide a means of sending remittance information in an EDI format through the ACH system. It is scheduled to be replaced by the CTX format in 1996.

- *Corporate Trade Exchange (CTX)* - The CTX format combines the record structure and enveloping required by the ACH system with flexible length standards of ASC X12. A CTX transfer is essentially an ASC X12 820 (Payment Order/Remittance Advice) or 835 (Health Care Claim Payment/Advice) transmitted using ACH communications protocols. This allows the remittance information contained in the ASC X12 820 or 835 to move through the ACH network rather than having to be separated from the payment and sent through a third-party network or through direct communication.

- *Changing Standards and Recent Developments* - As information needs change and companies gain experience in using EDI standards, the standards themselves evolve. Each year, most standards bodies publish revisions to the standards. While this process is necessary to adapt the standards to changing needs, it poses some problems for the EDI user. Some of a company's trading partners may be using different versions of the standard and an EDI user must often support multiple versions of the EDI standards. EDI software, VABs, and VANs will help to manage these problems.

B. EDI Software

EDI software is necessary to convert data into standard formats and communicate messages between trading partners.

1. *Steps Performed by EDI Software* - There are three basic steps which must be performed in the creation of an EDI transaction set. These steps must either be handled by EDI software or by a third-party service provider. In addition, the steps may be accomplished by one piece of integrated EDI software, or by several separate software programs exchanging information with each other. The order outlined below is for an outgoing EDI message; the order would be reversed for an incoming message. Exhibit 13.3 shows these steps.

   - *File Conversion* - The first step is to extract data stored in the company's business application and reformat (map) it for input into the formatting stage. The mapping of a paper document to an EDI transaction set is a necessary but time-consuming part of EDI. Each required element of the EDI transaction set must be matched to its corresponding data field in the application database. Software which provides mapping utilities makes EDI implementation easier and faster.

- *Formatting* - This stage, also known as translation, takes the input data from the file conversion step and translates it into the desired EDI standard format. Most software is capable of formatting data into any accepted cross-industry standard or industry convention. In essence, this step creates EDI transaction sets according to required formats and protocols.

- *Communication* - This portion of the software establishes communications either directly with the trading partner or with a VAN or VAB. It sends (or receives) the EDI formatted data to (or from) another party using mutually acceptable communication protocols.

EXHIBIT 13.3
Steps Performed by EDI Software

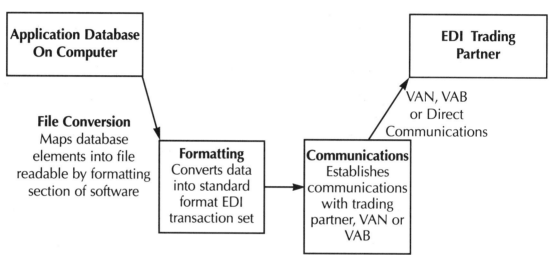

2. *Availability of EDI Software* - EDI software packages with mapping utilities are generally available for most computer platforms and operating systems. In addition, most EDI software is table-driven, meaning that all of the requirements and formats for EDI transaction sets are stored in easy-to-change tables. By changing these parameters, the software can produce any desired transaction set and can be easily updated as standards evolve.

C. Value Added Networks

A VAN is an intermediary which provides various services to the users of EDI or electronic commerce. VANs solve interface problems between two companies that have different computer systems, different format needs and different protocols. Thus, VANs make it easier for companies to implement EDI and to add new EDI trading partners. VANs offer many services to their customers. Among these services are the following:

- *Communications Capacity* - VANs maintain large numbers of communications lines with many different transmission speeds and communications protocols. Companies using VANs are assured of sufficient communications capacity to meet their EDI needs.

- *Mailboxing* - This permits one trading partner to send transaction sets to the other's mailbox for storage. When the other trading partner is ready, it retrieves the transaction sets. This solves the problem of finding a time when both partners can communicate.

- *Protocol Conversion* - This permits one partner to use a communication package with one transmission protocol and communicate with the other partner that uses another protocol.

- *Standards Conversion* - Some VANs offer the ability to receive a document in one format and translate it into another format before sending the information to the customer.

- *Line Speed Conversion* - This is provided so that messages may be received and sent at whatever line speed the parties require.

- *Gateway to Other VANs or VABs* - Gateways to other VANs or VABs permit companies to communicate with any of their trading partners, even if they use a different VAN or a VAB.

- *Implementation Assistance* - This is frequently offered in the form of consulting, software and training of trading partners.

D. Value-Added Banks

Some banks provide VAN services for information related to payments. These are called VABs. They solve the problem companies face when trading partners differ in their abilities to process the kind of electronic payment and remittance information the company wants to send. Some VABs may also provide EDI services which are not directly related to payments or FEDI.

1. *VAB Payment Services* - Integrated payables (see Chapter 8, Disbursements) is one of the services provided by VABs. There are several approaches to these types of services:

    - One approach is to have a company send a single data file to a third party (usually a financial institution) containing a listing of all its payments to be made. The file contains information on when to issue a disbursement and to whom, as well as instructions on the payment method to be used (i.e., check, wire or ACH). These instructions may be in a proprietary format or in an ASC X12 820 transaction set (Payment Order/Remittance Advice).

    - Alternatively, the third party maintains a database of a company's payees that includes detailed information such as preferred payment methods, specific remittance information, and receiving financial institutions. The database is periodically updated as new payees are added or an existing payee's remittance profile changes (i.e., payee switches to ACH instead of check for its standard payment type). In such cases, as a company makes a disbursement, it sends only limited payment information to the third party.

    - With either approach, the third party either issues the payments immediately or warehouses them until a future date as instructed by the data file. A company utilizing these types of services is outsourcing much of its disbursements functions and potentially reducing the overall costs of its accounts payables operations.

2. *VAB Collection Services* - Some banks offer a collection service that records the receipt of incoming payments (paper check, ACH, wire, etc.) and then reformats the data and transmits it to the company. This service is generally referred to as an electronic lockbox and provides the information to a company in whatever format it desires (i.e., a proprietary format, BAI lockbox format, or an ASC X12 format).

3.   *Electronic Clearing House Services (National & Regional)* - There are several electronic clearing house services operated by third parties or member banks which specialize in providing various types of EDI services to their members and/or customers. These clearing houses allow banks to offer a wider range of EDI services than they may be able to provide on their own.

E. Computer Hardware

EDI can be implemented on a variety of computers, ranging from single-user PCs to large mainframes. Some companies, particularly those new to EDI, may choose a PC for their initial implementations because of low cost and ease of start-up. As EDI transaction volumes increase, companies may choose to implement EDI on their mainframes or in a client-server environment.

IV. CREDIT TERMS AND EDI TRANSACTIONS

Most credit terms used today assume a paper-based environment with mailed invoices and checks.

A. Impact of EDI and EFT

EDI permits companies to complete paper-based processes more rapidly. EFT also removes much of the payment float due to mail, processing, and availability delays. Therefore, many companies are re-examining conventional credit terms. Other things being equal, faster payments are a disadvantage to buyers and an advantage to sellers. To compensate for changes in the cash flow timeline, companies are beginning to negotiate new EDI-based credit terms.

B. Negotiating Shared Benefits

EDI can bring significant cost savings to both parties. EDI makes it possible to shift the timing and/or amount of cash flows such that both buyer and seller realize significant savings. Buyers and sellers can transfer value by changing the terms of transactions. It is important to note that some companies will negotiate terms separately with each of their trading partners, while other companies may decide to unilaterally adjust terms for all of their trading partners. Two common approaches are:

1.   *Price Changes (Discount)* - The seller offers the buyer a cash discount to compensate for earlier payment. For example, a seller offers a 1.5% discount if a customer allows its account to be electronically debited on the day product or service is delivered. This may compare to normal payment under the paper system of 30 days or more.

2.   *Payment Timing Changes* - The buyer initiates later payment (compared to when paper checks were sent) to compensate for shorter delays involved in electronic payment (compared to the paper check process). For example, a customer initiates an ACH payment to its suppliers three days later than a check payment would have been mailed out. This neutralizes the float that the buyer gives up as a result of the switch to EFT.

C. Determination of Discount or Change in Payment Terms

The amount of the discount required to renegotiate credit terms successfully in an EDI environment depends on the present value impact of changing the payment timing and any transaction cost savings as a result of electronic versus paper-based payments. Companies utilizing a discount approach will set the discount for earlier electronic payment approximately equal to the present value cost of earlier payment.

Companies that change the timing of the payment will often determine a "float-neutral" solution to payment timing, which simply makes the electronic payment date equal to the paper payment date, plus the normal collection float. Regardless of the approach, a successful solution will be one which provides benefits to both the buyer and the seller.

V. EXAMPLES OF EC APPLICATIONS

EDI and EC play an integral part in the redesign of functions or processes in the treasury area. Two primary examples of this re-engineering are the implementation of evaluated receipts settlement and paid-on-production.

A. Evaluated Receipts Settlement

Evaluated receipts settlement (ERS) is a payment method designed to eliminate the need for a supplier to provide an invoice to the customer. The dollar amount for ERS payments is based not on an invoice, but on a calculation of the quantity actually received by the customer multiplied by the price on the purchase order. The supplier does not send an invoice, but rather is simply paid by the customer on an agreed date after receipt of the shipment. The use of ERS allows the customer to automate its payables process and the supplier to automate the receivables and payment application process.

B. Paid-on-Production

Paid-on-production is the process by which a payment record is created for goods and/or services based on a usage record rather than on shipping records. It is similar to consignment sales in retail, but is based on usage within a manufacturing environment. Typically there is only one supplier, and title to the product (or supply) transfers somewhere during the manufacturing process rather than at the shipping dock as in ERS. Because of legal concerns relating to liability, potential bankruptcy, and use of inventory assets for supporting loans, it is important to determine exactly when and where title to inventory transfers.

Questions

These chapter questions are to test and review the information in the text and are not examples of CCM examination questions, nor are they in the examination format.

Answers can be found at the back of the book on p. 333.

1. What are the primary benefits of electronic commerce (EC)?

2. What are the three basic types of electronic data interchange (EDI)?

3. What is the difference between EDI, FEDI, and EFT?

4. What are the costs which must be considered in an EC or EDI implementation?

5. What are the major barriers to EDI implementation?

6. What is UN/EDIFACT and how is it related to EDI in North America?

7. What are the primary ASC X12 financial transaction sets?

8. What are the primary NACHA formats for ACH payments?

9. What are the basic steps performed by EDI software?

10. What are the services offered by VANs to their customers?

11. What are the services offered by VABs to their customers?

12. How are credit terms affected by EDI?

13. What is evaluated receipts settlement (ERS)?

CHAPTER 14

Financial Risk Management

OVERVIEW

Financial risk due to interest rate and currency volatility exists for many companies. Methods have been developed for companies to manage their financial risk and to protect themselves against interest rate and currency movements. This chapter will cover the basics of financial risk management and various methods and instruments which can be used by companies to reduce their overall risk.

LEARNING OBJECTIVES

Upon completion of this chapter and the related study questions, the reader should know:

1. How the risk profile of a company affects its financial risk management.

2. The objectives of financial risk management.

3. The different types of instruments used in risk management.

4. The types of interest rate exposure.

5. What instruments companies can use to manage their interest rate exposure.

6. The types of foreign exchange exposure.

7. How the foreign exchange markets work.

8. How foreign exchange hedging contracts are used to manage foreign exchange exposure.

9. The types of commodity exposure.

10. What instruments companies can use to manage their commodities exposures.

11. The accounting issues relating to financial risk management.

OUTLINE

I. OVERVIEW OF FINANCIAL RISK MANAGEMENT

Financial risk management involves the identification, measurement, hedging, and monitoring of risk due to changing interest rates, foreign exchange rates, and/or commodity prices. This area is separate and distinct from the area known as insurance and risk management, which deals primarily with insurance related risk. Insurance and risk management is not covered in this text. The term financial risk has also been used in conjunction with a company's use of debt or financial leverage in its financial structure. This chapter will cover financial risk only as it relates to risk from changing interest rates, foreign exchange rates, and commodity prices, not as it relates to a company's use of financial leverage.

Financial risk for a company comes from a wide variety of sources. Some examples include:

• A company with a loan at a floating rate linked to a base rate such as LIBOR (London Inter-Bank Offered Rate) is exposed to interest rate risk.

- A company that borrows at fixed rates, for example in the bond market, is exposed to a possible opportunity cost if rates decline after it has borrowed. Investors may also be adversely affected.

- A company which agrees to pay or receive a foreign currency in the future is exposed to a change in the value of that currency relative to the U.S. dollar.

- A company whose cash flows may be impacted by changing commodity prices is also subject to financial risk. A company in the food processing industry could be impacted by changing prices in agricultural commodity markets, or a mining company might be impacted by changing prices in the commodity market for metals.

A. Risk Profile

An important part of risk management is the assessment of a company's risk profile. This is the determination of how much risk a company is willing to accept in each area of potential exposure. This risk profile, or attitude toward risk will change, depending on the nature of a company's business, its capital structure, its competition, and the general level of risk that its management is willing to accept.

There is generally a risk-return tradeoff to be considered. In most cases, taking on a higher level of risk offers the potential for higher returns or losses. Taking a more conservative, low-risk approach usually offers a lower range of possible returns or losses.

The management of a company must decide how aggressive the company should be toward risk where there is possible exposure. For example, a company may decide to be very aggressive (taking on high risk) relative to interest rate risk, but be conservative (taking on low risk) relative to foreign exchange and commodity risk. Because of the potential impact on the profitability of a company, its risk profile should be determined at the highest management level possible.

B. Hedging versus Speculating

It is critical for a company to recognize the difference between using various markets and instruments for hedging financial risk versus their use for speculative purposes. This distinction is important for both overall financial risk management and for possible tax and accounting consequences.

1. *Hedging* - Hedging is typically defined as utilizing financial instruments or contracts to reduce or eliminate the risk from future changes in rates or prices. When a company hedges a particular rate or price, it is essentially establishing a fixed price or rate for a future period. For example, a U.S. company expecting a future cash flow in a foreign currency is exposed to change in the value of that currency relative to the U.S. dollar. The company could hedge the future foreign currency flow by entering into a contract with another party to exchange the foreign currency for U.S. dollars in the future at a specific fixed rate. The purpose of hedging a transaction, therefore, is to replace an uncertain future cash flow, rate, or price, with a fixed and certain cash flow, rate, or price.

2. *Speculating* - In contrast to hedging, the purpose of speculation is to profit from a change in a future rate or price. **Speculating** involves the assumption of additional risk. In financial markets, speculation usually takes the form of a contract for deliv-

ery of a security, foreign currency, or commodity at some future date at a fixed price or rate. When such a contract is used for hedging, the company purchasing the contract expects delivery of a security, foreign currency, or commodity as part of its normal business operation to offset or cover the delivery required by the contract. When a company is using the contract for speculation, there is no such offsetting delivery expected and the company is taking an open or uncovered position in the financial asset.

3. *Tax and Accounting Impacts of Hedging and Speculation* - Current U.S. tax codes treat the gains and losses from hedging versus speculation in very different manners. Gains from both hedging and speculative transactions are generally reported as ordinary income. Losses from hedging transactions are treated as ordinary income; however, speculative losses may only be used to offset speculative gains. In some cases, a transaction deemed as speculative will receive a different accounting treatment than one where an underlying exposure exists.

II. OBJECTIVES OF FINANCIAL RISK MANAGEMENT

While the specific objectives of financial risk management will vary from company to company there are some general objectives that are common to almost all companies.

- *Determine Risk Profile* - This profile will establish the company's willingness to assume risk in each of the financial risk areas (interest rates, foreign exchange rates, and commodities).

- *Set Basic Goals* - The goals for each financial risk area will be determined by the associated risk profiles. The goals will provide specific guidelines for the level of risk relating to possible hedging or other risk reduction strategies for each area. A written policy and a set of established guidelines help to set forth these goals.

- *Identify and Measure the Level of Exposure* - Exposure will depend upon a company's line of business, international operations, and the impact to the company of changing interest rates, foreign exchange rates, or commodities. This measurement of exposure is necessary because it will enable a company to ascertain the impact of various risk management strategies on its overall risk.

- *Manage Exposure* - To manage a company's exposure, specific instruments and strategies must be selected and applied.

- *Monitor Exposure* - A company must monitor exposure on an ongoing basis and evaluate the effectiveness of the instruments and strategies used against a written policy and established guidelines.

III. GENERAL TYPES OF CONTRACTS USED IN FINANCIAL RISK MANAGEMENT

There are four basic categories of contracts or instruments used in financial risk management. These are as follows:

A. Forwards

Forwards are contracts between two parties that require some specific action at a later date. Many firms use these types of products in the currency, financial, and commodity markets to provide hedges against risk by allowing the user to lock-in a future price or rate on a financial asset, currency, or commodity item. In most cases, forwards involve the contractual obligation for delivery of an underlying asset.

- For currency forwards, a currency would be the underlying asset; for financial forwards, a government security is the underlying asset; and for the commodity market, a wide variety of standard agricultural and resource commodities (gold, pork bellies, lumber, oil, etc.) serve as the underlying assets.

- The forward markets are managed and supported by groups of banks, dealers, and/or traders who act as market-makers by providing forward contracts in financial securities, foreign currencies, and commodities.

- The most active of the forward markets are the foreign exchange (currency) and money markets (short-term government securities).

- The advantage of forwards is that they can usually be created for almost any asset, over any period of time, for any amount.

- The disadvantage of forwards is the cost of negotiating the contracts, especially for small amounts.

- A typical example of the forward market is a forward currency exchange. In this market a company could contract to exchange one currency for another at a specified rate of exchange on a specified future date. This allows a company to hedge its transaction-based risk of foreign exchange exposure.

B. Futures

Future contracts are similar to forwards in concept and in their ability to provide risk management and hedging. There are, however, several important differences:

- Futures are based on standardized contracts, with standard underlying assets, denomination amounts, delivery dates and terms. This may mean that a treasurer may not be able to exactly hedge an exposure in the futures market.

- Futures are normally bought and traded on organized exchanges and require both margin accounts and constant adjustment of the value of the future to market. The primary futures markets in the U.S. are the Chicago Board of Trade, the Chicago Mercantile Exchange, the New York Mercantile Exchange, and the Commodity Exchange (New York). The primary markets for currency futures are the International Money Market (IMM), which is part of the Chicago Mercantile Exchange, and the New York Futures Exchange.

- The existence of margin accounts on futures allows investors in the market to benefit from leverage on their holding of futures. Margin requirements vary with the underlying asset and the riskiness of the market. They also specify the percentage of the total position that must be held in the margin account.

- In order to protect the market participants, contracts are "marked to market" on a continual basis throughout the trading day. Marking to market means that the gains or losses are posted to the contract account as they occur. A margin call is issued if the value of a future (and thus the amount in the margin account) drops below a specified level. The holder of the contract is then required to either put additional funds into the margin account, or close out the position. Similarly, if the contract increases in value, the excess above the required margin may be removed from the account.

- Futures are rarely settled by actual delivery of the underlying asset, and normally are closed out prior to their maturity. The profit or loss from the futures position acts as the required hedge for the holder of the futures contract.

C. Swaps

Swaps are flexible instruments which have shown rapid growth in recent years, and are now an important tool in financial risk management. In its simplest form, a swap is an agreement between two parties to exchange an underlying asset (or the stream of cash flows associated with an asset) for a specified period of time. The value of the underlying asset is expressed as the **notional amount**.

Without an intermediary, it is often difficult for two parties to a potential swap opportunity to find each other. For many currency and interest rate swaps, a financial intermediary acts as a counter-party or swap dealer. The most common swap arrangements are as follows:

1. *Interest Rate Swaps* - These arrangements are used to convert fixed-rate obligations to floating-rate obligations and vice versa.

2. *Currency Swaps* - These arrangements are used to convert an obligation in one currency to an obligation in another currency.

3. *Commodity Swaps* - These arrangements are used to convert a floating price for a commodity into a fixed price for that commodity.

4. *Basis Swaps* - These arrangements (also known as rate-basis swaps) are used to convert a borrowing agreement from one rate basis to another.

D. Options

An option is a contract between two parties in which one of the parties (the purchaser of the option) has the right, but not the obligation, to buy or sell an underlying asset at a specified price during, or at the end of, some future time period.

- A **call option** gives the holder the right to buy an underlying asset (i.e., foreign currency, financial instrument, or commodity).

- A **put option** gives the holder the right to sell an underlying asset (i.e., foreign currency, financial instrument, or commodity).

- The price at which the option can be exercised in the market is called the strike price.

- The buyer of the option pays a premium to the seller of the option. If the buyer exercises the option, the option is binding on the seller.

- The seller of the option (usually called the writer of the option) keeps the premium, whether the purchaser exercises the option or not. In return, the writer has the obligation to fulfill the contract (buy or sell the underlying asset) if the buyer of the option chooses to exercise it.

- A typical use of an option is to provide the purchaser of the option with a strike price, which may be either a floor price for selling the underlying asset, or a ceiling price for buying the underlying asset. Options provide protection against adverse price movements, but allow unlimited potential for gain. This is a very different concept from futures and forwards which simply lock in a known price for some exchange in the future.

- Options exist for a wide variety of underlying assets including: stocks, currencies, market indices, futures, and commodities.

- Options are generally either American options or European options. An American option can be exercised at any time during its effective life. In contrast, a European option can be exercised only on the expiration date. European options are used almost exclusively for currency options, while both European and American options are used for other types of option contracts.

- Many options are listed and traded on organized exchanges such as the Chicago Board of Options Exchange. Most options in the United States are cleared through the Option Clearing Corporation located in Chicago.

IV. INTEREST RATE EXPOSURE

Many companies face financial risk due to exposure to changes in interest rates. This exposure may arise from financing activities, from short-term investments, or due to the nature of a company's business.

A. Examples of Exposures

Interest rate exposure is generally related to either a company's use of borrowed funds or its investment in interest-sensitive financial instruments. The key factor relating to interest rate exposure is the potential for losses (either financial or operating) due to changes in interest rates.

1. *Exposure Due to Falling Interest Rates* - Companies with variable interest rate investments face the possibility of reduced earnings and cash flows if interest rates fall.

2. *Exposure Due to Rising Interest Rates* - Companies with debt tied to variable interest rates face higher costs of borrowing if interest rates rise.

3. *Exposure Due to Short-Term versus Long-Term Interest Rates* - Companies with current short-term investments or debt, but a need for long-term investments or debt, face long-term interest rate exposure. Companies with current long-term investments or debt, but a need for short-term investments or debt, face short-term interest rate exposure.

B. Types of Contracts

There are several types of contracts or instruments which can be used to manage interest rate risk for a company.

1. *Forward Rate Agreements* - A **forward rate agreement** is a forward contract in which two parties agree on the interest rate to be paid at a future settlement date. The principal amounts are agreed upon, but never exchanged, and the contracts are settled in cash. Each party's exposure is limited to the difference in interest rates

between the agreed and actual rates at settlement. The majority of forward rate agreements are based on Eurodollar rates, although others are available.

2. *Interest Rate Futures* - **Interest rate futures** are legally binding commitments to sell financial instruments at a specified future date at a specified price. They are not generally used for buying and selling financial instruments, but for generating gains and losses on the value of specific financial instruments through the purchase and sale of futures contracts.

    • The short-term financial instruments most actively traded in the futures market are 90-day Eurodollar time deposits, 90-day Treasury bills (T-bills) and 90-day bank certificates of deposit. The most actively traded long-term instruments are 5-year and 10-year U.S. Treasury notes, and 30-year U.S. Treasury bonds.

    • For both the 90-day Eurodollar and the 90-day T-bill contracts, the face amount per contract is $1,000,000. Pricing for a Eurodollar contract is based on LIBOR, and pricing for a T-bill is based on the 90-day T-bill discount rate.

3. *Interest Rate Swaps* - An **interest rate swap** occurs when two parties agree to exchange interest obligations for a specified period of time or when the sale of a security is coupled with a simultaneous purchase of a similar security with a different coupon rate. The purpose of an interest rate swap between two parties is usually for one party to convert a fixed-interest rate payment into a variable-rate payment while the other party takes the opposite position.

4. *Interest Rate Options* - Interest rate options are options on financial instrument futures. If interest rates rise, the price of a financial future will fall, and if interest rates fall, the price of the future will rise.

5. *Interest Rate Caps, Floors, and Collars* - Caps, floors, and collars are option-like instruments that allow companies to benefit from the low cost of adjustable-rate financing while protecting themselves against interest rate movements.

    • *Interest Rate Caps* - **Interest rate caps** are arrangements by lenders guaranteeing that interest rates on floating-rate loans or variable-rate securities will not exceed specified levels. If a defined floating base rate such as LIBOR exceeds the cap, then the lender pays the difference to the borrower. When rates are lower than the level defined, the borrower enjoys the full benefit, minus the cost of the cap. Caps on investments limit the interest that will be paid to an investor.

    • *Interest Rate Floors* - **Interest rate floors** are minimum interest rates for a loan or variable-rate security. They guarantee that an investor will receive no less than an agreed-upon lower limit on interest rates. From the borrower's perspective, a floor sets a limit on how low the interest paid on a loan will be.

    • *Interest Rate Collars* - **Interest rate collars** are combinations of caps and floors, giving the holders ranges of minimum and maximum interest rates. Because the buyer of a collar is being paid for selling the floor in addition to buying the cap, a collar is less expensive than a cap.

V. FOREIGN EXCHANGE

For companies that deal in foreign currencies, it is important to understand what kinds of exposure the company faces, and how the markets work.

A. Types of Exposures

There are three different types of foreign exchange exposure: transaction, translation, and economic exposure.

1. *Transaction Exposure* - **Transaction exposure** is the exposure of balance sheet accounts such as accounts receivable, accounts payable or loans to a change in foreign exchange rates between the time a transaction is recorded and the time it is paid.

   For example, a U.S. exporter sells merchandise to a French buyer, agreeing to accept payment in French francs three months from now. The exporter records the account receivable now. The exporter is exposed to a possible loss if the value of the French franc declines relative to the U.S. dollar.

2. *Translation Exposure* - An exposure is created when a foreign subsidiary's financial statements are translated into U.S. dollars in order to be consolidated into the U.S. parent's financial statement. **Translation exposure** is the net total of the exposed assets less the exposed liabilities

3. *Economic Exposure* - **Economic exposure** is the long-term effect of transaction exposure on the present value of cash flows to the firm. For multinational firms, this arises primarily because the firm is doing business in many different currencies and, in the long term, will always be subject to additional fluctuations in its cash flows because of exchange rate changes.

B. Foreign Exchange Markets

For foreign exchange, there are two basic markets, the spot market and the forward market.

1. *Spot Market* - A rate quoted in the spot market for currency is called a **spot foreign exchange rate** (spot rate). These rates are generally quoted for delivery one or two business days from the date of the transaction. Delivery exceptions may be made, but usually at the expense of a rate higher than the quoted spot rate.

2. *Forward Market* - The forward foreign exchange market is a market in which an exchange rate for a future exchange of currencies can be fixed today.

   • A **forward foreign exchange** rate (forward rate) is an exchange rate established today for a currency transaction that settles more than two days in the future.

   • Forward foreign exchange rates are based on the spot exchange rate and the difference in interest rates for the two currencies. This is known as interest rate parity.

C. Rate-Quoting Conventions

Foreign exchange rates are quoted in a variety of ways, depending on the currencies and the markets involved.

1. *Foreign Exchange Rates* - A **foreign exchange rate** is the equivalent number of units of one currency per unit of a different currency. There are two ways to quote foreign exchange rates: the U.S. dollar equivalent of a unit of the foreign currency, or the amount of the foreign currency per U.S. dollar. The following example shows these quotation formats for selected foreign currencies.

Currency	U.S. $ Equivalent	Currency per U.S. $
British Pound (£)	1.54	0.65
German Deutschemark (DM)	0.73	1.37
Japanese Yen (¥)	.0099	101.01

In this example, a British Pound would cost $1.54 or a U.S. dollar would cost £0.65.

2. *Bid-Offer Spreads* - Banks and other dealers quote both bid and offer rates for foreign currency. The bid rate is the rate at which a bank is willing to purchase currency. The offer rate is the rate at which a bank is willing to sell currency. The spread between the bid rate and the offer rate provides income for the bank.

    For example, if the bank provided a quote of DM 1.37 .39 = $1, it would purchase a dollar for DM 1.37 (bid) and would sell a dollar for DM 1.39 (offer).

3. *Discounts, Premiums and Par* - The terms discount, premium and par, describe the relationship between spot and forward exchange rates. In the forward market, every currency can be said to trade at a discount, a premium or par with respect to the spot rate for that currency.

    • A currency is at a discount if it is worth less in the forward market than in the spot market.

    • A currency is at a premium if it is worth more in the forward market than it is in the spot market.

    • If the spot and forward values are the same, then the forward rate is at par to the spot rate.

D. Types of Contracts

Once a company has identified and quantified its foreign exchange exposure it can decide whether to hedge it fully, partially or not at all. The tax consequences of the various strategies should also be assessed before implementation.

1. *Forwards* - A **forward foreign exchange contract** is a commitment to buy or sell a specified quantity of foreign currency at an exchange rate set today for delivery on a specific future date. An importer arranges to buy the amount of currency needed when the payment is due. An exporter arranges to sell the amount of currency received when the payment is expected. Forward contracts are typically for six months or less but may be arranged for longer periods.

2. *Futures* - Foreign exchange futures are similar in concept to forwards but are highly standardized contracts offered for only a few major currencies like the British pound

and the Japanese yen. Futures contracts involve large amounts of the currency and mature at fixed dates. Because the contracts trade on their own, they do not require an underlying commercial transaction.

3. *Currency Swaps* - A **foreign currency swap** is a transaction in which two counter-parties initially exchange specific amounts of two different currencies, then repay these amounts over time with interest. The payment flows incorporate repayment of principal and the interest rates for each currency, which can be fixed or floating.

4. *Options* - An option is a right, but not an obligation, to buy or sell foreign currency at a specific price within a fixed period of time. Currency options provide a company with a low-cost method to limit its foreign currency exposure. For example, a U.S. company expecting a cash flow in yen could purchase a put option on yen which would provide a floor on the yen-to-U.S.-dollar exchange rate. Another example would be a company bidding on a contract which will create a foreign currency exposure if the company were to win the contract. For a fixed price, an option could provide protection against this potential exposure.

VI. COMMODITIES

Markets exist for many commodities which are either used by companies in their production process or which are sold by companies to their customers. The most common commodity markets are in the areas of agricultural and meat products, oil and gas, minerals, and metals. Companies with exposures related to products traded in these markets can utilize the markets to reduce their exposure.

A. Examples of Exposures

Companies face two basic types of exposures related to commodities.

1. *Price Exposure* - The primary exposure faced by companies relative to commodities is the potential for changes in the prices of those commodities. If a company uses commodities as inputs to its production process, rising prices on those commodities generates exposure for the company. Falling commodity prices would create a potential exposure for companies selling the commodities or items related to the commodities.

2. *Availability Exposure* - For companies whose business livelihood depends upon available supplies of a particular commodity, there is exposure related to possible shortages of that commodity.

B. Exchanges

The primary commodity exchanges are the Chicago Board of Trade, the Chicago Mercantile Exchange, and Commodity Exchange in New York. These markets and other regional and specialty commodity markets offer many different futures contracts.

C. Types of Contracts

As with the interest rate and foreign exchange markets, the commodity markets offer a variety of contracts.

1. *Forward* - A forward commodities contract is entered into between two parties who agree to exchange a specified amount of a commodity at a specified price at some future point in time. Except for certain highly traded commodities, forward contracts on commodities are not as readily available as those for interest rates or foreign exchange.

2. *Futures* - The futures markets for commodities are highly developed and available for a wide range of commodities and prices. The characteristics and use of these contracts are similar to futures contracts used in the interest rate and foreign exchange markets.

3. *Swaps* - Commodity swaps are used to convert a floating price for a commodity into a fixed price for that commodity. Commodity swaps can be approximated by using commodity futures and options to lock-in prices.

4. *Options* - The options markets for commodities are highly developed and available for a wide range of commodities and prices. The characteristics and use of these contracts are similar to options contracts used in the interest rate and foreign exchange markets.

VII. DERIVATIVES

Derivatives are financial products that derive their value from other assets, such as equities, debt, foreign currency, and commodities. Technically, instruments such as swaps, futures, options, and forwards are classified as derivatives. These standard derivatives are often traded on open exchanges and their risk characteristics are well-known and generally understood. However, other types of derivatives may be so complex that, in many instances, the buyers and sellers cannot easily understand the risks involved.

A. Use of Derivatives

Derivatives can be used either for hedging or speculative purposes. As discussed earlier in this chapter, there are some important differences between hedging and speculating. When used to hedge an existing exposure, a derivative can help to reduce the financial risk of a company. When used for speculation, a derivative can create additional financial exposure for a company.

B. Risks in Using Derivatives

The use of derivatives will have an impact on the risk profile of a company. Whether this causes an increase or a decrease in the overall risk is very much dependent on the exact mix of financing and instruments used by the firm. It also depends on whether the derivative is being used for hedging or speculation. It is also important to consider the overall risk placed on the financial markets by the increased use of these instruments (systemic risk). With many non-standard derivatives, there is also a risk that either the counter-party to a derivative transaction or the dealer facilitating the transaction will fail to fulfill their end of the contract. This could leave the other party to the transaction either in exposed position, or fail to provide the reduction in exposure expected. The financial condition of both the dealer and counter-party to the transaction should be carefully considered.

VIII. ACCOUNTING ISSUES

Due to the nature of the contracts used in financial risk management, there are special accounting issues which must be considered. Many of these issues are addressed by the Financial Accounting Standards Board (FASB) which issues Statements on Financial Accounting Standards (SFAS) pronouncements to guide in the accounting of financial risk and the instruments used in managing that risk. Some of the critical SFAS pronouncements relative to financial risk management include:

A. Financial Instruments Disclosure

The pronouncement concerning basic financial instruments disclosure (SFAS 105) covers the requirements for companies to disclose certain information about their investment in financial instruments. All companies are required to disclose the essential information about financial instruments with off-balance sheet risk of loss. This information includes contract amounts, nature and terms of instruments, potential accounting losses, collateral and security provisions, counter-party credit risk, and the fair market value of instruments. Additional requirements for the disclosure of derivative financial instruments are provided by SFAS 119.

B. Other Accounting Issues

Other accounting issues related to financial risk management are the following:

1. *Foreign Currency Translation* - SFAS 52 covers standards for foreign currency translations that are designed to:

    *   Provide information that is generally comparable to the expected economic effects of a rate change on an enterprise's cash flows and equity, and

    *   Reflect in consolidated statements the financial results and relationships as measured in the primary currency in which each entity conducts its business (referred to as its functional currency).

2. *Accounting for Taxes* - SFAS 109 primarily deals with the accounting for income taxes, but several of the sections have an impact on accounting for deferred tax liabilities related to foreign currency transactions.

Questions

These chapter questions are to test and review the information in the text and are not examples of CCM examination questions, nor are they in the examination format.

Answers can be found at the back of the book on p. 335.

1. What is financial risk management and where does it come from?

2. What is the risk profile of a company?

3. What is the difference between hedging and speculating?

4. What are the four basic types of contracts or instruments used in financial risk management?

5. What is the difference between a forward contract and a futures contract?

6. What are the primary types of interest rate exposure?

7. What are caps, collars, and floors?

8. What creates transaction exposure?

9. A bank provides a quote of SF 1.59 – .64 = $1. How much will it pay for one U.S. dollar?

10. How are forward exchange rates determined?

11. What are the primary types of contracts used to manage foreign exchange exposure?

12. What are the two types of commodity exposure?

13. What are the differences between derivatives and real securities and what are the risks involved in using derivatives?

14. What is the impact of SFAS 105 on financial risk management by a company?

CHAPTER 15

International Cash Management

OVERVIEW

This chapter describes the principal methods of international cash management including the application of cash management principles to the business environment of other countries and techniques specific to cross-border cash management. It describes the principal international trade payment methods, letters of credit, documentary collections and open accounts, and introduces export financing and insurance.

LEARNING OBJECTIVES

Upon completion of this chapter and the related study questions, the reader should know:

1. Why international cash management is important.

2. The objectives of international cash management.

3. How payment methods and banking systems vary among countries.

4. How cross-border check payments and wire transfers are made.

5. What techniques are used to help manage cash flows on an international basis.

6. How an exporter selects and uses letters of credit and documentary collections.

7. The principal methods of export financing and credit management.

8. What the tax considerations are for international cash management.

OUTLINE

I. **Introduction to International Cash Management**
   A. Increased Globalization of Business
   B. Increased Competition in the Domestic Marketplace
   C. Need for Cash Management Services on a Global Basis

I. INTRODUCTION TO INTERNATIONAL CASH MANAGEMENT

International cash management is becoming increasingly important as companies expand their presence in the global marketplace. This global marketplace, however, is a constantly changing and complex environment in which to operate. Each country operates under different sets of laws, business practices, and banking systems and practices. Compounding the problem of international cash management is the fact that the U.S. banking and payments system, with which most cash managers are familiar, is significantly different from those used elsewhere in the world.

A. Increased Globalization of Business

Almost every company in the U.S. is impacted by events on a global basis. Even small, localized companies use supplies with some foreign content, or are selling goods which compete with foreign products. Agreements such as the North American Free Trade Act (NAFTA) in 1994 and the General Agreement on Tariffs and Trade (GATT) have facilitated trade between countries, thus increasing the level of international business activity.

B. Increased Competition in the Domestic Marketplace

Increased competition in the domestic marketplace has caused many companies to look toward foreign markets as sources of additional revenue, either through export sales or expansion into foreign operations.

C. Need for Cash Management Services on a Global Basis

Companies expanding abroad have a need for the same kinds of cash management services they have in the U.S. Companies operating multinationally have many of the same concerns related to collection, concentration, disbursement, and information management that they have in the U.S., but these issues may have to be dealt with on very different basis. The selection of banks to assist a company in its international operations is a critical part of the international cash management process.

II. OBJECTIVES OF INTERNATIONAL CASH MANAGEMENT

The objectives of international cash management are similar to those for U.S. cash management. International cash management is the application of basic functions such as collection, concentration, disbursement, investment, borrowing, and information management to each international environment. International cash management is also concerned with cross-border funds movement, foreign exchange, and cash management practices within countries outside the U.S.

A. International Cash Management Issues

For a company involved in international cash management, many of the issues are the same as for domestic cash management, but with two additional challenges:

1. *More Complex Cash Flows* - A multinational company must deal with cash flows from different subsidiaries, suppliers, and customers in each of the countries in which it operates. As a result of widely differing regulations, banking systems, and information availability, companies operating internationally must manage a very complex series of cash flows in different currencies on a daily basis.

2. *Exposure Management* - In addition to the increased complexity of cash flows, a company must consider the impact of these cash flows on both the day-to-day and long-term foreign currency exposure to the company. (See also, Chapter 14, Financial Risk Management.)

B. International Cash Management Organization

The organization of the international cash management function may be centralized, decentralized or a combination of the two.

1. *Control* - Control may be either centralized or decentralized.

    *   *Centralized Control* - Some companies maintain centralized control over international cash management giving relatively little autonomy to non-domestic treasury personnel. A centralized function can result in economies of scale for services and lower costs to a company.

    *   *Decentralized Control* - Other companies with decentralized international treasury operations often require non-domestic treasury personnel to send in weekly and monthly reports summarizing bank balances, borrowing, investments and other indicators of performance. Headquarters personnel may make periodic visits to international offices to audit and train treasury personnel.

2. *Structure* - A company with relatively autonomous international subsidiaries operating as independent companies is more likely to be decentralized. A company with sales subsidiaries that interact primarily with the U.S. parent is more likely to be centralized.

III. CHARACTERISTICS OF INTERNATIONAL BANKING SYSTEMS

Each country's banking system has different regulations, capabilities, and services.

A. Central Bank

The central bank of a country will establish the conditions and restrictions under which foreign banks can operate. Changes in these conditions and restrictions are occurring rapidly in many countries. In general, these changes tend to create more competition and have a positive impact on the efficiency of local banks.

In the U.S., the central bank is the Federal Reserve, which performs a variety of functions, including operator of the payments system, bank regulator, lender of last resort, and controller of the money supply. Some of these functions may not be performed by central banks in other countries.

B. Number of Banks

In the U.S. there are thousands of independent financial institutions, many of them having only a single location. This is not generally the case in other countries, where there are a few banks which operate branches nationwide. Nationwide branching has a major impact on the operation and efficiency of collection, concentration, and disbursement systems.

C. Restrictions on Demand Deposit Accounts

In the U.S. there are restrictions which prevent the payment of interest on corporate demand deposit accounts offered by banks. In most other countries, banks pay interest on corporate demand deposit accounts with positive balances, and charge interest on accounts with negative balances. This makes many of the cash management services offered by U.S. banks, such as zero balance and sweep accounts, unnecessary in other countries.

D. Value Dating

In most countries other than the U.S., banks use value dating as compensation for services provided to their customers. Under a **value dating** system, the bank sets the dates upon which it grants credit for deposits or it debits the account for checks written.

- The forward value date is the date upon which the firm will be granted credit for deposited items.

- The back value date is the date upon which checks written on an account are debited from that account.

- Value dating may be negotiable, depending upon the bank and the country.

E. Characteristics of Banks and Banking Systems in Other Countries

Banks and banking systems vary widely from country to country, and are generally different from the U.S. banking system.

1. *Canada* - Canada is the largest trading partner of the U.S. and is a member of the North American Free Trade Agreement (NAFTA). As a result, many U.S. companies must deal with the Canadian banking system. In general, the Canadian banking system differs in many ways when compared to the U.S. system. Some of the characteristics of the Canadian banking system and financial institutions include:

    - The six largest Canadian financial institutions provide nationwide branching throughout the country.

    - The Canadian Payments Association is the operator of the national clearing and settlement system. Generally, all deposits receive same-day availability.

    - Lockboxes are used in Canada, but primarily to reduce mail and processing float, or for reductions in processing costs. They have no impact on availability float.

    - Canadian financial institutions, in contrast to U.S. institutions, offer corporate overdraft accounts and pay interest on corporate demand deposits.

    - Canadian financial institutions offer a variety of electronic services, including support for Electronic Data Interchange (EDI) transactions.

    - Many Canadian financial institutions offer support for cross-border transactions such as U.S.-dollar check settlements via U.S. dollar accounts in Canada or via U.S. Fed points.

2. *Europe* - With few exceptions, European banks are efficient and offer a full array of electronic services. Companies with significant cross-border flows often use institutions operating in regional banking centers such as London or Brussels. Cross-border banking requires specific branch and electronic capabilities, and only a limited number of banks are able to do this.

    Banking in Eastern Europe tends to be difficult, with local banks and foreign banks providing varying degrees of service.

3. *Pacific Rim/Asia* - Banking in this region is characterized by a high degree of regulation and a limited, but growing, foreign presence.

    Japanese banks are typically used for business within Japan since the local subsidiary management tends to prefer dealing with Japanese banks. Japanese banks continue to expand services available outside of Japan and are generally changing their style to be more like that of banks in Europe and the U.S.

    In the countries of South East Asia, local banking systems are often inefficient and banking services are limited. However, foreign banks that offer banking services are increasing their presence in these countries.

    In Australia and New Zealand, where the local banking systems are based on nationwide branch banking, most services are available to multinational customers.

4. *Latin America* - This region has a wide variety of banking systems. For example, Brazil's banking system is highly electronic, while systems in other countries in the region are still primarily paper-based. There are minimal cross-border flows within the region due in part to country regulations. Generally, companies use local banks for local services and use foreign banks only when cross-border banking is needed.

5. *Africa/Middle East* - The majority of commercial activity in these regions is conducted via letters of credit. There is increasing bank representation in the region led by European (mainly British and French) and U.S. banks. Companies operating here tend to use foreign banks for cross-border banking.

IV. CHARACTERISTICS OF INTERNATIONAL PAYMENT SYSTEMS

A. Check Clearing

There are several key issues in international check clearing. They include:

*   The check clearing process within a country varies significantly from country to country. Some countries have nationwide clearing, others do not. The clearing of checks may be accomplished by the central bank (as the Fed does in the U.S.), by several of the major banks acting as clearing agents, or by correspondent relationships between different banks.

*   The clearing of checks between countries is often a slow and complicated process. Inter-country checks generally clear as collection items which must be presented back to the bank in the country where they were drawn.

*   Some financial institutions offer specialized international check clearing services which speed up the process of international check clearing.

B. Electronic Payment Systems

Many countries offer different types of electronic systems for both corporate and consumer payments.

1. *Company-to-Company Electronic Payment Systems* - Electronic payment of company obligations is more common in some areas of the world than it is in the U.S. This is especially true in countries with poor postal services or slow check clearing

systems. The actual structure and operation of these payment systems vary from country to country, but they have some common characteristics:

- *Credit-Based Transactions* - Most company-to-company electronic payments are credit-type transactions, where the payor is sending money from its account to that of the company being paid. In this sense, these payments are similar to ACH credits or Fedwire transactions in the U.S. The method in which a company accesses its bank to initiate payment varies widely by country, bank, and company. Generally, the payment initiation systems are provided by the banks to their customers on a proprietary basis.

- *Transactions are Cleared Through Correspondent Balances* - The majority of electronic payments systems outside the U.S. are cleared through correspondent balances of the banks involved in the transfers. Between countries, this clearing is usually done bank-to-bank on a bilateral basis. Within a country, the clearing may be done on a bilateral basis, or through a netting system run by a few clearing banks. These systems are different from the Fedwire system in the U.S., where value is transferred by debits and credits to bank reserve balances at the Federal Reserve.

- *Role of SWIFT* - The Society for Worldwide Inter-bank Financial Telecommunications (SWIFT) offers a wide variety of services to banks, which in turn provide these benefits to their customers. Through SWIFT messages, a company can transfer balances, initiate foreign payments, receive information on foreign accounts and balances, and send documentation relating to letters of credit. Though SWIFT does not actually transfer value for payments, the messages sent via this system provide instructions for the value transfer. The actual clearing of the payments is done through correspondent balances, as are most other international electronic payments.

- *Use of Giros* - Most European countries have giro systems which generally operate through their postal systems. Giro systems allow payments from one giro account to another using direct debits and credits. Though these systems are primarily used for consumer-type payments, there is significant use for company-to-company payments in some countries.

2. *Consumer Electronic Payments Systems* - The use of electronic payments systems by consumers is also more common in many areas of the world than in the U.S. These types of payments would include those between consumers and companies and governments, as well as consumer-to-consumer payments. As in the case of company-to-company payments, the structure and operation of the payment systems will vary from country to country. Some of the most common systems and applications are as follows:

- *Consumer Use of Giros* - As stated above, many countries have giro systems which operate through their postal systems. Payments from consumers to companies and governments (for taxes) are generally the bulk of payment volumes in these systems. Consumers may use the giro system in place of checks through a bank for their payment of monthly bills and statements. In some countries these systems can be accessed by consumers via PCs, terminals, or telephone.

- *Debit Cards* - Debit cards outside the U.S. operate similarly to domestic cards. As consumers use these cards for purchases, the funds are debited from their bank or giro account and credited to the seller's account.

- *Smart Cards* - These cards are similar to debit cards, but may contain a microchip with additional information and security protections. The card keeps track of purchases and payments and can provide the user with a current account balance. It may also be used for pre-paid value transactions, where the consumer prepays the bank, Giro, or company issuing the card. The card keeps track of purchases and the remaining balance.

V. INTERNATIONAL CASH MANAGEMENT TECHNIQUES

A. Pooling

In most European countries, a procedure known as **pooling** is offered by banks. In pooling, excess funds in the accounts of some subsidiaries may be used to offset deficits in the accounts of other subsidiaries. This type of pooling arrangement typically is offered in a variety of currencies. Credit facilities of some kind are usually required by the banks to support any negative balances in the pool.

Positive and negative balances may be aggregated each day for the calculation of interest earned or due. Normally, no funds are actually transferred; only the interest calculation is made.

B. Netting

Netting is a system designed to reduce the number of cross-border payments among units of a company through the elimination or consolidation of individual funds flows typically denominated in a number of different currencies. Many countries impose restrictions on the use of netting systems, and formal approval may be required.

1. *Bilateral Netting* - In a **bilateral netting** system, purchases in a specific currency between two subsidiaries of the same company are netted against each other so that over time, typically one month, only the difference is transferred.

    For example, subsidiaries of a multinational company, one located in France and another in Germany, hold payments until one or two regularly scheduled times during the month. Prior to the settlement date, the payments in both directions are totaled, the net due one of the subsidiaries determined, and a single transfer is scheduled.

2. *Multilateral Netting* - The system is similar to bilateral netting, but with more than two units. Each unit informs a central treasury management center of all planned cross-border payments. To determine netting transactions, the payments between all subsidiaries are converted into a common, reference currency. Payments are combined into fewer, but larger, transactions and each unit is informed prior to the settlement date of the net amount to pay or to be received in its own currency. The netting center makes the necessary foreign exchange conversions. Although **multilateral netting** is used primarily for intra-company transactions, some companies include third-party payments or receipts in their systems.

    The mechanics of multilateral netting are illustrated in Exhibit 15.1.

EXHIBIT 15.1

Illustration of Multilateral Netting

Intercompany Cash Flows Before Netting

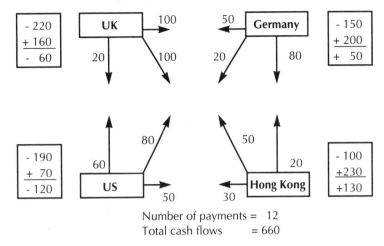

Number of payments = 12
Total cash flows = 660

Cash Flow with Multilateral Netting Center

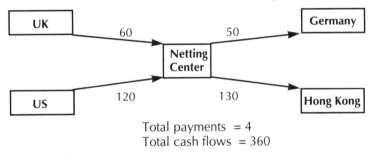

Total payments = 4
Total cash flows = 360

3. *Benefits* - The benefits of netting include:

    • The number of foreign exchange transactions, as well as cross-border wire transfer transactions, are reduced.

    • The larger scale foreign exchange transactions resulting from consolidation should improve rates.

    • Preplanning cross-border payments improves cash forecasting for both the subsidiary and the parent.

4. *Costs* - There are setup and maintenance costs which must be considered when starting and operating a netting system.

C. Leading and Lagging

Netting systems may be used to implement **leading and lagging**. Leading and lagging involves making cross-border payments between subsidiaries either ahead of schedule (leading) or behind schedule (lagging). Liquidity is moved from one subsidiary to the other. Leading can be helpful when a currency is expected to depreciate while lagging will be used when the currency is expected to appreciate relative to the parent's home currency. Leading and lagging are also effective in local cash management and mobilization.

D. Reinvoicing

Reinvoicing is a method of centralizing the responsibility for monitoring and collecting international accounts receivable and more effectively managing the related foreign exchange exposure. A reinvoicing center is a company-owned subsidiary that buys the goods from the an exporter and resells the goods to an importer. The exporting unit invoices and receives funds from the reinvoicing subsidiary in its own currency, while the importing unit is invoiced and pays funds to the reinvoicing subsidiary in its own currency. Establishing a reinvoicing center requires local government approval and negotiation on how the subsidiary will be taxed.

1. *Benefits* - The benefits of a reinvoicing center include:

   - Because each subsidiary deals primarily in its own currency, foreign exchange exposure is centralized in the reinvoicing center where it can be more effectively managed.

   - It can also improve a company's worldwide short-term liquidity management by providing flexibility in inter-subsidiary payments. For instance, it enables leading and lagging arrangements to be implemented easily, improves export trade financing and collections, reduces bank costs and improves foreign exchange rates by trading in larger amounts.

2. *Costs* - Reinvoicing center expenses include physical location and administration costs as well as costs specifically associated with netting centers.

   Reinvoicing is illustrated in Exhibit 15.2.

EXHIBIT 15.2

Illustration of Reinvoicing

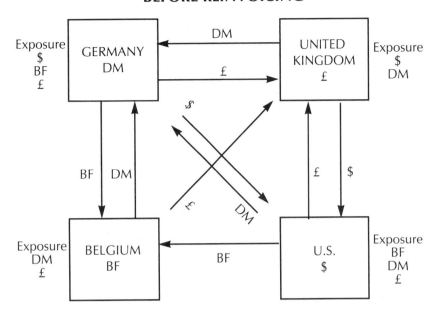

TRANSACTION EXPOSURES BEFORE REINVOICING

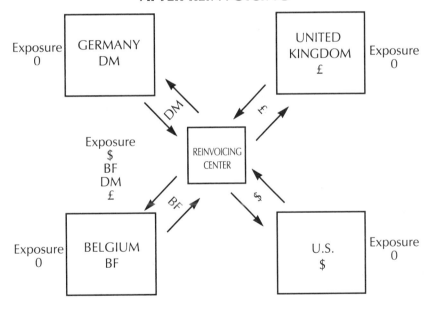

TRANSACTION EXPOSURES AFTER REINVOICING

E. Internal Factoring

The purpose of an internal factoring center is similar to that of reinvoicing. Rather than taking actual title to the goods as with reinvoicing, the internal factoring unit buys accounts receivable from the exporting unit and collects from the importing unit.

F. Multicurrency Accounts

A **multicurrency account** is an account that allows for the transfer of payments in any readily convertible currency to and from one designated account. The currency denomination of the account is at the discretion of the account holder.

G. Balance Reporting Services

Major banks in Europe and Asia have been offering balance reporting services and transactions electronically since the mid-1980s. Such reporting services allow both local and international access.

For example, the balances and debit and credit details for a Dutch subsidiary of a U.S. company can be reported to local management in the Netherlands as well as to the parent. Major international banks and third-party service providers can consolidate reporting by a company's banking network into a single daily report.

VI. INTERNATIONAL TRADE PAYMENT METHODS

In the U.S., it is customary for a seller to check the credit standing of a buyer prior to selling on open account. Invoices are often sent with each shipment and included in a statement of amounts due at the end of the month. When a seller is exporting goods to a non-domestic buyer, more credit protection is frequently needed, particularly for a new business relationship. The most frequently used international trade payment mechanisms, letters of credit, documentary collections, and open account, can be explained as a hierarchy. Letters of credit offer the seller the most protection, but they are also the most expensive. Open account terms offer the least protection but are also the least costly. Regardless of the method of trade payment, the currency to be used must be agreed upon by the buyer and seller. Payment is generally specified in either the buyer's currency or the seller's currency, but may be in a third currency if mutually acceptable to both parties. Exhibit 15.3 shows the hierarchy of trade payment mechanisms.

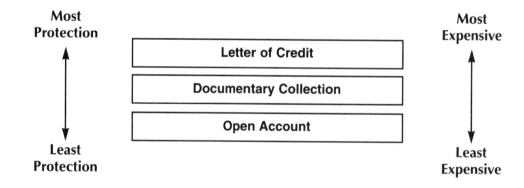

EXHIBIT 15.3
Hierarchy of International Trade Payment Methods

Most Protection — Least Protection
Letter of Credit
Documentary Collection
Open Account
Most Expensive — Least Expensive

A. Letters of Credit

A letter of credit (L/C) is an important method of payment for international trade. The characteristics and use of them are as follows:

1. *Definition* - A **letter of credit** is a document issued by a bank, guaranteeing the payment of a customer's draft up to a stated amount for a specified period if certain conditions are met. An L/C substitutes a bank's credit for that of the buyer, virtually eliminating the seller's risk.

2. *Role of Banks* - Banks may have the following roles in L/C transactions.

    *   *Issuing Bank* - The issuing bank is the buyer's (importer's) bank that issues the L/C in favor of the beneficiary (seller/exporter).

    *   *Advising Bank* - The advising bank advises the beneficiary of an L/C in its favor.

    *   *Negotiating Bank* - The negotiating bank examines the documents presented by the beneficiary, receives payment from the issuing bank, and pays the beneficiary. The advising and negotiating bank are often the same.

    *   *Confirming Bank* - The confirming bank confirms to the beneficiary that payment will be made if documents meet the terms and conditions of the L/C, regardless of the issuing bank's ability to pay.

3. *Commitment* - Letters of credit are generally irrevocable. This means the L/C cannot be canceled or amended without the agreement of all parties to the transaction. The parties that must agree are the buyer, beneficiary (seller), issuing bank, and, if the L/C is confirmed, the confirming bank.

4. *Payment Timing* - The L/C may provide for either immediate or deferred payment to the beneficiary (seller/exporter).

    *   When the L/C requires the presentment of a sight draft, which is a draft payable on demand, the negotiating bank pays the seller immediately, and is reimbursed by the issuing bank.

    *   The L/C may require presentment of a time draft which provides for payment at a future date. The use of time draft is a way for the seller to provide credit terms to the buyer. The seller may be able to receive payment prior to maturity by discounting (selling for its discounted value) the time draft to a local bank.

    *   A deferred payment L/C provides for presentation of one or more sight drafts at specified dates in the future, and this sometimes extends over several years. When medium-term financing is provided for the export of capital goods, a deferred payment L/C may be used in conjunction with a term loan agreement.

5. *Documentary Nature of L/C* - It is important to realize that an L/C is documentary in nature. This means that the bank's role in an L/C transaction is the examination of documents, not the underlying merchandise. It is the responsibility of the importer opening the credit to specify the documents that the exporter must present after shipment as a condition for payment. The use of documents has its limitation as a protective mechanism to ensure that the importer gets the exact merchandise it ordered.

6. *Commercial Letter of Credit* - A commercial letter of credit is issued by a bank in relation to a trade transaction involving the domestic or international shipment of merchandise. It is the intended mechanism of payment and typically requires presentment of a draft, commercial invoice, and related shipping documents.

7. *Standby Letter of Credit* - A **standby letter of credit** is an L/C issued on behalf of a bank's customer to secure that customer's payment or other form of performance in favor of the beneficiary. Unlike a commercial L/C, a standby L/C is not the intended mechanism of payment and is only drawn upon in the event of the bank's customer's non-payment or non-performance. It usually requires presentation of a draft along with a statement signed by the beneficiary stating that the bank's customer has not fulfilled its agreed upon obligation.

Exhibit 15.4 illustrates a typical international commercial letter of credit transaction.

EXHIBIT 15.4

Illustration of a Letter of Credit Transaction

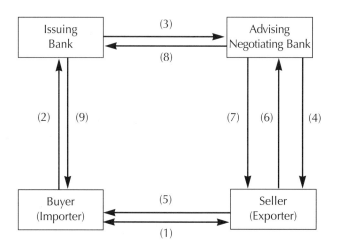

Step 1. The buyer and the seller agree to a sales contract in which the buyer is required to open an LC in favor of the seller.

Step 2. The buyer chooses a bank in its country and opens an LC in favor of the seller.

Step 3. The issuing (buyer's) bank sends the LC to a bank in the seller's country. The latter bank becomes the advising bank.

Step 4. The advising bank sends details of the credit to the seller, who is the beneficiary of the credit.

Step 5. The seller ships the merchandise to the buyer.

Step 6. The seller presents the draft and documents to the advising/negotiating bank.

Step 7. The advising/negotiating bank examines the documents and pays the seller if the documents meet the terms of the LC.

Step 8. The advising/negotiating bank sends the documents to the issuing bank and charges the issuing bank's account.

Step 9. The issuing bank examines the documents, charges the buyer's account, and releases the documents to the buyer. With the documents, the buyer is able to claim the merchandise.

B. Documentary Collections

Documentary collections are another method of payment used in international trade. The characteristics and use of this method follow:

1. *Definition* - A **documentary collection** is a payment method that processes the collection of a draft and accompanying shipping documents through international correspondent banks. Instructions regarding the specifics of the transaction are contained in a collection letter or form which accompanies the documentation. It is the responsibility of the seller (exporter) to determine the specific instructions to be used in the collection letter.

2. *Role of Banks* - The banks involved in a documentary collection act only as collecting and paying agents and, unlike a L/C, assume no direct obligation for ensuring that payment will be made. Banks involved in these transactions may play the following roles:

    *   *Remitting Bank* - The remitting bank is the seller's (exporter's) bank that prepares the collection letter and forwards documents to a correspondent bank in the buyer's (importer's) country.

    *   *Collecting Bank* - The collecting bank is the remitting bank's correspondent that is responsible for contacting the buyer (importer) and processing the collection of payment and release of the documents as instructed.

3. *Collection Letter* - A collection letter specifies the exact procedures to be followed before shipping documents are released to the importer. The buyer (importer) usually needs physical possession of the shipping documents in order to obtain the merchandise. Documents are typically released either against payment or acceptance as follows:

    *   Documents against payment use a sight draft and require that the collecting bank receive full and final payment of the amount owed prior to releasing the documents.

    *   Documents against acceptance use a time draft which must be accepted by the importer before the collecting bank may release documents. Upon maturity of the time draft, it is presented to the importer for payment.

4. *Final Payment* - Once final payment is received, the collecting bank sends the payment to the remitting bank, as instructed, for payment to the seller (exporter).

5. *Non-Payment or Non-Acceptance* - In the event of non-payment or non-acceptance, the exporter bears the risk and cost of having to remarket the goods to another buyer or possibly having the merchandise returned. The exporter may have the collecting bank initiate formal action against the importer for non-performance.

Exhibit 15.5 illustrates a documentary collection.

EXHIBIT 15.5

*Illustration of a
Documentary
Collection*

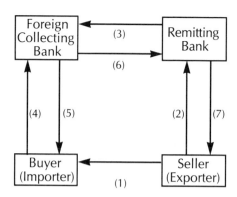

Step 1.   The seller/exporter ships merchandise to the buyer/importer.

Step 2.   The seller/exporter delivers the draft and documents to the remitting bank.

Step 3.   The remitting bank forwards the documents to the buyer/importer's bank, the foreign collecting bank.

Step 4.   The buyer/importer makes payment to the foreign collecting bank in the case of a sight draft, or accepts a time draft.

Step 5.   The foreign collecting bank releases the documents so that the buyer/importer may take delivery of the merchandise.

Step 6.   The foreign collecting bank remits funds to the remitting bank.

Step 7.   The remitting bank pays the seller/exporter.

C. Open Accounts

Under the open account method, the seller ships the merchandise and sends an invoice to the buyer.

- The open account method is the least secure, but also the least costly of the three most often used international trade payment methods (L/C, documentary collections and open account).

- The open account is the most frequently used method of payment for well-established relationships.

D. Other Trade Payment Methods

Other less frequently used international trade payment mechanisms include cash before delivery, consignment, barter, counter-trade and forfaiting.

1.   *Cash Before Delivery* - Cash before delivery (CBD) is used when the seller requires the total protection of receiving payment before shipment of goods.

2.   *Consignment* - The seller consigns goods to a foreign agent, but retains title to the goods. The agent pays the exporter when the goods are sold. Title generally remains with the seller until payment date. Regaining possession of the goods if they are not sold may be difficult and costly.

3. *Barter* - **Barter** is the direct exchange of goods and/or services without using money.

4. *Counter-trade* - **Counter-trade** is a method of payment used by companies that do not have access to sufficient hard currency (internationally traded currencies such as the U.S. dollar or the German Deutschmarks) to pay for imports from other countries. A seller in a country such as the U.S. ships merchandise to the counter-trading country, and takes in exchange merchandise that can be sold elsewhere in the world.

5. *Forfaiting* - **Forfaiting** is a specialized form of export financing which provides both short and medium-term financing. The seller accepts a note from the buyer which may have a maturity of up to three years. The note can be discounted in a specialized market in London. It may be useful in situations where confirmed letters of credit are not available.

6. *Trading Companies* - An exporter (seller) can also sell its products, at a discount, to an **export trading company** which, in turn, resells the products.

E. Banker's Acceptance

A banker's acceptance (BA) is most often used to finance the import, export or domestic shipment of goods, but can also be used to finance storage of those goods. BAs are commonly, but not necessarily, used in conjunction with letters of credit.

A banker's acceptance is a time draft, on the face of which the drawee has written the word accepted over its signature. The date and place payable are also indicated. The party accepting or agreeing unconditionally to pay the draft at a particular time and place is known as the acceptor.

By accepting the draft, the bank creates a banker's acceptance and indicates its commitment to pay the face amount at maturity to anyone who presents it for payment at that time. In this way, the bank backs the instrument with its name and credit and assumes the credit risk, but at the same time creates a short-term instrument that is negotiable in the money market. The bank can either hold the banker's acceptance in its own portfolio or sell it to an investor.

1. *Cost* - The cost of acceptance financing has two components: the discount rate (the rate earned by the investor) and the bank's acceptance commission.

2. *Eligibility* - Most acceptance financing is done with eligible acceptances. An eligible BA is an acceptance that may be discounted at the Federal Reserve. To be eligible for discount, the acceptance may not have a maturity of more than 180 days. Eligible underlying transactions include the following:

    *   Import or export of goods

    *   Domestic storage transactions with documents conveying title attached

    *   Storage of readily marketable staples secured by warehouse receipts

VII. EXPORT FINANCING AND TAX CONSIDERATIONS

Providing financing to a non-domestic buyer, obtaining export credit insurance, and considering tax implications are important competitive factors for an exporter.

A. Foreign Credit Evaluation

It may be difficult for a U.S. company or bank to evaluate the credit of a non-U.S. buyer because of the scarcity of credit information and differing accounting practices. Collecting delinquent accounts in other countries can be both difficult and expensive for a U.S. exporter.

B. Financing Foreign Buyers

A critical issue for many companies selling internationally is how to finance their sales to foreign buyers. For U.S.-based companies, the primary sources of financing are commercial banks and the Export-Import Bank of the U.S.

1. *Commercial Banks* - Some commercial banks in the U.S. specialize in providing direct financing to the foreign buyers of U.S. exports.

2. *Export-Import Bank of the U.S.* - The **Export-Import Bank of the U.S.** (Eximbank) is an independent agency of the U.S. government established to finance and guarantee payment for U.S. exports. The Eximbank is directed by its corporate charter to:

   • develop export financing programs that are competitive with those offered by other countries,

   • ensure that financing or repayment guarantees are made to borrowers with a reasonable capacity to repay, and

   • supplement, but not compete with, financing offered by private commercial banks.

   The Eximbank's programs include a working capital program aimed at small businesses, a loan guarantee program to encourage private-sector loans, and a direct loan program used in a situation in which the competition receives subsidized financing.

C. Export Credit Insurance

A common method of ensuring payment is through **export credit insurance**. This insurance is provided by the Eximbank and by certain private insurers. Export insurance can cover both political (sovereign) risk and commercial risk. Insurance coverage is available for shipment to almost every country with which the U.S. has diplomatic relations. The insurance obtained through the Eximbank is backed by the U.S. government.

D. Offshore Financing

Offshore financing involves raising funds outside a company's home country. Companies may finance outside their country for the following reasons:

1. *Diversification of Funding* - A company may want to diversify its funding sources rather than depend on one market:

    • Too much debt in a particular market may saturate investors' desire for a company's debt, and as a result, raise the cost of borrowing.

    • In times of tight credit, it is helpful to have relationships with a number of different lenders.

2. *Hedging in Foreign Currencies* - Long-term debt in a foreign currency can hedge a long-term investment in the same currency. Similarly, short-term debt can hedge current assets such as accounts receivable in the same currency. For example, if a U.S. company had accounts receivable denominated in British pounds sterling (£), it may consider short-term debt denominated in sterling. In both long and short-term cases, if foreign currency-denominated assets depreciate, liabilities denominated in the same foreign currency depreciate as well.

3. *Lower Borrowing Rates for Parent Company* - A U.S. parent company may be able to borrow in a foreign currency at a lower borrowing rate than its U.S. borrowing rate, even after hedging.

4. *Lower Borrowing Rate for Foreign Subsidiaries* - An international subsidiary may be able to borrow in its local market from one of its local banks at lower rates than it can through its parent company.

5. *Tax Advantages* - There may be tax advantages available in the subsidiary's home country.

Companies may also establish offshore financing subsidiaries to obtain funding and benefit from favorable tax regulations. A company may fund the needs of a number of subsidiaries in different countries through its offshore finance company, thus taking advantage of lower rates by borrowing in large amounts.

E. Tax Considerations

Multinational companies must deal with tax codes in all the countries in which they have operations or sales. Some of the more important considerations include:

1. *Foreign Tax Credits* - A U.S. company's income derived from its foreign operations may have to be included in its U.S. income tax return. This typically occurs when a dividend is paid from a foreign subsidiary to the U.S. parent. That same income may also have been taxed in the country in which the subsidiary is located, resulting in double taxation.

    To relieve the effect of this double taxation, the U.S. tax law allows a U.S. company a dollar-for-dollar tax credit against its total U.S. income tax liability for those foreign income taxes paid by the parent and its subsidiaries. This credit is called the foreign tax credit. It is allowed only for those foreign taxes paid which are income taxes and which do not exceed U.S. tax rates.

2. *Foreign Tax Planning* - The complexity of the law regarding the taxation of non-domestic income makes it important for treasury personnel to work with tax experts.

3. *Tax-Advantaged Business Centers* - To attract multinational businesses and related employment opportunities, a number of countries offer tax incentives for subsidiaries that perform certain administrative and financial functions.

Questions

These chapter questions are to test and review the information in the text and are not examples of CCM examination questions, nor are they in the examination format.

Answers can be found at the back of the book on p. 336.

1. Why is international cash management becoming increasingly important for companies?

2. What are some of the key characteristics in which international banking systems differ?

3. What is value dating?

4. What must a payee do if it receives a check drawn in a different country?

5. How do payment practices vary outside the U.S.?

6. What is pooling, as applied in non-U.S. banking systems?

7. What is a multi-currency account?

8. What are the major benefits of using a netting system?

9. What is a reinvoicing center?

10. What risk is eliminated by the use of a letter of credit?

11. What is an irrevocable letter of credit?

12. What is a stand-by letter of credit?

13. What is the major difference in the role of the banks under a documentary collection as opposed to a letter of credit?

14. What is counter-trade?

15. What is the maximum maturity for a banker's acceptance to remain eligible for discount at the Federal Reserve?

16. What is the Eximbank?

17. Why do companies use offshore financing?

CHAPTER 16

Relationship Management

OVERVIEW

This chapter describes the objectives of relationship management, the various issues in selecting financial institutions and other service providers, the role of account analysis in financial institution compensation, and the benefits of different methods of financial institution compensation.

LEARNING OBJECTIVES

Upon completion of this chapter and the related study questions, the reader should know:

1. The objectives of relationship management.

2. How companies select and evaluate financial institutions and other service providers.

3. What an account analysis statement is and how it is used in relationship management.

4. How to perform a collected balances and earnings credit calculation.

5. The options for compensating financial institutions.

OUTLINE

I. Objectives of Relationship Management

II. Service Provider Selection
    A. Selection Process
    B. Selection Criteria

III. Issues in Financial Institution Relationship Management
    A. Creditworthiness
    B. Rating Agencies
    C. Depository Financial Institution Strength
    D. Number of Relationships
    E. Relationship Documentation
    F. Audit and Control

I. OBJECTIVES OF RELATIONSHIP MANAGEMENT

Among the objectives of relationship management are the following:

- *Developing a Partnership Approach* - A partnership approach means that the relationship is mutually beneficial and mutually profitable.

- *Maintaining Access to Credit* - A company requires access to credit facilities to meet short-term working capital needs.

- *Developing Service Relationships* - A company requires access to such services as cash management, investment, trust, international, and risk management.

- *Managing Costs and Quality* - A company selects and monitors financial institutions and other service providers to ensure that the relationship is cost-effective for the quality of service and value received.

- *Monitoring Financial Institution Risk* - A company monitors the risk of a disruption in a financial institution relationship, whether by a change in management policy, merger, acquisition, or failure.

II. SERVICE PROVIDER SELECTION

The trend toward consolidation and specialization among financial institutions and other service providers has made the selection process a critical decision for many companies. The trend toward consolidation means that there are fewer major players in certain product areas. The trend toward specialization means that it is important to match a given company's needs with a particular provider's strengths.

A. Selection Process

1. *Informal* - Financial institution or service provider selection does not always involve a formal process. Sometimes a company may already have an established relationship with a provider or may have already targeted specific providers of a service. In such cases, the selection process does not involve a formal written proposal.

2. *Request for Information* - In some cases, a **Request for Information** (**RFI**) may be used in the selection process. An RFI is often used by a company simply to confirm that use of a current provider of a service is justified, or to narrow the field of potential providers before issuing a Request for Proposal. An RFI is also used to solicit ideas from service providers on how to solve a particular business or operational problem.

3. *A Request for Proposal* - A **Request for Proposal (RFP)** is a formal document prepared by a company which outlines its objectives and service requirements. An RFP can be used by a company to place out for bid, everything ranging from one particular service to its entire relationship. By law, some government entities are required to prepare RFPs on a periodic basis, usually every three to five years, to ensure that they are receiving comparable services at competitive prices. Many companies also periodically prepare RFPs for similar reasons. Outside consultants are sometimes used to assist in the preparation of and evaluation of responses to RFPs.

    Among the kinds of information requested in a typical RFP are the following:

    - Background information on the provider
    - Service descriptions
    - Service features and benefits
    - The provider's commitment to support and enhance services
    - Price schedule and a cost/benefit analysis
    - Pro forma account analysis statement (financial institutions only)
    - Sample service commitments or agreements
    - Customer references

B. Selection Criteria

The following are among the important criteria for selecting service providers:

- Willingness to be a reliable provider of credit at competitive rates
- Ability to structure flexible loan terms and conditions and provide financial advice
- Knowledge of a company and/or a specific industry
- Responsiveness to questions and understanding of needs
- Quality of customer service
- Pricing of services
- Commitment to a company, industry, or service
- Quality and expertise of relationship managers and technical specialists
- Financial strength of service provider
- Ability to customize services and innovation in developing new services
- Geographic considerations and convenience

III. ISSUES IN FINANCIAL INSTITUTION RELATIONSHIP MANAGEMENT

A. Creditworthiness

The creditworthiness of financial institutions has been an on-going concern of corporate treasurers and cash managers since the 1980s when many financial institutions failed or were acquired in lieu of being liquidated. Failures and acquisitions impact access to credit and other services that are crucial to a company's own business strategy and requirements.

B. Rating Agencies

Financial institution rating and analysis have become increasingly important. There are a number of agencies that offer services in this area. Some agencies offer only ratings, while others support their ratings with detailed reports. These reports may be based on both quantitative financial analyses and qualitative interviews with management.

C. Depository Financial Institution Strength

Among the most common measures of depository financial institution strength is the CAMEL rating, a system widely used by regulators. CAMEL is an acronym for Capital, Assets, Management, Earnings, and Liquidity. While management strength is qualitative, the other four factors can be quantified as follows:

- *Capital* - A U.S. depository financial institution's capital is rated according to one of four risk categories ranging from well capitalized to critically undercapitalized. A simple measure of capital adequacy is the ratio of shareholder equity to total assets. A second measure that has grown in importance factors in the riskiness of the depository financial institution's assets. As a result of these capital ratio measurements and tightening of regulatory requirements, some depository financial institutions have adjusted their business strategies. This can impact a company's choice of provider for certain services.

- *Asset Quality* - Asset quality is a measure of the quality of the total loans carried on the books of a depository financial institution. Asset quality can be measured by examining such factors as the percentage of non-performing loans, the amount of bad loan charge-offs, the loan loss reserve, and the provision for loan losses.

- *Earnings* - The level and stability of earnings are also important indicators of depository financial institution strength. Earnings can be measured by examining such factors as net interest margin (the difference between the yield on loans and investments and the cost of funds on a percentage basis), the ratio of operating expenses to income, and pre-tax operating profit.

- *Liquidity* - For a depository financial institution, liquidity represents its ability to pay depositors on demand. An institution should have sufficient liquid reserves to meet the day-to-day demand of depositors who withdraw funds. Liquidity is more difficult to measure than capital, asset quality, or earnings.

One of the factors that is not part of the CAMEL rating is the strength of a depository financial institution's holding company. Some agencies rate institutions on a consolidated basis. Other agencies rate institutions on both a consolidated and a parent basis.

D. Number of Relationships

For many companies, the number of financial institution relationships is dependent upon the following considerations:

- Many companies establish multiple relationships to ensure that they have adequate credit facilities or to diversify service providers.

- There are internal and external costs for each financial institution relationship, resulting in an incentive to optimize the number of relationships. There has been a trend toward fewer financial institution relationships.

- Each institution should serve a purpose in the company's business strategy. Because of increasing financial institution consolidation and specialization, there is a trend toward strengthening existing relationships or seeking new relationships based on particular services.

- When a company has multiple financial institution relationships, often one is designated a lead institution. There may be different lead institutions for credit and other services.

E. Relationship Documentation

Among the important documents associated with the establishment of a financial institution relationship are the following:

1. *Account Resolution* - This document is the basic account authorization and is usually a board of directors' resolution.

    - The resolution describes what functions can be performed by specific individuals or job titles, lists signers on the account, and covers a variety of liability issues.

    - The resolution may be rather broad in scope, or it may address very specific transactions and limit actions that can be taken on the part of the company.

    - The resolution can be a standard one used by all commercial customers of a given financial institution or can be customized for a given company.

    - Some companies have developed their own standard resolutions that they use for all their financial institution relationships.

2. *Signature Cards* - Most financial institutions require companies to furnish signatures of authorized signers or specimens of facsimile or computerized signatures.

3. *Service Agreements* - Service agreements are required for most services. The agreements may be standardized or customized. Among the elements that might be included in a service agreement are the following:

    - Operational policies and procedures, including the detailed processing requirements for the service, information needs, and identifying people who are authorized to make changes

    - Performance standards that define agreed upon service quality

    - Compensation policies, including pricing, method of payment, payment frequency, excess/deficit balance arrangements, contract length, and adjustments

    - Liability clauses defining responsibilities for risks

F. Audit and Control

Among the audit and control issues facing a company in managing its financial institution relationships are the following:

- Establishing and updating policies and procedures for opening accounts including, but not limited to,

  * an approved policy for opening accounts
  * a financial institution's corporate resolution or a company's own in-house developed resolution
  * a list of individuals authorized to open accounts or contract for services
  * a list of authorized signatories

- Establishing and updating policies and procedures for timely reconciliation of account statements and timely reporting of problems and exceptions. There should be a clear separation of transaction initiation, accounting, and reconciliation duties.

- Establishing and updating policies and procedures for account documentation and record-keeping, including corporate resolutions, contracts for services, and signatories on accounts.

G. Negotiation and Pricing

Negotiation and pricing play an important part in financial institution relationship management. This is especially true as financial institutions have developed more sophisticated methods for measuring relationship profitability.

For example, pricing of loans is often based on factors such as the cost of funds, risk, total loans committed and outstanding, service fees, deposit balances, and the range of other services used. Likewise, pricing of services is often based on such factors as business strategy, volume, customization and exception handling requirements, incremental costs of providing the service, deposit balances, operational overhead, and other services used. Increasingly, companies find that every aspect of a financial institution relationship requires negotiation.

H. Performance Measurement and Evaluation

Service quality is a very important criterion in evaluating financial institution relationships. One of the most difficult tasks for a company is to determine exactly what operating quality means and what the reasonable error rates are for the various services used. Two of the most common types of performance measurement are report cards and relationship reviews.

1. *Report Cards* - A report card is one of the tools used by companies to quantitatively measure the level of service and the responsiveness to problem resolution. Among some of the criteria commonly found in report cards are the following:

    - Number of errors by service

    - Reporting times for information services

    - Responsiveness to questions

    - Timeliness of error resolution

    - Effectiveness of personnel

    Report cards are generally prepared monthly, quarterly, or annually. Some companies that deal with many financial institutions and other service providers, rank them by their ability to meet its quality criteria on a service-by-service basis.

2. *Relationship Review* - A relationship review is one of the tools used by companies to qualitatively assess the level of service and the responsiveness of personnel. Relationship reviews can be either formal or informal. Formal reviews typically involve a quarterly, semi-annual, or annual meeting of the senior management representatives of both parties. Informal reviews typically involve weekly or monthly contacts by individuals who are responsible for the day-to-day management of the relationship.

    The Bank Administration Institute (BAI) has developed standards for measuring quality in cash management services.

IV. FINANCIAL INSTITUTION COMPENSATION AND ACCOUNT ANALYSIS

A. Relationship Approach

In every long-term relationship, both parties depend on each other for their mutual success. Among the factors that increase the success of a relationship and ensure profitability for both the company and its financial institutions are the following:

- Open and frequent two-way communications, both formal and informal

- Regular and timely feedback, both formal and informal

- Clear expectations as established by letters of agreement and legal contracts

- Fair compensation of the financial institution by the company, and fair pricing of services by the financial institution

- Complete disclosure by both parties of information that is essential to the success and ethical basis of the relationship

B. Account Analysis

The **account analysis statement** is a bank's paper or electronic report to its commercial customers of services provided, volumes processed, and charges assessed. It is essentially an invoice. Banks often describe similar services using varying terminology. Services and fees can be detailed and itemized, or bundled into a single line term, or some combination of the two. Fee structures are varied and complex, as are the account analysis formats in which they are reported.

1. *TMA Account Analysis Standard* - The Treasury Management Association (TMA) has developed a standard format for account analysis that includes a standard set of service codes. In 1993 a new and expanded set of service codes was published.

    The TMA standard account analysis consists of sections with the following information:

    - Customer information

    - Current and historic balance and compensation information

    - Adjustment detail

    - Management summary of accounts

    - Service codes and price information

2. *TMA Service Codes* - TMA service codes provide standard, uniform references and terms for identifying, describing, and reporting bank services and associated charges. By simplifying and organizing the varied and complex terminology often used to identify bank services, the service codes also help resolve errors in volume and pricing. Below are some examples of TMA service code product families:

   - *Lockbox Services (05)* - This product family includes services associated with wholesale and retail lockbox processing. Document handling, data capture, and programming are included in this product family, which also covers lockbox deposit reporting and information delivery.

   - *Depository Services (10)* - This product family includes services associated with the processing of coin, currency, and encoded and unencoded check deposits. Branch and vault deposits and supplies of coin and currency are included in this product family, as are services related to domestic collections and return item processing. It also includes deposit reconciliation services, reports, and software.

   - *Paper Disbursement Services (15)* - This product family includes services associated with the issuance, control, and processing of checks and drafts paid against an account. Controlled disbursement, positive pay, and payable through draft services are included in this product family. Also included are check inquiries and stop payments, returned checks, teller services, check sorting, microfilming and retention, and disbursement information reporting and software

   - *General Automated Clearing House (ACH) Services (25)* - This product family includes services associated with the origination and receipt of ACH transactions. Included are ACH input processing, ACH activity reporting, master file maintenance, ACH returns and exception processing, and ACH software.

3. *ASC X12 822 Account Analysis Format* - The American National Standards Institute ASC X12 committee has developed a standardized format (ASC X12 822 Customer Account Analysis) for financial institutions to use in sending account analysis statements to companies electronically. The ASC X12 822 transaction set can accommodate the TMA Standardized Account Analysis Format and incorporates TMA service codes.

4. *Account Analysis Terminology* - The following are among the common terms used in account analysis statements:

   - *Service Charges* - Service charges are the explicit fees or prices charged for services provided by a financial institution. Service charges are usually expressed in the form of a per item or per unit price.

   - *Collected Balances* - **Collected balance**s are calculated by subtracting deposit float, or uncollected funds, from the ledger balance.

   - *Collected Balances Required* - Collected balances required are the amount of balances which a company must maintain in order to cover the cost of services.

   - *Reserve Requirements* - **Reserve requirements** are the non-earning balances that must, by law, be maintained by financial institutions at the Federal Reserve. Reserve requirements are one of the key components of U.S. monetary policy. (See also Chapter 3, The U.S. Financial Environment.) For compensation purposes, a financial institution may use a reserve percentage other than the one required by the Federal Reserve.

   - *Earnings Credit Rate* - The **earnings credit rate** (**ECR**) is the value used to calculate the earnings credit. The method of determining this rate varies by financial institution. The most commonly used measure is the 90-day T-bill rate.

- *Earnings Credit* - The **earnings credit** is the total credit which can be used to off-set service charges incurred during the period. It is calculated by multiplying the collected balances (adjusted for reserve requirements) by the earnings credit rate for the period.

5. *Collected Balances Required Calculation* - The level of collected balances required can be computed as a function of monthly service charges and the earnings credit rate, adjusted for reserve requirements. The formula for this computation is:

$$\text{Collected Balances Required} = \frac{\text{Monthly Service Charges, Fees, or Costs}}{\left(\text{Earnings Credit Rate} \times \dfrac{\text{Days in Month}}{365}\right) \times (1 - \text{Reserve Requirement})}$$

$$CB = \frac{SC}{\left(ECR \times \dfrac{D}{365}\right) \times (1 - RR)}$$

Where:
CB = Collected balances required for services
SC = Service charges, fees, or costs
ECR = Earnings credit rate
RR = Reserve requirement
D = Number of days in the month

Note: Some banks use the earnings credit rate divided by 12 instead of using the actual number of days to determine this monthly calculation.

An example of the collected balances required calculation is provided in Exhibit 16.1.

EXHIBIT 16.1
Collected Balances Required Calculation

A company uses services with charges that total $10,000 per month. The earnings credit rate is 5%. The reserve requirement is 10%. Assuming a 30-day month, the average collected balances required to compensate the financial institution for the services used is as follows:

$$\text{Collected Balances Required} = \frac{\text{Monthly Service Charges, Fees, or Costs}}{\left(\dfrac{\text{Earnings Credit Rate} \times \text{Days in Month}}{365}\right) \times (1 - \text{Reserve Requirement})}$$

$$= \frac{\$10,000}{\left(.05 \times \dfrac{30}{365}\right) \times (1 - .10)} = \frac{\$10,000}{(.0041 \times .90)} = \frac{\$10,000}{.0037} = \$2,702,703$$

Note: If $1.00 is used as the service charge in the above formula, the balance multiplier is calculated. This number, 270.2703, multiplied by the charge for any service, gives the collected balances required to pay for this service.

6. *Earnings Credit Calculation* - The level of earnings credits can be determined by multiplying the collected balances (adjusted for reserve requirements) by the earnings credit rate for the period. The formula for converting collected balances into the earnings credit is:

$$\frac{\text{Earnings}}{\text{Credit}} = \frac{\text{Collected}}{\text{Balances}} \times \left(1 - \frac{\text{Reserve}}{\text{Requirement}} \right) \times \left(\frac{\text{Earnings Credit}}{\text{Rate}} \times \frac{\text{Days in Month}}{365} \right)$$

$$EC = CB \times (1 - RR) \times \left(ECR \times \frac{D}{365} \right)$$

Where:

EC = Earnings credit
CB = Actual collected balances
RR = Reserve requirement
ECR = Earnings credit rate
D = Number of days in the month

Note: Some banks use the earnings credit rate divided by 12 instead of using the actual number of days to determine this monthly calculation.

An example of the earnings credit calculation is provided in Exhibit 16.2.

EXHIBIT 16.2
Earnings Credit Calculation

Assumptions:

Average ledger balance	$250,000
Deposit float	$30,000
Reserve requirement	10%
Earnings credit rate	5%
Service charges for the month	$1,000
Days in month	30

Average Collected Balance Calculation:

Average ledger balance	$250,000
Less: deposit float	($ 30,000)
Equals: average collected balance	$220,000

$$\frac{\text{Earnings}}{\text{Credit}} = \frac{\text{Collected}}{\text{Balances}} \times (1-\text{Reserve Requirement}) \times \left(\frac{\text{Earnings}}{\text{Credit Rate}} \times \frac{\text{Days in Month}}{365} \right)$$

$$= \$220,000 \times (1 - .10) \times \left(.05 \times \frac{30}{365} \right) = \$220,000 \times .90 \times .0041 = \$811.80$$

If the current service charges are $1,000, but the amount of earnings credit is only $811.80, the company did not keep sufficient collected balances on deposit to cover the cost of services over the period. In effect, the company has a compensation deficit of $188.20 which is owed to the financial institution.

C. Financial Institution Compensation Policies

Compensation policies vary among financial institutions. Among some of the differences are the following:

- If a company has collected balances in excess of the amount required for compensation, the excess cannot be returned to the company as cash nor can interest be paid on the balances according to current regulations. Policies vary on how financial institutions treat the excess. Institutions may or may not allow these excesses to be carried forward to future periods.

- Deficit service charge amounts are collected by the financial institution either by direct debit of a customer's account or by invoicing the customer.

- Most financial institutions calculate the earnings credit on collected balances net of reserve requirements (net collected balances). Some apply this adjusted ECR rate to the monthly average net collected balance. Others apply it to the daily average net collected balances. If it is applied to the daily average, net collected balances are not allowed to be averaged over the course of a month. This may result in a borrowing rate being charged on days when there is a negative net collected balance.

- Accounts may be considered individually or on a combined basis for compensation. If accounts are combined, all balances are averaged together. This approach is helpful for a company that has excess balances in some accounts but deficit balances in others. By combining the balances, overall service charges can be reduced.

- A company that has multi-state locations may use a financial institution that has facilities in each of the states. In some cases, the financial institution will prepare a combined account analysis for all of the company's accounts in all states. In other cases, this is not possible due to management policies that vary from institution to institution or state to state. The practice of preparing a combined account analysis statement may become more common as interstate branching increases.

D. Comparing Service Charges

Companies compare financial institution service charges both during the initial selection process as well as during periodic relationship reviews. Among the factors that make service charge comparisons difficult are the following:

- Financial institutions have different pricing strategies.

- Service charges may be bundled or unbundled. Bundling is the practice of charging for a group of related services. Unbundling is charging individually for each service used.

  For example, with controlled disbursement, one provider may have all charges combined in a single per item price. Another provider may have a charge for each check paid, one for account reconcilement services, another for reporting the amount of checks clearing each day, and another for funding the account. As a result, to make valid comparisons between providers, it is necessary to know all the service charge components that make up a service. Some companies rebundle unbundled prices as a method for comparing total charges.

- Prices may vary depending on the level of service provided to a company.

E. Fee versus Balance Compensation

Financial institutions allow companies to pay for services in fees, collected balances, or a combination of both. The advantages and disadvantages vary depending on whether they are viewed from a company or a financial institution perspective.

1. *Fee Compensation: Company Perspective* - Among the factors favoring fee compensation for a company are the following:

    - *Opportunity Cost* - A company can generally earn higher rates of interest on its investments than financial institutions pay in an ECR on collected balances. The primary reasons for this are the deduction for the reserve requirement when balance compensation is calculated and the fact that the ECR is typically tied to short-term investment instruments with lower rates.

    - *Explicit Cost Control* - Fees can be budgeted and compared with other costs, while balances are not as directly comparable.

2. *Fee Compensation: Financial Institution Perspective* - Among the factors favoring fee compensation for a financial institution are the following:

    - *Annuity Factor* - Compared to interest income from loans, fees from services are a recurring, and generally lower risk, source of earnings for a financial institution.

    - *Capital Requirements* - Because deposit balances increase the liabilities on a financial institution's balance sheet, they can lead to a need for additional capital to meet regulatory or other requirements.

3. *Balance Compensation: Company Perspective* - Among the factors favoring balance compensation for a company are the following:

    - *Transaction Balances* - Daily transaction requirements often result in some collected balances in deposit accounts. If a company's concentration system does not mobilize all of these funds, the collected balances could be used for compensation.

    - *Relationship Considerations* - Some financial institutions price loans and other services more favorably if collected balances are maintained.

    - *Soft Dollar Budgeting* - Balance compensation is not as visible as fees for budgeting purposes.

    - *Differential Charges for Fee Compensation* - Some financial institutions' preference for deposit balances is so strong that they charge more if services are paid for in fees rather than balances.

4. *Balance Compensation: Financial Institution Perspective* - Among the factors favoring balance compensation for a financial institution are the following:

    - *Funding Strategies* - Some financial institutions' strategy involves attracting deposits to fund their loans and investments.

    - *Profitability Factor* - Because of the spread between the ECR it pays and the investment rates earned, services may be more profitable to a financial institution when paid for in balances rather than fees.

5. *Compensation by Both Fees and Balances* - If collected balances can be used as the compensation base with any deficiencies paid for in fees, a company can maximize the value of any transaction balances and may reduce its overall service costs.

Questions

These chapter questions are to test and review the information in the text and are not examples of CCM examination questions, nor are they in the examination format.

Answers can be found at the back of the book on p. 338.

1.   What are the major objectives of relationship management?

2.   What are some of the criteria for selecting service providers?

3.   What are the five components commonly used to measure a depository financial institution's strength?

4.   Why does a company seek to optimize the number of financial institutions with whom it has relationships?

5.   What are the major documents associated with the establishment of a relationship with a financial institution?

6.   What are the major audit and control issues regarding managing financial institution relationships?

7.   What types of performance are commonly graded on a service provider report card?

8.   What are the key factors in ensuring a successful relationship between a company and its financial institutions?

9.   What is an account analysis?

10. What are some of the basic product families of TMA Service Codes for account analysis?

11. A company uses services with charges that total $4,000 per month. The bank's earnings credit rate is 6% and the reserve requirement is 10%. Assuming a 30-day month, what is the average collected balance required to compensate the bank for services used?

12. The following information is provided:
Average ledger balance	$100,000
Deposit float	19,000
Reserve requirement	10%
Earnings credit rate	6%
Service charges for the month	$650
Days in the month	30

     Are the earnings credits sufficient to cover the service charges?

13. What is bundling of service charges?

14. How may financial institutions be compensated?

15. What are the major factors favoring fee compensation to a financial institution from the company perspective?

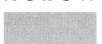

ACRONYMS

ABA - American Bankers Association or American Bar Association

ACH - Automated Clearing House

ANSI - American National Standards Institute

ASC - Accredited Standards Committee

ATM - automated teller machine

BA - banker's acceptance

BAI - Bank Administration Institute

BIF - Bank Insurance Fund

CAMEL - Capital, Assets, Management, Earnings, and Liquidity

CBD - cash before delivery

CBOT - Chicago Board of Trade

CCD - cash concentration or disbursement

CCD+ - cash concentration or disbursement plus addendum

CD - certificate of deposit

CEO - Chief Executive Officer

CFO - Chief Financial Officer

CHIPS - Clearing House Interbank Payments System

COD - cash on delivery

CP - commercial paper

CPU - central processing unit

CTP - corporate trade payment

CTX - corporate trade exchange

DDA - demand deposit account

DES - Data Encryption Standard

DIDMCA - Depository Institutions Deregulation and Monetary Control Act (1980)

DSO - days' sales outstanding

DTC - depository transfer check

ECCHO - Electronic Check Clearing House Organization

EC - electronic commerce

ECP - electronic check presentment

ECR - earnings credit rate

EDI - electronic data interchange

EDT - electronic depository transfer

EFAA - Expedited Funds Availability Act (1988)

EFT - electronic funds transfer

EFTA - Electronic Funds Transfer Act (1978)

EFTA - Electronic Funds Transfer Association

EFTPS - Electronic Federal Tax Payment System

ERISA - Employee Retirement Income and Security Act

FAS - Financial Accounting Standards

FASB - Financial Accounting Standards Board

FDIC - Federal Deposit Insurance Corporation

FEDI - Financial Electronic Data Interchange

FFCB - Federal Farm Credit Bank

FHLMC - Federal Home Loan Mortgage Corporation (Freddie Mac)

FIRREA - Financial Institutions Reform, Recovery and Enforcement Act (1989)

FMS - Financial Management Service

FNMA - Federal National Mortgage Association (Fannie Mae)

FOMC - Federal Open Market Committee

FTC - foreign tax credit

FTD - federal tax deposit

FX - foreign exchange

GAAP - Generally Accepted Accounting Principles

GATT - General Agreement on Tariffs and Trade

GIC - guaranteed income contract

GNMA - Government National Mortgage Association (Ginnie Mae)

HDGS - high dollar group sort

ICR - intelligent character recognition

IRB - industrial revenue bond

IRR - internal rate of return

IRS - Internal Revenue Service

ISDA - International Swap Dealers Association

LAN - local area network

L/C - letter of credit

LIBOR - London Interbank Offered Rate

MAC - message authentication code

MICR - Magnetic Ink Character Recognition

MIS - management information system

NACHA - National Automated Clearing House Association

NCHA - National Clearinghouse Association

NCUA - National Credit Union Administration

NOCH - National Organization of Clearing Houses

NOW - negotiable order of withdrawal

NYSE - New York Stock Exchange

OCC - Office of the Comptroller of the Currency

OCR - optical character recognition

PAD - Preauthorized debit

PC - personal computer

PID - payable if desired

PIN - personal identification number

POD - proof of deposit

POS - point of sale

PPD - prearranged payment or deposit

PTD - payable through draft

RCPC - Regional Check Processing Center

REPO - repurchase agreement

RFI - Request for Information

RFP - Request for Proposal

S&L - savings and loan association

SAIF - Savings Association Insurance Fund

SEC - Securities and Exchange Commission

SIA - Securities Industry Association

SLMA - Student Loan Marketing Association (Sallie Mae)

SWIFT - Society for Worldwide Interbank Financial Telecommunication

TMA - Treasury Management Association

TMIS - treasury management information system

TXP - tax payment format

UCC - Uniform Commercial Code

UN/EDIFACT - United Nations Rules for EDI for Administration, Commerce and Transport

VAB - value-added bank

VAN - value-added network

VRDB - variable-rate demand bond

WACC - weighted average cost of capital

WAN - wide area network

ZBA - zero balance account

GLOSSARY

Account analysis—A statement, usually prepared monthly for a company by each bank, summarizing a company's transaction activity, average balances, and service charges.

Accounts receivable—Assets resulting from the extension of trade credit to a company's customers.

Accounts receivable balance pattern—The percentage of credit sales in a time period (usually a month) that remains outstanding at the end of each subsequent time period.

Adjusted net income—Long-term cash forecasting method which uses a company's projected sources and uses of funds to derive projected cash flows.

Agency—A role in which a bank or trust institution manages assets in which the title remains with the owner.

Aging schedule—At a given point in time, a list of the percentages and/or amounts of outstanding accounts receivable classified as current or past due in 30-day increments.

All-in rate—This rate consists of a risk spread that is added to a base rate such as prime, the Fed funds rate, or LIBOR. The sum of these two components is referred to as the all-in rate. The all-in rate is normally variable and will adjust in relation to changes in the base rate.

ANSI—American National Standards Institute, the recognized coordinator and clearing house for information on national and international standards including those for electronic transaction formats that are used in electronic data interchange (EDI).

Anticipation—The initiation of a transfer before cash becomes available at the depository financial institution.

ASC X12—Accredited Standards Committee X12 of the American National Standards Institute (ANSI) was formed to develop general standards for electronic data interchange; acts as a coordinating body for the further development and support of EDI cross-industry standards in North America.

As-of adjustment—Adjustment of the value date of a transaction in order to calculate collected balances to a date different from the date the transaction occurred.

Asset-based borrowing—Lending based on the pledging of accounts receivable and inventory as loan collateral.

Automated Clearing House System (ACH)—A domestic payment system providing an electronic parallel to the Federal Reserve check clearing system. An ACH transfer can contain more information than a check and is generally more reliable and cost efficient.

Availability—When funds deposited will become available for use.

Availability float—The delay between the time a check is deposited and the time the company's account is credited with collected funds.

Availability schedule—A schedule that specifies when a bank or the Federal Reserve grants credit for deposited checks in the form of an increase in the depositor's available or collected balance.

Balance and transaction activity—Information on current ledger and collected balances, one- and two-day float, debit and credit detail, and adjustment items. Average balances and a balance history may also be reported.

Balloon payment—The majority of the principal balance is due in the final years of the loan term.

Bank Insurance Fund (BIF)—A fund administered by the Federal Deposit Insurance Corporation (FDIC), which insures the deposits of commercial banks and mutual savings banks.

Banker's acceptance (BA)—A short-term obligation of a bank usually arising from an international trade transaction, such as the shipment or storage of goods.

Barter—The direct exchange of goods and/or services without using money.

Base rate—Lenders may use a variety of base rates in determining pricing, including the prime rate and LIBOR.

Basis point—The minimum price change in interest rates is one basis point (0.01%).

Bearer security—A treasury security where the holder can collect interest or principal at maturity as well as sell the security.

Bilateral netting—System in which purchases between two subsidiaries of the same company are netted against each other, so that over time, typically one month, only the difference is transferred.

Bond—An interest-bearing certificate of debt by which the issuer becomes obligated to repay the principal on a specified maturity date and to pay periodic interest.

Bond equivalent yield—Nominal yield on a long-term instrument quoted on a 365-day basis.

Bond indenture agreement—Formal agreement between an issuer of bonds and the bondholder.

Book entry—Securities are stored at the Federal Reserve Bank of New York, and entries are made when ownership changes; book entry securities do not physically move when traded.

Bullet maturity payment—The entire principal is due on the final maturity date.

Call back—A return call to a company to ensure that a transaction has been authorized; a call is placed after the transaction has been entered, but before it is executed.

Call option—The holder of a security has the right, but not the obligation, to purchase the foreign currency at a given price.

CAMEL—An acronym for Capital, Assets, Management, Earnings, and Liquidity. CAMEL is among the most common measures of depository financial institution strength.

Capital market—A financial market that consists of both equity and debt instruments that mature in more than one year.

Captive finance company—Typically, a company's wholly-owned subsidiary whose major purpose is to perform credit operations and obtain receivables financing for its company.

Cash application—The process of matching and applying customer payments against outstanding accounts receivable.

Cash concentration—The movement of funds from outlying depository locations to a central bank account, where they can be utilized and managed most effectively.

Cash before delivery (CBD)—Credit terms requiring payment, often in the form of a check, a cashier's check, or a certified check, before the order is shipped.

Cash concentration or disbursement (CCD)—Electronic payment format used for concentration and disbursement of funds within or between companies.

Cash concentration or disbursement plus addendum (CCD+)—Electronic payment format identical to the CCD format, but containing one additional addendum record.

Cash forecasting—The process of predicting cash flow for the purposes of liquidity management and financial control.

Cash letter—A bundle of one or more checks accompanied by a list of individual items and dollar amounts together with deposit tickets and other control documents.

Cash on delivery (COD)—Credit terms in which goods are shipped and the buyer must pay upon delivery.

Cash terms—Credit terms in which the buyer generally has a week to 10 days to make the payment.

Cash transfer scheduling—The decision on when and how much cash to transfer.

Certificates of deposit (CDs)—Negotiable or non-negotiable obligations of a bank, that may have a fixed or a variable interest rate.

Check—A demand instrument to transfer funds from the payor to the payee.

Check clearing—The process by which a check is presented to and accepted by the drawee bank, the institution on which it is drawn.

Check retention service—The bank retains paid checks and microfilm records. Copies of checks can be obtained when needed.

Check truncation—The process by which essential information contained on a conventional paper check is captured electronically and the electronic information, not the paper check, is sent through the clearing system.

City items—Checks drawn on banks located in Federal Reserve cities.

Clearing float—The delay between the time the check is deposited and the time it is presented to the payor's bank for payment. It has two components: availability float and clearing slippage float.

Clearing House Automated Payment Service (CHAPS)—A London-based payment system for high-value, same-day settlement of transactions.

Clearing House Interbank Payment System (CHIPS)—An independent message-switching system that permits international financial transactions to be settled among New York banks. CHIPS is operated by the New York Clearing House Association.

Clearing houses—Associations formed by banks to exchange items drawn on the other participants.

Clearing slippage float—The delay between the time the payee receives collected funds and the time the payor's account is debited. Also called Fed float.

Collected balances—The difference between ledger balances and deposit float. Collected balances may be used to cover the cost of services provided by the financial institution.

Collection float—The delay between the time the payor mails a check and the time the payee receives available funds. It has three components: mail float, processing float, and availability float.

Commercial letter of credit—Letter of credit issued by a bank to another bank on behalf of a commercial customer stating that payment will be made if documents are presented as provided in the credit agreement.

Commercial paper—An unsecured promissory note issued for a specific amount with a maturity of 270 days or less.

Commitment fee—A component of pricing for a line of credit. A percentage fee, either on the total amount of the commitment or on the unused portion of the commitment.

Company processing center—A collection system in which the company does its own processing and depositing of payments.

Compensating balances—Balances held by a company in the form of collected balances to pay for bank services.

Controlled disbursement—A cash management service that provides same-day notification, usually by early or mid-morning, of the dollar amount of checks that will clear against the controlled disbursement account that day.

Convertible bond—A type of bond convertible into shares of the company's common stock at a defined price.

Corporate trade exchange (CTX)—Electronic payment format for corporate-to-corporate payments that contains additional addenda records in the ANSI ASC X12 format.

Corporate trustee—As a trustee for a corporate bond or preferred stock issue, a financial institution monitors compliance with the indenture agreements between issuers and investors.

Correspondent balances—Demand deposits held by one bank at another bank to facilitate check clearing, securities, letters of credit and other transactions.

Counter-trade—Method of payment, typically an exchange of merchandise, used by companies lacking access to sufficient hard currency to pay for imports.

Country items—Checks drawn on banks located outside the area served by a Federal Reserve city or RCPC.

Covenants—Provisions in loan agreements that restrict a borrower's activities in ways that protect the lender during the term of the agreement.

Credit enhancement—Use of an indemnity bond or letter of credit to back a debt issue, thereby substituting the creditworthiness of the guarantor for the borrower's creditworthiness.

Credit scoring—Statistical analysis used to estimate the creditworthiness of credit applicants.

Currency swaps—Agreements between borrowers with debt in different currencies to exchange payments in different currencies. They are normally arranged through financial institution intermediaries.

Daily cash position—A daily cash position assists a cash manager in determining a company's cash needs. Information about incoming and outgoing wire transfers, collection of large accounts receivable, clearing of large disbursement items, and Automated Clearing House (ACH) credits and debits is compiled to prepare a daily cash position.

Data exchange—The method by which multi-bank reporting is gathered. An arrangement is established by which one of a company's financial institutions or a third-party reporting service gathers and consolidates account balances and transaction activity from each of the company's financial institutions.

Daylight overdraft—An intra-day exposure of a bank when an account is in an overdraft position at any time during the business day.

Days' sales outstanding (DSO)—A credit measurement ratio calculated by dividing accounts receivable outstanding at the end of a time period by the average daily credit sales for the period.

Debit card—Debit card transactions post to bank deposit accounts as withdrawals. On-line settlement requires a Personal Identification Number (PIN) to initiate the transaction.

Demand deposit account (DDA)—Bank account from which funds can be transferred to a third party with a check, a wire transfer, or an ACH transfer.

Deposit float—The sum of each check deposited multiplied by its availability in days.

Deposit reconciliation—Service that enables deposits from multiple locations, being credited to a single corporate account, to be identified and reported. Also called branch consolidation services.

Depository Institutions Deregulation and Monetary Control Act of 1980 (DIDMCA)—Federal law that required the Federal Reserve to eliminate or price Fed float and to charge for its services explicitly. Commonly referred to as the Monetary Control Act.

Depository Transfer Check (DTC)—A preprinted, unsigned, restricted-payee instrument used by a company to transfer funds from one of its outlying depository locations to its concentration account.

Direct send—Cash letter that bypasses the local Federal Reserve clearing system and is sent via courier directly to a non-local Federal Reserve bank or to a correspondent bank.

Disbursement float—The delay between the time a payor issues the check and the time when the funds are debited from the payor's account. It has the following components: mail float, processing float, and clearing float.

Disbursement network—A system of check mailing locations and drawee banks based on disbursement studies and designed to maximize disbursement float.

Discount—The face value multiplied by the discount rate times the number of days divided by 360.

Discount rate—Interest rate charged by the Federal Reserve for loans to depository institutions; rate used to determine present value.

Distribution method—A forecasting technique used in cash scheduling wherein the distribution of cash flow over a given time period is estimated.

Documentary collections—Credit tied to a set of documents specifying the conditions of the sale. Also called draft bill of lading.

Dollar-days—The usual measurement for float, calculated by multiplying the time lag in collections by the dollar amount being delayed.

Douglas Amendment—Federal law enacted in 1956 that allows banks to merge across state lines if each of the states involved permits it. It also prohibits bank holding companies from acquiring banks across state lines.

Drawdown wire—A company initiates instructions to debit its own or another party's account. The party being debited must authorize the transfer.

Drawee bank—The bank on which the check is drawn, the payor's bank.

Earnings credit—A financial institution credit used to offset service charges.

Earnings credit rate (ECR)—A bank-specific rate used to calculate earnings credit; it is usually tied to the T-bill rate.

Economic exposure—The exposure reflected by the potential decline in the value of a company that may result from changes in the exchange rate.

Edge Act—Federal act that permits banks to invest in corporations that engage in international banking and finance and allows banks to develop domestic networks of Edge Act corporations devoted to international transactions.

Effective annual yield—A compounded, annualized yield calculated on a 365-day basis.

Electronic Check Presentment (ECP)—The drawee bank debits the payor's account based on MICR-line data captured by the depository bank and transmitted to the drawee bank.

Electronic commerce (EC)—Electronic Commerce is the exchange of business information from one organization to another in an electronic format in some mutually agreed standard. EC includes unstructured electronic messaging such as facsimile (fax) or electronic mail (E-mail) as well as Electronic Data Interchange (EDI) formats.

Electronic data interchange (EDI)—The movement of business data electronically between or within companies (including their agents or intermediaries) in a structured computer-processable data format that permits data to be transferred without re-keying.

Electronic depository transfer (EDT)—An ACH transaction used for concentration of funds.

Electronic Federal Tax Payment System (EFTPS)—Electronic system for collecting and accounting for taxes. By 1998, most organizations are scheduled to make federal tax deposits electronically.

Electronic funds transfer (EFT)—The movement of funds by non-paper means (i.e., electronically), usually through a payment system such as an automated clearing house network.

Electronic Funds Transfer Act—Federal law enacted in 1978 that defines the rights and responsibilities of users and providers of consumer EFT services.

Electronic lockbox—A collection service that records the receipt of incoming wire transfer and ACH payments, reformats the data, and transmits it to the company in whatever format it desires.

Electronic window—Information reporting systems are sometimes referred to as "window" products, when data is often obtained through multiple points of access; when a single point of access is used the technology is referred to as an electronic window.

Encryption—A process that scrambles a message so that it cannot be read by someone who may intercept it.

Equity warrant—A long-term option to buy a stated number of shares of stock at a specified price (exercise price). The value of a warrant moves in relation to the value of the underlying stock. At the time of their issuance, warrants usually have an exercise price greater than the current market price of the stock.

Eurobond—A bond issued outside the country where the currency of the bonds is domiciled.

Eurodollar CD—U.S. dollar-denominated CD issued by banks, including branches of U.S. banks, outside the U.S.

Eurodollar deposits—U.S. dollar-denominated deposits in banks or bank branches located outside the U.S., but not necessarily in Europe.

Eurodollar time deposits (Euro-TDs)—Non-negotiable, fixed-rate time deposits with maturities from overnight to several years, issued by non-U.S. banks and branches of U.S. banks outside the U.S.

Excess bank balances—Average collected balances in a company's bank account above the average required for bank compensation, or the level a company has chosen to maintain at a bank.

Eximbank—The Export-Import Bank of the U.S. (Eximbank) is an independent agency of the U.S. government established to finance and guarantee payment for U.S. exports.

Expedited Funds Availability Act (EFAA)—Federal law that defines check availability time periods, payable-through draft and check return procedures.

Exponential smoothing—A time series forecasting technique that assigns declining weights to past values.

Factoring—The sale or transfer of title of the accounts receivable to a third party (factor).

Federal Deposit Insurance Corporation (FDIC)—Independent federal agency that insures deposits in member banks. It has its own reserves and can borrow from the U.S. Treasury.

Federal Reserve System (Fed)—An independent agency of the U.S. government which plays a central role in monetary policy, domestic payments system, and the regulation of financial institutions.

Federal Reserve float (Fed float)—The difference in timing between the availability granted a clearing bank and the actual presentment of the item to the drawee bank.

Fed funds—Funds deposited by commercial banks at Federal Reserve banks, including funds in excess of bank reserve requirements. Banks may lend federal funds to each other on an overnight basis at the federal funds rate to help the borrowing bank satisfy its reserve requirements or liquidity needs.

Federal agency securities (Agencies)—Discount and coupon obligations of the federal agencies that were established by Congress to provide credit to specific sectors of the economy.

Fedwire—The real-time system operated by the Federal Reserve for funds transfer and supporting information.

Fee compensation—Compensation for bank services by direct, explicit fee payment.

Fiduciary—An individual or institution to whom certain property is given to hold in trust according to a trust agreement.

Financial Accounting Standards Board (FASB)—An independent accounting organization responsible for publishing the Generally Accepted Accounting Principles (GAAP). FASB is the public accounting profession's self-regulatory organization. It publishes Statements of Financial Accounting Standards (SFAS).

Financial EDI (FEDI)—The electronic transmission of payments and payment-related information in standard formats between company trading partners and/or their banks. FEDI includes electronic format for invoices, initiation of payments, lockbox deposit reports, and remittance information sent either directly to a trading partner or processed through a financial or communications intermediary.

Financial leverage—The use of debt to finance a company.

Floor planning—Type of financing frequently used to support the inventory of dealers who specialize in high cost durable goods such as automobiles, trucks, farm equipment, and major appliances.

Foreign bonds—Bonds issued in the country of their currency by non-residents of that country.

Foreign currency swap—A transaction in which specific amounts of two different currencies are exchanged, and the amounts are repaid over time.

Foreign exchange (FX) rate—The equivalent number of units of one currency per unit of a different currency.

Forfaiting—Specialized form of export financing in which the seller accepts a note from the buyer which can be discounted; useful where confirmed letters of credit are not available.

Forward foreign exchange contract—A contract to purchase or sell a specified quantity of a foreign currency at an exchange rate established today for delivery on a specific date in the future.

Forward foreign exchange rate—An exchange rate established today for a currency transaction that settles more than two days in the future.

Forward rate agreement—Forward contract in which two parties agree on the interest rate to be paid at a future settlement date.

Forwards—Contracts that require some specific action at a later date and allow lock-in of a future price or rate; forwards are typically used to provide a hedge against risk.

Fractional availability—Adjustment to a customer's availability to take into account missed availability deadlines; extends availability by the resulting fraction or part of a day.

Freight payment services—Specialized payment services offered by banks and third parties that effect payment for the client directly to freight carriers and offer data bases that assist in determining cost-efficient freight distribution methods.

Full reconciliation—Company supplies an electronic file of checks issued to its bank and the bank matches checks paid against the file. Bank supplies a listing, either as a paper report and/or electronic form, of checks paid and outstanding in check serial number order.

Futures contract—A standardized, normally exchange-traded contract for future delivery of a financial or real asset.

GAAP (Generally Accepted Accounting Principles)—See Financial Accounting Standards Board.

Garn-St. Germain Act—Federal law enacted in 1982 that extends the legal lending limit of banks.

GATT (General Agreement on Tariffs and Trade) —An international agreement to encourage trade by the reduction of tariffs and quotas on foreign goods and services.

General obligation securities—A form of municipal security backed by the issuer's resources and its pledge to levy taxes.

Giro systems—Centralized payment systems, common in Europe, generally operated by the postal service using direct debits and credits.

Glass-Steagall Act (Banking Act of 1933)—Federal law prohibiting commercial banks from securities underwriting. It required the Federal Reserve to establish interest rate ceilings and established the FDIC.

Grace period—Permits repayment of principal beginning at some specified future date. For example, an eight-year loan with a two-year grace period would mean that principal payments would not commence until the third year of the loan.

Grid notes—A type of bank credit arrangement in which a company signs a comprehensive promissory note under which borrowing takes place and is recorded on the note.

High Dollar Group Sort (HDGS)—A program of the Federal Reserve to expedite the processing of high-dollar checks through the system.

Imprest accounts—An account maintained at a prescribed level for a particular purpose or activity; it is periodically replenished to the prescribed level.

Industrial revenue bonds (IRBs)—A special class of municipal bonds issued to provide funds for a facility the municipality is trying to attract for the area.

Integrated or comprehensive payables—The outsourcing of accounts payable and/or disbursement functions to a third party.

Interest rate cap—A ceiling on the maximum interest rate for a loan or variable-rate security. Caps on investments limit the interest that will be paid to an investor.

Interest rate collar—Collars are combinations of caps and floors, giving the holders ranges of minimum and maximum interest rates. A collar is less expensive than a cap.

Interest rate floor — Minimum interest rates for a loan or variable-rate security.

Interest rate futures—Legally binding commitments to sell financial instruments at a specified future date and price.

Interest rate swap—A swap between two parties usually for one party to convert a fixed-interest rate payment into a variable-rate payment while the other party takes the opposite position.

Internal rate of return (IRR)—The discount rate at which the net present value is equal to zero.

Invoicing float—The delay between the purchase of goods and services and the receipt of the invoice by the customer.

Leading and lagging—A technique for making cross-border payments from one subsidiary to another either ahead of schedule (leading) or behind schedule (lagging) as a means of moving liquidity from one unit to another.

Ledger balances—Bank balances that reflect all accounting entries that affect a bank account, regardless of any deposit float.

Ledger cutoff time—The time after which deposits are credited as of the following business day.

Letter of credit (L/C)—A document issued by a bank, guaranteeing the payment of a customer's draft up to a stated amount for a specified period if certain conditions exist.

Line of credit—An agreement between a bank and a customer in which the customer can borrow up to a specified amount during a year.

Liquidity—The ability to convert assets into cash or cash equivalents without significant loss; the ability to pay obligations when they become due.

Loan participation—A bank agreement to share part of an existing bank loan with another lender.

Loan sale—A bank program where the bank makes a loan and sells all or a part of the loan to investors.

Lockbox—A collection system in which a bank or a third party receives, processes and deposits a company's mail receipts. Also known as a lockbox processor.

Lockbox networks—Collection systems that offer multiple locations to receive customer remittances through one organization.

London Interbank Offered Rate (LIBOR)—Rate offered by banks in the Eurodollar market for short-term placement of funds by other banks.

Magnetic Ink Character Recognition (MICR) Line—The lower part of a check, deposit ticket, or other item, that contains the special character information necessary to process items by machine.

Mail float—The delay between the time a check is mailed and the date it is received by the payee or at a processing site.

Master account—Account used to fund zero balance accounts automatically.

Master notes—A form of borrowing between highly rated companies and the trust departments of major banks. The amount loaned can fluctuate daily.

Matching—Purchase of a security with a maturity on the date that funds are required to meet an obligation.

McFadden Act—Federal law enacted in 1927 that established the state as the foremost party in determining geographic restrictions for commercial banks and prohibited banks from accepting deposits across state lines.

Memo posting—Posting an ACH credit or debit early in the day when the actual credit or debit will not be posted until later in the day.

Merchant's processor—Service provider that has entered into an agreement with a merchant to process credit card transactions. Also referred to as a merchant acquirer.

Message authentication—A digital signature used to protect the integrity of a message and ensure that it is unchanged.

Money market—Financial markets consisting of debt instruments that mature in one year or less.

Money market deposit accounts—Short-term deposit accounts created by Garn-St. Germain Act that pay an unregulated rate of interest determined by the bank and allow limited check-writing.

Money market yields—Nominal yield quoted on a 360-day basis.

Multi-bank reporting—An arrangement by which one of a company's financial institutions or a third-party reporting service gathers and consolidates account balances and transaction activity from each of the company's financial institutions.

Multicurrency accounts—An account that allows for the transfer of payments in any readily convertible currency to and from one designated account.

Multilateral netting—System in which purchases among participating non-domestic subsidiaries of the same company are netted so that each participant pays or receives only the net amount of its intracompany sales and purchases.

Multiple drawee checks—Checks that can be presented for payment at a bank other than the drawee bank; both bank names appear on the check. Also called payable-if-desired (PID) checks.

Municipal securities—Debt securities issued by state and local governments and their agencies.

NACHA—National Automated Clearing House Association, the membership organization that provides marketing and education and establishes rules, standards and procedures that enable financial institutions to exchange ACH payments on a national basis.

Netting—A system to reduce the number of cross-border payments among units of a company either through the elimination or consolidation of individual funds flow. There are two types: bilateral and multilateral.

Negotiable order of withdrawal (NOW)—Bank accounts that offer unrestricted check-writing and pay unregulated rates of interest.

Nominal yield—The quoted yield on an annual basis for most instruments is a simple annual rate.

OCC—The Office of the Comptroller of the Currency (OCC) grants charters to and regulates, supervises and examines national banks. It monitors bank performance, issues supervisory agreements and determines loan credit quality ratings.

Open account (Open book credit)—Type of commercial trade credit in the U.S. in which the seller issues an invoice, which is formal evidence of an obligation, and records the sale as an account receivable.

Open market activities—The purchase and sale of securities from the Federal Reserve's portfolio, respectively increasing or decreasing the money supply.

Opportunity cost—The price or rate of return that the best alternative course of action would provide.

Options—The holder has the right, but not the obligation to sell (put option) or buy (call option) financial instruments at a specified price (strike price) within a fixed period of time.

Over-the-counter/field deposit—Collection system in which funds are received and deposited by local operating units in the field in the form of cash, checks, or credit card vouchers.

Partial reconciliation—Checks paid are listed in numerical order by check serial number, or date paid.

Payable-if-desired (PID)—See multiple drawee checks.

Payable through draft (PTD)—A payment instrument resembling a check that is drawn against the payor, not the bank, and on which the payor has a period of time in which to honor or refuse payment.

Payee—The party to whom a check is payable.

Paying agent—Agent, usually a bank, that receives funds from an issuer of bonds or stock and in turn pays principal and interest to bondholders and dividends to stockholders.

Payment finality—The Federal Reserve's guarantee of funds received. For example, on Fedwire, the Fed guarantees the transferred funds to the receiving bank if the sending bank fails to settle.

Payment float—The delay between the receipt of an invoice and when payment is applied to the customer's account. It has two components: collection float and disbursement float.

Payor—The party who writes or draws a check.

Payor Bank Services—An information service in which the Federal Reserve electronically notifies controlled disbursement banks early in the morning of all checks that will be presented that day.

Percentage-of-sales—A forecasting method in which financial statements are projected based on future sales and the historical relationship between sales and balance sheet items.

Personal identification number (PIN)—A unique number assigned to an individual that is used to determine that the person is authorized to execute the transaction.

Pooling—A special procedure offered by banks in 05countries outside the U.S. in which excess funds in the accounts of some subsidiaries may be used to offset deficits in the accounts of other subsidiaries.

Positive Pay Service—A service used for fraud control. A list of checks issued by a company is transmitted to a financial institution which includes the serial number and the dollar amount. Only those checks that match this register information are paid.

Prearranged payment or deposit (PPD)—The automated consumer payment application by which a consumer may authorize debits or credits to a personal account by a company or financial institution.

Pre-authorized debit —A payment method in which the payor approves in advance the transfer of funds from the payor's bank account to the payee's bank account. The payee initiates the transaction.

Prenotifications (prenotes)—Zero-dollar entries that are sent through the ACH system at least ten days prior to live entries to provide a verification function at the receiving bank before entries for settlement are processed.

Prime rate—The interest rate banks charge to their most creditworthy customers; it applies primarily to middle-market companies.

Private placement—An unregistered direct sale of securities by a company to institutional investors.

Processing float—The delay between the time the payee or the processing center receives a check and the time the check is deposited.

Procurement/Purchasing card—The use of credit cards by a company for routine purchases of goods and services.

Promissory note—An unconditional promise to pay a specified amount plus interest at a specified rate either on demand or on a certain date.

Proof of deposit (POD)—A bank procedure for assigning availability to checks in the ACH system based on time of deposit and endpoints. Also called item-by-item.

Provisional credit—Credit given when a check is deposited, subject to final clearing; ledger credit.

Put options—The holder has the right to sell foreign currency, or other financial instruments at a given price.

RCPC items—Checks drawn on banks served by a Federal Reserve regional check processing center (RCPC).

Receipts and disbursements method—Basic method for short-term cash forecasting that uses schedules of cash receipts and disbursements prepared on a cash basis.

Registered securities—A treasury security registered in the name of an investor, and only that party can collect interest and principal or sell the security.

Registrar—Agencies responsible for monitoring the owners of bonds and the issuance of stock to ensure that no more than the authorized amount of stock is in circulation.

Regression analysis—A statistical technique that establishes the best linear relationship between the variable to be predicted, the independent variable and one or more input or explanatory variables.

Reinvoicing—A method for centralizing the responsibility for tracking and collecting international accounts receivable and for managing the related foreign exchange exposure.

Repurchase agreement (Repo)—A transaction between a securities dealer and an investor in which the dealer sells the security to the investor with an agreement to buy the security back at a specific time and price that will result in a predetermined yield for the investor.

Request for information (RFI)—A document used to confirm that use of a current provider of a service is justified or to narrow the field of potential providers before issuing a Request for Proposal. May also be used to solicit ideas from service providers on how to solve a particular business or operational problem.

Request for proposal (RFP)—A formal document used to place services out for bid.

Reserve requirements—Federal Reserve balances that must be maintained by depository financial institutions.

Retail lockbox—Lockboxes characterized by a large number of relatively small-dollar remittances, usually from consumers.

Return item—A check that is rejected by the institution on which it is drawn.

Reverse positive pay—Financial institution service that transmits to the issuing company a file of checks presented for payment which the company matches to its register data for check fraud control. The company contacts the financial institution if any items are to be returned. See also Positive Pay.

Reverse repurchase agreement (Reverse repo)—The borrower/investor sells the securities to a dealer with an agreement to buy back for a specific price at a specific time.

Revolving credit agreement (Revolver)—Multi-year bank credit facilities in which a borrower can borrow, repay and reborrow up to a defined amount.

Revolving credit terms—A form of trade and consumer credit in which credit is granted without requiring specific approval for each transaction as long as the account is current and below the maximum limit.

Riding the yield curve—The investor buys highly liquid and marketable securities that mature on a day different from the day a payment must be made.

Robinson-Patman Act—Federal law that prohibits price discrimination among customers when a cost basis cannot be demonstrated as the reason for price differences.

Same-day settlement—Fed rule designed to improve competition in check collection services. It requires a drawee bank to settle in same-day funds by the close of Fedwire on checks presented by 8 a.m. local time.

Savings Association Insurance Fund (SAIF)—A fund administered by the Federal Deposit Insurance Corporation (FDIC). It insures the deposits of savings and loan associations.

Seasonal dating—Credit terms that require payment near the end or after the buyer's selling season.

Securitization—A financing technique in which a company issues securities backed by selected financial assets.

Sender net debit cap—Limits set by the Federal Reserve and based on a bank's self-evaluation. These limits set the maximum intraday overdraft that a bank can incur over all the large-dollar payment systems.

Settlement dates—Dates of ACH transactions that determine the availability of funds.

Sight draft—A draft that is payable when presented. Generally it must be accompanied by other documents showing that the terms of a transaction have been met.

Simple moving averages—Extrapolative methods that base a forecast on a simple average of past values of the variable to be predicted.

Sinking fund—Used to ensure that adequate funds are available to pay a bond issue at its maturity. Periodic payments are accumulated in a separate custodial account that is used to redeem the securities.

Smart cards—Stored value cards. Plastic cards with embedded integrated computer chips and capable of storing data, including monetary value, that can be electronically replenished.

Society for Worldwide Interbank Financial Telecommunications (SWIFT)—The major international financial telecommunications network that transmits international payment instructions as well as other financial messages.

Sovereign risk—The risk that a foreign country will not allow an obligation to be paid.

Spot foreign exchange rate—Currency rates generally quoted for delivery two business days from the date of the transaction.

Standby letter of credit—A letter of credit used as a guarantee issued on behalf of a bank's customer in favor of a beneficiary stating that the bank will pay the latter upon presentation of a statement signed by the beneficiary stating that the bank's customer has not fulfilled the terms of the contract.

Statistical forecasting—Describes the relationship between the cash flow component to be predicted and one or more input variables. Useful when there is a large population to be sampled. Can be applied to the analysis of trends. Two of the more important statistical techniques are time series forecasting and regression analysis.

Swaps—Exchanges of securities for other securities of similar credit quality to improve yields.

Sweep account—A bank account that automatically transfers excess balances into an interest-earning account with the same bank.

SWIFT—See Society for Worldwide Interbank Financial Telecommunications.

Target balance—Average collected balance that must be maintained to compensate a bank for all the services provided to the company. Targets are often set monthly and monitored daily.

Target concentration—All funds above a target balance level are transferred to the concentration account.

Term loan—A loan for a fixed period of time, usually several years, often with a fixed repayment schedule.

Threshold concentration—Depository balance levels are allowed to build up to a predetermined level. Then most or all funds are transferred to the concentration account.

Time deposits—Deposits that must be held at a depository financial institution for a specified time period.

Time draft—A draft similar to a sight draft payable to a third party on a specified future date.

Time series forecasting—Forecasts a variable based only on past observations of that variable. Primary types of time series forecasting are simple moving average and exponential smoothing.

Trade credit—A form of credit granted to a company's customers through the extension of credit terms.

Transaction balances—Depository balances held by a company for collection and disbursement activities.

Transaction exposure—The exposure of balance sheet accounts to a change in foreign exchange rates between the time a transaction is booked and the time it is paid.

Transaction sets—The electronic equivalent of a paper business document or form.

Transfer agent—Individual or company that keeps a record of the shareholders of a corporation by name, address and number of shares.

Translation exposure—The exposure of balance sheet accounts when a non-domestic subsidiary's financial statements must be translated into U.S. dollars to be incorporated into the parent company's financial statement.

Treasury Bills (T-bills)—Discount instruments issued by the U.S. Treasury in original maturities of 13, 26, and 52 weeks.

Treasury Bonds (T-bonds)—Coupon securities issued by the U.S. Treasury with interest paid semi-annually in original maturities of ten to 30 years.

Treasury Notes (T-notes)—Interest-bearing securities issued by the U.S. Treasury with original maturities of two to ten years.

Treasury securities— "Full faith and credit" obligations of the U.S. Government issued by sale at periodic auctions, delivered and cleared electronically. There are two types: registered and bearer.

Treasury management information system (TMIS)—Configurations of hardware, software, and information sources designed to assist in the collection and formatting of information and routine calculations.

Treasury workstation—Typically a PC which has software that gathers information from both internal and external sources, then compiles the data for purposes of analysis and decision-making. It can be a stand-alone or part of a Local Area Network (LAN) or Wide Area Network (WAN).

UN/EDIFACT Standards —United Nations Rules for EDI for Administration, Commerce and Transport. UN/EDIFACT comprises a set of internationally agreed-upon standards, directories, and guidelines for the electronic interchange of structured data that relates, in particular, to trade in goods and services between independent computerized information systems. UN/EDIFACT standards are widely used in Europe and are also used in some Asian countries.

Uniform Commercial Code (UCC)—A uniform set of laws governing commercial transactions enacted separately in each state. It defines the rights and duties of the parties in a commercial transaction and provides a statutory definition of commonly used business practices.

Value-added bank (VAB)—A bank which provides non-financial EDI services in addition to payment-related FEDI service for its customers. This type of bank offers services similar to those of a VAN.

Value-added network (VAN)—Third-party communications provider that play a major role in EDI processing and serve as intermediaries between trading partners.

Value dating—A system used in some banks outside the U.S. in which the bank sets the dates at which it grants credit for deposits or debits the account for checks written. Value dates may not have any relationship to the actual deposit or clearing dates of checks.

Vendor Express—The U.S. Department of the Treasury program to pay government agency vendors electronically through the ACH.

Wholesale lockboxes—Lockboxes characterized by a moderate number of large-dollar remittances, usually from company payors.

Whole-tail lockbox—Processes both wholesale and retail lockbox payment types; useful for companies that have both consumers and businesses as customers, and small and large remittances. Characterized by customized processing and data capture requirements.

Yankee CDs—U.S. dollar-denominated CDs issued by non-domestic banks through their branches in the U.S. market.

Year basis—A factor affecting pricing is the lender's use of either a 360-day or 365-day year basis in calculating interest cost. Certain methods of borrowing have traditionally used one year basis over the other.

Yield—Income divided by principal, adjusted to be expressed as an annual percentage rate of return.

Yield curve—The relationship between current market interest rates (or yields) and time to maturity.

Zero balance account (ZBA)—A disbursement bank account on which checks are written even though the balances in the accounts are maintained at zero. Debits are covered by a transfer of funds from a master account at the same bank.

A N S W E R S

Chapter 1: The Role of Cash Management in Corporate Finance

1. The major objectives of cash management are:

    - Maintaining liquidity
    - Cash Optimization
    - Obtaining short- and long-term financing
    - Monitoring and controlling financial risk exposure
    - Coordinating decision-making with other departments in the firm

2. The operating cycle corresponds to the cash inflows and outflows occurring along the cash flow timeline. A company must first purchase the resources necessary to make its product or deliver its service. It then sells that product or service and finally collects the funds from the sale.

3. The three general types of cash flows are as follows:

    Cash Inflows - These are funds collected from customers or obtained from financial sources.

    Concentration and Liquidity Management Flows - Concentrated funds are those that are systematically transferred to create a centralized inventory of liquid reserves held as cash or invested in cash equivalents. Concentration funds include internal transfers among operating units of a company and between various bank accounts owned by a company.

    Cash Outflows - These funds are disbursed from liquid reserves to vendors, employees, lenders, shareholders, and other payees of the company.

4. The tools of cash management are designed to synchronize a company's cash flows, thereby promoting the efficient operation of the cash flow timeline. Products used in the collection, concentration, and disbursement of funds reduce the time periods between events occurring along the cash flow timeline.

5. The principal roles of the finance function are:

    Accounting - reporting and record-keeping function
    Funding - raising capital to finance projects
    Capital Budgeting - determining which projects in which to invest

6. The major decision areas are:

    - Investment decisions
    - Financing decisions
    - Dividend decisions

7. The key players in the finance function (other than the cash manager) are:

    - Chief Financial Officer (CFO)
    - Treasurer
    - Controller
    - Internal Auditor
    - Credit Manager

8. The typical cash management functions and responsibilities include:

    - Systems design, implementation, and evaluation
    - Funds management
    - Banking systems administration
    - Money market administration
    - Forecasting

9. The features that have traditionally distinguished the U.S. from other countries include the following:

    - a large number of banks
    - a lack of nationwide bank branching
    - an extensive use of mail for payment
    - a custom of paying most bills by check

10. The 1970s saw the introduction of remote disbursement and controlled disbursement.

11. Depository Institutions Deregulation and Monetary Control Act of 1980 had a major impact on bank services and prices.

12. The key issues in the current treasury environment are:

    - *Quality concerns* - Treasury departments are being challenged to provide a high level of quality results at an acceptable cost.

    - *Reorganization of treasury operations* - Many companies have restructured their treasury operations using such tools as: re-engineering, benchmarking, and out-sourcing.

Chapter 2: Accounting and Financial Concepts

1. GAAP (Generally Accepted Accounting Principles) are the detailed rules, developed by the Financial Accounting Standards Board, which govern financial reporting and record-keeping in the U.S.

2. A "red" book balance is a negative balance in a firm's cash account. A firm may avoid reporting it by combining cash and marketable securities on its balance sheet or by reporting checks written but not yet presented as a current liability.

3. The three basic financial statements are the balance sheet, the income statement, and the statement of cash flows.

4. The present value of $1,500 two years from now at an opportunity cost of 5% can be computed as follows:

$$\text{Present Value} = \frac{\text{Future Value}}{(1 + \text{Interest Rate})^{\text{Number of Periods}}}$$

$$= \frac{\$1,500}{(1 + .05)^2} = \$1,500 \times (1 + .05)^{-2}$$

$$= \frac{\$1,500}{(1.1025)} = \$1,500 \times (.9070) = \$1,360.50$$

5. Companies use debt for two basic reasons: 1) debt is less expensive, due to its tax-deductibility, and 2) the use of debt does not dilute the equity position of the shareholders.

6. A company needs liquidity for transaction requirements, precautionary requirements, and speculative requirements.

7. The ratios typically used to measure liquidity are the current ratio, quick ratio, cash flow to total debt ratio, and the cash conversion cycle.

8. The cash conversion cycle measures the time it takes a company to convert a cash outflow (for payment of inventory purchases) into a cash inflow (collection of accounts receivable). This measure uses the average age of the inventory, the average days of accounts receivable, and the average age of the accounts payable to indicate how efficiently a company is using its current assets and liabilities.

9. Among the disadvantages of traditional ratio measures are the following:

   • Traditional ratio measures usually reflect accounting rather than economic values.
   • Ratios express static relationships that do not take the variability of cash flows into account, except to the extent that the ratios themselves may vary.
   • Financial ratios provide indications but not answers. The evaluation of the company's worth is a matter of judgment.
   • Ratios are affected by differing methods of depreciation and by window dressing, the practice of adjusting certain accounts just prior to the end of the accounting period to make financial statements look better.

10. Float is caused by delays along the cash flow timeline. A company benefits from shortening all types of float associated with cash inflows, and lengthening all types of float associated with cash outflows. A company may be limited by its ability to extend or lengthen certain types of disbursement float.

Chapter 3: The U.S. Financial Environment

1. The major roles of commercial banks are:

   - Intermediation
   - Payments and Collections
   - Acting as Guarantor
   - Acting as Agent or Fiduciary
   - Consulting Services
   - Risk Management
   - Acting as Broker and Dealer

2. Underwriting is the principal function of an investment banking firm. It assures the issuer of stock or bonds of a definite sum of money for the issue at a definite time. The investment banker assumes the risk of price and marketability.

3. Savings and loan associations and mutual savings banks have traditionally been state chartered. The Garn-St. Germain Act of 1982 allows mutual savings banks to switch to a federal charter.

4. Unlike banks, credit unions are not-for-profit financial institutions with restricted membership.

5. The four major roles of the Federal Reserve are:

   - Supervising banks
   - Conducting monetary policy
   - Providing services for banks
   - Acting as the fiscal agent for the U.S. Treasury

6. National bank charters are granted by the Office of the Comptroller of the Currency (OCC).

7. The FDIC operates the Bank Insurance Fund (BIF) covering commercial banks and mutual savings banks, and the Savings Association Insurance Fund (SAIF), covering savings and loan associations.

8. The Edge Act allows U.S. banks to invest in corporations engaged in international banking.

9. The McFadden Act originally prohibited banks from accepting deposits across state lines. The Douglas Amendment allowed banks to merge across state lines if each state permitted it, but did not allow bank holding companies to acquire banks across state lines. The Interstate Banking and Branching Efficiency Act (1994) phases out, over a three year period, the state barriers against branching established by the McFadden Act. Full interstate branching can be achieved in June 1997.

10. The Glass-Steagall Act separates commercial banking from investment banking.

11. The Depository Institutions Deregulation and Monetary Control Act (DIDMCA) of 1980 included mandates that the Federal Reserve reduce and/or price float.

12. The Financial Institutions Reform Recovery and Enforcement Act (FIRREA) consolidated the two financial institution insurance funds under the FDIC.

13. The Interstate Bank and Branching Efficiency Act of 1994 has the following primary provisions:

    - Permits bank holding companies to acquire a bank located in any state effective September 1995.
    - Allows banks in one state to merge with banks in another state beginning June 1997, so long as neither state has taken legislative action to prohibit interstate mergers between the date of enactment and the end of May 1997.
    - Allows banks to establish new branches in states where they do not maintain a branch if the host state passes a law expressly permitting such branches.

14. The payment of interest on corporate demand deposits is prohibited by Regulation Q.

15. Federal Reserve Regulation CC required the disclosure of check availability policies by banks.

16. Article 3 of the Uniform Commercial Code (UCC) permits avoidance of inadvertent accord and satisfaction.

17. Under UCC Article 4, a firm has a maximum of 30 days to examine bank statements and report unauthorized signatures.

18. Under UCC Article 4A, banks are not responsible for consequential damages, which are losses resulting from the action or error made by the bank beyond the simple loss of funds. A bank incorrectly executing a payment order remains liable for interest losses or incidental expenses. The bank is liable for consequential damages only if it agrees to assume this liability in a written agreement with the customer.

Chapter 4: The Payments System

1. The payee is the receiver of a check and party to whom a payment is made. The payor is the party who writes or draws the check to remit funds.

2. The purpose of the Magnetic Ink Character Recognition (MICR) is to clear checks back to the bank on which the check is drawn and, when received by the drawee bank, to debit the payor's account.

3. Checks can be cleared through the following channels:

   - On-us clearing
   - Clearing house
   - Federal Reserve Bank
   - Correspondent bank

4. A cash letter is a bundle of checks, accompanied by a list of individual items and dollar amounts, together with deposit tickets and other control documents.

5. A direct send is a cash letter that bypasses the local Federal Reserve. A bank sends it directly to a correspondent bank or a non-local Federal Reserve bank.

6. An on-us item is a check deposited in the same bank on which it is drawn.

7. High Dollar Group Sort (HDGS) is the Fed's program to expedite the processing of high-dollar checks through the system. The HDGS program automatically involves making a second presentment to RCPC or country banks with more than $10 million of checks presented from outside their Fed districts.

8. A ledger balance reflects accounting entries to a bank account while collected balances reflect the transfer of value after the appropriate delay specified by the availability schedule.

9. Deposit float may be calculated on an item-by-item basis, as an average of all the bank's customers or on the basis of a sample of the company's deposited checks. In some cases availability maybe negotiated.

10. Factors that determine availability include:

    - Drawee's location
    - Time of deposit
    - Pre-encoding by the customer
    - Checks rejected during processing

11. Federal Reserve float represents the difference between the availability granted the clearing bank and the time required to debit the drawee bank's account.

12. PTD is drawn against the payor and not a bank.

13. A sight draft is payable when presented while a time draft is payable at a specified future date.

14. The most commonly used ACH formats are:

- Prearranged Payment or Deposit (PPD) used for consumer transactions
- Cash Concentration and Disbursement (CCD) used to move funds within or between companies
- Cash Concentration and Disbursement plus Addendum (CCD+) used for the U.S. Treasury Department's Vendor Express program and corporate-to-corporate payments
- Corporate Trade Payments (CTP) used for corporate-to-corporate payments
- Corporate Trade Exchange (CTX) used for corporate-to-corporate payments

15. In an ACH transaction settlement occurs one or two days after transmission of the payment information to the ODFI, with the debit and credit occurring simultaneously.

16. Settlement through Fedwire is immediate rather than on a one- or two-day cycle like the ACH.

17. A repetitive wire transfer is used when a company makes frequent transfers between the same debit and credit parties. A line number is used to identify each transfer with only the date and dollar amount allowed to be changed. A non-repetitive wire requires all information for a wire transfer to be given when making the wire.

18. CHIPS is both a message and a settlement system, while SWIFT is not a funds transfer network. SWIFT sends payment instructions, while settlement occurs through another means like Fedwire, CHIPS or a correspondent bank account.

19. A daylight overdraft is an intra-day exposure that occurs when an account is overdrawn during a business day. Because the Federal Reserve is guarantor of a wire transfer to the receiving bank, it could be forced to make good a wire transfer initiated by a bank that subsequently fails. The Federal Reserve has set a cap on the daylight overdraft allowed for each financial institution to lessen the risk.

20. Among examples of the types of security procedures that are commonly used are the following:

- Use of physical security and limited access at both the company and the bank
- Use of passwords and Personal Identification Numbers (PINs) to identify authorized users
- Use of repetitive wires to limit where funds can be transferred
- Use of dual release (one person enters the wire and another reviews and releases it)
- Use of electronic security methods such as encryption (the scrambling of a message by the sender and the unscrambling of the message by the receiver) and message authentication (a digital signature which prevents an unauthorized person from changing a wire)

Chapter 5: Credit and Accounts Receivable Management

1. The major objectives of credit management are:
    - Creating, preserving, and collecting accounts receivable
    - Establishing and communicating a company's credit policies
    - Evaluating customer creditworthiness and setting customer credit lines
    - Establishing terms of sale consistent with overall company objectives
    - Ensuring prompt and accurate customer billing in conjunction with the customer service or billing departments
    - Maintaining up-to-date records of accounts receivable
    - Following up on overdue accounts and initiating collection procedures when necessary

2. A credit policy consists of setting credit standards, specifying credit terms, and establishing a collection policy.

3. The formula for calculating the effective cost of not taking a discount is as follows:

$$\frac{\text{Annualized Cost}}{\text{of Trade Credit}} = \frac{\text{Early Pmt Discount}}{(1 - \text{Early Pmt Discount})} \times \frac{365}{(\text{Net Pmt Period} - \text{Discount Pmt Period})}$$

Given terms of 3/20, Net 60, the cost of not taking the discount (i.e., paying the net amount on day 60, rather than the discounted amount on day 20) can be calculated as:

$$\text{Cost of Trade Credit} = \frac{.03}{(1-.03)} \times \frac{365}{(60-20)} = 28.22\%$$

4. The five C's of credit are:

    - *Character* - willingness to pay
    - *Capacity* - ability to pay
    - *Capital* - financial strength
    - *Collateral* - protection for the lender
    - *Conditions* - economic environment

5. Credit scoring is a technique used to estimate creditworthiness of credit applicants based on statistical profiles of prior credit applicants. Various elements on the applications are weighted and compared to historical profiles.

6. Revolving credit terms involve the granting of credit without requiring specific approval of each transaction as long as the credit limit is not exceeded, and required minimum payments are made on time.

7. Seasonal dating is a special credit term used in industries with highly seasonal sales. Payment is due near the end of the buyer's selling season although sliding discounts may be offered to encourage early payment.

8. Days' sales outstanding (DSO) in this question is determined as follows:

$$\text{Average Daily Credit Sales} = \frac{(\$75,000 + \$100,000 + \$90,000)}{90} = \$2,944.44$$

$$\text{DSO} = \frac{\text{Outstanding Accounts Receivable}}{\text{Average Daily Credit Sales}} = \frac{\$125,000.00}{\$2,944.44} = 42.45 \text{ Days}$$

9. Factoring is the sale or transfer of title of an accounts receivable to a factoring company. The factoring company provides credit evaluation and collection services.

10. The Robinson-Patman Act is federal legislation which prohibits price discrimination.

11. The Truth-in-Lending Act is federal legislation which requires disclosure of the true cost of a loan.

Chapter 6: Collections

1. The major objectives of a collection system are to mobilize funds, provide timely and accurate information, update accounts receivable, and support audit trails for both internal and external auditors.

2. Companies may collect through the following methods:

    - through an over-the-counter/field deposit system
    - by mail payments to the company or to a lockbox
    - electronically via a wire transfer or through the ACH system

3. In designing a collection system, a company must take into consideration the following issues:

    - commonly accepted payment practices
    - the nature of the payments system
    - the nature of its own business
    - characteristics of the payment instrument used
    - the cost of float and system administration
    - the differences between wholesale and retail businesses

4. Collection float is composed of mail float, processing float, and availability float.

5. Availability float is determined by the depository bank's availability schedule.

6. The average daily cost of float and the annual cost of float are determined as follows:

    - Average daily float = $2,120,000 / 30 = $70,667
    - Annual cost of float = $70,667 x .07 = $4,947

7. The selection of either a company processing center or a lockbox is a function of the volume of checks processed and the dollar size of the checks. For example, a low volume of checks with large dollar amounts usually supports the use of a lockbox system.

8. A lockbox system reduces mail, processing, and availability float; provides economies of scale in processing; and establishes an audit trail outside the company.

9. A wholesale lockbox is used primarily for corporate-to-corporate payments where large-dollar remittances are involved. A retail lockbox is used for large-volume, small-dollar remittance payments like consumer payments.

10. The determination of the net benefit of the lockbox is as follows:

   - Average float with lockbox = $1,010,000 / 30   = $ 33,667
   - Annual cost of float with lockbox = $33,667 x .07   = 2,357
   - Float savings with lockbox = $4,947 - 2,357   = 2,590
   - Fixed lockbox cost   = (1,000)
   - Variable lockbox cost = (6,000 x .30)   = (1,800)
   - Savings of internal processing cost = (6,000 x . 20)   = 1,200
   - Net benefit of lockbox   = $ 990
   - A lockbox is profitable in this situation.

11. Lockbox studies are used to determine the optimal number and location of lockbox collecting points that will minimize collection float.

12. An electronic lockbox allows companies to receive customer payments by wire transfer or through the ACH.

13. An over-the-counter field deposit system is a collection system in which funds are received and deposited by local operating units of the company such as division offices or retail stores.

14. A pre-authorized debit involves the advance approval of a payor for the payee to transfer funds from the payor's account. An example of this application is the automatic withdrawal of insurance premiums from a policyholder's account.

15. Net settlement systems benefit companies in the same industry that buy and sell from each other on a regular basis by requiring only periodic transfers of the net amount due to other companies.

16. Image technology is used to facilitate processing of both wholesale and retail payments. This technology allows paper documents to be scanned, converted to a digital image, and stored for subsequent handling and processing. The documents scanned can be both checks and remittance advices. Potential benefits of applying image technology to the remittance processing function include reduced overall processing costs, increased productivity, improved accuracy, and the ability to capture data for automated posting to accounts receivable.

17. The major types of retail collection systems include credit cards, debit cards, automated teller machine (ATM) networks, telephone banking, bill paying services, home banking, agents, and smart cards.

18. A whole-tail lockbox combines aspects of both wholesale and retail lockbox operations. It is able to process both payment types. Automated cash application data can be combined and sent to the company in a single transmission. Whole-tail lockboxes are often characterized by customized processing and data capture requirements.

19. The key applications in ACH corporate-to-corporate payments are as follows:

    • Federal Government Vendor Express program
    • Manufacturer/supplier EDI programs
    • Dealers with floor plans
    • Corporate-to-corporate ACH debit programs

Chapter 7: Cash Concentration

1. The objectives of a cash concentration system include:

   • Simplifying cash management
   • Improving control of funds
   • Pooling funds for investment or debt reduction
   • Minimizing excess balances
   • Reducing transfer expenses

2. EDT stands for electronic depository transfer, which is an ACH transaction used to concentrate funds. These transactions are transmitted in the CCD format.

3. Wire transfers may also be used for concentration. They are generally used when the amounts are large enough to justify their cost.

4. A depository transfer check (DTC) is an unsigned, restricted payee instrument used to concentrate funds. After a DTC is deposited, it clears in the same manner as a regular check.

5. The major cost components of a cash concentration system are excess balances in the company's banks, costs to transfer funds and the administrative costs of operating the concentration system.

6. Excess balances may arise through delays in deposit reporting, clearing, or the initiation of transfers.

7. Anticipation is the initiation of a transfer before funds become available at the deposit bank. Availability anticipation initiates the transfers on the basis of actual deposit information, while deposit anticipation is done on the basis of unreported, expected deposits.

8. Threshold concentration allows bank balances to build to a predetermined level and then a transfer is initiated to the concentration bank.

9. The minimum wire transfer required to break even is determined as follows:

$$\text{Minimum Transfer} \quad = \quad \frac{\text{Wire Cost} \ - \ \text{EDT Cost}}{\text{Days Accelerated} \ \times \ \dfrac{\text{Opportunity Cost}}{365 \ \text{Days}}}$$

$$= \quad \frac{\$22.00 \ - \ \$1.00}{1 \ \text{Day} \ \times \ \dfrac{.08}{365 \ \text{Days}}}$$

$$= \quad \$95,812.50$$

10. Fraud may be prevented by having different reports prepared by different people, by conducting surprise audits, by requiring daily reporting, and by instructing banks to allow no overdrafts.

11. Pooling funds is a valuable objective of cash concentration because it permits a company to buy larger blocks of short-term securities which tend to earn higher yields. Alternatively, pooled funds can be used to reduce debt or take advantage of supplier discount opportunities.

12. Among a company's concentration system considerations are its collection system, disbursement system, funds transfer alternatives, and banking network.

Chapter 8: Disbursement and Accounts Payable Management

1. A cash disbursement system should:

   • Reduce the net cost of making payments
   • Provide timely information
   • Help maintain good payee relations
   • Protect against fraud
   • Manage disbursement float

2. Disbursement systems may be centralized or decentralized. In a centralized system check writing and account reconciliation are controlled from headquarters, while in a decentralized system checks are drawn on a local disbursement bank and account reconciliation is performed at the local level. It is also possible for check issuance and account reconciliation to be performed at the local level but drawn on a centralized disbursement account.

3. Disbursement float is composed of mail float, processing float and clearing float (availability float plus clearing slippage float).

4. Control and fraud prevention measures include the following:

    - Formal, written policy and procedures for each type of disbursement.
    - Separation of functional authority for collection and disbursement.
    - Separation of expense approval, check-signing authority and account reconciliation.
    - Use of check stock printed on safety paper and/or use of difficult to reproduce watermarks.
    - Use of reputable printing companies.
    - Storing checks and signature plates in a secure area with limited access.
    - Using a printing process that does not require preprinted check stock (i.e. laser printing of checks and MICR lines).
    - Use of Positive Pay, a service that matches check serial numbers and dollar amounts to a database to determine the checks to be paid.
    - Setting a specific dollar amount limit for each type of account. Checks issued above this limit are returned to the depositor as unauthorized.
    - Increasing the use of electronic payment methods.

5. Controlled disbursement is a bank service that provides same-day notification, usually by early or mid-morning, of the dollar amount of checks that will clear against the controlled disbursement account that day. The disbursement bank must receive its final cash letter of the day from the local Fed early in the morning so that the checks can be sorted and the company notified of its funding requirement. Payor bank services are often used to aid in this process.

6. A zero balance account is a bank disbursement product which is an account on which checks are written even though the balance in the account is zero. The checks are covered by a transfer of funds from the company's master account in that bank.

7. The current method for collecting and accounting for taxes withheld by employers from individuals' salaries and wages, as well as corporate business and excise taxes, is being changed to an electronic system called Electronic Federal Tax Payment System (EFTPS). Effective January 1995, the largest taxpayers were mandated to make all tax deposits electronically. In succeeding years, additional organizations are to be mandated. By 1998, most organizations are scheduled to make these deposits electronically.

8. Same-day presentment items are checks drawn on a disbursement bank which are directly presented from another bank by 8:00 a.m. According to Fed regulations, these checks must be paid the same day they are presented. These same-day presentment items may need to be handled by a different processing method than the rest of the controlled disbursement checks in order to have them included in the controlled disbursement totals. Banks also have the option of designating the local Federal Reserve Bank as the clearing point for same-day presentment items.

9. Payor bank services are an information service provided by the Federal Reserve to notify banks of a day's presentments.

10. A controlled disbursement bank should be evaluated on the following criteria:

    - Timeliness of reporting
    - Accuracy in processing
    - Volume capacity
    - Reporting detail and reconciliation services
    - Cost effectiveness
    - Customer service support

11. Positive Pay is a service used for fraud control. The company transmits a file of checks issued. The bank matches serial numbers and dollar amounts and pays only those checks that match.

12. In a partial reconciliation service, a bank lists all checks paid in numerical order by check serial number, or date paid. For each item, the paid report shows the check serial number, dollar amount, and date paid. The listing is available as a paper report and/or electronic form. In a full reconciliation service, a company supplies an electronic file of checks issued to its bank and the bank matches checks paid against the file. The bank supplies a listing, either as a paper report and/or electronic form, of checks paid and outstanding in check serial number order.

13. There are two situations in which a bank has credit exposure. These are:

    - With delayed funding, there is risk that an EDT or DTC may be returned by the bank on which these items are drawn. By the time the returned EDT or DTC reaches the disbursement bank, it may be too late to return any disbursement checks being funded by the EDT or DTC. The disbursement bank is owed funds and becomes a creditor of the company.
    - With the use of an affiliated bank for disbursing with funding through the parent bank, there is no problem if the affiliate bank is funded directly on a same-day basis by a wire transfer. However, if the company funds the parent bank and the parent bank automatically funds the affiliate with immediate funds, there is a potential overdraft problem at the parent bank. Since the affiliate bank does not have an overdrawn account, it cannot legally refuse to pay the checks even though there may be an overdraft at the parent bank.

14. There are two basic approaches to managing an integrated or comprehensive payables service:

    - One approach is to have a company send a single data file to a third party containing a listing of all its payments to be made. The file contains information on when to issue a disbursement and to whom, as well as instructions on the payment method to be used (i.e., check, wire, or ACH).
    - Alternatively, the third party maintains a database of a company's payees that includes detailed information such as preferred payment methods, specific remittance information, and receiving financial institutions. The database is periodically updated as new payees are added or an existing payee's remittance profile changes (i.e., payee switches to ACH instead of check for its standard payment type). In such cases, as a company makes a disbursement, it sends to the third party only limited payment information.

15. Procurement or purchasing cards are credit cards used by a company for the purchase of supplies, inventory, equipment, and service contracts. Companies who have implemented such systems have been able to reduce the costs involved in purchasing, while still maintaining adequate levels of control.

16. Image processing is being used in a variety of disbursement services. The front and back of checks are optically scanned and converted into digital information. Check images (all of them or selected ones) may be transmitted to a company's computer and stored there, or sent to a fax machine. The check images may also be stored in a bank computer which a company can access to view or retrieve the images. Any of these methods allows a company faster access to check information. Imaging services are particularly useful in conjunction with positive pay services.

Chapter 9: Short-Term Investments

1. A firm has a short-term investment portfolio in order to hold temporary excess funds, maintain a liquidity reserve, and generate income with an acceptable degree of risk.

2. A company's investment policy is influenced by:

   - Purpose and objectives for short-term investments
   - Timing of cash flows
   - Tax status of firm
   - Qualified staff
   - Legal or internal restrictions
   - Financial reporting requirements

3. A company will examine the time to maturity, credit quality, and marketability of a financial instrument in order to determine its fit with the company's short-term investment portfolio.

4. Financial markets may be divided into long-term or capital markets with instruments that mature in more than one year, and the money market, which consists of short-term debt instruments maturing in one year or less.

5. In a book entry transaction, the physical securities do not move when traded. Treasury securities, for example, remain in a vault at the Federal Reserve Bank of New York, and book entries are made when ownership changes.

6. The U.S. Treasury issues T-bills with maturities of 3 months to one year, T-notes with maturities from 2 to 10 years, and T-bonds with maturities of 10 to 30 years.

7. Federal agency securities are debt instruments issued by agencies of the U.S. Government. Agencies act as financial intermediaries in certain credit markets. For example, the Federal National Mortgage Association (Fannie Mae) helps provide liquidity to the mortgage market.

8. Municipal securities are classified as general obligation securities or revenue securities. General obligation securities are backed by the taxing power of the issuing entity, while revenue securities pay their principal and interest from proceeds of a specific project.

9. The income from municipal obligations is exempt from federal income tax and is often exempt from taxes in the state in which they are issued.

10. Eurodollar CDs are U.S. dollar-denominated certificates of deposit issued by banks, including branches of U.S. banks, outside the U.S.

11. Banker's acceptances are short-term obligations of a bank created in financing an international trade transaction.

12. Repo is an abbreviation for a repurchase agreement which is a transaction between a securities dealer and an investor in which the dealer sells securities to the investor with an agreement to repurchase them at a specific time and price to produce a predetermined yield to the investor.

13. Commercial paper is an unsecured promissory note which matures in 270 days or less.

14. Money market preferred is preferred stock in which the dividend rate is adjusted every 49 days on the basis of current Treasury yields.

15. Yield is influenced by:

    - *Maturity* - normally the shorter the time to maturity, the lower the yield
    - *Marketability* - securities without an active secondary market tend to have higher yields
    - *Default Risk* - the lower the credit rating of the instrument, the higher its yield
    - *Tax-Status* - tax-exempt securities, like municipal securities, will have a lower pre-tax yield than a taxable instrument of similar risk

16. An inverted yield curve means that yields on long-term securities are not as high as those of short-term securities. This is due to investor expectations of falling short-term interest rates.

17. The purchase price of a 182-day, $100,000 T-bill sold at a 4.53% discount rate is calculated as follows:

$$\text{Dollar Discount} = (\text{Discount Rate x Face Value}) \times \frac{\text{Days to Maturity}}{360}$$

$$= (.0453 \times \$100,000) \times \frac{182}{360} = \$2,290.17$$

$$\text{Purchase Price} = \text{Face Value - Dollar Discount}$$

$$= \$100,000 - \$2,290.17 = \$97,709.83$$

18. The bond equivalent yield of the T-bill in Question 18 is calculated as follows:

$$\text{Bond Equivalent Yield (BEY)} = \left(\frac{\text{Dollar Discount}}{\text{Purchase Price}} \right) \times \left(\frac{365}{\text{Days to Maturity}} \right)$$

$$= \left(\frac{\$2,290.17}{\$97,709.83} \right) \times \left(\frac{365}{182} \right) = 4.70\%$$

19. Banks provide sweep accounts, which automatically transfer excess balances into an interest-earning account.

20. The two major active investment strategies are 1) matching, which involves purchasing a security which matures on the date funds are required; and 2) "riding the yield curve," which requires purchasing a security which will mature beyond the cash need if with a normal yield curve, or which will mature prior to the cash need if with an inverted yield curve.

21. The development, implementation, and periodic review of investment guidelines are critical factors in the management of short-term investments. They are usually determined by the CFO and/or the board of directors. The important considerations are: acceptable instruments, diversification, acceptable dealers/issuers, and investment authority.

Chapter 10: Borrowing

1. The objectives of a company's borrowing program include:

    • Maintaining availability of credit
    • Optimizing the cost of funds
    • Minimizing risk
    • Maintaining flexibility

2. The London Interbank Offered Rate (LIBOR) is the rate offered by banks in the Eurodollar market for the short- term placement of funds by other banks.

3. Credit enhancement is a process in which a bank or an insurance company guarantees the debt obligation of the borrower using an indemnity bond or letter of credit. The borrower's debt is traded at a level that reflects the credit rating of the guarantor.

4. A committed line of credit involves a formal loan agreement with the bank requiring balance or fee compensation and obligating the bank to provide funding up to the established credit limit, provided the agreement is not in default.

5. The effective annual borrowing rate (interest cost) of the loan can be determined as follows:

$$\text{Effective Annual Borrowing Rate} = \left(\frac{(.07 \times \$200,000) + (.0025 \times \$3,000,000)}{\$200,000} \right) \times \left(\frac{365}{365} \right)$$

$$= \left(\frac{\$14,000 + \$750}{\$200,000} \right) \times (1) = 7.38\%$$

6. Commercial paper issuers have lines of credit to be used if market conditions are not conducive to issuing commercial paper.

7. The effective annual percentage cost of issuing the commercial paper can be determined as follows:

$$\text{Usable Funds} = \text{Face Value} \times \left[1 - \left(\text{Discount Rate} \times \frac{\text{Maturity}}{360} \right) \right]$$

$$= \$10,000,000 \times \left[1 - \left(.06 \times \frac{60}{360} \right) \right] = \$990,000$$

$$\text{Interest Cost} = \text{Face Value} - \text{Usable Funds} = \$1,000,000 - \$990,000 = \$10,000$$

$$\text{Pro-Rated Dealer Cost} = (\text{Annual Dealer Charge} \times \text{Face Value}) \times \left(\frac{\text{Maturity}}{360} \right)$$

$$= (.0025 \times \$1,000,000) \times \left(\frac{60}{360} \right) = \$417$$

$$\text{Total Issue Costs} = \text{Interest Cost} + \text{Pro-Rated Dealer Cost}$$

$$= \$10,000 + \$417 = \$10,417$$

$$\text{Effective Annual Cost of Issue} = \left(\frac{\text{Total Issue Costs}}{\text{Usable Funds}} \right) \times \left(\frac{365}{\text{Maturity}} \right)$$

$$= \left(\frac{\$10,417}{\$990,000} \right) \times \left(\frac{365}{60} \right) = 6.40\%$$

8. A loan participation is an arrangement whereby a bank signs an agreement to share part of an existing loan with another lender. This is generally done with the borrower's approval.

9. An asset suitable for securitization should have a predictable, steady cash flow and a low level of historical loss experience.

10. A bond indenture is the formal agreement among all parties to a bond issue defining the details of the issue, such as the collateral, if any, and the duties of the trustee.

11. A leasing arrangement can be structured as either on- or off-balance-sheet. On balance sheet is referred to as a capital lease; off balance sheet is referred to as an operating lease. Accounting and tax issues must be evaluated to determine a lease's proper classification.

12. A sinking fund is used to insure that adequate funds are available to pay a bond issue at its maturity. Periodic payments are accumulated in a separate custodial account that is used to redeem the securities.

13. Because of the potential value of the equity feature, convertible bonds in order to borrow at a lower rate than possible with non-convertible bonds.

14. If a default occurs the lender may demand repayment of the debt prior to maturity, terminate the agreement, or do both.

Chapter 11: Information and Technology Management

1. The objectives of daily cash management include the following:

   • Determine cash requirements
   • Track activity
   • Identify opportunities
   • Update forecasts
   • Update management information

2. The typical tasks a cash manager performs on a daily basis include the following:

   • Obtain account balances and transaction detail from external sources
   • Obtain from appropriate sources internal information that impacts the cash flow timeline
   • Consolidate the external and internal information into the cash position worksheet
   • Integrate data on current day transfers and large transactions
   • Determine cash position
   • Initiate transfers
   • Execute investment and/or borrowing decisions
   • Update the cash position worksheet and the short-term cash forecast

3. The types of internal data exchanged between the treasury area and other areas of the company include the following:

   • Sales summary reports
   • Purchase summary reports
   • Cash receipt and disbursement forecast
   • Aging schedules
   • Investment schedules
   • Debt repayment schedules

4. The sources of current day information for the cash manager include the following:

   - Lockbox deposits
   - Controlled disbursement
   - Cash concentration reports
   - Wire transfers
   - ACH transfers
   - Money market and foreign exchange rates

5. Multi-bank reporting is a service used by companies with two or more banking relationships. An arrangement is established by which one of the company's financial institutions or a third party reporting service gathers and consolidates the account balances and transaction activity from each of the company's financial institutions.

6. The four most common types of reporting mechanisms are telephone reporting, facsimile transmission (fax), PC/terminal access, and CPU to CPU transmission.

7. A treasury workstation is typically a PC which has software that gathers information from both internal and external sources, then compiles the data for purposes of analysis and decision-making. A treasury workstation can either be stand-alone or part of a LAN or WAN.

8. The modules typically found in treasury workstation systems include the following:

   - Account balance report
   - Target balance report
   - Cash position worksheet
   - Transaction detail report
   - Investment
   - Borrowing
   - Letters of credit

9. The types of transactions which can typically be initiated through a treasury workstation include the following:

   - Wire transfers
   - Cash concentration transfers
   - ACH debits and credits
   - Stop payments
   - Letters of credit
   - Investment purchases and sales
   - Loan drawdowns
   - Foreign exchange transactions

10. The benefits associated with TMIS technology include the following:

    • Improves productivity
    • Expedites data gathering, compiling, and analysis
    • Increases forecasting accuracy
    • Reduces borrowing expense
    • Improves investment earnings
    • Improves management reporting

    The costs associated with TMIS technology include the following:

    • Start-up and training expense
    • Hardware and software costs
    • Administrative, maintenance, and overhead expenses
    • Telecommunications charges
    • Transaction service charges
    • Security expense

11. The three most common types of security risks related to TMIS systems are loss of data, unauthorized user access, and computer viruses.

12. The basic types of security safeguards for TMIS systems are as follows:

    • Create a security officer/administrator position
    • Develop written policies and procedures
    • Establish physical security
    • Institute basic access requirements
    • Establish different levels of access
    • Require backup storage
    • Institute computer virus protection methods
    • Use electronic security

13. A disaster recovery plan is a blueprint for reconstructing a TMIS in the event it is disabled or destroyed, or in the event a similar disaster occurs at one of the company's banks. Such a plan should include regular back-up of data and the plan should also be tested regularly.

Chapter 12: Forecasting Cash Flows

1. The objectives of cash forecasting are:

    • Liquidity management
    • Financial control
    • Supporting strategic objectives
    • Supporting capital budgets
    • Cost management
    • Managing currency exposure

2. The steps in the forecasting process include the following:

   • Determine the forecast horizons
   • Divide the cash flows into their major components
   • Categorize the cash flows by their degree of certainty
   • Identify and organize the data to be used in the forecast
   • Select a forecast method
   • Validate the forecast

3. Short-term forecasts can be prepared using either the receipts and disbursements method or the distribution method.

4. A pro forma statement is prepared using the percentage-of-sales method. This presumes the next financial statement period will retain the same relationship between sales and other income statement and balance sheet items as it did in the prior period.

5. The major sources of cash are cash flows from operations, decreases in assets and increases in liabilities. The major uses of cash are increases in assets, decreases in liabilities, capital expenditures and dividend payments..

6. The primary types of time series forecasting are simple moving average and exponential smoothing.

7. The moving average forecast is: (100+150+250+210) / 4= 177.5

8. Exponential smoothing is a variation on the simple moving average that weights each observation with more recent observations given heavier weights. This enables trends and seasonality to be captured in the forecast.

9. The steps in selecting a forecasting method are as follows:

   • Establish data relationships
   • Select a method
   • Test the relationship
   • Manage the costs of the forecast system and data

10. The three types of forecast validation are in-sample validation, out-of-sample validation, and ongoing validation.

11. Regression analysis is a statistical technique that systematically identifies the relationship between a variable to be predicted (the dependent variable) and other data which may be available (explanatory or independent variables).

Chapter 13: Electronic Commerce

1. The primary benefits of electronic commerce (EC) include the following:

   - Information moves faster, and with greater accuracy
   - Costs related to paper processing are reduced
   - Inventories may be lowered
   - Customer and supplier relationships are redefined
   - Treasury functions and duties are changed

2. The three basic types of electronic data interchange (EDI) are cross-industry EDI, industry convention EDI, and proprietary EDI.

3. EDI refers to the general area of electronic data interchange which includes all EDI transaction sets across all areas of a company. Financial EDI (FEDI) more specifically refers to the electronic transmission of payments and payment related information in standard formats between company trading partners and/or their banks. Electronic Funds Transfer (EFT) is the exchange of value which requires the involvement of financial intermediaries such as banks to send and receive electronic payments.

4. The costs which must be considered in an EC or EDI implementation are as follows:

   - Software
   - Hardware
   - Communications
   - Encryption and authentication
   - Education and training
   - Trading partner selling and support
   - Negotiating with trading partners

5. In addition to the costs of EDI, additional barriers to EDI are:

   - Convenience of paper-based systems
   - Versatility of check processing system
   - Tradition of paper-based system
   - Dual systems may be required initially
   - Number of EDI capable banks

6. Parallel efforts in EDI standards development have been proceeding in many countries, leading to the development of the UN/EDIFACT standards (United Nations Rules for EDI for Administration, Commerce and Transport). UN/EDIFACT comprises a set of internationally agreed-upon standards, directories, and guidelines for the electronic interchange of structure data that relates, in particular, to trade in goods and services between independent computerized information systems. UN/EDIFACT standards are widely used in Europe and are also used in some Asian countries.

7. The primary ASC X12 financial transaction sets are the following:

    - 810 Invoice
    - 820 Payment Order/Remittance Advice
    - 821 Financial Information Reporting
    - 822 Customer Account Analysis
    - 823 Lockbox Information
    - 824 Application Advice
    - 828 Debit Authorization
    - 835 Health Care Claim Payment/Advice
    - 997 Functional Acknowledgement

8. The primary NACHA formats for ACH payments are the following:

    - *PPD* - Prearranged Payments or Deposits
    - *CCD* - Cash Concentration or Disbursement
    - *CCD+* - CCD plus Addenda
    - *TXP* - Tax Payment Format
    - *CTP* - Corporate Trade Payment
    - *CTX* - Corporate Trade Exchange

9. The basic steps performed by EDI software are file conversion, formatting, and communication.

10. The services offered by VANs to their customers are the following:

    - Communications capacity
    - Mailboxing
    - Protocol conversion
    - Standards conversion
    - Line speed conversion
    - Gateway to other VANs or VABs
    - Implementation assistance

11. VABs offer EDI services related to payments. They may also provide EDI services which are not directly related to payments or Financial EDI.

12. EDI permits companies to complete paper processing more rapidly. This along with EFT generally results in faster payments, which are a disadvantage to buyers and an advantage to sellers. To compensate for changes in the cash flow timeline, companies are beginning to negotiate new EDI-based credit terms.

13. Evaluated Receipts Settlement (ERS) is a payment method designed to eliminate the need for a supplier to provide an invoice to the customer. The dollar amount for ERS payments is based not on an invoice, but on a calculation of the quantity actually received by the customer multiplied by the price on the purchase order. The supplier does not send an invoice, but rather is simply paid by the customer on an agreed date after receipt of the shipment.

Chapter 14: Financial Risk Management

1. Financial risk management involves the identification, measurement, hedging, and monitoring of risk due to changing interest rates, foreign exchange rates, and/or commodity prices. This area is separate and distinct from the area known as insurance and risk management, which deals primarily with insurance related risk.

2. The risk profile of a company is the determination of how much risk a company is willing to accept in each area of potential exposure. This risk profile, or attitude toward risk, will change, depending on the nature of a company's business, its capital structure, its competition, and the general level of risk that its management is willing to accept.

3. Hedging is typically defined as utilizing financial instruments or contracts to reduce or eliminate the risk from future changes in rates or prices. In contrast to hedging, the purpose of speculation is to profit from a change in a future rate or price. Speculating involves the assumption of additional risk.

4. The four basic types of contracts or instruments used in financial risk management are forwards, futures, swaps, and options.

5. Though futures are similar in purpose to forwards, there are several important differences:

   - Futures are based on standardized contracts, with standard underlying assets.
   - Futures are normally bought and traded on organized exchanges and require both margin accounts and constant adjustment of the value of the future to market.
   - The existence of margin accounts on futures allows investors in the market to benefit from leverage on their holding of futures.
   - Futures are rarely settled by actual delivery of the underlying assets, and normally are closed out prior to their maturity.

6. The primary types of interest rate exposure are due to falling interest rates, rising interest rates, and fixed versus variable rates.

7. Caps, floors, and collars are option-like instruments that allow companies to benefit from the low cost of adjustable-rate financing while protecting themselves against interest rate movements.

8. Transaction exposure is the exposure of balance sheet accounts such as accounts receivable, accounts payable or loans to a change in foreign exchange rates between the time a transaction is recorded and the time it is paid.

9. A quote of SF 1.59 - .64 = $1 means the bank will pay (bid) 1.59 Swiss francs for one U.S. dollar. The offer rate of 1.64 Swiss francs is the rate at which it will sell one U.S. dollar.

10. Forward exchange rates are based on the spot exchange rate and the level of borrowing and lending interest rates in the two currencies.

11. Foreign exchange exposure can be hedged using forward contracts, futures, options, or currency swaps.

12. The two basic types of commodity exposure are price exposure and availability exposure.

13. Derivatives are financial products that derive their value from other assets, such as equities, debt, foreign currency, and commodities. Derivatives can be used either for hedging or speculative purposes. The use of derivatives will have an impact on the risk profile of a company. Whether this causes an increase or a decrease in the overall risk is very much dependent on the exact mix of financing and instruments used by the firm. It also depends on whether the derivative is being used for hedging or speculation. It is also important to consider the overall risk placed on the financial markets by the increased use of these instruments (systemic risk).

14. The pronouncement concerning basic financial instruments disclosure (SFAS 105) covers the requirements for companies to disclose certain information about their investment in financial instruments. All companies are required to disclose the essential information about financial instruments with off-balance-sheet risk of loss. This information includes: contract amounts, nature and terms of instruments, potential accounting losses, collateral and security provisions, counter-party credit risk, and the fair market value of instruments. Additional requirements for the disclosure of derivative financial instruments are provided by SFAS 119.

Chapter 15: International Cash Management

1. International cash management is becoming increasingly important due to the increased globalization of business, increased competition in the domestic marketplace, and the need for cash management services on a global basis.

2. The key characteristics in which international banking systems differ are the following:

   • Central bank operations
   • Number of banks and branching
   • Restrictions on demand deposit accounts
   • Value dating

3. In most countries other than the U.S., banks use value dating as compensation for services provided to their customers. Under a value dating system, the bank sets the dates upon which it grants credit for deposits or it debits the account for checks written.

4. The clearing of checks between countries is often a slow and complicated process. Inter-country checks generally clear as collection items which must be presented back to the bank in the country where they were drawn.

5. The check clearing process within a country varies significantly from country to country. Some countries have nationwide clearing, others do not. The clearing of checks may be accomplished by the central bank (as the Fed does in the U.S.), by

several of the major banks acting as clearing agents, or by correspondent relationships between different banks. Other differences include the significant use of electronic payments for both corporate and consumer payments.

6. Pooling is the practice of allowing excess balances in the accounts of some subsidiaries to be used to offset deficits in the accounts of other subsidiaries.

7. A multicurrency account is an account that allows for the transfer of payments in any readily convertible currency to and from one designated account. The currency denomination of the account is at the discretion of the account holder.

8. A netting system reduces the number of foreign exchange transactions and therefore lowers the transactions cost. There is favorable pricing for larger foreign exchange transactions, and cash forecasting is improved. Netting can eliminate float and result in greater certainty regarding value dating.

9. A reinvoicing center is a company-owned subsidiary that buys goods from the exporter and sells goods to the importer. Each party conducts the transaction in its own currency.

10. A letter of credit substitutes a bank's credit for that of the buyer. Consequently, it eliminates the risk of non-payment to the seller.

11. An irrevocable letter of credit requires the issuing bank to honor all drafts presented by the seller as long as all necessary documentation is provided.

12. A stand-by letter of credit states that a bank will pay the beneficiary upon presentation of a signed statement by the beneficiary that the bank's customer has not fulfilled the terms of the contract.

13. Banks under a documentary collection do not assume credit risk but act only as agents in the collection process.

14. Counter-trade is a method of payment in which a purchaser in a country with an insufficient amount of hard currency agrees to exchange merchandise for sale in the buyer's country rather than making a money payment.

15. To be eligible for discount at the Federal Reserve, a banker's acceptance may not have a maturity of more than 180 days.

16. The Export-Import Bank of the United States (Eximbank) is an independent agency of the United States government established to finance and guarantee U.S. export loans.

17. A company may seek off shore financing in order to:

- Diversify its funding sources
- Hedge long-term investments in that currency
- Lower borrowing rates for parent company
- Lower borrowing rates for foreign subsidiaries
- Gain tax advantages

Chapter 16: Relationship Management

1. The major objectives of relationship management include:

   • Developing a partnership approach
   • Maintaining access to credit
   • Developing service relationships
   • Managing costs and quality
   • Monitoring financial institution risk

2. The criteria for selecting service providers include:

   • Willingness to be a reliable provider of credit at competitive rates
   • Ability to structure flexible loan terms and conditions and provide financial advice
   • Knowledge of a company and/or a specific industry
   • Responsiveness to questions and understanding of needs
   • Quality of customer service
   • Pricing of services
   • Commitment to a company, industry, or service
   • Quality and expertise of relationship managers and technical specialists
   • Financial strength of service provider
   • Ability to customize services and innovation in developing new services
   • Geographic considerations and convenience

3. The five components commonly used to measure a depository financial institution's strength are referred as a CAMEL rating. CAMEL is an acronym for Capital, Assets, Management, Earnings, and Liquidity.

4. A company will want to optimize the number of financial institutions with which it has a relationship because there are internal and external costs for each relationship. As a result, there is an incentive to avoid having more relationships than are necessary.

5. Among the major documents associated with a financial institution relationship are the account resolution, signature cards and service agreements.

6. Among the audit and control issues facing a company in managing its financial institution relationships are the following:

   • Establishing and updating policies and procedures for opening accounts.
   • Establishing and updating policies and procedures for timely reconciliation of account statements and timely reporting of problems and exceptions
   • Establishing and updating polices and procedures for account documentation and record-keeping, including corporate resolutions, contracts for services, and signatories on accounts.

7. A service provider report card often includes the following items:

   - Number of errors by service
   - Reporting times for information services
   - Responsiveness to questions
   - Timeliness of error resolution
   - Effectiveness of personnel

8. Among the factors that increase the success and profitability of a relationship for both parties are the following:

   - Open and frequent two-way communications, both formal and informal
   - Regular and timely feedback, both formal and informal
   - Clear expectations as established by letters of agreement and legal contracts
   - Fair compensation of the financial institution by the company, and fair pricing of services by the financial institution
   - Complete disclosure by both parties of information that is essential to the success and ethical basis of the relationship

9. The account analysis statement is a bank's paper or electronic report to its commercial customers of services provided, volumes processed, and charges assessed. It is essentially an invoice. Services and fees can be detailed and itemized, or bundled into a single line term, or some combination of the two.

10. The basic product families of TMA Service Codes for account analysis include the following:

    - Lockbox Services (05)
    - Depository Services (10)
    - Paper Disbursement Services (15)
    - General ACH Services (25)

11. The average collected balance required to compensate the bank for services used are computed as follows:

$$\text{Collected Balances Required} = \frac{\text{Monthly Service Charges, Fees, or Costs}}{\left(\text{Earnings Credit Rate} \times \dfrac{\text{Days in Month}}{365}\right) \times (1 - \text{Reserve Requirement})}$$

$$= \frac{\$4,000}{\left(.06 \times \dfrac{30}{365}\right) \times (1 - .10)}$$

$$= \frac{\$4,000}{.0044383} = \$901,246$$

12. Given the information in this problem, the earnings credit can be calculated as follows:

$$\frac{\text{Earnings}}{\text{Credit}} = \frac{\text{Collected}}{\text{Balances}} \times \left(1 - \frac{\text{Reserve}}{\text{Requirement}}\right) \times \left(\frac{\text{Earnings Credit}}{\text{Rate}} \times \frac{\text{Days in Month}}{365}\right)$$

$$= (\$100{,}000 - \$19{,}000) \times (1 - .10) \times (.06 \times 30/365)$$

$$= \$81{,}000 \times .90 \times (.0049315)$$

$$= \$359.50$$

In this example, the earnings credit of $359.50 is not sufficient to cover the $650 of bank services for the month. The company will owe the bank $290.50.

13. Service charges may be bundled or unbundled. Bundling is the practice of charging for a group of related services. Unbundling is charging individually for each service used.

14. Financial institutions may allow companies to pay for services in fees, balances, or a combination of both.

15. The major factors favoring fee compensation from the company perspective are the following:

- A company can generally earn higher rates of interest on its investments than a financial institution can pay in an ECR on collected balances.
- Fees can be budgeted and compared with other costs, while balances are not as directly comparable.

INDEX

D

E

F

H

Hardware, 65, 200, 202-203, 220, 225-226, 232, 308

Hedging, 235-239, 246, 248, 267

High dollar group sort (HDGS), 57, 70, 140

Home banking, 115

I

Imaging

imaging services, 134, 145-146

imaging technology, 110

Imprest account, 143

Income recognition, 16

Income statement, 15-18, 20, 211-213

Indenture agreement, 184

Industrial credit and capital companies, 39

Industrial revenue bonds, 184, 299

Information security, 202

Intangible assets, 19

Integrated or comprehensive payables, 134, 144-146, 299

Interest rate

cap, 69, 242, 299, 306

collar, 242, 299

exposure management, 251

floor, 111, 182, 240, 242, 245, 298, 300

futures, 11, 37-38, 152, 159, 236, 239-242, 244-246, 248, 299-300

options, 11, 37-38, 79, 87, 100, 152-153, 159, 170, 186, 236, 240-242, 245-246, 271, 302, 304

swaps, 11, 37-38, 170, 236, 240, 242, 245-246, 294, 307

Intermediation, 34, 38

Internal auditor, 7

International banking systems, 250, 252, 269

International cash management, 157, 181, 183, 249-269

International trade payment methods, 249-250, 260, 264

Interstate Banking and Branching Efficiency Act, 12, 34, 44, 46

Inventory, 4, 9, 16, 19, 27-28, 35, 78, 81, 111, 145, 157, 176, 181-182, 206, 211-214, 224, 233, 289, 298

Inverted yield curve, 159-160, 168, 171

Investment

investment banking, 33, 36-38, 50, 179

investment guidelines, 147-152, 171

investment instruments, 147-148, 150, 153, 162, 282

long-term investment, 158, 267

investment objectives, 148-149, 152

investment policy, 150, 171

short-term investment, 147-171, 206, 282

Invoicing float, 15, 31, 78, 300

L

Leading and lagging, 250, 257-258, 300

Leasing, 36, 39, 77, 174, 185-186

Ledger balances, 11, 57, 292, 300

Ledger cutoff time, 59, 109, 300

Letter of credit (L/C)

commercial letter of credit, 80, 262, 293

standby letter of credit, 151, 158, 179, 262, 306

Level of exposure, 238

Leverage ratios, 78

Liabilities

current liabilities, 19-21, 26-27

long-term liabilities, 20

Line of credit, 21, 26, 36, 173, 176-180, 188-189, 196, 206, 293, 300

Line speed conversion, 231

Liquidity, 3-4, 7, 15, 19, 21, 25-28, 32, 39, 43, 75, 77-78, 87, 120, 148-155, 157-159, 176, 206, 257-258, 274, 285, 291, 297, 300

Liquidity ratios, 28, 77-78

Loan participation, 151, 189, 300

Loan sale

Local area network, 194, 286, 308

Lockbox, 9, 48, 64, 89-90, 93-94, 98, 101-110, 116-117, 121-124, 126-128, 195-197, 199, 206, 221, 223, 228, 231, 278, 296, 298, 300, 305, 309

lockbox cost benefit analysis, 94, 105-106

NOTES

NOTES